C O D E

CODE

version 2.0

LAWRENCE LESSIG

BASIC
BOOKS

A Member of the Perseus Books Group
New York

Published by Basic Books
A Member of the Perseus Books Group

Printed in the United States of America. For information, address Basic Books, 387 Park Avenue South, New York, NY 10016–8810.

Books published by Basic Books are available at special discounts for bulk purchases in the United States by corporations, institutions, and other organizations. For more information, please contact the Special Markets Department at the Perseus Books Group, 11 Cambridge Center, Cambridge MA 02142, or call (617) 252-5298, (800) 255-1514 or e-mail special.markets@perseusbooks.com.

CIP catalog record for this book is available from the Library of Congress.

ISBN-10: 0–465–03914–6
ISBN-13: 978–0–465–03914–2

06 07 08 09 / 10 9 8 7 6 5 4 3 2 1

Code version 1.0

FOR CHARLIE NESSON, WHOSE EVERY IDEA

SEEMS CRAZY FOR ABOUT A YEAR.

Code version 2.0

TO WIKIPEDIA,

THE ONE SURPRISE THAT TEACHES MORE THAN EVERYTHING HERE.

CONTENTS

PART V: RESPONSES

PREFACE TO THE SECOND EDITION

This is a translation of an old book—indeed, in Internet time, it is a translation of an ancient text. The first edition of this book was published in 1999. It was written in a very different context, and, in many ways, it was written in opposition to that context. As I describe in the first chapter, the dominant idea among those who raved about cyberspace then was that cyberspace was beyond the reach of real-space regulation. Governments couldn't touch life online. And hence, life online would be different, and separate, from the dynamic of life offline. *Code* v1 was an argument against that then common view.

In the years since, that common view has faded. The confidence of the Internet exceptionalists has waned. The idea—and even the desire—that the Internet would remain unregulated is gone. And thus, in accepting the invitation to update this book, I faced a difficult choice: whether to write a new book, or to update the old, to make it relevant and readable in a radically different time.

I've done the latter. The basic structure of the first edition remains, and the argument advanced is the same. But I've changed the framing of particular examples, and, I hope, the clarity of the writing. I've also extended the argument in some parts, and added brief links to later work in order to better integrate the argument of the original book.

One thing I have not done, however, is extend the argument of this book in the places that others have worked. Nor have I succumbed to the (insanely powerful) temptation to rewrite the book as a response to critics, both sympathetic and not. I have included direction in the notes for those wanting to follow the arguments others have made in response. But, even more than when it was first published, this book is just a small part of a much bigger debate. Thus, you shouldn't read this to the exclusion of extraordinary later work. Two books in particular already published nicely complement the argument made here—Goldsmith and Wu's *Who Controls the Net?* (2006), and Benkler's *The Wealth of Networks* (2006)—and a third by Zittrain, expected in 2007, significantly extends the same argument.

I have also not tried to enumerate the mistakes, real and alleged, made in the first edition. Some I've simply corrected, and some I've kept, because, however mistaken others take them to be, I continue to believe that they are not mistakes. The most important of the second type is my view that the infrastructure of the Net will become increasingly controlled and regulable through digital identity technologies. Friends have called this "mistake" a "whopper." It is not. I'm not sure what time horizon I had in mind in 1999, and I concede that some of the predictions made there have not come to pass—yet. But I am more confident today than I was then, and thus I have chosen to stick with this "fundamental mistake." Perhaps this is simply to hedge my bets: If I'm right, then I have the reward of understanding. If I'm wrong, then we'll have an Internet closer to the values of its original design.

The genesis of the revisions found here was a wiki. Basic Books allowed me to post the original edition of the book in a wiki hosted by Jotspot, and a team of "chapter captains" helped facilitate a conversation about the text. There were some edits to the text itself, and many more valuable comments and criticisms.[1] I then took that text as of the end of 2005 and added my own edits to produce this book. While I wouldn't go as far as the musician Jeff Tweedy ("Half of it's you, half is me"), an important part of this is not my work. In recognition of that, I've committed the royalties from this book to the nonprofit Creative Commons.

I am grateful to JotSpot (<jot.com>) for donating the wiki and hosting services that were used to edit *Code* v1. That wiki was managed by an extraordinary Stanford undergraduate, Jake Wachman, who gave this project more time than he had. Each chapter of the book, while living on the wiki, had a "chapter captain." I am grateful to each of them—Ann Bartow, Richard Belew, Seth Finkelstein, Joel Flynn, Mia Garlick, Matt Goodell, Paul Gowder, Peter Harter, Brian Honermann, Brad Johnson, Jay Kesan, John Logie, Tom Maddox, Ellen Rigsby, and Jon Stewart—for the work they volunteered to do, and to the many volunteers who spent their time trying to make *Code* v1 better. I am especially grateful to Andy Oram for his extensive contributions to the wiki.

In addition to these volunteers, Stanford helped me gather an army of law students to help complete the research that *Code* v2 required. This work began with four—David Ryan Brumberg, Jyh-An Lee, Bret Logue, and Adam Pugh—who spent a summer collecting all the work that built upon or criticized *Code* v1. I relied upon that research in part to decide how to modify *Code* v1. During the fall semester, 2005, a seminar of Stanford students added their own critical take, as well as classes at Cardozo Law School. And then during the year, two other students, John Eden and Avi Lev Robinson-

Mosher, spent many hours helping me complete the research necessary to finish a reasonable draft of *Code* v2.

No student, however, contributed as much to the final version of *Code* v2 as Christina Gagnier. In the final months of this project, she took command of the research, completing a gaggle of unresolved questions, putting the results of this 18-month process in a form that could be published, and supervising a check of all citations to verify their completeness and accuracy. Without her work, this book would not have been completed.

I am also grateful to friends and colleagues who have helped me see how this work needed to change—especially Ed Felten, David Johnson, Jorge Lima, Alan Rothman, and Tim Wu. Jason Ralls designed the graphics for *Code* v2. And finally, I am indebted beyond words to Elaine Adolfo, whose talent and patience are far beyond anything I've ever known, and without whom I could not have done this, or much else in the past few years.

PREFACE TO THE FIRST EDITION

In the spring of 1996, at an annual conference organized under the title "Computers, Freedom, and Privacy" (CFP), two science-fiction writers were invited to tell stories about cyberspace's future. Vernor Vinge spoke about "ubiquitous law enforcement" made possible by "fine-grained distributed systems," in which the technology that will enable our future way of life also feeds data to, and accepts commands from, the government. The architecture that would enable this was already being built—it was the Internet—and technologists were already describing ways in which it could be extended. As this network which could allow such control became woven into every part of social life, it would be just a matter of time, Vinge said, before the government claimed control over vital parts of this system. As the system matured, each new generation of system code would increase the power of government. Our digital selves—and increasingly, our physical selves—would live in a world of perfect regulation, and the architecture of this distributed computing—what we today call the Internet and its successors—would make that regulatory perfection possible.

Tom Maddox followed Vinge and told a similar story, though with a slightly different cast. The government's power would not come just from chips, he argued. Instead, it would be reinforced by an alliance between government and commerce. Commerce, like government, fares better in a well-regulated world. Commerce would, whether directly or indirectly, help supply resources to build a well-regulated world. Cyberspace would thus change to take on characteristics favorable to these two powerful forces of social order. Accountability would emerge from the fledgling, wild Internet.

Code and commerce.

When these two authors spoke, the future they described was not yet present. Cyberspace was increasingly everywhere, but it was very hard for those in the audience to imagine it tamed to serve the ends of government. And at that time, commerce was certainly interested in cyberspace, though credit card companies were still warning customers to stay far away from the Net. The Net was an exploding social space of something. But it was hard to see it as an exploding space of social control.

I didn't see either speech. I first listened to them through my computer, three years after they were given. Their words had been recorded; they now sit archived on a server at MIT.[1] It takes a second to tune in and launch the recording of their speeches. The very act of listening to these lectures given years before—served on a reliable and indexed platform that no doubt recorded the fact that I had listened, across high-speed, commercial Internet lines that feed my house both the Internet and ABC News—confirmed something of their account. One can hear in the audience's reaction a recognition that these authors were talking fiction—they were science-fiction writers, after all. But the fiction they spoke terrified those who listened.

Ten years later, these tales are no longer fiction. It is no longer hard to understand how the Net could become a more perfectly regulated space or how the forces behind commerce could play a role in facilitating that regulation.

The ongoing battle over peer-to-peer filesharing is an easy example of this dynamic. As an astonishing quantity of music files (among others) was made available for free (and against the law of copyright) through P2P applications, the recording industry has fought back. Its strategy has included vigorous prosecution of those downloading music illegally, extraordinary efforts to secure new legislation to add new protections for their copyrighted content, and a host of new technical measures designed to change a feature of the original architecture of the network—namely that the Net copies content blind to the rules of copyright that stand behind that content. The battle is thus joined, and the outcome will have implications for more than just music distribution. But the form of the battle is clear: commerce and government working to change the infrastructure to make better control possible.

Vinge and Maddox were first-generation theorists of cyberspace. They could tell their stories about perfect control because they lived in a world that couldn't be controlled. They could connect with their audience because it wanted to resist the future they described. Envisioning this impossible world was sport.

Now the impossible is increasingly real. Much of the control in Vinge's and Maddox's stories that struck many of their listeners as Orwellian now seems to many quite reasonable. It is possible to imagine the system of perfect regulation that Vinge described, and some even like what they see. It is inevitable that an increasingly large part of the Internet will be fed by commerce. Most don't see anything wrong with that either. The "terrifying" has now become normal, and only the historians (or authors of old books like this) will notice the difference.

This book continues Vinge's and Maddox's stories. I share their view of the Net's future; much of this book is about the expanding architecture of regulation that the Internet will become. But I don't share the complacency of the self-congratulatory cheers echoing in the background of that 1996 recording. It may well have been obvious in 1996 who "the enemy" was. But it is not obvious now.

The argument of this book is that our future is neither Vinge's nor Maddox's accounts standing alone. Our future is the two woven together. If we were only in for the dystopia described by Vinge, we would have an obvious and powerful response: Orwell gave us the tools, and Stalin gave us the resolve to resist the totalitarian state. After 9/11, we may well see a spying and invasive Net. But even that will have limits. Totalitarian control by Washington is not our future. *1984* is solidly in our past.

Likewise, if we were only in for the future that Maddox described, many of our citizens would call that utopia, not science fiction. A world where "the market" runs free and the "evil" of government is defeated would be, for them, a world of perfect freedom.

But when you tie the futures described by Vinge and Maddox together, it is a different picture altogether: A future of control in large part exercised by technologies of commerce, backed by the rule of law (or at least what's left of the rule of law).

The challenge for our generation is to reconcile these two forces. How do we protect liberty when the architectures of control are managed as much by the government as by the private sector? How do we assure privacy when the ether perpetually spies? How do we guarantee free thought when the push is to propertize every idea? How do we guarantee self-determination when the architectures of control are perpetually determined elsewhere? How, in other words, do we build a world of liberty in the face of the dangers that Vinge and Maddox together describe?

The answer is not in the knee-jerk antigovernment rhetoric of a libertarian past: Governments are necessary to protect liberty, even if they are also able to destroy it. But neither does the answer lie in a return to Roosevelt's New Deal. Statism has failed. Liberty is not to be found in some new D.C. alphabet soup (WPA, FCC, FDA . . .) of bureaucracy.

A second generation takes the ideals of the first and works them out against a different background. It knows the old debates; it has mapped the dead-end arguments of the preceding thirty years. The objective of a second generation is to ask questions that avoid dead-ends and move beyond them.

There is great work from both generations. Esther Dyson and John Perry Barlow, and Todd Lapin still inspire, and still move one (Dyson is editor at large at CNET Networks; Barlow now spends time at Harvard). And in the second generation, the work of Andrew Shapiro, David Shenk, and Steven Johnson is becoming well known and is compelling.

My aim is this second generation. As fits my profession (I'm a lawyer), my contribution is more long-winded, more obscure, more technical, and more obtuse than the best of either generation. But as fits my profession, I'll offer it anyway. In the debates that rage right now, what I have to say will not please anyone very much. And as I peck these last words before e-mailing the manuscript off to the publisher, I can already hear the reactions: "Can't you tell the difference between the power of the sheriff and the power of Walt Disney?" "Do you really think we need a government agency regulating software code?" And from the other side: "How can you argue for an architecture of cyberspace (free software) that disables government's ability to do good?"

But I am also a teacher. If my writing produces angry reactions, then it might also effect a more balanced reflection. These are hard times to get it right, but the easy answers to yesterday's debate won't get it right.

I have learned an extraordinary amount from the teachers and critics who have helped me write this book. Hal Abelson, Bruce Ackerman, James Boyle, Jack Goldsmith, and Richard Posner gave patient and excellent advice on earlier drafts. I am grateful for their patience and extremely fortunate to have had their advice. Larry Vale and Sarah Whiting guided my reading in the field of architecture, though no doubt I was not as patient a student as I should have been. Sonya Mead helped me put into pictures what it would take a lawyer ten thousand words to say.

An army of students did most of the battle on earlier drafts of this book. Carolyn Bane, Rachel Barber, Enoch Chang, Ben Edelman, Timothy Ehrlich, Dawn Farber, Melanie Glickson, Bethany Glover, Nerlyn Gonzalez, Shannon Johnson, Karen King, Alex Macgillivray, Marcus Maher, David Melaugh, Teresa Ou, Laura Pirri, and Wendy Seltzer provided extensive, if respectful, criticism. And my assistants, Lee Hopkins and Catherine Cho, were crucial in keeping this army in line (and at bay).

Three students in particular have influenced my argument, though none are fairly called "students." Harold Reeves takes the lead in Chapter 10. Tim Wu forced me to rethink much of Part I. And Andrew Shapiro showed me the hopefulness in a future that I have described in very dark terms.

I am especially indebted to Catherine Marguerite Manley, whose extraordinary talent, both as a writer and a researcher, made it possible to finish this work long before it otherwise could have been finished. Thanks also to Tawen Chang and James Stahir for their careful review of the notes and work to keep them honest.

This is a not a field where one learns by living in libraries. I have learned everything I know from the conversations I have had, or watched, with an extraordinary community of academics and activists, who have been struggling over the last five years both to understand what cyberspace is and to make it better. This community includes the scholars and writers I discuss in the text, especially the lawyers Yochai Benkler, James Boyle, Mark Lemley, David Post, and Pam Samuelson. I've also benefited greatly from conversations with nonlawyers, especially Hal Abelson, John Perry Barlow, Todd Lapin, Joseph Reagle, Paul Resnick, and Danny Weitzner. But perhaps more importantly, I've benefited from discussions with the activists, in particular the Center for Democracy and Technology, the Electronic Frontier Foundation, and the American Civil Liberties Union. They have made the issues real, and they have done much to defend at least some of the values that I think important.

This book would not have been written, however, but for a story by Julian Dibbell, a conference organized by Henry J. Perritt, and many arguments with David Johnson. I am grateful to all three for what they have taught.

I began this project as a fellow at Harvard's Program on Ethics and the Professions. I am grateful to Dennis Thompson for his skeptical encouragement that year. The Berkman Center for Internet and Society at Harvard Law School has made much of my research possible. I am grateful in particular to Lillian and Myles Berkman for that support, and especially to the center's co-director and my sometime coteacher, Jonathan Zittrain, for his support and, more important, friendship. I've dedicated this book to the other co-director of the Berkman Center, Charlie Nesson, who has given me the space and support to do this work and a certain inspiration to push it differently.

But more significant than any of that support has been the patience, and love, of the person to whom I've dedicated my life, Bettina Neuefeind. Her love will seem crazy, and wonderful, for much more than a year.

CODE

ONE

code is law

ALMOST TWO DECADES AGO, IN THE SPRING OF 1989, COMMUNISM IN EUROPE
died—collapsed, like a tent, its main post removed. The end was not brought
by war or revolution. The end was exhaustion. A new political regime was
born in its place across Central and Eastern Europe, the beginnings of a new
political society.

For constitutionalists (like me), this was a heady time. I had graduated
from law school in 1989, and in 1991 I began teaching at the University of
Chicago. At that time, Chicago had a center devoted to the study of the emerging democracies in Central and Eastern Europe. I was a part of that center.
Over the next five years I spent more hours on airplanes, and more mornings
drinking bad coffee, than I care to remember.

Eastern and Central Europe were filled with Americans telling former
Communists how they should govern. The advice was endless. And silly. Some
of these visitors literally sold translated constitutions to the emerging constitutional republics; the rest had innumerable half-baked ideas about how the
new nations should be governed. These Americans came from a nation where
constitutionalism seemed to work, yet they had no clue why.

The Center's mission, however, was not to advise. We knew too little to
guide. Our aim was to watch and gather data about the transitions and how
they progressed. We wanted to understand the change, not direct it.

What we saw was striking, if understandable. Those first moments after
communism's collapse were filled with antigovernmental passion—a surge of
anger directed against the state and against state regulation. Leave us alone,
the people seemed to say. Let the market and nongovernmental organizations—a new society—take government's place. After generations of communism, this reaction was completely understandable. Government was the

1

oppressor. What compromise could there be with the instrument of your repression?

A certain kind of libertarianism seemed to many to support much in this reaction. If the market were to reign, and the government were kept out of the way, freedom and prosperity would inevitably grow. Things would take care of themselves. There was no need, and could be no place, for extensive regulation by the state.

But things didn't take care of themselves. Markets didn't flourish. Governments were crippled, and crippled governments are no elixir of freedom. Power didn't disappear—it shifted from the state to mafiosi, themselves often created by the state. The need for traditional state functions—police, courts, schools, health care—didn't go away, and private interests didn't emerge to fill that need. Instead, the needs were simply unmet. Security evaporated. A modern if plodding anarchy replaced the bland communism of the previous three generations: neon lights flashed advertisements for Nike; pensioners were swindled out of their life savings by fraudulent stock deals; bankers were murdered in broad daylight on Moscow streets. One system of control had been replaced by another. Neither was what Western libertarians would call "freedom."

About a decade ago, in the mid-1990s, just about the time when this post-communist euphoria was beginning to wane, there emerged in the West another "new society," to many just as exciting as the new societies promised in post-communist Europe. This was the Internet, or as I'll define a bit later, "cyberspace." First in universities and centers of research, and then throughout society in general, cyberspace became a new target for libertarian utopianism. *Here* freedom from the state would reign. If not in Moscow or Tblisi, then in cyberspace would we find the ideal libertarian society.

The catalyst for this change was likewise unplanned. Born in a research project in the Defense Department,[1] cyberspace too arose from the unplanned displacement of a certain architecture of control. The tolled, single-purpose network of telephones was displaced by the untolled and multipurpose network of packet-switched data. And thus the old one-to-many architectures of publishing (television, radio, newspapers, books) were complemented by a world in which anyone could become a publisher. People could communicate and associate in ways that they had never done before. The space seemed to promise a kind of society that real space would never allow—freedom without anarchy, control without government, consensus without power. In the words of a manifesto that defined this ideal: "We reject: kings, presidents and voting. We believe in: rough consensus and running code."[2]

As in post-Communist Europe, these first thoughts about freedom in cyberspace tied freedom to the disappearance of the state. As John Parry Barlow, former lyricist for the Grateful Dead and co-founder of the Electronic Frontier Foundation, declared in his "Declaration of Independence for Cyberspace,"

> Governments of the Industrial World, you weary giants of flesh and steel, I come from Cyberspace, the new home of Mind. On behalf of the future, I ask you of the past to leave us alone. You are not welcome among us. You have no sovereignty where we gather.

But here the bond between freedom and the absence of the state was said to be even stronger than in post-Communist Europe. The claim for cyberspace was not just that government would not regulate cyberspace—it was that government *could not* regulate cyberspace. Cyberspace was, by nature, unavoidably free. Governments could threaten, but behavior could not be controlled; laws could be passed, but they would have no real effect. There was no choice about what kind of government to install—none could reign. Cyberspace would be a society of a very different sort. There would be definition and direction, but built from the bottom-up. The society of this space would be a fully self-ordering entity, cleansed of governors and free from political hacks.

I taught in Central Europe during the summers of the early 1990s; I witnessed through my students the transformation in attitudes about communism that I described above. And so I felt a bit of déjà vu when, in the spring of 1995, while teaching the law of cyberspace, I saw in my students these very same post-communist thoughts about freedom and government. Even at Yale—not known for libertarian passions—the students seemed drunk with what James Boyle would later call the "libertarian gotcha":[3] no government could survive without the Internet's riches, yet no government could control the life that went on there. Real-space governments would become as pathetic as the last Communist regimes: It was the withering of the state that Marx had promised, jolted out of existence by trillions of gigabytes flashing across the ether of cyberspace.

But what was never made clear in the midst of this celebration was *why*. Why was cyberspace incapable of regulation? What made it so? The word itself suggests not freedom but control. Its etymology reaches beyond a novel by William Gibson (*Neuromancer*, published in 1984) to the world of "cybernetics," the study of control at a distance through devices.[4] So it was doubly puzzling to see this celebration of "perfect freedom" under a banner that aspires (to anyone who knows the origin, at least) to perfect control.

As I said, I am a constitutionalist. I teach and write about constitutional law. I believe that these first thoughts about government and cyberspace were just as misguided as the first thoughts about government after communism. Liberty in cyberspace will not come from the absence of the state. Liberty there, as anywhere, will come from a state of a certain kind. We build a world where freedom can flourish not by removing from society any self-conscious control, but by setting it in a place where a particular kind of self-conscious control survives. We build liberty as our founders did, by setting society upon a certain *constitution*.

But by "constitution" I don't mean a legal text. Unlike my countrymen in Eastern Europe in the early 1990s, I am not trying to sell a document that our framers wrote in 1787. Rather, as the British understand when they speak of their "constitution," I mean an architecture—not just a legal text but a way of life—that structures and constrains social and legal power, to the end of protecting fundamental values. (One student asked, "constitution" in the sense of "just one tool among many, one simple flashlight that keeps us from fumbling in the dark, or, alternatively . . . more like a lighthouse that we constantly call upon?" I mean constitution as in lighthouse—a guide that helps anchor fundamental values.)

Constitutions in this sense are built, they are not found. Foundations get laid, they don't magically appear. Just as the founders of our nation learned from the anarchy that followed the revolution (remember: our first constitution, the Articles of Confederation, was a miserable failure of do-nothingness), so too are we beginning to understand about cyberspace that this building, or laying, is not the work of an invisible hand. There is no reason to believe that the foundation for liberty in cyberspace will simply emerge. Indeed, the passion for that anarchy—as in America by the late 1780s, and as in the former Eastern bloc by the late 1990s—has faded. Thus, as our framers learned, and as the Russians saw, we have every reason to believe that cyberspace, left to itself, will not fulfill the promise of freedom. Left to itself, cyberspace will become a perfect tool of control.

Control. Not necessarily control by government, and not necessarily control to some evil, fascist end. But the argument of this book is that the invisible hand of cyberspace is building an architecture that is quite the opposite of its architecture at its birth. This invisible hand, pushed by government and by commerce, is constructing an architecture that will perfect control and make highly efficient regulation possible. The struggle in that world will not be government's. It will be to assure that essential liberties are preserved in this environment of perfect control. As Siva Vaidhyanathan puts it,

While once it seemed obvious and easy to declare the rise of a "network society" in which individuals would realign themselves, empower themselves, and undermine traditional methods of social and cultural control, it seems clear that networked digital communication need not serve such liberating ends.[5]

This book is about the change from a cyberspace of anarchy to a cyberspace of control. When we see the path that cyberspace is on now—an evolution I describe below in Part I—we see that much of the "liberty" present at cyberspace's founding will be removed in its future. Values originally considered fundamental will not survive. On the path we have chosen, we will remake what cyberspace was. Some of that remaking will make many of us happy. But some of that remaking, I argue, we should all regret.

Yet whether you celebrate or regret the changes that I will describe, it is critical to understand how they happen. What produced the "liberty" of cyberspace, and what will change to remake that liberty? That lesson will then suggest a second about the source of regulation in cyberspace.

That understanding is the aim of Part II. Cyberspace demands a new understanding of how regulation works. It compels us to look beyond the traditional lawyer's scope—beyond laws, or even norms. It requires a broader account of "regulation," and most importantly, the recognition of a newly salient regulator.

That regulator is the obscurity in this book's title—Code. In real space, we recognize how laws regulate—through constitutions, statutes, and other legal codes. In cyberspace we must understand how a different "code" regulates—how the software and hardware (i.e., the "code" of cyberspace) that make cyberspace what it is also regulate cyberspace as it is. As William Mitchell puts it, this code is cyberspace's "law."[6] "Lex Informatica," as Joel Reidenberg first put it,[7] or better, "code is law."

Lawyers and legal theorists get bothered, however, when I echo this slogan. There are differences, they insist, between the regulatory effects produced by code and the regulatory effects produced by law, not the least of which is the difference in the "internal perspective" that runs with each kind of regulation. We understand the internal perspective of legal regulation—for example, that the restrictions the law might impose on a company's freedom to pollute are a product of self-conscious regulation, reflecting values of the society imposing that regulation. That perspective is harder to recognize with code. It could be there, but it need not. And no doubt this is just one of many important differences between "code" and "law."

I don't deny these differences. I only assert that we learn something useful from ignoring them for a bit. Justice Holmes famously focused the regulator on the "bad man."[8] He offered a theory of regulation that assumed that "bad man" at its core. His point was not that everyone was a "bad man"; the point instead was about how we could best construct systems of regulation.

My point is the same. I suggest we learn something if we think about the "bot man" theory of regulation—one focused on the regulation of code. We will learn something important, in other words, if we imagine the target of regulation as a maximizing entity, and consider the range of tools the regulator has to control that machine.

Code will be a central tool in this analysis. It will present the greatest threat to both liberal and libertarian ideals, as well as their greatest promise. We can build, or architect, or *code* cyberspace to protect values that we believe are fundamental. Or we can build, or architect, or code cyberspace to allow those values to disappear. There is no middle ground. There is no choice that does not include some kind of building. Code is never found; it is only ever made, and only ever made by us. As Mark Stefik puts it, "Different versions of [cyberspace] support different kinds of dreams. We choose, wisely or not."[9] Or again, code "determines which people can access which digital objects . . . How such programming regulates human interactions . . . depends on the choices made."[10] Or, more precisely, a code of cyberspace, defining the freedoms and controls of cyberspace, will be built. About that there can be no debate. But by whom, and with what values? That is the only choice we have left to make.

My argument is not for some top-down form of control. The claim is not that regulators must occupy Microsoft. A constitution envisions an environment; as Justice Holmes said, it "call[s] into life a being the development of which [cannot be] foreseen."[11] Thus, to speak of a constitution is not to describe a hundred-day plan. It is instead to identify the values that a space should guarantee. It is not to describe a "government"; it is not even to select (as if a single choice must be made) between bottom-up or top-down control. In speaking of a constitution in cyberspace we are simply asking: What values should be protected there? What values should be built into the space to encourage what forms of life?

The "values" at stake here are of two sorts—substantive and structural. In the American constitutional tradition, we worried about the second first. The framers of the Constitution of 1787 (enacted without a Bill of Rights) were focused on structures of government. Their aim was to ensure that a particular government (the federal government) did not become too powerful. And so they built into the Constitution's design checks on the power of the federal government and limits on its reach over the states.

Opponents of that Constitution insisted that more checks were needed, that the Constitution needed to impose substantive limits on government's power as well as structural limits. And thus was the Bill of Rights born. Ratified in 1791, the Bill of Rights promised that the federal government would not remove certain freedoms—of speech, privacy, and due process. And it guaranteed that the commitment to these substantive values would remain despite the passing fancies of normal, or ordinary, government. These values—both substantive and structural—were thus entrenched through our constitutional design. They can be changed, but only through a cumbersome and costly process.

We face the same questions in constituting cyberspace, but we have approached them from the opposite direction.[12] Already we are struggling with substance: Will cyberspace promise privacy or access? Will it enable a free culture or a permission culture? Will it preserve a space for free speech? These are choices of substantive value, and they are the subject of much of this book.

But structure matters as well, though we have not even begun to understand how to limit, or regulate, arbitrary regulatory power. What "checks and balances" are possible in this space? How do we separate powers? How do we ensure that one regulator, or one government, doesn't become too powerful? How do we guarantee it is powerful enough?

Theorists of cyberspace have been talking about these questions since its birth.[13] But as a culture, we are just beginning to get it. As we slowly come to see how different structures within cyberspace affect us—how its architecture, in a sense I will define below, "regulates" us—we slowly come to ask how these structures should be defined. The first generation of these architectures was built by a noncommercial sector—researchers and hackers, focused upon building a network. The second generation has been built by commerce. And the third, not yet off the drawing board, could well be the product of government. Which regulator do we prefer? Which regulators should be controlled? How does society exercise that control over entities that aim to control it?

In Part III, I bring these questions back down to the ground. I consider three areas of controversy—intellectual property, privacy, and free speech—and identify the values within each that cyberspace will change. These values are the product of the interaction between law and technology. How that interaction plays out is often counter-intuitive. My aim in this part is to map that interaction, so as to map a way that we might, using the tools of Part II, preserve the values that are important to us within each context.

Part IV internationalizes these questions. Cyberspace is everywhere, meaning those who populate cyberspace come from everywhere. How will the sovereigns of everywhere live with the claimed "sovereignty" of cyberspace? I map a particular response that seems to me inevitable, and will reinforce the conclusion of Part I.

The final part, Part V, is the darkest. The central lesson of this book is that cyberspace requires choices. Some of these are, and should be, private: Whether an author wants to enforce her copyright; how a citizen wants to protect his privacy. But some of these choices involve values that are collective. I end by asking whether we—meaning Americans—are up to the challenge that these choices present. Are we able to respond rationally—meaning both (1) are we able to respond without undue or irrational passion, and (2) do we have institutions capable of understanding and responding to these choices?

My strong sense is that we are not, at least now, able to respond rationally to these challenges. We are at a stage in our history when we urgently need to make fundamental choices about values, but we should trust no institution of government to make such choices. Courts cannot do it, because as a legal culture we don't want courts choosing among contested matters of values. Congress should not do it because, as a political culture, we are deeply skeptical (and rightly so) about the product of this government. There is much to be proud of in our history and traditions. But the government we now have is a failure. Nothing important should be trusted to its control, even though everything important is.

Change is possible. I don't doubt that revolutions remain in our future. But I fear that it is too easy for the government, or specially powered interests, to dislodge these revolutions, and that too much will be at stake for it to allow real change to succeed. Our government has already criminalized the core ethic of this movement, transforming the meaning of *hacker* into something quite alien to its original sense. Through extremism in copyright regulation, it is criminalizing the core creativity that this network could produce. And this is only the beginning.

Things could be different. They are different elsewhere. But I don't see how they could be different for us just now. This no doubt is simply a confession of the limits of my own imagination. I would be grateful to be proven wrong. I would be grateful to watch as we relearn—as the citizens of the former Communist republics are learning—how to escape these disabling ideas about the possibilities for governance. But nothing in the past decade, and especially nothing in the past five years, has convinced me that my skepticism about governance was misplaced. Indeed, events have only reinforced that pessimism.

TWO

four puzzles from cyberspace

EVERYONE WHO IS READING THIS BOOK HAS USED THE INTERNET. SOME HAVE BEEN in "cyberspace." The Internet is that medium through which your e-mail is delivered and web pages get published. It's what you use to order books on Amazon or to check the times for local movies at Fandango. Google is on the Internet, as are Microsoft "help pages."

But "cyberspace" is something more. Though built on top of the Internet, cyberspace is a richer experience. Cyberspace is something you get pulled "into," perhaps by the intimacy of instant message chat or the intricacy of "massively multiple online games" ("MMOGs" for short, or if the game is a role-playing game, then "MMORPGs"). Some in cyberspace believe they're in a community; some confuse their lives with their cyberspace existence. Of course, no sharp line divides cyberspace from the Internet. But there is an important difference in experience between the two. Those who see the Internet simply as a kind of Yellow-Pages-on-steroids won't recognize what citizens of cyberspace speak of. For them, "cyberspace" is simply obscure.

Some of this difference is generational. For most of us over the age of 40, there is no "cyberspace," even if there is an Internet. Most of us don't live a life online that would qualify as a life in "cyberspace." But for our kids, cyberspace is increasingly their second life. There are millions who spend hundreds of hours a month in the alternative worlds of cyberspace—later on we will focus on one of these worlds, a game called "Second Life."[1] And thus while you may think to yourself, this alien space is nothing I need worry about because it's nowhere I'll ever be, if you care to understand anything about the world the next generation will inhabit, you should spend some time understanding "cyberspace."

That is the aim of two of the stories that follow. These two describe cyberspace. The other two describe aspects of the Internet more generally. My aim through these four very different stories is to orient by sometimes disorienting. My hope is that you'll come to understand four themes that will recur throughout this book. At the end of this chapter, I come clean about the themes and provide a map. For now, just focus on the stories.

BORDERS

It was a very ordinary dispute, this argument between Martha Jones and her neighbors.[2] It was the sort of dispute that people have had since the start of neighborhoods. It didn't begin in anger. It began with a misunderstanding. In this world, misunderstandings like this are far too common. Martha thought about that as she wondered whether she should stay; there were other places she could go. Leaving would mean abandoning what she had built, but frustrations like this were beginning to get to her. Maybe, she thought, it was time to move on.

The argument was about borders—about where her land stopped. It seemed like a simple idea, one you would have thought the powers-that-be would have worked out many years before. But here they were, her neighbor Dank and she, still fighting about borders. Or rather, about something fuzzy at the borders—about something of Martha's that spilled over into the land of others. This was the fight, and it all related to what Martha did.

Martha grew flowers. Not just any flowers, but flowers with an odd sort of power. They were beautiful flowers, and their scent entranced. But, however beautiful, these flowers were also poisonous. This was Martha's weird idea: to make flowers of extraordinary beauty which, if touched, would kill. Strange no doubt, but no one said that Martha wasn't strange. She was unusual, as was this neighborhood. But sadly, disputes like this were not.

The start of the argument was predictable enough. Martha's neighbor, Dank, had a dog. Dank's dog died. The dog died because it had eaten a petal from one of Martha's flowers. A beautiful petal, and now a dead dog. Dank had his own ideas about these flowers, and about this neighbor, and he expressed those ideas—perhaps with a bit too much anger, or perhaps with anger appropriate to the situation.

"There is no reason to grow deadly flowers," Dank yelled across the fence. "There's no reason to get so upset about a few dead dogs," Martha replied. "A dog can always be replaced. And anyway, why have a dog that suffers when dying? Get yourself a pain-free-death dog, and my petals will cause no harm."

I came into the argument at about this time. I was walking by, in the way one walks in this space. (At first I had teleported to get near, but we needn't complicate the story with jargon. Let's just say I was walking.) I saw the two neighbors becoming increasingly angry with each other. I had heard about the disputed

flowers—about how their petals carried poison. It seemed to me a simple problem to solve, but I guess it's simple only if you understand how problems like this
are created.

Dank and Martha were angry because in a sense they were stuck. Both had
built a life in the neighborhood; they had invested many hours there. But both
were coming to understand its limits. This is a common condition: We all build
our lives in places with limits. We are all disappointed at times. What was different about Dank and Martha?

One difference was the nature of the space, or context, where their argument
was happening. This was not "real space" but virtual space. It was part of what I
call "cyberspace." The environment was a "massively multiple online game"
("MMOG"), and MMOG space is quite different from the space we call real.

Real space is the place where you are right now: your office, your den, maybe
by a pool. It's a world defined by both laws that are man-made and others that are
not. "Limited liability" for corporations is a man-made law. It means that the
directors of a corporation (usually) cannot be held personally liable for the sins
of the company. Limited life for humans is not a man-made law: That we all will
die is not the result of a decision that Congress made. In real space, our lives are
subject to both sorts of law, though in principle we could change one sort.

But there are other sorts of laws in real space as well. You bought this book,
I trust, or you borrowed it from someone who did. If you stole it, you are a thief,
whether you are caught or not. Our language is a norm; norms are collectively
determined. As our norms have been determined, your "stealing" makes you a
thief, and not just because you took it. There are plenty of ways to take something
but not be thought of as a thief. If you came across a dollar blowing in the wind,
taking the money will not make you a thief; indeed, not taking the money makes
you a chump. But stealing this book from the bookstore (even when there are so
many left for others) marks you as a thief. Social norms make it so, and we live
life subject to these norms.

Some of these norms can be changed collectively, if not individually. I can
choose to burn my draft card, but I cannot choose whether doing so will make
me a hero or a traitor. I can refuse an invitation to lunch, but I cannot choose
whether doing so will make me rude. I have choices in real life, but escaping the
consequences of the choices I make is not one of them. Norms in this sense constrain us in ways that are so familiar as to be all but invisible.

MMOG space is different. It is, first of all, a virtual space—like a cartoon on
a television screen, sometimes rendered to look three-dimensional. But unlike a
cartoon, MMOG space enables you to control the characters on the screen in real
time. At least, you control your character—one among many characters controlled by many others in this space. One builds the world one will inhabit here.

As a child, you grew up learning the physics that governed the world of Road Runner and Wile E. Coyote (violent but forgiving); your children will grow up making the world of Road Runner and Wile E. Coyote (still violent, but maybe not so forgiving). They will define the space and then live out the story. Their choices will make the laws of that space real.

This is not to say that MMOG space is unreal. There is real life in MMOG space, constituted by how people interact. The "space" describes where people interact—much as they interact in real space no doubt, but with some important differences. In MMOG space the interaction is in a virtual medium. This interaction is "in" cyberspace. In 1990s terms, people "jack" into these virtual spaces, and they do things there. And "they" turns out to be many many people. As Edward Castronova estimates, "an absolute minimum figure would be 10 million [but my] guess is that it is perhaps 20 to 30 million" participating in these virtual worlds.[3] The "[t]ypical user spends 20–30 hours per week inside the fantasy. Power users spend every available moment."[4] As one essay estimates, "assuming just average contact time among these 9.4 million people, subscribers to virtual worlds could be devoting over 213 million hours per week to build their virtual lives."[5]

The things people do there are highly varied. Some play role-playing games: working within a guild of other players to advance in status and power to some ultimate end. Some simply get together and gab: They appear (in a form they select, with qualities they choose and biographies they have written) in a virtual room and type messages to each other. Or they walk around (again, the ambiguity is not a slight one) and talk to people. My friend Rick does this as a cat—a male cat, he insists. As a male cat, Rick parades around this space and talks to anyone who's interested. He aims to flush out the cat-loving sorts. The rest, he reports, he punishes.

Others do much more than gab. Some, for example, homestead. Depending on the world and its laws, citizens are given or buy plots of undeveloped land, which they then develop. People spend extraordinary amounts of time building a life on these plots. (Isn't it incredible the way these people waste time? While you and I spend up to seventy hours a week working for firms we don't own and building futures we're not sure we'll enjoy, these people are designing and building things and making a life, even if only a virtual one. Scandalous!) They build houses—by designing and then constructing them—have family or friends move in, and pursue hobbies or raise pets. They may grow trees or odd plants—like Martha's.

MMOG space grew out of "MUD" or "MOO" space.[6] MUDs and MOOs are virtual worlds, too, but they are text-based virtual worlds. There are no real graphics in a MUD or MOO, just text, reporting what someone says and does.

You can construct objects in MOO space and then have them do things. But the objects act only through the mediation of text. (Their actions are generally quite simple, but even simple can be funny. One year, in a MUD that was part of a cyberlaw class, someone built a character named JPosner. If you poked JPosner, he muttered, "Poking is inefficient." Another character was FEaster-brook. Stand in a room with FEasterbrook and use the word "fair," and FEast-erbrook would repeat what you said, substituting the word "efficient." "It's not fair" became "You mean, it's not efficient.")

Although it was easy for people who liked texts or who wrote well to under-stand the attraction of these text-based realities, it was not so easy for the many who didn't have that same fondness. MMOG space lifts that limit just a bit. It is the movie version of a cyberspace novel. You build things here, and they survive your leaving. You can build a house, and people walking down the street see it. You can let them come in, and in coming into your house, they see things about you. They can see how you construct your world. If a particular MMOG space permits it, they might even see how you've changed the laws of the real world. In real space, for instance, people "slip and fall" on wet floors. In the MMOG space you've built, that "law" may not exist. Instead, in your world, wet floors may make people "slip and dance."

The best example of this space today is the extraordinary community of Second Life. In it, people create both things and community, the avatars are amazingly well crafted, and their owners spend hundreds of thousands of hours building things in this space that others see, and some enjoy. Some make clothes or hair styles, some make machines that make music. Whatever object or service the programming language allows, creators in Second Life are creating it. There are more than 100,000 residents of Second Life at the time of this writing. They occupy close to 2,000 servers housed in downtown San Francisco, and suck 250 kilowatts of electricity just to run the computers—about the equivalent of 160 homes.

But here we get back to Martha and Dank. In their exchange—when Martha blamed Dank for having a dog that died with pain—they revealed what was most amazing about that particular MMOG. Martha's remarks ("Why do you have a dog that suffers when dying? Get yourself a pain-free-death dog, and my petals will cause no harm") should have struck you as odd. You may have thought, "How weird that someone would think that the fault lay not in the poi-sonous petals but in a dog that died with pain." But in this space, Dank did have a choice about how his dog would die. Maybe not a choice about whether "poi-son" would "kill" a dog, but a choice about whether the dog would "suffer" when it "died." He also had a choice about whether a copy of the dog could be made, so that if it died it could be "revived." In MMOG space, these possibilities are not given by God. Or rather, if they are defined by God, then the players share the power of God. For the possibilities in MMOG space are determined by the code—the software, or architecture, that makes the MMOG space what it is. "What happens when" is a statement of logic; it asserts a relationship that is manifested in code. In real space we don't have much control over that code. In MMOG space we do.

So, when Martha said what she said about the dog, Dank made what seemed to me an obvious response. "Why do your flowers have to stay poisonous once they leave your land? Why not make the petals poisonous only when on your land? When they leave your land—when, for example, they are blown onto my land—why not make them harmless?"

It was an idea. But it didn't really help. For Martha made her living selling these poisonous plants. Others (ok not many, but some) also liked the idea of this art tied to death. So it was no solution to make poisonous plants that were poisonous only on Martha's property, unless Martha was also interested in collecting a lot of very weird people on her land.

But the idea did suggest another. "Okay," said Dank, "why not make the petals poisonous only when in the possession of someone who has 'purchased' them? If they are stolen, or if they blow away, then let the petals lose their poison. But when kept by the owner of the plant, the petals keep their poison. Isn't that a solution to the problem that both of us face?"

The idea was ingenious. Not only did it help Dank, it helped Martha as well. As the code existed, it allowed theft.[7] (People want reality in that virtual space; there will be time enough for heaven when heaven comes.) But if Martha could modify the code slightly so that theft[8] removed a plant's poison, then "theft" would also remove the plant's value. That change would protect the profit in her plants as well as protect Dank's dogs. Here was a solution that made both neighbors better off—what economists call a pareto superior move. And it was a solution that was as possible as any other. All it required was a change of code.

Think for a second about what's involved here. "Theft" entails (at minimum) a change in possession. But in MMOG space "possession" is just a relation defined by the software that defines the space. That same code must also define the properties that possession yields. It might, like real space, distinguish between having a cake and eating it. Or it might erase that distinction, meaning you can "eat" your cake, but once it's "eaten," it magically reappears. In MMOG space you can feed a crowd with five loaves and two fishes, and it isn't even a miracle.[9]

So why not craft the same solution to Martha and Dank's problem? Why not define ownership to include the quality of poisonousness, and possession without ownership to be possession without poison? If the world is designed this way, then it could resolve the dispute between Martha and Dank, not by making one of them change his or her behavior, but by changing the laws of nature to eliminate the conflict altogether.

We're a short way into this not so short book, though what I'm about to say may make it a very short book indeed (for you at least). This book is all about the question raised by this simple story, and about any simplicity in this apparently simple answer. This is not a book about MMOG space or avatars. The story about Martha and Dank is the first and last example that will include avatars. But it is a book about cyberspace. My claim is that both "on the Internet" and "in cyberspace," we will confront precisely the questions that Martha and Dank faced, as well as the questions that their solution raised. Both "on the Internet" and "in cyberspace," technology constitutes the environment of the space, and it will give us a much wider range of control over how interactions work in that space than in real space. Problems can be programmed or "coded" into the story, and they can be "coded" away. And while the experience with gamers so far is that they don't want virtual worlds to deviate too far from the real, the important point for now is that there is the capacity to make these worlds different. It is this capacity that raises the question that is at the core of this book: What does it mean to live in a world where problems can be coded away? And when, in that world, should we code problems away, rather than learn to work them out, or punish those who cause them?

It is not MMOG space that makes these questions interesting problems for law; the very same problems will arise outside of MMOG space, and outside MUDs and MOOs. The problems of these spaces are problems of the Internet in general. And as more of our life becomes wired (and weird), in the sense that more of our life moves online, these questions will become more pressing.

But I have learned enough in this business to know that I can't convince you of this with an argument. (I've spent the last 12 years talking about this subject; at least I know what doesn't work.) If you see the point, good for you. If you don't, I must show you. So my method for readers of the second sort must be more indirect. Proof, for them, will come in a string of stories, which aim to introduce and disorient. That, again, is the purpose of this chapter.

Let me describe a few other places and the oddities that inhabit them.

GOVERNORS

A state—call it "Boral"—doesn't like its citizens gambling, even if many of its citizens do like gambling. But the state is the boss; the people have voted; the law is as it is. Gambling in the state of Boral is illegal.

Then along comes the Internet. With the Net streaming into their homes through phones or cable lines, some citizens of Boral decide that Internet gambling is the next "killer app." A citizen of Boral sets up a "server" (a computer that is accessible on the Internet) that provides access to online gambling. The state doesn't like it. It tells this citizen, "Shut down your server or we will lock you up."

Wise, if evasive, the gambling Boralian agrees to shut his server down—at least in the state of Boral. But he doesn't choose to leave the gambling business. Instead, he rents space on a server in an "offshore haven." This offshore web server hums away, once again making gambling available on the Net and accessible to the people of Boral via the Internet. Here's the important point: Given the architecture of the Internet (at least as it was circa 1999), it doesn't really matter where in real space the server is. Access doesn't depend on geography. Nor, depending on how clever the gambling sorts are, does access require that the user know anything about who owns, or runs, the real server. The user's access can be passed through anonymizing sites that make it practically impossible in the end to know *what* went on *where* and with whom.

The Boral attorney general thus now faces a difficult problem. She may have moved the server out of her state, but she hasn't succeeded in reducing Boralian gambling. Before the Net, she would have had a group of people she could punish—those running gambling sites, and those who give those places custom. Now, the Net has made them potentially free from punishment—at the least because it is more difficult to know who is running the server or who is gambling. The world for this attorney general has changed. By going online, the gamblers moved into a world where this behavior is no longer *regulable*.

By "regulable" I mean simply that a certain behavior is capable of regulation. The term is comparative, not absolute—in some place, at some time, a certain behavior will be more regulable than at another place and in another time. My claim about Boral is simply that the Net makes gambling less regulable there than it was before the Net. Or at least, in a sense that will become clearer as the story continues, with the architecture of the Net as it originally was, life on the Net is less regulable than life off the Net.

JAKE'S COMMUNITIES

If you had met Jake at a party in Ann Arbor (were Jake at a party in Ann Arbor), you would have forgotten him.[10] If you didn't forget him, you might have thought, here's another quiet, dweeby University of Michigan undergraduate, terrified of the world, or, at least, of the people in the world.

You wouldn't have figured Jake for an author—indeed, quite a famous short-story author, at least within his circles. In fact, Jake is not just a famous author, he was also a character in his own stories. But who he was in his stories was quite different from who he was in "real" life—if, that is, after reading his stories you still thought this distinction between "real life" and "not real life" made much sense.

Jake wrote stories about violence—about sex as well, but mainly about violence. They seethed with hatred, especially of women. It wasn't enough to rape a woman, she had to be killed. And it wasn't enough that she was killed, she had to be killed in a particularly painful and tortured way. This is, however unfortunate, a genre of writing. Jake was a master of this genre.

In real space Jake had quite successfully hidden this propensity. He was one of a million boys: unremarkable, indistinguishable, harmless. Yet however inoffensive in real space, the harmfulness he penned in cyberspace was increasingly well known. His stories were published in USENET, in a group called alt.sex.stories.

USENET isn't itself a network, except in the sense that the personal ads of a national newspaper are part of a network. Strictly speaking, USENET is the product of a protocol—a set of rules named the network news transfer protocol (NNTP)—for exchanging messages intended for public viewing. These messages are organized into "newsgroups," and the newsgroups are organized into subjects. Most of the subjects are quite technical, many are related to hobbies, and some are related to sex. Some messages newsgroups come with pictures or movies, but some, like Jake's, are simply stories.

There are thousands of newsgroups, each carrying hundreds of messages at any one time. Anyone with access to a USENET server can get access to the messages (or at least to the ones his administrator wants him to read), and anyone with access can post a message or respond to one already posted. Imagine a public bulletin board on which people post questions or comments. Anyone can read the board and add his or her own thoughts. Now imagine 15,000 boards, each with hundreds of "threads" (strings of arguments, each tied to the next). That, in any one place, is USENET. Now imagine these 15,000 boards, with hundreds of threads each, on millions of computers across the world. Post a message in one group, and it is added to that group's board everywhere. That, for the world, is USENET.

Jake, as I said, posted to a group called alt.sex.stories. "Alt" in that name refers to the hierarchy that the group sits within. Initially, there were seven primary hierarchies.[11] "Alt" was created in reaction to this initial seven: Groups are added to the seven through a formal voting process among participants in the groups. But groups are added to "alt" based solely on whether administrators choose to carry them, and, generally, administrators will carry them if they are popular, as long as their popularity is not controversial.

Among these groups that are carried only on demand, alt.sex.stories is quite popular. As with any writing space, if stories are "good" by the standards of the space—if they are stories that users of the space demand—they are followed and their authors become well known.

Jake's stuff was very valuable in just this sense. His stories, about kidnapping, torturing, raping, and killing women, were as graphic and repulsive as any such story could be—which is why Jake was so famous among like-minded sorts. He was a supplier to these people, a constant and consistent fix. They needed these accounts of innocent women being violated, and Jake supplied them for free.

One night in Moscow, a sixteen-year-old girl read a story by Jake. She showed it to her father, who showed it in turn to Richard DuVal, a Michigan alum. DuVal was shocked at the story, and angry that it bore the tag "umich.edu" on the story's header. He called his alma mater and complained. They took the complaint seriously.[12]

The university contacted the police; the police contacted Jake—with handcuffs and a jail cell. A slew of doctors examined him. Some concluded that he was a threat. The local prosecutors agreed with these doctors, especially after his computer was seized and e-mails were discovered between Jake and a Canadian fan who was planning to re-enact in real space one of the stories Jake published in cyberspace. At least, that's what the e-mails said. No one could tell for certain what the two men really intended. Jake said it was all pure fiction, and indeed, there was no evidence to prove otherwise.

Nonetheless, federal charges were brought against Jake for the transmission of a threat. Jake said that his stories were only words, protected by the First Amendment to the U.S. Constitution. A month and a half later, a court agreed. The charges were dropped,[13] and Jake returned to the special kind of obscurity that had defined his life before.

I don't care so much just now about whether Jake Baker's words should have been protected by the Constitution. My concern is Jake Baker himself, a person normed into apparent harmlessness in real space, but set free in cyberspace to become the author of this violence. People said Jake was brave, but he wasn't "brave" in real space. He didn't express his hatred in classes, among friends, or in the school newspaper. He slithered away to cyberspace, and only there did his deviancy flourish.

He did this because of something about him and something about cyberspace. Jake was the sort who wanted to spread stories of violence, at least if he could do so without public account. Cyberspace gave Jake this power. Jake was in effect an author and publisher in one. He wrote stories, and as quickly as he finished them he published them—to some thirty million computers across the world within a few days. His potential audience was larger than twice that for the top fifteen best-selling novels combined, and though he made nothing from his work, the demand for it was high. Jake had discovered a way to mainline his depravity into the veins of a public for whom this stuff was otherwise quite difficult to find. (Even *Hustler* wouldn't publish the likes of this.)

Of course, there were other ways Jake could have published. He could have offered his work to *Hustler,* or worse. But no real-world publication would have given Jake a comparable audience. Jake's readership was potentially millions, stretching across country and continent, across culture and taste.

This reach was made possible by the power in the network: Anyone anywhere could publish to everyone everywhere. The network allowed publication without filtering, editing, or, perhaps most importantly, responsibility. One could write what one wanted, sign it or not, post it to machines across the world, and within hours the words would be everywhere. The network removed the most important constraint on speech in real space—the separation of publisher from author. There is vanity publishing in real space, but only the rich can use it to reach a broad audience. For the rest of us, real space affords only the access that the publishers want to give us.

Thus cyberspace is different because of the reach it allows. But it is also different because of the relative anonymity it permits. Cyberspace permitted Jake to escape the constraints of real space. He didn't "go to" cyberspace when he wrote his stories, in the sense that he didn't "leave" Ann Arbor. But when he was "in" cyberspace, it allowed him to escape the norms of Ann Arbor. He was free of real-life constraints, of the norms and understandings that had successfully formed him into a member of a college community. Maybe he wasn't perfectly at home; maybe he wasn't the happiest. But the world of the University of Michigan had succeeded in steering him away from the life of a psychopath— except when it gave him access to the Net. On the Net he was someone else.

As the Internet has grown, it has produced many more opportunities for Jake-like characters—characters that do things in the virtual world that they would never do in the real world. One of the most popular MMOGs is a game called "Grand Theft Auto." In this game, one practices committing crimes. And one of the most troubling uses of video chat is the practice of virtual-prostitution by children. As the *New York Times* recently reported, thousands of children spend hundreds of hours prostituting themselves online. Sitting in the "privacy" of their own bedroom, using the iSight camera their parents gave them for Christmas, a 13-year-old girl or boy enacts the sexual behavior demanded by the audience. The audience gets their fix of sexual perversion. The kid gets money, and whatever psychological baggage this behavior creates.[14]

It is impossibly difficult to look across this range of Jake-like characters and not think that, at some point, the virtual has crossed over into something real. Or, at least, the virtual has real effects—either on those who live it, or on those who live with them.[15] When Jake was prosecuted, many First Amendment defenders argued his words, however vivid, never crossed into reality. And no doubt, there is a difference between writing about rape and raping, just as there is a difference between an actor enacting rape and actually raping someone. But I take it that all concede a line is crossed somewhere as we move across this range of Jake-like characters. If a parent was untroubled by the virtual prostitution of her son in his bedroom, we would not understand that to be principled free speech activism, even if the only "prostitution" was the son describing in text how he was molested by those in the chat.

But my point is not to draw lines between the acceptable virtual dual-lives and the unacceptable. It is instead to remark that this space enables more of this duality. And though part of this duality is always "only virtual," and sometimes "only words," real-space regulators (whether parents or governments) will feel compelled to react. The Net enables lives that were previously impossible, or inconvenient, or uncommon. At least some of those virtual lives will have effects on non-virtual lives—both the lives of the people living in the virtual space, and the lives of those around them.

WORMS THAT SNIFF

A "worm" is a bit of computer code that is spit out on the Net and works its way into the systems of vulnerable computers. It is not a "virus" because it doesn't attach itself to other programs and interfere with their operation. It is just a bit of extra code that does what the code writer says. The code could be harmless and simply sit on someone's machine. Or it could be harmful and corrupt files or do other damage that its author commands.

Imagine a worm designed to do good (at least in the minds of some). Imagine that the code writer is the FBI and that the FBI is looking for a particular document belonging to the National Security Agency (NSA). Suppose that this document is classified and illegal to possess without the proper clearance. Imagine that the worm propagates itself on the Net, finding its way onto hard disks wherever it can. Once on a computer's hard disk, it scans the entire disk. If it finds the NSA document, it sends a message back to the FBI saying as much. If it doesn't, it erases itself. Finally, assume that it can do all this without "interfering" with the operation of the machine. No one would know it was there; it would report back nothing except that the NSA document was on the hard disk.

Is this an unconstitutional worm? This is a hard question that at first seems to have an easy answer. The worm is engaging in a government-initiated search of citizens' disks. There is no reasonable suspicion (as the law ordinarily requires) that the disk holds the document for which the government is searching. It is a generalized, suspicionless search of private spaces by the government.

From the standpoint of the Constitution—the Fourth Amendment in particular—you don't get any worse than that. The Fourth Amendment was written against the background of just this sort of abuse. Kings George II and George III would give officers a "general warrant" authorizing them to search through private homes looking for evidence of a crime.[16] No suspicion was needed before the officer ransacked your house, but because he had a warrant, you were not able to sue the officer for trespass. The aim of the Fourth Amendment was to require at least suspicion, so that the burden of the search fell on a reasonably chosen class.[17]

But is the worm really the same as the King's general search? One important difference is this: Unlike the victims of the general searches that the Framers of our Constitution were concerned about, the computer user never knows that his or her disk is being searched by the worm. With the general search, the police were breaking into a house and rummaging through private stuff. With the worm, it is a bit of computer code that does the breaking, and (I've assumed) it can "see" only one thing. And perhaps more importantly, unlike the general search, the worm learns little and leaves no damage after it's finished: The code can't read private letters; it doesn't break down doors; it doesn't interfere with ordinary life. And the innocent have nothing to fear.

The worm is silent in a way that King George's troops were not. It searches perfectly and invisibly, discovering only the guilty. It does not burden the innocent; it does not trouble the ordinary citizen; it captures only what is outside the protection of the law.

This difference complicates the constitutional question. The worm's behavior is like a generalized search in that it is a search without suspicion. But it is unlike the historical generalized search in that it creates no disruption of ordinary life and "discovers" only contraband. In this way, the worm is like a dog sniff—which at least at airports is constitutionally permissible without probable cause[18]—but better. Unlike the dog sniff, the worm doesn't even let the computer user know when there is a search (and hence the user suffers no particularized anxiety).

Is the worm, then, constitutional? That depends on your conception of what the Fourth Amendment protects. In one view, the amendment protects against suspicionless governmental invasions, whether those invasions are burdensome or not. In a second view, the amendment protects against invasions that are burdensome, allowing only those for which there is adequate suspicion that guilt will be uncovered. The paradigm case that motivated the framers does not distinguish between these two very different types of protections, because the technology of the time wouldn't distinguish either. You couldn't—technically—have a perfectly burdenless generalized search in 1791. So they didn't—technically—express a view about whether such a search should be constitutionally proscribed. It is instead we who must choose what the amendment is to mean.

Let's take the example one step further. Imagine that the worm does not search every machine it encounters, but instead can be put on a machine only with judicial authorization—say, a warrant. Now the suspicionless-search part of the problem has been removed. But now imagine a second part to this rule: The government requires that networks be constructed so that a worm, with judicial authorization, could be placed on any machine. Machines in this regime, in other words, must be made worm-ready, even though worms will be deployed only with judicial warrant.

Is there any constitutional problem with this? I explore this question in much greater detail in Chapter 11, but for now, notice its salient feature. In both cases, we are describing a regime that allows the government to collect data about us in a highly efficient manner—inexpensively, that is, for both the government and the innocent. This efficiency is made possible by technology, which permits searches that before would have been far too burdensome and invasive. In both cases, then, the question comes to this: When the ability to search without burden increases, does the government's power to search increase as well? Or, more darkly, as James Boyle puts it: "Is freedom inversely related to the efficiency of the available means of surveillance?" For if it is, as Boyle puts it, then "we have much to fear."[19]

This question, of course, is not limited to the government. One of the defining features of modern life is the emergence of technologies that make data collection and processing extraordinarily efficient. Most of what we do—hence, most of what we are—is recorded outside our homes. When you make telephone calls, data are recorded about whom you called, when, how long you spoke, and how frequently you made such calls.[20] When you use your credit cards, data are recorded about when, where, what, and from whom you made purchases. When you take a flight, your itinerary is recorded and possibly profiled by the government to determine whether you are likely to be a terrorist.[21] If you drive a car in London, cameras record your license plate to determine whether you've paid the proper "congestion tax." No doubt Hollywood's image of counter-terrorist units—where one person sitting behind a terminal instantly tracks the life of another—is wrong. But it need not be terribly wrong for much longer. It may not be easy to imagine systems that follow an individual wherever he goes, but it is easy to imagine technologies that gather an extraordinary amount of data about everything we do and make those data accessible to those with the proper authorization. The intrusiveness would be slight, and the payoff could be great.

Both private and public monitoring in the digital age, then, have the same salient feature: monitoring, or searching, can increase without increasing the burden on the individual searched. Both present a similar question: How should we think about this change? How should the protection the framers gave us be applied to a world the framers couldn't even imagine?

THEMES

Four stories, four themes, each a window into one aspect of cyberspace that will be central in all that follows. My aim in the balance of this book is to work through the issues raised by these four themes. I thus end this chapter with a map of the four, laid out in the order they will appear in the balance of the book. That order begins with story number two.

Regulability

"Regulability" is the capacity of a government to regulate behavior within its proper reach. In the context of the Internet, that means the ability of the government to regulate the behavior of (at least) its citizens while on the Net. The story about Boral was thus a story about regulability, or more specifically, about the changes in regulability that cyberspace brings. Before the Internet, it was relatively easy for the attorney general of Boral to control commercial gambling within her jurisdiction; after the Internet, when the servers moved outside of Boral, regulation became much more difficult.

For the regulator, this is just a particular instance of a much more general story. To regulate well, you need to know (1) who someone is, (2) where they are, and (3) what they're doing. But because of the way the Internet was originally designed (and more on this below), there was no simple way to know (1) who someone is, (2) where they are, and (3) what they're doing. Thus, as life moved onto (this version of) the Internet, the regulability of that life decreased. The architecture of the space—at least as it was—rendered life in this space less regulable.

The balance of Part I is about regulability. Can we imagine a more regulable cyberspace? Is this the cyberspace we are coming to know?

Regulation by Code

The story about Martha and Dank is a clue to answering this question about regulability. If in MMOG space we can change the laws of nature—make possible what before was impossible, or make impossible what before was possible—why can't we change regulability in cyberspace? Why can't we imagine an Internet or a cyberspace where behavior can be controlled because code now enables that control?

For this, importantly, is just what MMOG space is. MMOG space is "regulated," though the regulation is special. In MMOG space regulation comes through code. Important rules are imposed, not through social sanctions, and not by the state, but by the very architecture of the particular space. A rule is defined, not through a statute, but through the code that governs the space.

This is the second theme of this book: There is regulation of behavior on the Internet and in cyberspace, but that regulation is imposed primarily through code. The differences in the regulations effected through code distinguish different parts of the Internet and cyberspace. In some places, life is fairly free; in other places, it is more controlled. And the difference between these spaces is simply a difference in the architectures of control—that is, a difference in code.

If we combine the first two themes, then, we come to a central argument of the book: The regulability described in the first theme depends on the code described in the second. Some architectures of cyberspace are more regulable than others; some architectures enable better control than others. Therefore, whether a part of cyberspace—or the Internet generally—can be regulated turns on the nature of its code. Its architecture will affect whether behavior can be controlled. To follow Mitch Kapor, its architecture is its politics.[22]

And from this a further point follows: If some architectures are more regulable than others—if some give governments more control than others—then governments will favor some architectures more than others. Favor, in turn, can translate into action, either by governments, or for governments. Either way, the architectures that render space less regulable can themselves be changed to make the space more regulable. (By whom, and why, is a matter we take up later.)

This fact about regulability is a threat to those who worry about governmental power; it is a reality for those who depend upon governmental power. Some designs enable government more than others; some designs enable government differently; some designs should be chosen over others, depending upon the values at stake.

Latent Ambiguity

The worm tells a different story still. Though it is a technology for searching, the worm's function differs from "searching" in real space. In real space, a search carries costs: the burdens of the search, the insecurities it might create, the exposure it might make possible to invasions beyond a legitimate reach.[23] The worm erases those costs: The burden is gone, the search is (practically) invisible, and the searching technology is programmed to find only what is illegal. This raises a question about how such a search should, under the Constitution, be understood.

A fair view of the Constitution's protections could go in either of two ways. It may be that we see the worm's invasion as inconsistent with the dignity that the amendment was written to protect,[24] or it may be that we see the invasion of the worm as so unobtrusive as to be reasonable. The answer could be either, which means that the change reveals what I will call "a latent ambiguity" in the original constitutional rule. In the original context, the rule was clear (no generalized search), but in the current context, the rule depends upon which value the Constitution was meant to protect. The question is now ambiguous between (at least) two different answers. Either answer is possible, depending upon the value, so now we must choose one or the other.

You may not buy my story about the worm. You may think it is pure science fiction. But by the end of the book, I will convince you that there are any number of cases in which a similar ambiguity troubles our constitutional past. In many of them our Constitution yields no answer to the question of how it should be applied, because at least two answers are possible—in light of the choices that the framers actually made and given the technologies of today.

For Americans, this ambiguity creates a problem. If we lived in an era when courts felt entitled to select the value that produced an answer that made the most sense in the context, there would be no problem. Latent ambiguities would be answered by choices made by judges—the framers could have gone either way, but our judges choose to go *this* way.

But we don't live in such an era, and so we don't have a way for courts to resolve these ambiguities. As a result, we must rely on other institutions. My claim is a dark one: We have no such institutions. If our ways don't change, our constitution in cyberspace will be a thinner and thinner regime.

Cyberspace will present us with ambiguities over and over again. It will press this question of how best to go on. We have tools from real space that will help resolve the interpretive questions by pointing us in one direction or another, at least some of the time. But in the end the tools will guide us even less than they do in real space and time. When the gap between their guidance and what we do becomes obvious, we will be forced to do something we're not very good at doing—deciding what we want, and what is right.

Competing Sovereigns

But regulation by whom? For the rules are different in one place versus another.

This was one important issue raised by Jake Baker. Jake lived in Ann Arbor, Michigan. His life there was subject to the norms of Ann Arbor, and he apparently adapted to these norms reasonably well. The authority of that space governed Jake, and, as far as anyone knew, it appeared to govern him exclusively.

But in cyberspace, Jake's behavior changed, in part because the norms of the space were different. That created the problem. For when Jake "went to" cyberspace, he didn't leave real space. In particular, he never left Ann Arbor. While sitting in a dorm at the University of Michigan, he was able to teleport himself—in the only normatively significant sense—to a different world where the norms of civility and decency that governed outside his dorm room did not reign. Cyberspace gave Jake the chance to escape Ann Arbor norms and to live according to the norms of another place. It created a competing authority for Jake and gave him the chance to select between these competing authorities merely by switching his computer on or off.

Again, my point is not that no similar possibility exists in real space—it plainly does. There is no doubt a Jake living in Hackensack, New Jersey (a suburban town with suburban values), who drives every night into lower Manhattan and lives for a few hours according to the "rules" of lower Manhattan. Those rules are not the rules of Hackensack; that life is different. Like Ann Arbor Jake, the Hackensack Jake lives under competing authorities. But between the lives of these two Jakes, there is a difference in degree that ripens into a difference in kind: It is at least conceivable that the Ann Arbor Jake raises a more significant problem for Ann Arbor than the Hackensack Jake raises for Hackensack. The differences could well be greater, and the effect more pervasive.

Nor should we think too narrowly about the competing normative communities into which a Jake might move. "Escape" here can be good or bad. It is escape when a gay teen in an intolerant small town can leave the norms of that town through a gay chat room on America Online;[25] it is escape when a child predator escapes the norms of ordinary society and engages a child in online sex.[26] Both escapes are enabled by the architecture of cyberspace as we now know it. Our attitudes about each, however, are very different. I call the first escape liberating and the second criminal. There are some who would call both escapes criminal, and some who would call both liberating. But the question isn't about name-calling, it's about the consequences of living in a world where we can occupy both sorts of space at the same time. When 50 people from 25 jurisdictions around the world spend 2,000 hours building a virtual community in Second Life that is housed on servers in San Francisco, what claim should real world jurisdictions have over that activity? Which of the 25 jurisdictions matters most? Which sovereign should govern?

These four themes frame everything that follows. They also map the understanding that I want this book to provide. Regulation in cyberspace can help us see something important about how all regulation works. That's the lesson of the first theme, "regulability." It will also introduce a regulator ("code") whose significance we don't yet fully understand. That's the second theme, "Regulation by Code." That regulation will render ambiguous certain values that are fundamental to our tradition. Thus, the third theme, "latent ambiguity." That ambiguity will require us, the United States, to make a choice. But this choice is just one among many that many sovereigns will have to make. In the end the hardest problem will be to reckon these "competing sovereigns," as they each act to mark this space with their own distinctive values.

I explore these four themes against a background that, as I said at the start, has changed significantly since the first edition of this book. When I first wrote the book, two ideas seemed to dominate debate about the Net: first, that the government could never regulate the Net, and second, that this was a good thing. Today, attitudes are different. There is still the commonplace that government can't regulate, but in a world drowning in spam, computer viruses, identity theft, copyright "piracy," and the sexual exploitation of children, the resolve against regulation has weakened. We all love the Net. But if some government could really deliver on the promise to erase all the bads of this space, most of us would gladly sign up.

Yet while attitudes about the Net have progressed, my own views have not. I still believe the Net can be regulated. I still believe that the obvious consequence of obvious influences will be to radically increase the ability of governments to regulate this Net. I also still believe that, in principle, this is not a bad thing. I am not against regulation, properly done. I believe regulation is essential to preserving and defending certain fundamental liberties. But I also still believe that we are far from a time when our government in particular can properly regulate in this context. This is both because of a general skepticism about government—grounded in a disgust about the particular form of corruption that defines how our government functions—and a particular skepticism about government—that it has not yet fully recognized just how regulation in the digital age works.

No doubt this particular mix of views will continue to puzzle some. How can I believe in regulation and yet be so skeptical about government? But it doesn't take much imagination to understand how these apparently conflicting views can go together. I take it we all believe in the potential of medicine. But imagine your attitude if you were confronted with a "doctor" carrying a vial of leeches. There's much we could do in this context, or at least, that is my view. But there's a very good reason not to want to do anything with this particular doctor.

PART ONE

"regulability"

It is said that cyberspace can't be regulated. But what does it mean to say that something could be regulated? What makes regulation possible? That's the question raised in this Part. If the Internet can't be regulated, why? And whatever the reason, can it change? Might an unregulable space be tamed? Might the Wild West be won, and how?

THREE

---

i s - i s m :

is the way it is the way it must be?

The rise of an electronic medium that disregards geographical bound-
aries throws the law into disarray by creating entirely new phenomena
that need to become the subject of clear legal rules but that cannot be
governed, satisfactorily, by any current territorially based sovereign.
                                              David Johnson and David Post[1]

Some things never change about governing the Web. Most prominent is
its innate ability to resist governance in almost any form.
                                              Tom Steinert-Threlkeld[2]

IF THERE WAS A MEME THAT RULED TALK ABOUT CYBERSPACE, IT WAS THAT CYBERSPACE
was a place that could not be regulated. That it "cannot be governed"; that its
"nature" is to resist regulation. Not that cyberspace cannot be broken, or that
government cannot shut it down. But if cyberspace exists, so first-generation
thinking goes, government's power over behavior there is quite limited. In its
essence, cyberspace is a space of no control.

Nature. Essence. Innate. The way things are. This kind of rhetoric should
raise suspicions in any context. It should especially raise suspicion here. If
there is any place where nature has no rule, it is in cyberspace. If there is any
place that is constructed, cyberspace is it. Yet the rhetoric of "essence" hides
this constructedness. It misleads our intuitions in dangerous ways.

31

This is the fallacy of "is-ism"—the mistake of confusing how some-thing is with how it must be. There is certainly a way that cyberspace *is*. But how cyberspace *is* is not how cyberspace has to be. There is no single way that the Net has to be; no single architecture that defines the nature of the Net. The possible architectures of something that we would call "the Net" are many, and the character of life within those different architectures is diverse.

That most of us commit this fallacy is not surprising. Most of us haven't a clue about how networks work. We therefore have no clue about how they could be different. We assume that the way we find things is the way things have to be. We are not trained to think about all the different ways technology could achieve the same ends through different means. That sort of training is what technologists get. Most of us are not technol-ogists.

But underlying everything in this book is a single normative plea: that all of us must learn at least enough to see that technology is plastic. It can be remade to do things differently. And that if there is a mistake that we who know too little about technology should make, it is the mistake of imagining technology to be too plastic, rather than not plastic enough. We should expect—and demand—that it can be made to reflect any set of val-ues that we think important. The burden should be on the technologists to show us why that demand can't be met.

The particular is-ism that I begin with here is the claim that cyberspace can't be regulated. As this, and the following chapters argue, that view is wrong. Whether cyberspace can be regulated depends upon its architecture. The original architecture of the Internet made regulation extremely diffi-cult. But that original architecture can change. And there is all the evidence in the world that it is changing. Indeed, under the architecture that I believe will emerge, cyberspace will be the most regulable space humans have ever known. The "nature" of the Net might once have been its unreg-ulability; that "nature" is about to flip.

To see the flip, you must first see a contrast between two different cyber-places. These two cyber-places are ideal types, and, indeed, one of the two ideals no longer exists anywhere on the Net. That fact is confirmation of the point this section aims to make: that we're moving from one Internet to another, and the one we're moving to will be significantly more regula-ble.

The following descriptions are not technical; I don't offer them as com-plete definitions of types of networks or types of control. I offer them to illustrate—to sketch enough to see a far more general point.

CYBER-PLACES: HARVARD VERSUS CHICAGO

The Internet was born at universities in the United States. Its first subscribers were researchers. But as a form of life, its birth was tied to university life. It swept students online, pulling them away from life in real space. The Net was one of many intoxicants on college campuses in the mid-1990s, and its significance only grew through time. As former *New York Times* columnist J. C. Herz wrote in her first book about cyberspace:

> When I look up, it's four-thirty in the morning. "No way." I look from the clock to my watch. Way. I've been in front of this screen for six hours, and it seems like no time at all. I'm not even remotely tired. Dazed and thirsty, but not tired. In fact, I'm euphoric. I stuff a disheveled heap of textbooks, photocopied articles, hilighters and notes into my backpack and run like a madwoman up the concrete steps, past the security guard, and outside into the predawn mist. . . .
>
> I stop where a wet walkway meets a dry one and stand for a sec. . . . [I] start thinking about this thing that buzzes around the entire world, through the phone lines, all day and all night long. It's right under our noses and it's invisible. It's like Narnia, or Magritte, or *Star Trek,* an entire goddamned world. Except it doesn't physically exist. It's just the collective consciousness of however many people are on it.
>
> This really is outstandingly weird.[3]

Yet not all universities adopted the Net in the same way. Or put differently, the access universities granted was not all the same. The rules were different. The freedoms allowed were different. One example of this difference comes from two places I knew quite well, though many other examples could make the same point.

In the middle 1990s at the University of Chicago, if you wanted access to the Internet, you simply connected your machine to Ethernet jacks located throughout the university.[4] Any machine with an Ethernet connection could be plugged into these jacks. Once connected, your machine had full access to the Internet—access, that is, that was complete, anonymous, and free.

The reason for this freedom was a decision by an administrator—the then-Provost, Geoffrey Stone, a former dean of the law school and a prominent free speech scholar. When the university was designing its net, the technicians asked Stone whether anonymous communication should be permitted. Stone, citing the principle that the rules regulating speech at the university should be as protective of free speech as the First Amendment, said yes: People should have the right to communicate at the university anonymously, because the First Amendment to the Constitution guarantees the same right vis-à-vis governments. From that policy decision flowed the architecture of the University of Chicago's net.

At Harvard, the rules are different. If you plug your machine into an Ethernet jack at the Harvard Law School, you will not gain access to the Net. You cannot connect your machine to the Net at Harvard unless the machine is registered—licensed, approved, verified. Only members of the university community can register their machines. Once registered, all interactions with the network are monitored and identified to a particular machine. To join the network, users have to "sign" a user agreement. The agreement acknowledges this pervasive practice of monitoring. Anonymous speech on this network is not permitted—it is against the rules. Access can be controlled based on who you are, and interactions can be traced based on what you did.

This design also arose from the decision of an administrator, one less focused on the protections of the First Amendment. Control was the ideal at Harvard; access was the ideal at Chicago. Harvard chose technologies that made control possible; Chicago chose technologies that made access easy.

These two networks differ in at least two important ways. First and most obviously, they differ in the values they embrace.[5] That difference is by design. At the University of Chicago, First Amendment values determined network design; different values determined Harvard's design.

But they differ in a second way as well. Because access is controlled at Harvard and identity is known, actions can be traced back to their root in the network. Because access is not controlled at Chicago, and identity is not known, actions cannot be traced back to their root in the network. Monitoring or tracking behavior at Chicago is harder than it is at Harvard. Behavior in the Harvard network is more controllable than in the University of Chicago network.

The networks thus differ in the extent to which they make behavior within each network regulable. This difference is simply a matter of code—a difference in the software and hardware that grants users access. Different code makes differently regulable networks. Regulability is thus a function of design.

These two networks are just two points on a spectrum of possible network designs. At one extreme we might place the Internet—a network defined by a suite of protocols that are open and nonproprietary and that require no personal identification to be accessed and used. At the other extreme are traditional closed, proprietary networks, which grant access only to those with express authorization; control, therefore, is tight. In between are networks that mix elements of both. These mixed networks add a layer of control to the otherwise uncontrolled Internet. They layer elements of control on top.

Thus the original—there have been some changes in the last years[6]—University of Chicago network was close to the norm for Internet access in the middle of the 1990s.[7] Let's call it Net95. At the other extreme are closed networks that both predate the Internet and still exist today—for example, the ATM network, which makes it possible to get cash from your California bank at 2:00 A.M. while in Tblisi. And in the middle are Harvard-type networks—networks that add a layer of control on top of the suite of protocols that define "the Internet." These protocols are called "TCP/IP." I describe them more extensively in Chapter 4. But the essential feature of the Harvard network is that this suite was supplemented. You get access to the Internet only after you've passed through this layer of control.

All three designs are communication networks that are "like" the Internet. But their differences raise an obvious question: When people say that the Internet is "unregulable," which network are they describing? And if they're talking about an unregulable network, why is it unregulable? What features in its design make it unregulable? And could those features be different?

Consider three aspects of Net95's design that make it hard for a regulator to control behavior there. From the perspective of an anonymity-loving user, these are "features" of Net95—aspects that make that network more valuable. But from the perspective of the regulator, these features are "bugs"—imperfections that limit the data that the Net collects, either about the user or about the material he or she is using.

The first imperfection is information about users—who the someone is who is using the Internet. In the words of the famous *New Yorker* cartoon of two dogs sitting in front of a PC, "On the Internet, nobody knows you're a dog."[8] No one knows, because the Internet protocols don't require that you credential who you are before you use the Internet. Again, the *Internet* protocol doesn't require that credential; your local access point, like the Harvard network, might. But even then, the information that ties the individual to a certain network transaction is held by the access provider. It is not a part of your Internet transaction.

The second "imperfection" is information about geography—where the someone is who is using the Internet. As I will describe more in Chapter 4, although the Internet is constituted by addresses, those addresses were initially simply logical addresses. They didn't map to any particular location in the physical world. Thus, when I receive a packet of data sent by you through the Internet, it is certainly possible for me to know the Internet address from which your packet comes, but I will not know the physical address.

And finally, the third "imperfection" is information about use—what is the data being sent across this network; what is its use? The Internet does not require any particular labeling system for data being sent across the Internet. Again, as we'll see in more detail below, there are norms that say something, but no rule to assure data gets distributed just according to the norms. Nothing puts the bits into a context of meaning, at least not in a way that a machine can use. Net95 had no requirement that data be labeled. "Packets" of data are labeled, in the sense of having an address. But beyond that, the packets could contain anything at all.

These three "imperfections" tie together: Because there is no simple way to know who someone is, where they come from, and what they're doing, there is no simple way to regulate how people behave on the Net. If you can't discover who did what and where, you can't easily impose rules that say "don't do this, or at least, don't do it there." Put differently, what you can't know determines what you can control.

Consider an example to make the point clearer. Let's say the state of Pennsylvania wants to block kids from porn. It thus passes a rule that says "No kid in Pennsylvania can get access to porn." To enforce that rule, Pennsylvania has got to know (1) whether someone is a kid, (2) where they come from (i.e., Pennsylvania or Maine), and (3) what they're looking at (porn or marzipan). Net95, however, won't be of much help to Pennsylvania as it tries to enforce this rule. People accessing content in Pennsylvania using Net95 need not reveal anything about who they are or where they come from, and nothing in the design of Net95 requires sites to describe what content they carry. These gaps in data make regulating hard. Thus from the perspective of the regulator, these are imperfections in the Net's original design.

But the Harvard network suggests that it is at least possible for the "bugs" in Net95 to be eliminated. The Net could know the credentials of the user (identity and location) and the nature of the data being sent. That knowledge could be layered onto the Internet without destroying its functionality. The choice, in other words, is not between the Internet and no Internet, or between the Internet and a closed proprietary network. Harvard suggests a middle way. Architectures of control could be layered on top of the Net to "correct" or eliminate "imperfections." And these architectures could, in other words, facilitate control.[9]

That is the first, very small, claim of this early chapter in a story about emerging control: Architectures of control are possible; they could be added to the Internet that we already know. If they were added, that would radically change the character of the network. Whether these architectures should be added depends upon what we want to use the network for.

I say this is a small claim because, while it is important, it is the sort of point that one recognizes as obvious even if one didn't see it originally. More than obvious, the point should be pedestrian. We see it in lots of contexts. Think, for example, of the post office. When I was growing up, the Post Office was a haven for anonymous speech. The job of the Post Office was simply to deliver packages. Like Net95, it didn't worry about who a piece of mail was from, or what was in the envelope or package. There was no enforced requirement that you register before you send a letter. There was no enforced requirement that the letter have a return address or that the return address be correct. If you were careful to avoid fingerprints, you could use this government-subsidized facility to send perfectly anonymous messages.

Obviously, the Post Office could be architected differently. The service could require, for example, a return address. It could require that you verify that the return address was correct (for example, by checking your ID before it accepted a package). It could even require inspection before it shipped a particular package or envelope. All of these changes in the procedures for the post would produce a world in which mail was more easily monitored and tracked. The government makes that choice when it designs the Post Office as it does. If monitoring becomes important, the government can change the system to facilitate it. If not, they can leave the postal system as it (largely) is. But if it does change the system to make monitoring more simple, that will reflect changes in values that inform the design of that network.

The claim of this book is that there are sufficient interests to move the Net95 from a default of anonymity to a default of identification. But nothing I've said yet shows how. What would get us from the relatively unregulable libertarian Net to a highly regulable Net of control?

This is the question for the balance of Part I. I move in two steps. In Chapter 4, my claim is that even without the government's help, we will see the Net move to an architecture of control. In Chapter 5, I sketch how government might help. The trends promise a highly regulable Net—not the libertarian's utopia, not the Net your father (or more likely your daughter or son) knew, but a Net whose essence is the character of control.

An Internet, in other words, that flips the Internet as it was.

F O U R

architectures of control

THE INVISIBLE MAN DOESN'T FEAR THE STATE. HE KNOWS HIS NATURE PUTS HIM beyond its reach (unless he gets stupid, and of course, he always gets stupid). His story is the key to a general lesson: If you can't know who someone is, or where he is, or what he's doing, you can't regulate him. His behavior is as he wants it to be. There's little the state can do to change it.

So too with the original Internet: Everyone was an invisible man. As cyberspace was originally architected, there was no simple way to know who someone was, where he was, or what he was doing. As the Internet was originally architected, then, there was no simple way to regulate behavior there.

The aim of the last chapter, however, was to add a small but important point to this obvious idea: Whatever cyberspace was, there's no reason it has to stay this way. The "nature" of the Internet is not God's will. Its nature is simply the product of its design. That design could be different. The Net could be designed to reveal who someone is, where they are, and what they're doing. And if it were so designed, then the Net could become, as I will argue throughout this part, the most regulable space that man has ever known.

In this chapter, I describe the changes that could—and are—pushing the Net from the unregulable space it was, to the perfectly regulable space it could be. These changes are not being architected by government. They are instead being demanded by users and deployed by commerce. They are not the product of some *1984*-inspired conspiracy; they are the consequence of changes made for purely pragmatic, commercial ends.

This obviously doesn't make these changes bad or good. My purpose just now is not normative, but descriptive. We should understand where we are going, and why, before we ask whether this is where, or who, we want to be.

The history of the future of the Internet was written in Germany in January 1995. German law regulated porn. In Bavaria, it regulated porn heavily. CompuServe made (a moderate amount of, through USENET,) porn available to its users. CompuServe was serving Bavaria's citizens. Bavaria told CompuServe to remove the porn from its servers, or its executives would be punished.

CompuServe at first objected that there was nothing it could do—save removing the porn from every server, everywhere in the world. That didn't trouble the Germans much, but it did trouble CompuServe. So in January 1995, CompuServe announced a technical fix: Rather than blocking access to the USENET newsgroups that the Bavarians had complained about for all members of CompuServe, CompuServe had devised a technology to filter content on a country-by-country basis.[1]

To make that fix work, CompuServe had to begin to reckon who a user was, what they were doing, and where they were doing it. Technology could give them access to the data that needed reckoning. And with that shift, the future was set. An obvious response to a problem of regulability would begin to repeat itself.

CompuServe, of course, was not the Internet. But its response suggests the pattern that the Internet will follow. In this Chapter, I map just how the Internet can effectively be made to run (in this respect at least) like CompuServe.

WHO DID WHAT, WHERE?

To regulate, the state needs a way to know the who, in "Who did what, where?" To see how the Net will show the state "who," we need to think a bit more carefully about how "identification" works in general, and how it might work on the Internet.

Identity and Authentication: Real Space

To make sense of the technologies we use to identify who someone is, consider the relationship among three familiar ideas—(1) "identity," (2) "authentication," and (3) "credential."

By "identity" I mean something more than just who you are. I mean as well your "attributes," or more broadly, all the facts about you (or a corporation, or a thing) that are true. Your identity, in this sense, includes your name, your sex, where you live, what your education is, your driver's license number, your social security number, your purchases on Amazon.com, whether you're a lawyer—and so on.

These attributes are known by others when they are communicated. In real space, some are communicated automatically: for most, sex, skin color, height, age range, and whether you have a good smile get transmitted automatically. Other attributes can't be known unless they are revealed either by you, or by someone else: your GPA in high school, your favorite color, your social security number, your last purchase on Amazon, whether you've passed a bar exam.

Just because an attribute has been asserted, however, does not mean the attribute is believed. ("You passed the bar?!") Rather belief will often depend upon a process of "authentication." In general, we "authenticate" when we want to become more confident about the truth about some asserted claim than appears on its face. "I'm married," you say. "Show me the ring," she says. The first statement is an assertion about an attribute you claim you have. The second is a demand for authentication. We could imagine (in a comedy at least) that demand continuing. "Oh come on, that's not a wedding ring. Show me your marriage license." At some point, the demands stop, either when enough confidence has been achieved, or when the inquiry has just become too weird.

Sometimes this process of authentication is relatively automatic. Some attributes, that is, are relatively self-authenticating: You say you're a woman; I'm likely to believe it when I see you. You say you're a native speaker; I'm likely to believe it once I speak with you. Of course, in both cases, I could be fooled. Thus, if my life depended upon it, I might take other steps to be absolutely confident of what otherwise appears plain. But for most purposes, with most familiar sorts of attributes, we learn how to evaluate without much more than our own individual judgment.

Some attributes, however, cannot be self-authenticating. You say you're licensed to fly an airplane; I want to see the license. You say you're a member of the California bar; I want to see your certificate. You say you're qualified to perform open heart surgery on my father; I want to see things that make me confident that your claim is true. Once again, these authenticating "things" could be forged, and my confidence could be unjustified. But if I'm careful to match the process for authentication with the level of confidence that I need, I'm behaving quite rationally. And most of us can usually get by without a terribly complicated process of authentication.

One important tool sometimes used in this process of authentication is a credential. By "credential," I mean a standardized device for authenticating (to some level of confidence) an assertion made. A driver's license is a credential in this sense. Its purpose is to authenticate the status of a driver. We're generally familiar with the form of such licenses; that gives us some confidence that we'll be able to determine whether a particular license is valid. A passport is also a credential in this sense. Its purpose is to establish the citizenship of the person it identifies, and it identifies a person through relatively self-authenticating attributes. Once again, we are familiar with the form of this credential, and that gives us a relatively high level of confidence about the facts asserted in that passport.

Obviously, some credentials are better than others. Some are architected to give more confidence than others; some are more efficient at delivering their confidence than others. But we select among the credentials available depending upon the level of confidence that we need.

So take an obvious example to bring these points together: Imagine you're a bank teller. Someone appears in front of you and declares that she is the owner of account # 654–543231. She says she would like to withdraw all the money from that account.

In the sense I've described, this someone (call her Ms. X) has asserted a fact about her identity—that she is the owner of account # 654–543231. Your job now is to authenticate that assertion. So you pull up on your computer the records for the account, and you discover that there's lots of money in it. Now your desire to be confident about the authentication you make is even stronger. You ask Ms. X her name; that name matches the name on the account. That gives you some confidence. You ask Ms. X for two forms of identification. Both match to Ms. X. Now you have even more confidence. You ask Ms. X to sign a withdrawal slip. The signatures seem to match; more confidence still. Finally, you note in the record that the account was established by your manager. You ask her whether she knows Ms. X. She confirms that she does, and that the "Ms. X" standing at the counter is indeed Ms. X. Now you're sufficiently confident to turn over the money.

Notice that throughout this process, you've used technologies to help you authenticate the attribute asserted by Ms. X to be true. Your computer links a name to an account number. A driver's license or passport ties a picture to a name. The computer keeps a copy of a signature. These are all technologies to increase confidence.

And notice too that we could imagine even better technologies to increase this confidence. Credit cards, for example, were developed at a time when merely possessing the credit card authenticated its use. That design creates the incentive to steal a credit card. ATM cards are different—in addition to possession, ATM cards require a password. That design reduces the value of stolen cards. But some write their passwords on their ATM cards, or keep them in their wallets with their ATMs. This means the risk from theft is not totally removed. But that risk could be further reduced by other technologies of authentication. For example, certain biometric technologies, such as thumbprint readers or eye scans, would increase the confidence that the holder of a card was an authorized user. (Though these technologies themselves can create their own risks: At a conference I heard a vendor describing a new technology for identifying someone based upon his handprint; a participant in the conference asked whether the hand had to be alive for the authentication to work. The vendor went very pale. After a moment, he replied, "I guess not.")

We are constantly negotiating these processes of authentication in real life, and in this process, better technologies and better credentials enable more distant authentication. In a small town, in a quieter time, credentials were not necessary. You were known by your face, and your face carried with it a reference (held in the common knowledge of the community) about your character. But as life becomes more fluid, social institutions depend upon other technologies to build confidence around important identity assertions. Credentials thus become an unavoidable tool for securing such authentication.

If technologies of authentication can be better or worse, then, obviously, many have an interest in these technologies becoming better. We each would be better off if we could more easily and confidently authenticate certain facts about us. Commerce, too, would certainly be better off with better technologies of authentication. Poor technologies begat fraud; fraud is an unproductive cost for business. If better technology could eliminate that cost, then prices could be lower and profits possibly higher.

And finally, governments benefit from better technologies of authentication. If it is simple to authenticate your age, then rules that are triggered based upon age are more easily enforced (drinking ages, or limits on cigarettes). And if it is simple to authenticate who you are, then it will be easier for the government to trace who did what.

Fundamentally, the regulability of life in real-space depends upon certain architectures of authentication. The fact that witnesses can identify who committed a crime, either because they know the person or because of self-authenticating features such as "he was a white male, six feet tall," enhances the ability of the state to regulate against that crime. If criminals were invisible or witnesses had no memory, crime would increase. The fact that fingerprints are hard to change and are now automatically traced to convicted felons increases the likelihood that felons will be caught again. Relying on a more changeable physical characteristic would reduce the ability of the police to track repeat offenders. The fact that cars have license plates and are registered by their owners increases the likelihood that a hit-and-run driver will be caught. Without licenses, and without systems registering owners, it would be extremely difficult to track car-related crime. In all these cases, and in many more, technologies of authentication of real-space life make regulating that life possible.

These three separate interests therefore point to a common interest. That's not to say that every technology of authentication meets that common interest, nor is it to say that these interests will be enough to facilitate more efficient authentication. But it does mean that we can see which way these interests push. Better authentication can benefit everyone.

Identity and Authentication: Cyberspace

Identity and authentication in cyberspace and real space are in theory the same. In practice they are quite different. To see that difference, however, we need to see more about the technical detail of how the Net is built.

As I've already said, the Internet is built from a suite of protocols referred to collectively as "TCP/IP." At its core, the TCP/IP suite includes protocols for exchanging packets of data between two machines "on" the Net.[2] Brutally simplified, the system takes a bunch of data (a file, for example), chops it up into packets, and slaps on the address to which the packet is to be sent and the address from which it is sent. The addresses are called Internet Protocol addresses, and they look like this: 128.34.35.204. Once properly addressed, the packets are then sent across the Internet to their intended destination. Machines along the way ("routers") look at the address to which the packet is sent, and depending upon an (increasingly complicated) algorithm, the machines decide to which machine the packet should be sent next. A packet could make many "hops" between its start and its end. But as the network becomes faster and more robust, those many hops seem almost instantaneous.

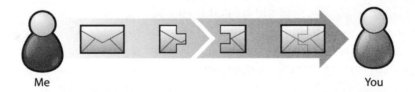

Me   You

In the terms I've described, there are many attributes that might be associated with any packet of data sent across the network. For example, the packet might come from an e-mail written by Al Gore. That means the e-mail is written by a former vice president of the United States, by a man knowledgeable about global warming, by a man over the age of 50, by a tall man, by an American citizen, by a former member of the United States Senate, and so on. Imagine also that the e-mail was written while Al Gore was in Germany, and that it is about negotiations for climate control. The identity of that packet of information might be said to include all these attributes.

But the e-mail itself authenticates none of these facts. The e-mail may say it's from Al Gore, but the TCP/IP protocol alone gives us no way to be sure. It may have been written while Gore was in Germany, but he could have sent it through a server in Washington. And of course, while the system eventually will figure out that the packet is part of an e-mail, the information traveling across TCP/IP itself does not contain anything that would indicate what the content was. The protocol thus doesn't authenticate who sent the packet, where they sent it from, and what the packet is. All it purports to assert is an IP address to which the packet is to be sent, and an IP address from which the packet comes. From the perspective of the network, this other information is unnecessary surplus. Like a daydreaming postal worker, the network simply moves the data and leaves its interpretation to the applications at either end.

This minimalism in the Internet's design was not an accident. It reflects a decision about how best to design a network to perform a wide range over very different functions. Rather than build into this network a complex set of functionality thought to be needed by every single application, this network philosophy pushes complexity to the edge of the network—to the applications that run on the network, rather than the network's core. The core is kept as simple as possible. Thus if authentication about who is using the network is necessary, that functionality should be performed by an application connected to the network, not by the network itself. Or if content needs to be encrypted, that functionality should be performed by an application connected to the network, not by the network itself.

This design principle was named by network architects Jerome Saltzer, David Clark, and David Reed as the end-to-end principle.[3] It has been a core principle of the Internet's architecture, and, in my view, one of the most important reasons that the Internet produced the innovation and growth that it has enjoyed. But its consequences for purposes of identification and authentication make both extremely difficult with the basic protocols of the Internet alone. It is as if you were in a carnival funhouse with the lights dimmed to darkness and voices coming from around you, but from people you do not know and from places you cannot identify. The system knows that there are entities out there interacting with it, but it knows nothing about who those entities are. While in real space—and here is the important point—anonymity has to be created, in cyberspace anonymity is the given.

Identity and Authentication: Regulability

This difference in the architectures of real space and cyberspace makes a big difference in the regulability of behavior in each. The absence of relatively self-authenticating facts in cyberspace makes it extremely difficult to regulate behavior there. If we could all walk around as "The Invisible Man" in real space, the same would be true about real space as well. That we're not capable of becoming invisible in real space (or at least not easily) is an important reason that regulation can work.

Thus, for example, if a state wants to control children's access to "indecent" speech on the Internet, the original Internet architecture provides little help. The state can say to websites, "don't let kids see porn." But the website operators can't know—from the data provided by the TCP/IP protocols at least—whether the entity accessing its web page is a kid or an adult. That's different, again, from real space. If a kid walks into a porn shop wearing a mustache and stilts, his effort to conceal is likely to fail. The attribute "being a kid" is asserted in real space, even if efforts to conceal it are possible. But in cyberspace, there's no need to conceal, because the facts you might want to conceal about your identity (i.e., that you're a kid) are not asserted anyway.

All this is true, at least, under the basic Internet architecture. But as the last ten years have made clear, none of this is true by necessity. To the extent that the lack of efficient technologies for authenticating facts about individuals makes it harder to regulate behavior, there are architectures that could be layered onto the TCP/IP protocol to create efficient authentication. We're far enough into the history of the Internet to see what these technologies could look like. We're far enough into this history to see that the trend toward this authentication is unstoppable. The only question is whether we will build into this system of authentication the kinds of protections for privacy and autonomy that are needed.

Architectures of Identification

Most who use the Internet have no real sense about whether their behavior is monitored, or traceable. Instead, the experience of the Net suggests anonymity. Wikipedia doesn't say "Welcome Back, Larry" when I surf to its site to look up an entry, and neither does Google. Most, I expect, take this lack of acknowledgement to mean that no one is noticing.

But appearances are quite deceiving. In fact, as the Internet has matured, the technologies for linking behavior with an identity have increased dramatically. You can still take steps to assure anonymity on the Net, and many depend upon that ability to do good (human rights workers in Burma) or evil (coordinating terrorist plots). But to achieve that anonymity takes effort. For most of us, our use of the Internet has been made at least traceable in ways most of us would never even consider possible.

Consider first the traceability resulting from the basic protocols of the Internet—TCP/IP. Whenever you make a request to view a page on the Web, the web server needs to know where to sent the packets of data that will appear as a web page in your browser. Your computer thus tells the web server where you are—in IP space at least—by revealing an IP address.

As I've already described, the IP address itself doesn't reveal anything about who you are, or where in physical space you come from. But it does enable a certain kind of trace. If (1) you have gotten access to the web through an Internet Service Provider (ISP) that assigns you an IP address while you're on the Internet and (2) that ISP keeps the logs of that assignment, then it's perfectly possible to trace your surfing back to you.

How?

Well, imagine you're angry at your boss. You think she's a blowhard who is driving the company into bankruptcy. After months of frustration, you decide to go public. Not "public" as in a press conference, but public as in a posting to an online forum within which your company is being discussed.

You know you'd get in lots of trouble if your criticism were tied back to you. So you take steps to be "anonymous" on the forum. Maybe you create an account in the forum under a fictitious name, and that fictitious name makes you feel safe. Your boss may see the nasty post, but even if she succeeds in getting the forum host to reveal what you said when you signed up, all that stuff was bogus. Your secret, you believe, is safe.

Wrong. In addition to the identification that your username might, or might not, provide, if the forum is on the web, then it knows the IP address from which you made your post. With that IP address, and the time you made your post, using "a reverse DNS look-up,"[4] it is simple to identify the Internet Service Provider that gave you access to the Internet. And increasingly, it is relatively simple for the Internet Service Provider to check its records to reveal which account was using that IP address at that specified time. Thus, the ISP could (if required) say that it was your account that was using the IP address that posted the nasty message about your boss. Try as you will to deny it

("Hey, on the Internet, no one knows you're a dog!"), I'd advise you to give up quickly. They've got you. You've been trapped by the Net. Dog or no, you're definitely in the doghouse.

Now again, what made this tracing possible? No plan by the NSA. No strategy of Microsoft. Instead, what made this tracing possible was a by-product of the architecture of the Web and the architecture of ISPs charging access to the Web. The Web must know an IP address; ISPs require identification before they assign an IP address to a customer. So long as the log records of the ISP are kept, the transaction is traceable. Bottom line: If you want anonymity, use a pay phone!

This traceability in the Internet raised some important concerns at the beginning of 2006. Google announced it would fight a demand by the government to produce one million sample searches. (MSN and Yahoo! had both complied with the same request.) That request was made as part of an investigation the government was conducting to support its defense of a statute designed to block kids from porn. And though the request promised the data would be used for no other purpose, it raised deep concerns in the Internet community. Depending upon the data that Google kept, the request showed in principle that it was possible to trace legally troubling searches back to individual IP addresses (and to individuals with Google accounts). Thus, for example, if your Internet address at work is a fixed-IP address, then every search you've ever made from work is at least possibly kept by Google. Does that make you concerned? And assume for the moment you are not a terrorist: Would you still be concerned?

A link back to an IP address, however, only facilitates tracing, and again, even then not perfect traceability. ISPs don't keep data for long (ordinarily); some don't even keep assignment records at all. And if you've accessed the Internet at an Internet café, then there's no reason to believe anything could be traced back to you. So still, the Internet provides at least some anonymity.

But IP tracing isn't the only technology of identification that has been layered onto the Internet. A much more pervasive technology was developed early in the history of the Web to make the web more valuable to commerce and its customers. This is the technology referred to as "cookies."

When the World Wide Web was first deployed, the protocol simply enabled people to view content that had been marked up in a special programming language. This language (HTML) made it easy to link to other pages, and it made it simple to apply basic formatting to the content (bold, or italics, for example).

But the one thing the protocol didn't enable was a simple way for a website to know which machines had accessed it. The protocol was "state-less."

When a web server received a request to serve a web page, it didn't know anything about the state of the requester before that request was made.[5]

From the perspective of privacy, this sounds like a great feature for the Web. Why should a website know anything about me if I go to that site to view certain content? You don't have to be a criminal to appreciate the value in anonymous browsing. Imagine libraries kept records of every time you opened a book at the library, even for just a second.

Yet from the perspective of commerce, this "feature" of the original Web is plainly a bug, and not because commercial sites necessarily want to know everything there is to know about you. Instead, the problem is much more pragmatic. Say you go to Amazon.com and indicate you want to buy 20 copies of my latest book. (Try it. It's fun.) Now your "shopping cart" has 20 copies of my book. You then click on the icon to check out, and you notice your shopping cart is empty. Why? Well because, as originally architected, the Web had no easy way to recognize that you were the same entity that just ordered 20 books. Or put differently, the web server would simply forget you. The Web as originally built had no way to remember you from one page to another. And thus, the Web as originally built would not be of much use to commerce.

But as I've said again and again, the way the Web was is not the way the Web had to be. And so those who were building the infrastructure of the Web quickly began to think through how the web could be "improved" to make it easy for commerce to happen. "Cookies" were the solution. In 1994, Netscape introduced a protocol to make it possible for a web server to deposit a small bit of data on your computer when you accessed that server. That small bit of data—the "cookie"—made it possible for the server to recognize you when you traveled to a different page. Of course, there are lots of other concerns about what that cookie might enable. We'll get to those in the chapter about privacy. The point that's important here, however, is not the dangers this technology creates. The point is the potential and how that potential was built. A small change in the protocol for client-server interaction now makes it possible for websites to monitor and track those who use the site.

This is a small step toward authenticated identity. It's far from that, but it is a step toward it. Your computer isn't you (yet). But cookies make it possible for the computer to authenticate that it is the same machine that was accessing a website a moment before. And it is upon this technology that the whole of web commerce initially was built. Servers could now "know" that this machine is the same machine that was here before. And from that knowledge, they could build a great deal of value.

Now again, strictly speaking, cookies are nothing more than a tracing technology. They make it simple to trace a machine across web pages. That tracing doesn't necessarily reveal any information about the user. Just as we could follow a trail of cookie crumbs in real space to an empty room, a web server could follow a trail of "mouse droppings" from the first entry on the site until the user leaves. In both cases, nothing is necessarily revealed about the user.

But sometimes something important is revealed about the user by association with data stored elsewhere. For example, imagine you enter a site, and it asks you to reveal your name, your telephone number, and your e-mail address as a condition of entering a contest. You trust the website, and do that, and then you leave the website. The next day, you come back, and you browse through a number of pages on that website. In this interaction, of course, you've revealed nothing. But if a cookie was deposited on your machine through your browser (and you have not taken steps to remove it), then when you return to the site, the website again "knows" all these facts about you. The cookie traces your machine, and this trace links back to a place where you provided information the machine would not otherwise know.

The traceability of IP addresses and cookies is the default on the Internet now. Again, steps can be taken to avoid this traceability, but the vast majority of us don't take them. Fortunately, for society and for most of us, what we do on the Net doesn't really concern anyone. But if it did concern someone, it wouldn't be hard to track us down. We are a people who leave our "mouse droppings" everywhere.

This default traceability, however, is not enough for some. They require something more. That was Harvard's view, as I noted in the previous chapter. That is also the view of just about all private networks today. A variety of technologies have developed that enable stronger authentication by those who use the Net. I will describe two of these technologies in this section. But it is the second of these two that will, in my view, prove to be the most important.

The first of these technologies is the Single Sign-on (SSO) technology. This technology allows someone to "sign-on" to a network once, and then get access to a wide range of resources on that network without needing to authenticate again. Think of it as a badge you wear at your place of work. Depending upon what the badge says ("visitor" or "researcher") you get different access to different parts of the building. And like a badge at a place of work, you get the credential by giving up other data. You give the receptionist an ID; he gives you a badge; you wear that badge wherever you go while at the business.

The most commonly deployed SSO is a system called Kerberos. But there are many different SSOs out there—Microsoft's Passport system is an example—and there is a strong push to build federated SSOs for linking many different sites on the Internet. Thus, for example, in a federated system, I might authenticate myself to my university, but then I could move across any domain within the federation without authenticating again. The big advantage in this architecture is that I can authenticate to the institution I trust without spreading lots of data about myself to institutions I don't trust.

SSOs have been very important in building identity into the Internet. But a second technology, I believe, will become the most important tool for identification in the next ten years. This is because this alternative respects important architectural features of the Internet, and because the demand for better technologies of identification will continue to be strong. Forget the hassle of typing your name and address at every site you want to buy something from. You only need to think about the extraordinary growth in identity theft to recognize there are many who would be eager to see something better come along.

To understand this second system, think first about how credentials work in real space.[6] You've got a wallet. In it is likely to be a driver's license, some credit cards, a health insurance card, an ID for where you work, and, if you're lucky, some money. Each of these cards can be used to authenticate some fact about you—again, with very different levels of confidence. The driver's license has a picture and a list of physical characteristics. That's enough for a wine store, but not enough for the NSA. The credit card has your signature. Vendors are supposed to use that data to authenticate that the person who signs the bill is the owner of the card. If the vendor becomes suspicious, she might demand that you show an ID as well.

Notice the critical features of this "wallet" architecture. First, these credentials are issued by different entities. Second, depending upon their technology, they offer different levels of confidence. Third, I'm free to use these credentials in ways never originally planned or intended by the issuer of the credential. The Department of Motor Vehicles never coordinated with Visa to enable driver's licenses to be used to authenticate the holder of a credit card. But once the one was prevalent, the other could use it. And fourth, nothing requires that I show all my cards when I can use just one. That is, to show my driver's license, I don't also reveal my health insurance card. Or to use my Visa, I don't also have to reveal my American Express card.

These same features are at the core of what may prove to be the most important addition to the effective architecture of the Internet since its birth. This is a project being led by Microsoft to essentially develop an Identity Metasystem—a new layer of the Internet, an Identity Layer, that would complement the existing network layers to add a new kind of functionality. This

Identity Layer is not Microsoft Passport, or some other Single Sign-On tech-nology. Instead it is a protocol to enable a kind of virtual wallet of credentials, with all the same attributes of the credentials in your wallet—except better. This virtual wallet will not only be more reliable than the wallet in your pocket, it will also give you the ability to control more precisely what data about you is revealed to those who demand data about you.

For example, in real space, your wallet can easily be stolen. If it's stolen, then there's a period of time when it's relatively easy for the thief to use the cards to buy stuff. In cyberspace, these wallets are not easily stolen. Indeed, if they're architected well, it would be practically impossible to "steal" them. Remove the cards from their holder, and they become useless digital objects.

Or again, in real space, if you want to authenticate that you're over 21 and therefore can buy a six-pack of beer, you show the clerk your driver's license. With that, he authenticates your age. But with that bit of data, he also gets access to your name, your address, and in some states, your social security number. Those other bits of data are not necessary for him to know. In some contexts, depending on how creepy he is, these data are exactly the sort you don't want him to know. But the inefficiencies of real-space technologies reveal these data. This loss of privacy is a cost of doing business.

The virtual wallet would be different. If you need to authenticate your age, the technology could authenticate that fact alone—indeed, it could authenti-cate simply that you're over 21, or over 65, or under 18, without revealing any-thing more. Or if you need to authenticate your citizenship, that fact can be certified without revealing your name, or where you live, or your passport number. The technology is crafted to reveal just what you want it to reveal, without also revealing other stuff. (As one of the key architects for this meta-system, Kim Cameron, described it: "To me, that's the center of the system."[7]) And, most importantly, using the power of cryptography, the protocol makes it possible for the other side to be confident about the fact you reveal without requiring any more data.

The brilliance in this solution to the problems of identification is first that it mirrors the basic architecture of the Internet. There's no central repos-itory for data; there's no network technology that everyone must adopt. There is instead a platform for building identity technologies that encourages com-petition among different privacy and security providers—TCP/IP for identity. Microsoft may be leading the project, but anyone can build for this protocol. Nothing ties the protocol to the Windows operating system. Or to any other specific vendor. As Cameron wisely puts it, "it can't be owned by any one company or any one country . . . or just have the technology stamp of any one engineer."[8]

The Identity Layer is infrastructure for the Internet. It gives value (and raises concerns) to many beyond Microsoft. But though Microsoft's work is an important gift to the Internet, the Identity Layer is not altruism. "Microsoft's strategy is based on web services," Cameron described to me. "Web services are impossible without identity."[9] There is important public value here, but private interest is driving the deployment of this public value.

The Identity Layer would benefit individuals, businesses, and the government, but each differently. Individuals could more easily protect themselves from identity theft;[10] if you get an e-mail from PayPal demanding you update your account, you'll know whether the website is actually PayPal. Or if you want to protect yourself against spam, you could block all e-mail that doesn't come from an authenticated server. In either case, the technology is increasing confidence about the Internet. And the harms that come from a lack of confidence—mainly fraud—would therefore be reduced.

Commerce too would benefit from this form of technology. It too benefits from the reduction of fraud. And it too would benefit from a more secure infrastructure for conducting online transactions.

And finally, the government would benefit from this infrastructure of trust. If there were a simple way to demand that people authenticate facts about themselves, it would be easier for the government to insist that they do so. If it were easier to have high confidence that the person on the website was who he said he was, then it would be cheaper to deliver certain information across the web.

But while individuals, commerce, and government would all benefit from this sort of technology, there is also something that each could lose.

Individuals right now can be effectively anonymous on the Net. A platform for authenticated identity would make anonymity much harder. We might imagine, for example, a norm developing to block access to a website by anyone not carrying a token that at least made it possible to trace back to the user—a kind of driver's license for the Internet. That norm, plus this technology, would make anonymous speech extremely difficult.

Commerce could also lose something from this design. To the extent that there are simple ways to authenticate that I am the authorized user of this credit card, for example, it's less necessary for websites to demand all sorts of data about me—my address, my telephone numbers, and in one case I recently encountered, my birthday. That fact could build a norm against revealing extraneous data. But that data may be valuable to business beyond simply confirming a charge.

And governments, too, may lose something from this architecture of identification. Just as commerce may lose the extra data that individuals need to reveal to authenticate themselves, so too will the government lose that. It may feel that such data is necessary for some other purpose, but gathering it would become more difficult.

Each of these benefits and costs can be adjusted, depending upon how the technology is implemented. And as the resulting mix of privacy and security is the product of competition and an equilibrium between individuals and businesses, there's no way up front to predict what it will be.

But for our purposes, the only important fact to notice is that this infrastructure could effectively answer the first question that regulability requires answering: *Who* did what where? With an infrastructure enabling cheap identification wherever you are, the frequency of unidentified activity falls dramatically.

This final example of an identification technology throws into relief an important fact about encryption technology. The Identity Layer depends upon cryptography. It thus demonstrates the sense in which cryptography is Janus-faced. As Stewart Baker and Paul Hurst put it, cryptography "surely is the best of technologies and the worst of technologies. It will stop crimes and it will create new crimes. It will undermine dictatorships, and it will drive them to new excesses. It will make us all anonymous, and it will track our every transaction."[11]

Cryptography can be all these things, both good and bad, because encryption can serve two fundamentally different ends. In its "confidentiality" function it can be "used to keep communications secret." In its "identification" function it can be "used to provide forgery-proof digital identities."[12] It enables freedom from regulation (as it enhances confidentiality), but it can also enable more efficient regulation (as it enhances identification).[13]

Its traditional use is secrets. Encrypt a message, and only those with the proper key can open and read it. This type of encryption has been around as long as language itself. But until the mid-1970s it suffered from an important weakness: the same key that was used to encrypt a message was also used to decrypt it. So if you lost that key, all the messages hidden with that key were also rendered vulnerable. If a large number of messages were encrypted with the same key, losing the key compromised the whole archive of secrets protected by the key. This risk was significant. You always had to "transport" the key needed to unlock the message, and inherent in that transport was the risk that the key would be lost.

In the mid-1970s, however, a breakthrough in encryption technique was announced by two computer scientists, Whitfield Diffie and Martin Hellman.[14] Rather than relying on a single key, the Diffie-Hellman system used two keys—one public, the other private. What is encrypted with one can be decrypted only with the other. Even with one key there is no way to infer the other.

This discovery was the clue to an architecture that could build an extraordinary range of confidence into any network, whether or not the physical network itself was secure.[15] And again, that confidence could both make me confident that my secrets won't be revealed and make me confident that the person using my site just now is you. The technology therefore works to keep secrets, but it also makes it harder to keep secrets. It works to make stuff less regulable, and more regulable.

In the Internet's first life, encryption technology was on the side of privacy. Its most common use was to keep information secret. But in the Internet's next life, encryption technology's most important role will be in making the Net more regulable. As an Identity Layer gets built into the Net, the easy ability to demand some form of identity as a condition to accessing the resources of the Net increases. As that ability increases, its prevalence will increase as well. Indeed, as Shawn Helms describes, the next generation of the Internet Protocol—IPv6—"marks each packet with an encryption 'key' that cannot be altered or forged, thus securely identifying the packet's origin. This authentication function can identify every sender and receiver of information over the Internet, thus making it nearly impossible for people to remain anonymous on the Internet."[16]

And even if not impossible, sufficiently difficult for the vast majority of us. Our packets will be marked. We—or something about us—will be known.

WHO DID *WHAT*, WHERE?

Regulability also depends upon knowing the "what" in "who did what, where?" But again, the Internet as originally designed didn't help the regulator here either. If the Internet protocol simply cuts up data into packets and stamps an address on them, then nothing in the basic protocol would tell anyone looking at the packet what the packet was for.

For example, imagine you're a telephone company providing broadband Internet access (DSL) across your telephone lines. Some smart innovator develops Voice-over-IP (VOIP)—an application that makes it possible to use the Internet to make telephone calls. You, the phone company, aren't happy about that, because now people using your DSL service can make unmetered telephone calls. That freedom cuts into your profit.

Is there anything you can do about this? Relying upon just the Internet protocols, the answer is no. The "packets" of data that contain the simulated-telephone calls look just like any packet of data. They don't come labeled with VOIP or any other consistent moniker. Instead, packets are simply marked with addresses. They are not marked with explanations of what is going on with each.

But as my example is meant to suggest, we can easily understand why some would be very keen to understand what packets are flowing across their network, and not just for anti-competitive purposes. Network administrators trying to decide whether to add new capacity need to know what the existing capacity is being used for. Businesses keen to avoid their employees wasting time with sports or porn have a strong interest in knowing just what their employees are doing. Universities trying to avoid viruses or malware being installed on network computers need to know what kind of packets are flowing onto their network. In all these cases, there's an obvious and valid *will* to identify what packets are flowing on the network. And as they say, where there's a will, there's a way.

The way follows the same technique described in the section above. Again, the TCP/IP protocol doesn't include technology for identifying the content carried in TCP/IP packets. But it also doesn't interfere with applications that might examine TCP/IP packets and report what those packets are about.

So, for example, consider a package produced by Ipanema Technologies. This technology enables a network owner to inspect the packets traveling on its network. As its webpage promises,

> The Ipanema Systems "deep" layer 7 packet inspection automatically recognizes all critical business and recreational application flows running over the network. Real-time graphical interfaces as well as minute-by-minute reports are available to rapidly discover newly deployed applications.[17]

Using the data gathered by this technology, the system generates reports about the applications being used in the network, and who's using them. These technologies make it possible to control network use, either to economize on bandwidth costs, or to block uses that the network owner doesn't permit.

Another example of this kind of content control is a product called "iProtectYou."[18] This product also scans packets on a network, but this control is implemented at the level of a particular machine. Parents load this software on a computer; the software then monitors all network traffic with that computer. As the company describes, the program can then "filter harmful websites and newsgroups; restrict Internet time to a predetermined schedule; decide which programs can have Internet access; limit the amount of data that can be sent or received to/from your computer; block e-mails, online chats, instant messages and P2P connections containing inappropriate words; [and produce] detailed Internet activity logs." Once again, this is an application that sits on top of the network and watches. It intervenes in network activity when it identifies the activity as the kind the administrator wants to control.

In addition to these technologies of control, programmers have developed a wide range of programs to monitor networks. Perhaps the dominant application in this context is called "nmap"—a program

> for network exploration or security auditing . . . designed to rapidly scan large networks. . . . Nmap uses raw IP packets in novel ways to determine what hosts are available on the network, what services (application name and version) those hosts are offering, what operating systems (and OS versions) they are running, what type of packet filters/firewalls are in use, and dozens of other characteristics.[19]

This software is "free software," meaning the source code is available, and any modifications of the source code must be made available as well. These conditions essentially guarantee that the code necessary to engage in this monitoring will always be available.

Finally, coders have developed "packet filtering" technology, which, as one popular example describes, "is the selective passing or blocking of data packets as they pass through a network interface. . . . The most often used criteria are source and destination address, source and destination port, and protocol." This again is a technology that's monitoring "what" is carried within packets, and decides what's allowed based upon what it finds.

In each of these cases, a layer of code complements the TCP/IP protocol, to give network administrators something TCP/IP alone would not—namely, knowledge about "what" is carried in the network packets. That knowledge increases the "regulability" of network use. If a company doesn't want its employees using IM chat, then these technologies will enforce that rule—by blocking the packets containing IM chat. Or if a company wants to know which employees use sexually explicit speech in Internet communication, these technologies will reveal that as well. Again, there are plenty of perfectly respectable reasons why network administrators might want to exercise this regulatory authority—even if there are plenty of cases where such power would be an abuse. Because of this legitimate demand, software products like this are developed.

Now, of course, there are countermeasures that users can adopt to avoid just this sort of monitoring. A user who encrypts the data he sends across the network will avoid any filtering on the basis of key words. And there are plenty of technologies designed to "anonymize" behavior on the Net, so administrators can't easily know what an individual is doing on a network. But these countermeasures require a significant investment for a particular user to deploy—whether of time or money. The vast majority won't bother, and the ability of network administrators to monitor content and use of the network will be preserved.

Thus, as with changes that increased the ability to identify "who" someone is who is using a network, here too, private interests provide a sufficient incentive to develop technologies that make it increasingly easy to say "what" someone is doing who is using a network. A gap in the knowledge provided by the plain vanilla Internet is thus plugged by these privately developed technologies.

WHO DID WHAT, *WHERE?*

Finally, as long as different jurisdictions impose different requirements, the third bit of data necessary to regulate efficiently is knowing where the target of regulation is. If France forbids the selling of Nazi paraphernalia, but the United States does not, then a website wanting to respect the laws of France must know something about where the person accessing the Internet is coming from.

But once again, the Internet protocols didn't provide that data. And thus, it would be extremely difficult to regulate or zone access to content on the basis of geography.

The original Internet made such regulation extremely difficult. As originally deployed, as one court put it:

> The Internet is wholly insensitive to geographic distinctions. In almost every case, users of the Internet neither know nor care about the physical location of the Internet resources they access. Internet protocols were designed to ignore rather than document geographic location; while computers on the network do have "addresses," they are logical addresses on the network rather than geographic addresses in real space. The majority of Internet addresses contain no geographic clues and, even where an Internet address provides such a clue, it may be misleading.[20]

But once again, commerce has come to the rescue of regulability. There are obvious reasons why it would useful to be able to identify where someone is when they access some website. Some of those reasons have to do with regulation—again, blocking Nazi material from the French, or porn from kids in Kansas. We'll consider these reasons more extensively later in this book. For now, however, the most interesting reasons are those tied purely to commerce.

And, again, these commercial reasons are sufficient to induce the development of this technology.

Once again, the gap in the data necessary to identify someone's location is the product of the way IP addresses are assigned. IP addresses are virtual addresses; they don't refer to a particular geographic place. They refer to a logical place on the network. Thus, two IP addresses in principle could be very close to each other in number, but very far from each other in geography. That's not the way, for example, zip codes work. If your zip code is one digit from mine (e.g., 94115 vs. 94116), we're practically neighbors.

But this gap in data is simply the gap in data about where someone is deducible from his IP address. That means, while there's no simple way to deduce from 23.214.23.15 that someone is in California, it is certainly possible to gather the data necessary to map where someone is, given the IP address. To do this, one needs to construct a table of IP addresses and geographic locations, and then track both the ultimate IP address and the path along which a packet has traveled to where you are from where it was sent. Thus while the TCP/IP protocol can't reveal where someone is directly, it can be used indirectly to reveal at least the origin or destination of an IP packet.

The commercial motivations for this knowledge are obvious. Jack Goldsmith and Tim Wu tell the story of a particularly famous entrepreneur, Cyril Houri, who was inspired to develop IP mapping technology. Sitting in his hotel in Paris one night, he accessed his e-mail account in the United States. His e-mail was hosted on a web server, but he noticed that the banner ads at the top of the website were advertising an American flower company. That gave him a (now obvious) idea: Why not build a tool to make it easy for a website to know from where it is being accessed, so it can serve relevant ads to those users?[21]

Houri's idea has been copied by many. Geoselect, for example, is a company that provides IP mapping services. Just browse to their webpage, and they're 99 percent likely to be able to tell you automatically where you are browsing from. Using their services, you can get a geographical report listing the location of the people who visit your site, and you can use their products to automatically update log files on your web server with geographic data. You can automatically change the greeting on your website depending upon where the user comes from, and you can automatically redirect a user based upon her location. All of this functionality is invisible to the user. All he sees is a web page constructed by tools that know something that the TCP/IP alone doesn't reveal—where someone is from.

So what commercial reasons do websites have for using such software? One company, MaxMind,[22] lists the major reason as credit card fraud: If your customer comes from a "high risk IP address"—meaning a location where it's likely the person is engaged in credit card fraud—then MaxMind's service will flag the transaction and direct that it have greater security verification. Max-Mind also promises the service will be valuable for "targeted advertising." Using its product, a client can target a message based upon country, state, or city, as well as a "metropolitan code," an area code, and connection speed of the user (no need to advertise DVD downloads to a person on a dial-up connection).

Here too there is an important and powerful open source application that provides the same IP mapping functions. Hostip.info gives website operators—for free—the ability to "geolocate" the users of their site.[23] This again means that the core functionality of IP mapping is not held exclusively by corporations or a few individuals. Any application developer—including a government—could incorporate the function into its applications. The knowledge and functionality is free.

Thus, again, one of the original gaps in the data necessary to make behavior regulable on the Internet—geographic identity—has been filled. But it has not been filled by government mandate or secret NSA operations (or so I hope). Instead, the gap has been filled by a commercial interest in providing the data the network itself didn't. Technology now layers onto the Internet to produce the data the network needs.

But it is still possible to evade identification. Civil liberty activist Seth Finkelstein has testified to the relative ease with which one can evade this tracking.[24] Yet as I will describe more below, even easily evaded tracking can be effective tracking. And when tied to the architectures for identity described above, this sort will become quite effective.

RESULTS

In the last chapter, we saw that the unregulability of the Internet was a product of design: that the failure of that network to identify who someone is, what they're doing, and where they're from meant that it would be particularly difficult to enforce rules upon individuals using the network. Not impossible, but difficult. Not for all people, but for enough to matter. The Internet as it originally was gave everyone a "Ring of Gyges," the ring which, as Plato reports in *The Republic*, made Gyges the shepherd invisible. The dilemma for regulation in such a world is precisely the fear Plato had about this ring: With such a ring, "no man can be imagined to be of such an iron nature that he would stand fast in justice."[25]

And if such a man did choose justice, even with the power of the ring, then "he would be thought by the lookers-on to be a most wretched idiot, although they would praise him to one another's faces, and keep up appearances with one another from a fear that they too might suffer injustice."

But these gaps in the Internet's original design are not necessary. We can imagine networks that interact seamlessly with the Internet but which don't have these "imperfections." And, more importantly, we can see why there would be an important commercial interest in eliminating these gaps.

Yet you may still be skeptical. Even if most Internet activity is traceable using the technologies that I've described, you may still believe there are significant gaps. Indeed, the explosion of spam, viruses, ID theft, and the like are strong testimony to the fact that there's still a lot of unregulable behavior. Commerce acting alone has not yet eliminated these threats, to both commerce and civil life. For reasons I explore later in this book, it's not even clear commerce could.

But commerce is not the only actor here. Government is also an important ally, and the framework of regulability that commerce has built could be built on again by government.

Government can, in other words, help commerce and help itself. How it does so is the subject of the chapter that follows.

FIVE

regulating code

COMMERCE HAS DONE ITS PART—FOR COMMERCE, AND INDIRECTLY, FOR governments. Technologies that make commerce more efficient are also technologies that make regulation simpler. The one supports the other. There are a host of technologies now that make it easier to know who someone is on the Net, what they're doing, and where they're doing it. These technologies were built to make business work better. They make life on the Internet safer. But the by-product of these technologies is to make the Net more regulable.

More regulable. Not perfectly regulable. These tools alone do a great deal. As Joel Reidenberg notes, they are already leading courts to recognize how behavior on the Net can be reached—and regulated.[1] But they don't yet create the incentives to build regulability into the heart of the Net. That final step will require action by the government.[2]

When I wrote the first version of this book, I certainly expected that the government would eventually take these steps. Events since 1999—including the birth of Z-theory described below—have only increased my confidence. In the United States, the identification of "an enemy"—terrorism—has weakened the resolve to resist government action to make government more powerful and regulation more effective. There's a limit, or at least I hope there is, but there is also no doubt that the line has been moved. And in any case, there is not much more that the government would need to do in order to radically increase the regulability of the net. These steps would not themselves excite any significant resistance. The government has the means, and the motive. This chapter maps the opportunity.

The trick is obvious once it is seen. It may well be difficult for the government to regulate behavior directly, given the architecture of the Internet as it is. But that doesn't mean it is difficult for the government to regulate the architecture of the Internet as it is. The trick, then, is for the government to take steps that induce the development of an architecture that makes behavior more regulable.

In this context, I don't mean by "architecture" the regulation of TCP/IP itself. Instead, I simply mean regulation that changes the effective constraints of the architecture of the Internet, by altering the code at any layer within that space. If technologies of identification are lacking, then regulating the architecture in this sense means steps the government can take to induce the deployment of technologies of identification.

If the government takes these steps, it will increase the regulability of behavior on the Internet. And depending upon the substance of these steps taken, it could render the Internet the most perfectly regulable space we've known. As Michael Geist describes it, "governments may have been willing to step aside during the commercial Internet's nascent years, but no longer."[3]

REGULATING ARCHITECTURE: THE REGULATORY TWO-STEP

We can call this the "regulatory two-step": In a context in which behavior is relatively unregulable, the government takes steps to increase regulability. And once framed, there are any number of examples that set the pattern for the two-step in cyberspace.

Car Congestion

London had a problem with traffic. There were too many cars in the central district, and there was no simple way to keep "unnecessary" cars out.

So London did three things. It first mandated a license plate that a video camera could read, and then it installed video cameras on as many public fixtures as it would take to monitor—perpetually—what cars were where.

Then, beginning in February 2003, the city imposed a congestion tax: Initially £5 per day (between 7 A.M. and 6:30 P.M.) for any car (save taxis and residents paying a special fee), raised to £8 in July 2005. After 18 months in operation, the system was working "better than expected." Traffic delays were down 32 percent, traffic within the city was down 15 percent, and delays on main routes into the zones were down 20 percent. London is now exploring new technologies to make it even easier to charge for access more accurately. These include new tagging technologies, as well as GPS and GSM technologies that would monitor the car while within London.[4]

Telephones

The architecture of telephone networks has undergone a radical shift in the past decade. After resisting the design of the Internet for many years,[5] telephone networks are now shifting from circuit-switched to packet-switched networks. As with the Internet, packets of information are spewed across the system, and nothing ensures that they will travel in the same way, or along the same path. Packets take the most efficient path, which depends on the demand at any one time.

This design, however, creates problems for law enforcement—in particular, that part of law enforcement that depends upon wiretaps to do their job. In the circuit-switched network, it was relatively simple to identify which wires to tap. In the packet-switched network, where there are no predictable paths for packets of data to travel, wiretapping becomes much more difficult.

At least it is difficult under one design of a packet-switched network. Different designs will be differently difficult. And that potential led Congress in 1994 to enact the Communications Assistance for Law Enforcement Act (CALEA). CALEA requires that networks be designed to preserve the ability of law enforcement to conduct electronic surveillance. This requirement has been negotiated in a series of "safe harbor" agreements that specify the standards networks must meet to satisfy the requirements of the law.

CALEA is a classic example of the kind of regulation that I mean this chapter to flag. The industry created one network architecture. That architecture didn't adequately serve the interests of government. The response of the government was to regulate the design of the network so it better served the government's ends. (Luckily for the networks, the government, at least initially, agreed to pick up part of the cost.[6]) As Susan Crawford writes,

> Most critically for the future of the Internet, law enforcement . . . has made clear that it wants to ensure that it reviews all possibly relevant new services for compliance with unstated information-gathering and information-forwarding requirements before these services are launched. All prudent businesses will want to run their services by law enforcement, suggests the DOJ: "Service providers would be well advised to seek guidance early, preferably well before deployment of a service, if they believe that their service is not covered by CALEA. . . . DOJ would certainly consider a service provider's failure to request such guidance in any enforcement action."[7]

CALEA is a "signal," Crawford describes, that the "FCC may take the view that permission will be needed from government authorities when designing

a wide variety of services, computers, and web sites that use the Internet protocol. . . . [I]nformation flow membranes will be governmentally mandated as
part of the design process for online products and services."[8] That hint has
continued: In August 2005, the Federal Communications Commission (FCC)
ruled that Voice-over-IP services "must be designed so as to make government
wiretapping easier."[9]

Of course, regulating the architecture of the network was not the only
means that Congress had. Congress could have compensated for any loss in
crime prevention that resulted from the decreased ability to wiretap by
increasing criminal punishments.[10] Or Congress could have increased the
resources devoted to criminal investigation. Both of these changes would have
altered the incentives that criminals face without using the network's potential
to help track and convict criminals. But instead, Congress acted to change the
architecture of the telephone networks, thus using the networks directly to
change the incentives of criminals indirectly.

This is law regulating code. Its indirect effect is to improve law enforcement, and it does so by modifying code-based constraints on law enforcement.

Regulation like this works well with telephone companies. There are few
companies, and the regulation is relatively easy to verify. Telephone companies
are thus regulable intermediaries: Rules directed against them are likely to be
enforced.

But what about when telephone service (or rather "telephone service")
begins to be carried across the Internet? Vonage, or Skype, rather than Bell
South? Are these entities similarly regulable?[11]

The answer is that they are, though for different reasons. Skype and Vonage, as well as many other VOIP providers, seek to maximize their value as
corporations. That value comes in part from demonstrating reliably regulable
behavior. Failing to comply with the rules of the United States government is
not a foundation upon which to build a healthy, profitable company. That's as
true for General Motors as it is for eBay.

Telephones: Part 2

Four years after Congress enacted CALEA, the FBI petitioned the Federal
Communications Commission to enhance even further government's power
to regulate. Among the amendments the FBI proposed was a regulation
designed to require disclosure of the locations of individuals using cellular
phones by requiring the phone companies to report the cell tower from which
the call was served.[12] Cellular phone systems need this data to ensure seamless

switching between transmitters. But beyond this and billing, the phone companies have no further need for this information.

The FBI, however, has interests beyond those of the companies. It would like that data made available whenever it has a "legitimate law enforcement reason" for requesting it. The proposed amendment to CALEA would require the cellular company to provide this information, which is a way of indirectly requiring that it write its code to make the information retrievable.[13]

The original motivation for this requirement was reasonable enough: Emergency service providers needed a simple way to determine where an emergency cellular phone call was coming from. Thus, revealing location data was necessary, at least in those cases. But the FBI was keen to extend the reach of location data beyond cases where someone was calling 911, so they pushed to require the collection of this information whenever a call is made.

So far, the FBI has been successful in its requests with the regulators but less so with courts. But the limits the courts have imposed simply require the FBI to meet a high burden of proof to get access to the data. Whatever the standard, the effect of the regulation has been to force cell phone companies to build their systems to collect and preserve a kind of data that only aids the government.

Data Retention

Computers gather data about how they're used. These data are collected in logs. The logs can be verbose or not—meaning they might gather lots of data, or little. And the more they gather, the easier it will be to trace who did what.

Governments are beginning to recognize this. And some are making sure they can take advantage of it. The United States is beginning to "mull,"[14] and the European Union has adopted, legislation to regulate "data generated or processed in connection with the provision of publicly available electronic communications," by requiring that providers retain specified data to better enable law enforcement. This includes data to determine the source, destination, time, duration, type, and equipment used in a given communication.[15] Rules such as this will build a layer of traceability into the platform of electronic communication, making it easier for governments to track individual behavior. (By contrast, in 2006, Congressman Ed Markey of Massachusetts proposed legislation to forbid certain Internet companies, primarily search engines, from keeping logs that make Internet behavior traceable.[16] We'll see how far that proposed rule gets.)

Encryption

The examples so far have involved regulations directed to code writers as a way indirectly to change behavior. But sometimes, the government is doubly indirect: Sometimes it creates market incentives as a way to change code writing, so that the code writing will indirectly change behavior. An example is the U.S. government's failed attempt to secure Clipper as the standard for encryption technology.[17]

I have already sketched the Janus-faced nature of encryption: The same technology enables both confidentiality and identification. The government is concerned with the confidentiality part. Encryption allows individuals to make their conversations or data exchanges untranslatable except by someone with a key. How untranslatable is a matter of debate,[18] but we can put that debate aside for the moment, because, regardless, it is too untranslatable for the government's liking. So the government sought to control the use of encryption technology by getting the Clipper chip accepted as a standard for encryption.

The mechanics of the Clipper chip are not easily summarized, but its aim was to encourage encryption technologies that left a back door open for the government.[19] A conversation could be encrypted so that others could not understand it, but the government would have the ability (in most cases with a court order) to decrypt the conversation using a special key.

The question for the government then was how it could spread the Clipper chip technology. At first, the Clinton administration thought that the best way was simply to ban all other encryption technology. This strategy proved very controversial, so the government then fixed on a different technique: It subsidized the development and deployment of the Clipper chip.[20]

The thinking was obvious: If the government could get industry to use Clipper by making Clipper the cheapest technology, then it could indirectly regulate the use of encryption. The market would do the regulation for the government.[21]

The subsidy plan failed. Skepticism about the quality of the code itself, and about the secrecy with which it had been developed, as well as strong opposition to any governmentally directed encryption regime (especially a U.S.-sponsored regime), led most to reject the technology. This forced the government to take another path.

That alternative is for our purposes the most interesting. For a time, some were pushing for authority to regulate authors of encryption code directly—with a requirement that they build into their code a back door through which the government could gain access.[22] While the proposals have been various, they all aim at ensuring that the government has a way to crack whatever encryption code a user selects.

Compared with other strategies—banning the use of encryption or flooding the market with an alternative encryption standard—this mode presents a number of advantages.

First, unlike banning the use of encryption, this mode of regulation does not directly interfere with the rights of use by individuals. It therefore is not vulnerable to a strong, if yet unproven constitutional claim that an individual has a right "to speak through encryption." It aims only to change the mix of encryption technologies available, not to control directly any particular use by an individual. State regulation of the writing of encryption code is just like state regulation of the design of automobiles: Individual use is not regulated. Second, unlike the technique of subsidizing one market solution, this solution allows the market to compete to provide the best encryption system, given this regulatory constraint. Finally, unlike both other solutions, this one involves the regulation of only a relatively small number of actors, since manufacturers of encryption technology are far fewer in number than users or buyers of encryption systems.

Like the other examples in this section, then, this solution is an example of the government regulating code directly so as to better regulate behavior indirectly; the government uses the architecture of the code to reach a particular substantive end. Here the end, as with digital telephony, is to ensure that the government's ability to search certain conversations is not blocked by emerging technology. And again, the government pursues that end not by regulating primary behavior but by regulating the conditions under which primary behavior happens.

REGULATING CODE TO INCREASE REGULABILITY

All five of these examples address a behavior that the government wants to regulate, but which it cannot (easily) regulate directly. In all five, the government thus regulates that behavior indirectly by directly regulating technologies that affect that behavior. Those regulated technologies in turn influence or constrain the targeted behavior differently. They "influence the development of code."[23] They are regulations of code that in turn make behavior more regulable.

The question that began this chapter was whether there were similar ways that the government might regulate code on the Internet to make behavior on the Net more regulable. The answer is obviously yes. There are many steps the government might take to make behavior on the network more regulable, and there are obvious reasons for taking those steps.

If done properly, these steps would reduce and isolate untraceable Internet behavior. That in turn would increase the probability that bad behavior would be detected. Increased detection would significantly reduce the expected return from maliciousness. For some significant range of malevolent actors, that shift would drive their bad behavior elsewhere.

This would not work perfectly, of course. No effort of control could ever be perfect in either assuring traceability or tracking misbehavior. But perfection is not the standard. The question is whether the government could put enough incentives into the mix of the network to induce a shift towards traceability as a default. For obvious reasons, again, the answer is yes.

The General Form

If the government's aim is to facilitate traceability, that can be achieved by attaching an identity to actors on the network. One conceivable way to do that would be to require network providers to block actions by individuals not displaying a government-issued ID. That strategy, however, is unlikely, as it is politically impossible. Americans are antsy enough about a national identity card;[24] they are not likely to be interested in an Internet identity card.

But even if the government can't *force* cyber citizens to carry IDs, it is not difficult to create strong *incentives* for individuals to carry IDs. There is no requirement that all citizens have a driver's license, but you would find it very hard to get around without one, even if you do not drive. The government does not require that you keep state-issued identification on your person, but if you want to fly to another city, you must show at least one form of it. The point is obvious: Make the incentive to carry ID so strong that it tips the normal requirements of interacting on the Net.

In the same way, the government could create incentives to enable digital IDs, not by regulating individuals directly but by regulating intermediaries. Intermediaries are fewer, their interests are usually commercial, and they are ordinarily pliant targets of regulation. ISPs will be the "most important and obvious" targets—"focal points of Internet control."[25]

Consider first the means the government has to induce the spread of "digital IDs." I will then describe more what these "digital IDs" would have to be.

First, government means:

- Sites on the Net have the ability to condition access based on whether someone carries the proper credential. The government has the power to require sites to impose this condition. For example, the state could require that gambling sites check the age and residency of anyone trying to use the site. Many sites could be required to check the citizenship of potential users, or any number of other credentials. As more and more sites complied with this requirement, individuals would have a greater and greater incentive to carry the proper credentials. The more credentials they carried, the easier it would be to impose regulations on them.[26]

- The government could give a tax break to anyone who filed his or her income tax with a proper credential.
- The government could impose a 10 percent Internet sales tax and then exempt anyone who purchased goods with a certificate that authenticated their state of residence; the state would then be able to collect whatever local tax applied when it was informed of the purchase.[27]
- The government could charge users for government publications unless they gained access to the site with a properly authenticated certificate.
- As in other Western democracies, the government could mandate voting[28]— and then establish Internet voting; voters would come to the virtual polls with a digital identity that certified them as registered.
- The government could make credit card companies liable for the full cost of any credit card or debit card online fraud whenever the transaction was processed without a qualified ID.
- The government could require the establishment of a secure registry of e-mail servers that would be used to fight spam. That list would encourage others to begin to require some further level of authentication before sending e-mail. That authentication could be supplied by a digital ID.

The effect of each of these strategies would be to increase the prevalence of digital IDs. And at some point, there would be a tipping. There is an obvious benefit to many on the Net to be able to increase confidence about the entity with whom they are dealing. These digital IDs would be a tool to increase that confidence. Thus, even if a site permits itself to be accessed without any certification by the user, any step beyond that initial contact could require carrying the proper ID. The norm would be to travel in cyberspace with an ID; those who refuse would find the cyberspace that they could inhabit radically reduced.

The consequence of this tipping would be to effectively stamp every action on the Internet—at a minimum—with a kind of digital fingerprint. That fingerprint—at a minimum—would enable authorities to trace any action back to the party responsible for it. That tracing—at a minimum— could require judicial oversight before any trace could be effected. And that oversight—at a minimum—could track the ordinary requirements of the Fourth Amendment.

At a minimum. For the critical part in this story is not that the government could induce an ID-rich Internet. Obviously it could. Instead, the important question is the kind of ID-rich Internet the government induces.

Compare two very different sorts of digital IDs, both of which we can understand in terms of the "wallet" metaphor used in Chapter 4 to describe the evolving technology of identity that Microsoft is helping to lead.

One sort of ID would work like this: Every time you need to identify yourself, you turn over your wallet. The party demanding identification rummages through the wallet, gathering whatever data he wants.

The second sort of ID works along the lines of the Identity Layer described in Chapter 4: When you need to identify yourself, you can provide the minimal identification necessary. So if you need to certify that you're an American, only that bit gets revealed. Or if you need to certify that you're over 18, only that fact gets revealed.

On the model of the second form of the digital ID, it becomes possible to imagine then an ultra-minimal ID—an identification that reveals nothing on its face, but facilitates traceability. Again, a kind of digital fingerprint which is meaningless unless decoded, and, once decoded, links back to a responsible agent.

These two architectures stand at opposite ends of a spectrum. They produce radically different consequences for privacy and anonymity. Perfect anonymity is possible with neither; the minimal effect of both is to make behavior traceable. But with the second mode, that traceability itself can be heavily regulated. Thus, there should be no possible traceability when the only action at issue is protected speech. And where a trace is to be permitted, it should only be permitted if authorized by proper judicial action. Thus the system would preserve the capacity to identify who did what when, but it would only realize that capacity under authorized circumstances.

The difference between these two ID-enabled worlds, then, is all the difference in the world. And critically, which world we get depends completely upon the values that guide the development of this architecture. ID-type 1 would be a disaster for privacy as well as security. ID-type 2 could radically increase privacy, as well as security, for all except those whose behavior can legitimately be tracked.

Now, the feasibility of the government effecting either ID depends crucially upon the target of regulation. It depends upon there being an entity responsible for the code that individuals use, and it requires that these entities can be effectively regulated. Is this assumption really true? The government may be able to regulate the telephone companies, but can it regulate a diversity of code writers? In particular, can it regulate code writers who are committed to resisting precisely such regulation?

In a world where the code writers were the sort of people who governed the Internet Engineering Task Force[29] of a few years ago, the answer is probably no. The underpaid heroes who built the Net have ideological reasons to resist government's mandate. They were not likely to yield to its threats. Thus, they would provide an important check on the government's power over the architectures of cyberspace.

But as code writing becomes commercial—as it becomes the product of a smaller number of large companies—the government's ability to regulate it increases. The more money there is at stake, the less inclined businesses (and their backers) are to bear the costs of promoting an ideology.

The best example is the history of encryption. From the very start of the debate over the government's control of encryption, techies have argued that such regulations are silly. Code can always be exported; bits know no borders. So the idea that a law of Congress would control the flow of code was, these people argued, absurd.

The fact is, however, that the regulations had a substantial effect. Not on the techies—who could easily get encryption technologies from any number of places on the Net—but on the businesses writing software that would incorporate such technology. Netscape or IBM was not about to build and sell software in violation of U.S. regulations. The United States has a fairly powerful threat against these two companies. As the techies predicted, regulation did not control the flow of bits. But it did quite substantially inhibit the development of software that would use these bits.[30]

The effect has been profound. Companies that were once bastions of unregulability are now becoming producers of technologies that facilitate regulation. For example, Network Associates, inheritor of the encryption program PGP, was originally a strong opponent of regulation of encryption; now it offers products that facilitate corporate control of encryption and recovery of keys.[31] Key recovery creates a corporate back door, which, in many contexts, is far less restricted than a governmental back door.

Cisco is a second example.[32] In 1998 Cisco announced a router product that would enable an ISP to encrypt Internet traffic at the link level—between gateways, that is.[33] But this router would also have a switch that would disable the encryption of the router data and facilitate the collection of unencrypted Internet traffic. This switch could be flipped at the government's command; in other words, the data would be encrypted only when the government allowed it to be.

The point in both cases is that the government is a player in the market for software. It affects the market both by creating rules and by purchasing products. Either way, it influences the supply of commercial software providers who exist to provide what the market demands.

Veterans of the early days of the Net might ask these suppliers, "How could you?"

"It's just business," is the obvious reply.

EAST COAST AND WEST COAST CODES

Throughout this section, I've been speaking of two sorts of code. One is the "code" that Congress enacts (as in the tax code or "the U.S. Code"). Congress passes an endless array of statutes that say in words how to behave. Some statutes direct people; others direct companies; some direct bureaucrats. The technique is as old as government itself: using commands to control. In our country, it is a primarily East Coast (Washington, D.C.) activity. Call it "East Coast Code."

The other is the code that code writers "enact"—the instructions imbedded in the software and hardware that make cyberspace work. This is code in its modern sense. It regulates in the ways I've begun to describe. The code of Net95, for example, regulated to disable centralized control; code that encrypts regulates to protect privacy. In our country (MIT excepted), this kind of code writing is increasingly a West Coast (Silicon Valley, Redmond) activity. We can call it "West Coast Code."

West Coast and East Coast Code can get along perfectly when they're not paying much attention to each other. Each, that is, can regulate within its own domain. But the story of this chapter is "When East Meets West": what happens when East Coast Code recognizes how West Coast Code affects regulability, and when East Coast Code sees how it might interact with West Coast Code to induce it to regulate differently.

This interaction has changed. The power of East Coast Code over West Coast Code has increased. When software was the product of hackers and individuals located outside of any institution of effective control (for example, the University of Illinois or MIT), East Coast Code could do little to control West Coast Code.[34] But as code has become the product of companies, the power of East Coast Code has increased. When commerce writes code, then code can be controlled, because commercial entities can be controlled. Thus, the power of East over West increases as West Coast Code becomes increasingly commercial.

There is a long history of power moving west. It tells of the clash of ways between the old and the new. The pattern is familiar. The East reaches out to control the West; the West resists. But that resistance is never complete. Values from the East become integrated with the West. The new takes on a bit of the old.

That is precisely what is happening on the Internet. When West Coast Code was born, there was little in its DNA that cared at all about East Coast Code concerns. The Internet's aim was end-to-end communication. Regulation at the middle was simply disabled.

Over time, the concerns of East Coast Coders have become much more salient. Everyone hates the pathologies of the Internet—viruses, ID theft, and spam, to pick the least controversial. That universal hatred has warmed West Coast Coders to finding a remedy. They are now primed for the influence East Coast Code requires: adding complements to the Internet architecture that will bring regulability to the Net.

Now, some will continue to resist my claim that the government can effect a regulable Net. This resistance has a common form: Even if architectures of identification emerge, and even if they become common, there is nothing to show that they will become universal, and nothing to show that at any one time they could not be evaded. Individuals can always work around these technologies of identity. No control that they could effect would ever be perfect.

True. The control of an ID-rich Internet would never be complete. There will always be ways to escape.

But there is an important fallacy lurking in the argument: Just because perfect control is not possible does not mean that effective control is not possible. Locks can be picked, but that does not mean locks are useless. In the context of the Internet, even partial control would have powerful effects.

A fundamental principle of bovinity is operating here and elsewhere. Tiny controls, consistently enforced, are enough to direct very large animals. The controls of a certificate-rich Internet are tiny, I agree. But we are large animals. I think it is as likely that the majority of people would resist these small but efficient regulators of the Net as it is that cows would resist wire fences. This is who we are, and this is why these regulations work.

So imagine the world in which we all could simply establish our credentials simply by looking into a camera or swiping our finger on a thumbprint reader. In a second, without easily forgotten passwords, or easily forged authentication, we get access to the Net, with all of the attributes that are ours, reliably and simply assertable.

What will happen then? When you can choose between remembering a pass-phrase, typing it every time you want access to your computer, and simply using your thumb to authenticate who you are? Or if not your thumb, then your iris, or whatever body part turns out to be cheapest to certify? When it is easiest simply to give identity up, will anyone resist?

If this is selling your soul, then trust that there are truly wonderful benefits to be had. Imagine a world where all your documents exist on the Internet in a "virtual private network," accessible by you from any machine on the Net and perfectly secured by a biometric key.[35] You could sit at any machine, call up your documents, do your work, answer your e-mail, and move on—everything perfectly secure and safe, locked up by a key certified by the markings in your eye.

This is the easiest and most efficient architecture to imagine. And it comes at (what some think) is a very low price—authentication. Just say who you are, plug into an architecture that certifies facts about you, give your identity away, and all this could be yours.

Z-THEORY

"So, like, it didn't happen, Lessig. You said in 1999 that commerce and government would work together to build the perfectly regulable net. As I look through my spam-infested inbox, while my virus checker runs in the background, I wonder what you think now. Whatever was possible hasn't happened. Doesn't that show that you're wrong?"

So writes a friend to me as I began this project to update *Code* v1. And while I never actually said anything about *when* the change I was predicting would happen, there is something in the criticism. The theory of *Code* v1 is missing a part: Whatever incentives there are to push in small ways to the perfectly regulable Net, the theory doesn't explain what would motivate the final push. What gets us over the tipping point?

The answer is not fully written, but its introduction was published this year. In May 2006, the *Harvard Law Review* gave Professor Jonathan Zittrain (hence "Z-theory") 67 pages to explain "The Generative Internet."[36] The article is brilliant; the book will be even better; and the argument is the missing piece in *Code* v1.

Much of *The Generative Internet* will be familiar to readers of this book. General-purpose computers plus an end-to-end network, Zittrain argues, have produced an extraordinarily innovative ("generative") platform for invention. We celebrate the good stuff this platform has produced. But we (I especially) who so celebrate don't pay enough attention to the bad. For the very same design that makes it possible for an Indian immigrant to invent HoTMaiL, or Stanford dropouts to create Google, also makes it possible for malcontents and worse to create viruses and worse. These sorts use the generative Internet to generate evil. And as Zittrain rightly observes, we've just begun to see the evil this malware will produce. Consider just a few of his examples:

- In 2003, in a test designed to measure the sophistication of spammers in finding "open relay" servers through which they could send their spam undetected, within 10 hours spammers had found the server. Within 66 hours they had sent more than 3.3 million messages to 229,468 people.[37]
- In 2004, the Sasser worm was able to compromise more than 500,000 computers—in just 3 days.[38] The year before, the Slammer worm infected 90 percent of a particular Microsoft server—in just 15 minutes.[39]
- In 2003, the SoBig.F e-mail virus accounted for almost 70 percent of the e-mails sent while it was spreading. More than 23.2 million messages were sent to AOL users alone.[40]

These are of course not isolated events. They are instead part of a growing pattern. As the U.S. Computer Emergency Readiness Team calculates, there has been an explosion of security incidents reported to CERT. Here is the graph Zittrain produced from the data:[41]

Number of Security Incidents Reported to CERT/CC, 1988-2003

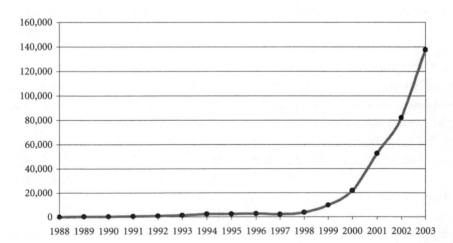

The graph ends in 2004 because CERT concluded that the incidents were so "commonplace and widespread as to be indistinguishable from one another."[42]

That there is malware on the Internet isn't surprising. That it is growing isn't surprising either. What is surprising is that, so far at least, this malware has not been as destructive as it could be. Given the ability of malware authors to get their malicious code on many machines very quickly, why haven't more tried to do real harm?

For example, imagine a worm that worked itself onto a million machines, and in a synchronized attack, simultaneously deleted the hard drive of all million machines. Zittrain's point is not that this is easy, but rather, that it is just as difficult as the kind of worms that are already successfully spreading themselves everywhere. So why doesn't one of the malicious code writers do real damage? What's stopping cyber-Armageddon?

The answer is that there's no good answer. And when there's no good explanation for why something hasn't happened yet, there's good reason to worry that it will happen. And when this happens—when a malware author produces a really devastatingly destructive worm—that will trigger the political resolve to do what so far governments have not done: push to complete the work of transforming the Net into a regulable space.

This is the crucial (and once you see it, obvious) insight of Z-theory. Terror motivates radical change. Think about, for example, the changes in law enforcement (and the protection of civil rights) effected by the "Patriot Act."[43] This massively extensive piece of legislation was enacted 45 days after the terror attacks on 9/11. But most of that bill had been written long before 9/11. The authors knew that until there was a serious terrorist attack, there would be insufficient political will to change law enforcement significantly. But once the trigger of 9/11 was pulled, radical change was possible.

The same will be true of the Internet. The malware we've seen so far has caused great damage. We've suffered this damage as annoyance rather than threat. But when the Internet's equivalent of 9/11 happens—whether sponsored by "terrorists" or not—annoyance will mature into political will. And that political will will produce real change.

Zittrain's aim is to prepare us for that change. His powerful and extensive analysis works through the trade-offs we could make as we change the Internet into something less generative. And while his analysis is worthy of a book of its own, I'll let him write it. My goal in pointing to it here is to provide an outline to an answer that plugs the hole in the theory of *Code* v1. *Code* v1 described the means. Z-theory provides the motive.

There was an awful movie released in 1996 called *Independence Day.* The story is about an invasion by aliens. When the aliens first appear, many earthlings are eager to welcome them. For these idealists, there is no reason to assume hostility, and so a general joy spreads among the hopeful across the globe in reaction to what before had seemed just a dream: really cool alien life.

Soon after the aliens appear, however, and well into the celebration, the mood changes. Quite suddenly, Earth's leaders realize that the intentions of these aliens are not at all friendly. Indeed, they are quite hostile. Within a very short time of this realization, Earth is captured. (Only Jeff Goldblum realizes what's going on beforehand, but he always gets it first.)

My story here is similar (though I hope not as awful). We have been as welcoming and joyous about the Net as the earthlings were about the aliens in *Independence Day;* we have accepted its growth in our lives without questioning its final effect. But at some point, we too will come to see a potential threat. We will see that cyberspace does not guarantee its own freedom but instead carries an extraordinary potential for control. And then we will ask: How should we respond?

I have spent many pages making a point that some may find obvious. But I have found that, for some reason, the people for whom this point should be most important do not get it. Too many take this freedom as nature. Too many believe liberty will take care of itself. Too many miss how different architectures embed different values, and that only by selecting these different architectures—these different codes—can we establish and promote our values.

Now it should be apparent why I began this book with an account of the rediscovery of the role for self-government, or control, that has marked recent history in post-Communist Europe. Market forces encourage architectures of identity to facilitate online commerce. Government needs to do very little—indeed, nothing at all—to induce just this sort of development. The market forces are too powerful; the potential here is too great. If anything is certain, it is that an architecture of identity will develop on the Net—and thereby fundamentally transform its regulability.

But isn't it clear that government should do something to make this architecture consistent with important public values? If commerce is going to define the emerging architectures of cyberspace, isn't the role of government to ensure that those public values that are not in commerce's interest are also built into the architecture?

Architecture is a kind of law: It determines what people can and cannot do. When commercial interests determine the architecture, they create a kind of privatized law. I am not against private enterprise; my strong presumption in most cases is to let the market produce. But isn't it absolutely clear that there must be limits to this presumption? That public values are not exhausted by the sum of what IBM might desire? That what is good for America Online is not necessarily good for America?

Ordinarily, when we describe competing collections of values, and the choices we make among them, we call these choices "political." They are choices about how the world will be ordered and about which values will be given precedence.

Choices among values, choices about regulation, about control, choices about the definition of spaces of freedom—all this is the stuff of politics. Code codifies values, and yet, oddly, most people speak as if code were just a question of engineering. Or as if code is best left to the market. Or best left unaddressed by government.

But these attitudes are mistaken. Politics is that process by which we collectively decide how we should live. That is not to say it is a space where we collectivize—a collective can choose a libertarian form of government. The point is not the substance of the choice. The point about politics is process. Politics is the process by which we reason about how things ought to be.

Two decades ago, in a powerful trilogy drawing together a movement in legal theory, Roberto Unger preached that "it's all politics."[44] He meant that we should not accept that any part of what defines the world is removed from politics—everything should be considered "up for grabs" and subject to reform.

Many believed Unger was arguing that we should put everything up for grabs all the time, that nothing should be certain or fixed, that everything should be in constant flux. But that is not what he meant.

His meaning was instead just this: That we should interrogate the necessities of any particular social order and ask whether they are in fact necessities, and we should demand that those necessities justify the powers that they order. As Bruce Ackerman puts it, we must ask of every exercise of power: Why?[45] Perhaps not exactly at the moment when the power is exercised, but sometime.

"Power," in this account, is just another word for constraints that humans can do something about. Meteors crashing to earth are not "power" within the domain of "it's all politics." Where the meteor hits is not politics, though the consequences may well be. Where it hits, instead, is nothing we can do anything about.

But the architecture of cyberspace is power in this sense; how it is could be different. Politics is about how we decide, how that power is exercised, and by whom.

If code is law, then, as William Mitchell writes, "control of code is power": "For citizens of cyberspace, . . . code . . . is becoming a crucial focus of political contest. Who shall write that software that increasingly structures our daily lives?"[46] As the world is now, code writers are increasingly lawmakers. They determine what the defaults of the Internet will be; whether privacy will be protected; the degree to which anonymity will be allowed; the extent to which access will be guaranteed. They are the ones who set its nature. Their decisions, now made in the interstices of how the Net is coded, define what the Net is.

How the code regulates, who the code writers are, and who controls the code writers—these are questions on which any practice of justice must focus in the age of cyberspace. The answers reveal how cyberspace is regulated. My claim in this part of the book is that cyberspace is regulated by its code, and that the code is changing. Its regulation is its code, and its code is changing.

We are entering an age when the power of regulation will be relocated to a structure whose properties and possibilities are fundamentally different. As I said about Russia at the start of this book, one form of power may be destroyed, but another is taking its place.

Our aim must be to understand this power and to ask whether it is properly exercised. As David Brin asks, "If we admire the Net, should not a burden of proof fall on those who would change the basic assumptions that brought it about in the first place?"[47]

These "basic assumptions" were grounded in liberty and openness. An invisible hand now threatens both. We need to understand how.

One example of the developing struggle over cyber freedoms is the still-not-free China. The Chinese government has taken an increasingly aggressive stand against behavior in cyberspace that violates real-space norms. Purveyors of porn get 10 years in jail. Critics of the government get the same. If this is the people's republic, this is the people's tough love.

To make these prosecutions possible, the Chinese need the help of network providers. And local law requires that network providers in China help. So story after story now reports major network providers—including Yahoo! and Microsoft—helping the government do the sort of stuff that would make our Constitution cringe.

The extremes are bad enough. But the more revealing example of the pattern I'm describing here is Google. Google is (rightly) famous for its fantastic search engine. Its brand has been built on the idea that no irrelevant factor controls its search results. Companies can buy search words, but their results are bracketed and separate from the main search results. The central search results—that part of the screen your eyes instinctively go to—are not to be tampered with.

Unless the company seeking to tamper with the results is China, Inc. For China, Google has promised to build a special routine.[48] Sites China wants to block won't appear in the Google.CN search engine. No notice will be presented. No system will inform searchers that the search results they are reading have been filtered by Chinese censors. Instead, to the Chinese viewer, this will look like normal old Google. And because Google is so great, the Chinese government knows most will be driven to Google, even if Google filters what the government doesn't want its people to have.

Here is the perfect dance of commerce with government. Google can build the technology the Chinese need to make China's regulation more perfectly enabled, and China can extract that talent from Google by mandating it as a condition of being in China's market.

The value of that market is thus worth more to Google than the value of its "neutral search" principle. Or at least, it better be, if this deal makes any sense.

My purpose here is not to criticize Google—or Microsoft, or Yahoo! These companies have stockholders; maximizing corporate value is their charge. Were I running any of these companies, I'm not sure I would have acted differently.

But that in the end is my point: Commerce has a purpose, and government can exploit that to its own end. It will, increasingly and more frequently, and when it does, the character of the Net will change.

Radically so.

PART TWO

regulation by code

The lesson of the last part was that the interaction between commerce and government will change the effective architecture of the Internet. That change will increase the regulability of behavior on the Internet. Powder will be sprayed on the invisible men of cyberspace, and after the spray, their exploits will be more easily known.

But so far my story has not changed the basic mode by which government regulates. So far, the government threatens punishment, and that threat is intended to create the incentive for individuals to obey the government's rule. The changes in the effective architecture of cyberspace that I have described would simply make it easier for the state to make good on its threat, and that would reduce the expected value of criminal behavior (preferably below zero). Traceability will increase effective enforcement; effective enforcement will increase the costs of deviating from a state-specified rule.

In this part, I consider a different kind of regulation. The question here is not how the architecture of the Net will make it easier for traditional regulation to happen. The issue here is how the architecture of the Net—or its "code"—itself becomes a regulator. In this context, the rule applied to an individual does not find its force from the threat of consequences enforced by the law—fines, jail, or even shame. Instead, the rule is applied to an individual through a kind of physics. A locked door is not a command "do not enter" backed up with the threat of punishment by the state. A locked door is a physical constraint on the liberty of someone to enter some space.

My claim is that this form of regulation will become increasingly common in cyberspace. And it has, moreover, a distinctive and often counter-intuitive character. The aim of this part is to explore this distinctive mode of regulation as a step to understanding more systematically the interaction between technology and policy.

SIX

cyberspaces

I'VE SAID WE CAN DISTINGUISH THE INTERNET FROM CYBERSPACE. TO MAKE THE distinctive form of regulation that is the subject of this part salient, we need to say a bit more about this distinction. The Internet is a medium of communication. People do things "on" the Internet. Most of those things are trivial, even if important. People pay bills on the Internet, they make reservations at restaurants. They get their news from the Internet. They send news to family members using e-mail or IM chat. These uses are important in the sense that they affect the economy and make life easier and harder for those using the Internet. But they're not important in the sense that they change how people live. It's very cool that you can buy books with one click at Amazon. I buy tons (maybe literally) of books I wouldn't otherwise have bought. But my life has not been changed by one-click (even if my bank account has). It's been made easier and more literate, but not anything fundamentally different.

Cyberspace, by contrast, is not just about making life easier. It is about making life different, or perhaps better. It is about making a different (or second) life. It evokes, or calls to life, ways of interacting that were not possible before. I don't mean that the interaction is new—we've always had communities; these communities have always produced something close to what I will describe cyberspace to have produced. But these cyberspace communities create a difference in degree that has matured into a difference in kind. There is something unique about the interactions in these spaces, and something especially unique about how they are regulated.

Life in cyberspace is regulated primarily through the code of cyberspace. Not regulated in the sense of Part I—my point is not that the code makes it easy to know who did what so that penalties can be visited upon those who behaved badly. Regulated in the sense that bars on a prison regulate the movement of a prisoner, or regulated in the sense that stairs regulate the access of the disabled. Code is a regulator in cyberspace because it defines the terms upon which cyberspace is offered. And those who set those terms increasingly recognize the code as a means to achieving the behaviors that benefit them best.

And so too with the Internet. Code on the Internet is also a regulator, and people live life on the Internet subject to that regulation. But my strategy in this chapter is to begin with the more obscure as a way to build recognition about the familiar. Once you see the technique applied to worlds you are unlikely to inhabit, you will recognize the technique applied to the world you inhabit all the time.

Cyberspace is not one place. It is many places. And the character of these many places differ in ways that are fundamental. These differences come in part from differences in the people who populate these places, but demographics alone don't explain the variance. Something more is going on.

Here is a test. Read the following passage, and ask yourself whether the description rings true for you:

> I believe virtual communities promise to restore to Americans at the end of the twentieth century what many of us feel was lost in the decades at the beginning of the century—a stable sense of community, of place. Ask those who've been members of such a virtual community, and they'll tell you that what happens there is more than an exchange of electronic impulses in the wires. It's not just virtual barn raising. . . . It's also the comfort from others that a man like Phil Catalfo of the WELL can experience when he's up late at night caring for a child suffering from leukemia, and he logs on to the WELL and pours out his anguish and fears. People really do care for each other and fall in love over the Net, just as they do in geographic communities. And that "virtual" connectedness is a real sign of hope in a nation that's increasingly anxious about the fragmentation of public life and the polarization of interest groups and the alienation of urban existence.[1]

There are two sorts of reactions to talk like this. To those who have been in "cyberspace" for some time, such talk is extremely familiar. These people have been on different kinds of "nets" from the start. They moved to the Internet from more isolated communities—from a local BBS (bulletin board service), or, as Mike Godwin (the author of the passage) puts it, from a "tony" address like The WELL. For them the Net is a space for conversation, connections, and exchange—a wildly promising location for making life in real space different.

But if you are a recent immigrant to this "space" (the old-timers call you "newbies"), or if all you do on the Internet is check your stocks or look up movie times, you are likely to be impatient with talk like this. When people talk about "community," about special ways to connect, or about the amazing power of this space to alter lives, you are likely to ask, "What is this idea of cyberspace as a place?" For newbies, those who have simply e-mailed or surfed the Web, the "community" of the Net is an odd sort of mysticism. How can anyone think of these pages full of advertisements and spinning icons as a community, or even as a space? To the sober newbie, this just sounds like hype high on java.[2]

Newbies are the silent majority of today's Net.[3] However much one romanticizes the old days when the Net was a place for conversation and exchange, this is not its function for most of its users now. There are exploding communities of bloggers and creativity. But bloggers are still just 3 percent of Internet users; the vast majority of Internet use has no connection to any ideal of community.

Cyberspace has changed in its feel.[4] How it looks, what you can do there, how you are connected there—all this has changed. *Why* it has changed is a complicated question—a complete answer to which I can't provide. Cyberspace has changed in part because the people—who they are, what their interests are—have changed, and in part because the capabilities provided by the space have changed.

But part of the change has to do with the space itself. Communities, exchange, and conversation all flourish in a certain type of space; they are extinguished in a different type of space.[5] My hope is to illuminate the differences between these two environments.

The next sections describe different cyber-places. The aim is to build intuitions about how to think through the differences that we observe. These intuitions, in turn, will help us see something about where cyberspace is moving.

THE VALUES OF A SPACE

Spaces have values.[6] They manifest these values through the practices or lives that they enable or disable. As Mark Stefik puts it:

> [B]arriers within cyberspace—separate chat rooms, intranet gateways, digital
> envelopes, and other systems to limit access—resemble the effects of national
> borders, physical boundaries, and distance. Programming determines which
> people can access which digital objects and which digital objects can interact

with other digital objects. How such programming regulates human interactions—and thus modulates change—depends on the choices made.[7]

Choices mean that differently constituted spaces enable and disable differently. This is the first idea to make plain. Here is an example.

At the start of the Internet, communication was through text. Media such as USENET newsgroups, Internet Relay Chat, and e-mail all confined exchange to text—to words on a screen, typed by a person (or so one thought).

The reason for this limitation is fairly obvious: The bandwidth of early Net life was very thin. In an environment where most users connected at 1,200 baud, if they were lucky, graphics and streaming video would have taken an unbearably long time to download, if they downloaded at all. What was needed was an efficient mode of communication—and text is one of the most efficient.[8]

Most think of this fact about the early Net as a limitation. Technically, it was. But this technical description does not exhaust its normative description as an architecture that made possible a certain kind of life. From this perspective, limitations can be features; they can enable as well as disable. And this particular limitation enabled classes of people who were disabled in real-space life.

Think about three such classes—the blind, the deaf, and the "ugly." In real space these people face an extraordinary array of constraints on their ability to communicate. The blind person in real space is constantly confronted with architectures that presume he can see; he bears an extraordinary cost in retrofitting real-space architectures so that this presumption is not totally exclusionary. The deaf person in real space confronts architectures that presume she can hear; she too bears an extraordinary cost in retrofitting these architectures. The "ugly" person in real space (think of a bar or a social club) confronts architectures of social norms that make his appearance a barrier to a certain sort of intimacy. He endures extraordinary suffering in conforming to these architectures.

In real space these three groups are confronted with architectures that disable them relative to "the rest of us." But in cyberspace, in its first iteration, they did not.

The blind could easily implement speech programs that read the (by definition machine-readable) text and could respond by typing. Other people on the Net would have no way of knowing that the person typing the message was blind, unless he claimed to be. The blind were equal to the seeing.

The same with the deaf. There was no need to hear anything in this early Internet. For the first time many of the deaf could have conversations, or exchanges, in which the most salient feature was not that the person was deaf. The deaf were equal to the hearing.

And the same with the "ugly." Because your appearance was not transmitted with every exchange, the unattractive could have an intimate conversation with others that was not automatically defined by what they looked like. They could flirt or play or be sexual without their bodies (in an extremely underappreciated sense) getting in the way. This first version of the Net made these people equal to "the beautiful." In a virtual chat room, stunning eyes, a captivating smile, or impressive biceps don't do it. Wit, engagement, and articulateness do.

The architecture of this original cyberspace gave these groups something that they did not have in real space. More generally, it changed the mix of benefits and burdens that people faced—the literate were enabled and the attractive disabled relative to real space. Architectures produced these enablings and disablings.

I've told this story as if it matters only to those who in real space are "disabled." But of course, "disabled" is a relative term.[9] It is more accurate to say that the space changes the meaning of the enabled. A friend—a strikingly beautiful and powerful woman, married, and successful—described for me why she spends hours in political chat spaces, arguing with others about all sorts of political topics:

> You don't understand what it's like to be me. You have lived your whole life in a world where your words are taken for their meaning; where what you say is heard for what it says. I've never had a space, before this space, where my words were taken for what they meant. Always, before, they were words of "this babe," or "wife," or "mother." I could never speak as I. But here, I am as I speak.

Clearly, the space is enabling her, even though one would not have said that in real space she was "disabled."[10]

Over time, as bandwidth has expanded, this architecture has changed, and so has the mix of benefits and burdens. When graphics entered the Net through the World Wide Web, the blind became "blind" again. As sound files or speech in virtual spaces have been created, the deaf have become "deaf" again. And as chat rooms have started segregating into spaces where videocams capture real images of the people chatting and spaces where there is just text, the video-unappealing are again unappealing.[11] As the architectures change, definitions of who is "disabled" change as well.

My point is not to argue that the Net should not change—though of course, if it can change in ways that minimize the disabling effect of sound and graphics, then it no doubt should.[12] However important, my point is not really about the "disabled" at all. I use this example simply to highlight a link—between these structures of code and the world this code enables. Codes constitute cyberspaces; spaces enable and disable individuals and groups. The selections about code are therefore in part a selection about who, what, and, most important, what ways of life will be enabled and disabled.

CYBER-PLACES

We can build on this point by looking at a number of "communities" that are constituted differently and that constitute different forms of life and by considering what makes these differences possible.

America Online

America Online (AOL) is an online service provider—"by far the largest ISP in the world"[13] with some 12 million subscribers in 1998 and 27 million today.[14] But despite having the population of New York and New Jersey combined, AOL still describes itself as a "community." A large community perhaps, but a community nonetheless.

This community has a constitution—not in the sense of a written document (though there is that as well), but in the sense of a way of life for those who live there. Its founding vision was that community would make this place sing. So from its start, AOL's emphasis has been on enabling people to interact, through chat, bulletin boards, and e-mail. (Today, AOL hosts the exchange of more messages daily than does the U.S. Post Office.[15]) Earlier providers, obsessed with providing content or advertising, limited or ignored the possibilities for interaction and exchange, but AOL saw interaction as the stuff that makes cyberspace different. It built itself on building a community and establishing itself as a place where people could say what they wanted.[16]

This interaction is governed by the rules of the place. Some of these rules are formal, others customary. Among the formal are express terms to which every member subscribes upon joining AOL. These terms regulate a wide range of behaviors in this space, including the behavior of AOL members anywhere on the Internet.[17]

Increasingly, these rules have become controversial. AOL policies have been called "Big Brother" practices. Arguments that get heated produce exchanges that are rude. But rudeness, or offensiveness, is not permitted in AOL's community. When these exchanges are expunged, claims of "censorship" arise.[18]

My aim here, however, is not to criticize these rules of "netiquette." AOL also has other rules that regulate AOL members—rules expressed not in contracts but rather through the very architectures of the space. These rules are the most important part of AOL's constitution, but they are probably the part considered last when we think about what regulates behavior in this cyberplace.

Consider some examples:

For most of AOL's life,[19] as a member of AOL you could be any one of five people. This was just one amazing feature of the space. When you started an account on AOL, you had the right to establish up to five identities, through five different "screen names" that in effect establish five different accounts. Some users, of course, used the five screen names to give other family members access to AOL. But not everyone used an AOL account like this. Think about the single woman, signing up for her first AOL account. AOL gave her up to five identities that she can define as she wishes—five different personae she can use in cyberspace.

What does that mean? A screen name is just a label for identifying who you are when you are on the system. It need not (indeed, often cannot) be your own name. If your screen name is "StrayCat," then people can reach you by sending e-mail to "straycat@aol.com." If you are online, people can try to talk to you by paging StrayCat on the AOL system; a dialogue would then appear on your screen asking whether you want to talk to the person who paged you. If you enter a chat room, the list of residents there will add you as "StrayCat."

But who is StrayCat? Here is a second dimension of control. StrayCat is who StrayCat says she is. She can choose to define herself as no one at all. If she chooses to place a description of herself in the members' directory, that description can be as complete or incomplete as she wishes. It can be true or false, explicit or vague, inviting or not. A member stumbling across StrayCat, then, in a chat room set up for stamp collectors could get her profile and read that StrayCat lives in Cleveland and is single and female. What happens next is anyone's guess.

Yet this need only be one of StrayCat's five identities. Let's say there is a different persona that StrayCat likes to have when she wanders through chat rooms. She can then select another screen name and define it in the directory as she wishes. Perhaps when StrayCat is having a serious discussion in a newsgroup or political list she prefers to speak as herself. She could then select a screen name close to her own name and define it according to who she really is. At other times StrayCat may like to pretend to be a man—engaging in virtual cross-dressing and all that might bring with it. One of her screen names could then be a man's. And so on. The point is the multiplicity that AOL allows, and the freedom this multiplicity permits.

No one except StrayCat needs to know which screen names are hers. She is not required to publish the full list of her identities, and no one can find out who she is (unless she breaks the rules). (After revealing to the U.S. Navy the name of one of its members so that the Navy could prosecute the person for being a homosexual, AOL adopted a very strict privacy policy that promises never to allow a similar transgression to happen again.)[20]

So in AOL you were given a fantastic power of pseudonymity that the "code writers" of real space simply do not give. You could, of course, try in real space to live the same range of multiple lives, and to the extent that these lives are not incompatible or inconsistent, you could quite often get away with it. For instance, you could be a Cubs fan during the summer and an opera buff during the winter. But unless you take extraordinary steps to hide your identity, in real space you are always tied back to you. You cannot simply define a different character; you must make it, and more important (and difficult), you must sustain its separation from your original identity.

That is a first feature of the constitution of AOL—a feature constituted by its code. A second is tied to speech—what you can say, and where.

Within the limits of decency, and so long as you are in the proper place, you can say what you want on AOL. But beyond these limits, speech on AOL is constrained in a more interesting way: not by rules, but by the character of the potential audience. There are places in AOL where people can gather; there are places where people can go and read messages posted by others. But there is no space where everyone gathers at one time, or even a space that everyone must sooner or later pass through. There is no public space where you could address all members of AOL. There is no town hall or town meeting where people can complain in public and have their complaints heard by others. There is no space large enough for citizens to create a riot. The owners of AOL, however, can speak to all. Steve Case, the founder of AOL, used to write "chatty" letters to the members as the community's "town mayor."[21] Case left AOL in 2005, and apparently no one has stepped into his speaker shoes. AOL does still advertise to all its members and can send everyone an e-mail, but only the owners and those they authorize can do so. The rest of the members of AOL can speak to crowds only where they notice a crowd—and never to a crowd greater than thirty-six (up from twenty-three when the first edition of this book was published).

This is another feature of the constitution of the space that AOL is, and it too is defined by code. That only twenty-three people can be in a chat room at once is a choice of the code engineers. While their reasons could be many, the effect is clear. One can't imagine easily exciting members of AOL into public action, such as picketing the latest pricing policy. There are places to go to complain, but you have to take the trouble to go there yourself. There is no place where members can complain en masse.

Real space is different in this respect. Much of free speech law is devoted to preserving spaces where dissent can occur—spaces that can be noticed, and must be confronted, by nondissenting citizens.[22] In real space there are places where people can gather, places where they can leaflet. People have a right to the sidewalks, public streets, and other traditional public forums. They may go there and talk about issues of public import or otherwise say whatever they want. Constitutional law in real space protects the right of the passionate and the weird to get in the face of the rest. But no such design is built into AOL.[23] As Dawn Nunziato writes,

> AOL explains in its Community Guidelines that "like any city, we take pride in—and are protective of—our community." Unlike any other city, however, AOL enjoys the unfettered discretion to censor constitutionally-protected speech in its discussion forums and other online spaces, including "vulgar language" (which, it warns, is "no more appropriate online than [it] would be at Thanksgiving dinner"), "crude conversations about sex," and "discussions about . . . illegal drug abuse that imply it is acceptable."[24]

This is not to romanticize the power of real-space public forums. (Nor is it to pick on AOL: As Nunziato continues, "users seeking stronger protection for their expression might turn to an ISP other than AOL. They will find, however, similar restrictions on speech imposed by many other major ISPs."[25]) We have become such an apolitical society that if you actually exercised this constitutionally protected right, people would think you were a nut. If you stood on a street corner and attacked the latest tax proposal in Congress, your friends would be likely to worry—and not about the tax proposal. There are exceptions—events can make salient the need for protest—but in the main, though real space has fewer controls through code on who can speak where, it has many more controls through norms on what people can say where. Perhaps in the end real space is much like AOL—the effective space for public speech is limited and often unimportant. That may well be. But my aim here is to identify the feature and to isolate what is responsible for it. And once again, it turns out to be a feature built into the code.

A third feature of AOL's constitution also comes from its code. This is traceability. While members are within the exclusive AOL content area (in other words, when they're not using AOL as a gateway to the Internet), AOL can (and no doubt does) trace your activities and collect information about them. What files you download, what areas you frequent, who your "buddies" are—all this is available to AOL. These data are extremely valuable; they help AOL structure its space to fit customer demand. But gaining the ability to collect these data required a design decision. This decision too was part of the constitution that is AOL—again, a part constituted by its code. It is a decision that gives some but not others the power to watch.

AOL is not exclusive in this enabling capacity. It shares the power. One wonderful feature of the online space is something called "buddy lists." Add someone to your buddy list, and when he comes online you hear the sound of a creaking door and are notified that he is online. (The "buddy" need not know he is being watched, though he can, if he knows, block the watching.) If that person goes into a chat area and you "locate" him, you will be told in what chat area he is. This power, given to ordinary users, can have complicated consequences. (Imagine sitting at work with your buddy feature turned on, watching your spouse come online, enter a chat area, and—you get the point.) This ability to monitor is built into the space. Individuals can turn it off, at least for a single watcher, but only if they know about it and think to change it.

Consider one final feature of the constitution of AOL, closely linked to the last: commerce. In AOL you can buy things. You can buy things and download them, or buy things and have them sent to your home. When you buy, you buy with a screen name, and when you buy with a screen name, AOL knows (even if no one else does) just who you are. It knows who you are, it knows where you live in real space, and most important, it knows your credit card number and the security it provides.

AOL knows who you are—this is a feature of its design. All your behavior on AOL is watched; all of it is monitored and tracked back to you as a user. AOL promises not to collect data about you individually, but it certainly collects data about you as part of a collective. And with this collective, and the link it provides back to you, AOL is a space that can better, and more efficiently, sell to you.

These four features mark AOL space as different from other places in cyberspace. It is easier for AOL to identify who you are, and harder for individuals to find out who you are; easier for AOL to speak to all its "citizens" as it wishes, and harder for dissidents to organize against AOL's views about how things ought to be; easier for AOL to market, and harder for individuals to hide. AOL is a different normative world; it can create this different world because it is in control of the architecture of that world. Members in that space face, in a sense, a different set of laws of nature; AOL makes those laws.

Again, my aim is not to criticize the creation of this world or to say that it is improper. No doubt AOL makes promises to its members that are designed to allay some of the concern that this control creates, and no doubt if the place became oppressive, the market would provide plenty of alternatives.

Rather my objective is to impart a sense of what makes AOL the way it is. It is not just written rules; it is not just custom; it is not just the supply and demand of a knowing consuming public. What makes AOL is in large part the structure of the space. You enter AOL and you find it to be a certain universe. This space is constituted by its code. You can resist this code—you can resist how you find it, just as you can resist cold weather by putting on a sweater. But you are not going to change how it is. You do not have the power to change AOL's code, and there is no place where you could rally AOL members to force AOL to change the code. You live life in AOL subject to its terms; if you do not like them, you go elsewhere.

These features of the AOL space have important implications for how it is regulated. Imagine there is a problem on AOL that AOL wants to stop. It wants to prevent or at least control a certain behavior. What tools does AOL have?

First, it has all the tools that any club, fraternity, or "community" might have. It can announce rules for its members (and AOL certainly does). Or it can try to stigmatize the behavior, to use the norms of the community to help regulate the problem. This AOL does as well. Alternatively, if the problem comes from the overuse of a particular resource, then the managers at AOL can price that resource differently by exacting a tax to reduce its usage or a different price for those who use it too much.

But AOL has something more at hand. If AOL does not like a certain behavior, then in at least some cases it can regulate that behavior by changing its architecture. If AOL is trying to control indecent language, it can write routines that monitor language usage; if there is improper mixing between adults and kids, AOL can track who is talking to whom; if there is a virus problem caused by people uploading infected files, it can run the files automatically through virus checkers; if there is stalking or harassing or threatening behavior, AOL can block the connection between any two individuals.

In short, AOL can deal with certain types of problems by changing its code. Because the universe that AOL members know (while in AOL) is defined by this code, AOL can use the code to regulate its members.

Think a bit about the power I am describing—and again, I am not complaining or criticizing or questioning this power, only describing it. As you move through this space that AOL defines—entering a chat area, posting a message to a bulletin board, entering a discussion space, sending instant-messages to another person, watching or following other people, uploading or downloading files from sites, turning to certain channels and reading certain articles, or obsessively paging through a space looking for pictures of a certain actor or actress—as you do any of these things, AOL is, in an important sense, there. It is as if the system gives you a space suit that you use to navigate the space but that simultaneously monitors your every move.

In principle, the potential for control is extraordinary. Imagine AOL slowing the response time for a certain kind of service it wants to discourage, or channeling the surfer through ads that it wants customers to see, or identifying patterns of behavior that its monitors would watch, based on the fear that people with patterns like X are typically dangerous to people of type Y. I do not think AOL engages in activities like these, and I am not saying that there would be anything wrong if it did. But it is important to note that the potential for control in this "community" is unlimited—not in the sense that AOL could make life miserable (since people would then leave), but in the sense that it has a regulatory tool that others, in both real space and other cyberspaces, do not. Its power is, of course, checked by the market, but it has a tool of control that others in the market, but outside cyberspace, do not have.

In principle, then, AOL must choose. Every time AOL decides that it wants to regulate a certain kind of behavior, it must select from among at least four modalities—rules, norms, prices, or architecture. And when selecting one of these four modalities, selecting architecture as a regulator will often make the most sense.

Counsel Connect

David Johnson began Counsel Connect (CC) in 1992 as an online lawyers' cooperative. The idea was simple: Give subscribers access to each other; let them engage in conversations with each other; and through this access and these conversations, value would be created. Lawyers would give and take work; they would contribute ideas as they found ideas in the space. A different kind of law practice would emerge—less insular, less exclusive, more broadly based.

I thought the idea amazing, though many thought it nuts. For a time the system was carried by Lexis; in 1996 it was sold to American Lawyer Media, L.P.; in 1997 it migrated to the Internet, and it closed in 1999.[26] At its peak, it boasted thousands of subscribers, though it is hard to know how many of them contributed to the discussion online. Most simply watched the discussions of others, perhaps linking three or four discussion groups of their particular interest, plus a few of more general interest. But many saw the emerging culture as something amazing and new (for lawyers at least). As its founder, David Johnson, described it, "Think of The Well for lawyers, with its own highly unique evolution, emergence, maintenance, and adaptation."[27] Members got to know each other well. "Inevitably, this led to numerous real world meetings. . . . Of those I attended, it always resemble[d] a get together of long-time acquaintances even though many of us ha[d] not previously met face to face."[28]

The discussion was organized into legal topics. Each topic was divided into discussion groups, with each group led by a discussion leader. The leader was not a moderator; he or she had no power to cancel a post. The leader was there to inspire conversation—to induce others to speak by being encouraging or provocative.

At its height, there were some 90 groups in this space. The poster of a particular message may have had it removed, but if the poster did not remove it, it stayed—at first in the list of topics being discussed, and later in an archive that could be searched by any member.

Members paid a fee to join and get an account with their real name on it. Postings use members' real names, and anyone wondering who someone is could simply link to a directory. Members of CC must be members of the bar, unless they are journalists. Others have no right to access; the community here is exclusive.

Postings in the space look very much like postings in a USENET newsgroup. A thread could be started by anyone, and replies to a thread were appended to the end. Because messages did not move off the system, one could easily read from the start of a thread to its end. The whole conversation, not just a snippet, was preserved.

These features of CC space were obviously designed; the architects chose to enable certain features and to disable others. We can list here some of the effects of these choices.

First, there was the effect from being required to use your own name. You were more likely to think before speaking and to be careful about being right before saying something definitive. You were constrained by the community, which would judge what you said, and in this community you could not escape from being linked to what you said. Responsibility was a consequence of this architecture, but so was a certain inhibition. Does a senior partner at a leading law firm really want to ask a question that will announce his ignorance about a certain area of law? Names cannot be changed to protect the ignorant, so they will often simply not speak.

Second, there was an effect from forcing all discussion into threads. Postings were kept together; a question was asked, and the discussion began from the question. If you wanted to contribute to this discussion, you had to first read through the other postings before responding. Of course, this was not a technical requirement—you certainly had a choice not to read. But if you did not read through the entire thread, you could well end up repeating what another had said and so reveal that you were speaking without listening. Again, the use of real names ties members' behavior to the norms of the community.

Third, there was the effect of reputation: The reputation you built in this space was based on the kind of advice you gave. Your reputation survived any particular post and was, of course, affected by any subsequent posts. These posts were archived and searchable. If you said one thing about topic X and then the opposite later on, you were at least open to a question about consistency.

Fourth, there was the effect of tying reputation to a real name in a real community of professionals. Misbehaving here mattered elsewhere. CC thus got the benefit of that community—it got the benefit, that is, of the norms of a particular community. These norms might have supported relatively productive community behavior—more productive, that is, than the behavior of a group whose members are fundamentally mixed. They might also have supported punishing those who deviated from appropriate behavior. Thus, CC got the benefit of community sanction to control improper behavior, whereas AOL had to rely on its own content police to ensure that people stayed properly on topic.

We can describe the world of CC that these features constitute in two different ways, just as we can describe the world AOL constitutes in two different ways. One is the life that CC's features made possible—highly dialogic and engaged, but monitored and with consequences. The other is the regulability by the manager of the life that goes on in the CC space. And here we can see a significant difference between this space and AOL.

CC could have used the norms of a community to regulate more effectively than AOL can. CC benefited from the norms of the legal community; it knew that any misbehavior would be sanctioned by that community. There was, of course, less "behavior" in this space than in AOL (you did fewer things here), but such as it was, CC behavior was quite significantly regulated by the reputations of members and the consequences of using their real names.

These differences together had an effect on CC's ability to regulate its members. They enabled a regulation through modalities other than code.

They made behavior in CC more regulable by norms than behavior in AOL is. CC in turn may have had less control than AOL does (since the controlling norms are those of the legal community), but it also bore less of the burden of regulating its members' behavior. Limiting the population, making members' behavior public, tying them to their real names—these are the tools of self-regulation in this virtual space.

But CC was like AOL in one important way: It was not a democracy and neither is AOL. Management in both cases controls what will happen in the space—again, not without constraint, because the market is an important constraint. But in neither place do "the people" have the power to control what goes on. Perhaps they did, indirectly, in CC more than AOL, since it is the norms of "the people" that regulate behavior in CC. But these norms cannot be used against CC directly. The decisions of CC and AOL managers may have been affected by market forces—individuals can exit, competitors can steal customers away. But voting doesn't direct where AOL goes, and it didn't with CC either.

That's not the case with the next cyber-place. At least, not anymore.

LambdaMOO

LambdaMOO is a text-based virtual reality. People from across the world (today close to six thousand of them) link to this space and interact in ways that the space permits. The reality is the product of this interaction. Individuals can participate in the construction of this reality—sometimes for upwards of eighty hours a week. For some this interaction is the most sustained human contact of their entire lives. For most it is a kind of interaction unmatched by anything else they know.

In the main, people just talk here. But it is not the talk of an AOL chat room. The talk in a MUD is in the service of construction—of constructing a character and a community. You interact in part by talking, and this talking is tied to a name. This name, and the memories of what it has done, live in the space, and over time people in the space come to know the person by what these memories recall.

The life within these MUDs differ. Elizabeth Reid describes two different "styles"[29]—social-style MUD and an adventure or game-style MUD. Social MUDs are simply online communities where people talk and build characters or elements for the MUD. Adventure MUDs are games, with (virtual) prizes or power to be won through the deployment of skill in capturing resources or defeating an enemy. In either context, the communities survive a particular interaction. They become virtual clubs, though with different purposes. Members build reputations through their behavior in these clubs.

You get a character simply by joining the MOO (though in LambdaMOO the waiting list for a character extends over many months). When
you join the space, you define the character you will have. At least, you
define certain features of your character. You select a name and a gender (no
gender is an option as well) and describe your character. Some descriptions
are quite ordinary (Johnny Manhattan is "tall and thin, pale as string cheese,
wearing a neighborhood hat").[30] Others, however, are quite extraordinary.
(Legba, for instance, is a Haitian trickster spirit of indeterminate gender,
brown-skinned and wearing an expensive pearl gray suit, top hat, and dark
glasses.)[31]

Julian Dibbell broke the story of this space to the nonvirtual world in an
article in the *Village Voice*.[32] The story that was the focus of Dibbell's article
involved a character called Mr. Bungle who, it turns out, was actually a group
of NYU undergraduates sharing this single identity. Bungle entered a room
late one evening and found a group of characters well known in that space.
The full story cannot be told any better than Dibbell tells it. For our purposes,
the facts will be enough.[33]

Bungle had a special sort of power. By earning special standing in the
LambdaMOO community, he had "voodoo" power: he could take over the
voices and actions of other characters and make them appear to do things
they did not really do. This Bungle did that night to a group of women and at
least one person of ambiguous gender. He invoked this power, in this public
space, and took over the voices of these people. Once they were in his control,
Bungle "raped" these women, violently and sadistically, and made it seem as
if they enjoyed the rape.

The "rape" was virtual in the sense that the event happened only on the
wires. "No bodies touched," as Dibbell describes it.

> Whatever physical interaction occurred consisted of a mingling of electronic
> signals sent from sites spread out between New York City and Sydney, Australia.
> . . . He commenced his assault entirely unprovoked at, or about 10 P.M. Pacific
> Standard Time. . . . [H]e began by using his voodoo doll to force one of the
> room's occupants to sexually service him in a variety of more or less conven-
> tional ways. That this victim was exu. . . . He turned his attentions now to Moon-
> dreamer . . . forcing her into unwanted liaisons with other individuals present in
> the room. . . . His actions grew progressively violent. . . . He caused Moon-
> dreamer to violate herself with a piece of kitchen cutlery. He could not be
> stopped until at last someone summoned Iggy . . . who brought with him a gun
> of near wizardly powers, a gun that didn't kill but enveloped its targets in a cage
> impermeable even to a voodoo doll's powers.[34]

Rape is a difficult word to use in any context, but particularly here. Some will object that whatever happened in this virtual space, it has nothing to do with rape. Yet even if "it" was not "rape," all will see a link between rape and what happened to these women there. Bungle used his power over these women for his own (and against their) sexual desire; he sexualized his violence and denied them even the dignity of registering their protest.

For our purposes, whether what happened here was really rape is beside the point. What matters is how the community reacted. The community was outraged by what Bungle had done, and many thought something should be done in response.

They gathered, this community of members of LambdaMOO, in a virtual room at a set time, to discuss what to do. Some thirty showed up, the largest meeting the community had known. Some thought that Bungle should be expelled—"toaded," as it is described, killed for purposes of the MOO. Others thought that nothing should be done; Bungle was certainly a creep, but the best thing to do to creeps was simply to ignore them. Some called on the Wizards of the space—the creators, the gods—to intervene to deal with this character. The Wizards declined: Their job, they replied, was to create the world; the members had to learn to live within it.

There was really no law that governed what Bungle had done. No real-space law reached sexual pranks like this, and neither did any explicit rule of LambdaMOO.[35] This troubled many who wanted to do something. Invoking real-space ideals about fair notice and due process, these people argued that Bungle could not be punished for violating rules that did not exist at the time.

Two extremes eventually emerged. One side urged vigilantism: Bungle was a miscreant, and something should be done about him. But what shouldn't be done, they argued, was for LambdaMOO to respond by creating a world of regulation. LambdaMOO did not need a state; it needed a few good vigilantes. It needed people who would enforce the will of the community without the permanent intrusion of some central force called the state. Bungle should be expelled, killed, or "toaded"—and someone would do it. But only if the group resisted the call to organize itself into a state.

The other side promoted just one idea: democracy. With the cooperation of the Wizards, LambdaMOO should establish a way to vote on rules that would govern how people in the space behaved. Any question could be made the subject of a ballot; there was no constitution limiting the scope of what democracy could decide. An issue decided by the ballot would be implemented by the Wizards. From then on, it would be a rule.

Both extremes had their virtues, and both invited certain vices. The anarchy of the first risked chaos. It was easy to imagine the community turning against people with little or no warning; one imagined vigilantes roaming the space, unconstrained by any rules, "toading" people whose crimes happened to strike them as "awful." For those who took this place less seriously than real space, this compromise was tolerable. But what was tolerable for some was intolerable to others—as Bungle had learned.

Democracy seemed natural, yet many resisted it as well. The idea that politics could exist in LambdaMOO seemed to sully the space. The thought that ideas would have to be debated and then voted on was just another burden. Sure, rules would be known and behavior could be regulated, but it all began to seem like work. The work took something from the fun the space was to have been.

In the end, both happened. The debate that evening wound down after almost three hours. No clear resolution had found its way in. But a resolution of sorts did occur. As Dibbell describes it:

> It was also at this point, most likely, that TomTraceback reached his decision. Tom-Traceback was a wizard, a taciturn sort of fellow who'd sat brooding on the sidelines all evening. He hadn't said a lot, but what he had said indicated that he took the crime committed against exu and Moondreamer very seriously, and that he felt no particular compassion toward the character who had committed it. But on the other hand he had made it equally plain that he took the elimination of a fellow player just as seriously, and moreover that he had no desire to return to the days of wizardly intervention. It must have been difficult, therefore, to reconcile the conflicting impulses churning within him at that moment. In fact, it was probably impossible, for . . . as much as he would have liked to make himself an instrument of the MOO's collective will, [he surely realized that under the present order of things] he must in the final analysis either act alone or not act at all.
>
> So TomTraceback acted alone.
>
> He told the lingering few players in the room that he had to go, and then he went. It was a minute or two before 10 P.M. He did it quietly and he did it privately, but all anyone had to do to know he'd done it was to type the @who command, which was normally what you typed if you wanted to know a player's present location and the time he last logged in. But if you had run an @who on Mr. Bungle not too long after TomTraceback left emmeline's room, the database would have told you something different.
>
> "Mr_Bungle," it would have said, "is not the name of any player."
>
> The date, as it happened, was April Fool's Day, but this was no joke: Mr. Bungle was truly dead and truly gone.[36]

When the Wizards saw this, they moved to the other extreme. With no formal decision by the citizens, the Wizards called forth a democracy. Starting May 1, 1993,[37] any matter could be decided by ballot, and any proposition receiving at least twice as many votes for as against would become the law.[38] Many wondered whether this was an advance or not.

There is a lot to think about in this story, even in my savagely abridged version.[39] But I want to focus on the sense of loss that accompanied the Wizards' decision. There is a certain romance tied to the idea of establishing a democracy—Kodak commercials with tearful Berliners as the Wall comes down and all that. The romance is the idea of self-government and of establishing structures that facilitate it. But LambdaMOO's move to self-government, through structures of democracy, was not just an achievement. It was also a failure. The space had failed. It had failed, we could say, to self-regulate. It had failed to engender values in its population sufficient to avoid just the sort of evil Bungle had perpetrated. The debate marked the passage of the space from one kind of place to another. From a space self-regulated to a space regulated by self.

It might seem odd that there would be a place where the emergence of democracy would so depress people. But this kind of reaction is not uncommon in cyber-places. Katie Hafner and Matthew Lyon tell a story of the emergence of a "widget" called the FINGER command on UNIX, that would allow users to see when the last time another user had been on the computer, and whether she had read her mail. Some thought (not surprisingly, I should think) that this command was something of an invasion of privacy. Whose business was it when I was last at my machine, and why should they get to know whether I have read my mail?

A programmer at Carnegie Mellon University, Ivor Durham, changed the command to give the user the power to avoid this spying finger. The result? "Durham was flamed without mercy. He was called everything from spineless to socially irresponsible to a petty politician, and worse—but not for protecting privacy. He was criticized for monkeying with the openness of the network."[40]

The values of the UNIX world were different. They were values embedded in the code of UNIX. To change the code was to change the values, and members of the community fought that change.

So too with the changes to LambdaMOO. Before the balloting, LambdaMOO was regulated through norms. These regulations of social structures were sustained by the constant policing of individual citizens. They were the regulations of a community; the rise of democracy marked the fall of this community. Although norms would no doubt survive the establishment of a democracy, their status was forever changed. Before the democracy, a struggle over which norms should prevail could be resolved only by consensus—by certain views prevailing in a decentralized way. Now such a struggle could be resolved by the power of a majority—not through what a majority did, but through how they voted.

I've romanticized this bizarre little world far more than I intended. I do not mean to suggest that the world of LambdaMOO before democracy was necessarily better than the one after. I want only to mark a particular change. Like CC, and unlike AOL, LambdaMOO is a place where norms regulate. But unlike CC, LambdaMOO is now a place where members have control over restructuring the norms.

Such control changes things. Norms become different when ballots can overrule them, and code becomes different when ballots can order Wizards to change the world. These changes mark a movement from one kind of normative space to another, from one kind of regulation to another.

In all three of these cyber-places, code is a regulator. But there are important differences among the three. Norms have a relevance in CC and LambdaMOO that they do not in AOL; democracy has a relevance in LambdaMOO that it does not have in CC or AOL. And monitoring has a relevance in AOL that it does not have in LambdaMOO or CC (since neither of the latter two use data about individuals for commercial purposes, either internal or external to the organization). Code constitutes these three communities; as Jennifer Mnookin says of LambdaMOO, "politics [is] implemented through technology."[41] Differences in the code constitute them differently, but some code makes community thicker than others. Where community is thick, norms can regulate.

The next space in this survey is also constituted by code, though in this case the "management" has less ability to change its basic architecture. This code is net code—a protocol of the Internet that is not easily changed by a single user. At least it was not easy for me.

.law.cyber

His name was IBEX, and no one knew who he was. I probably could have figured it out—I had the data to track him down—but after he did what he did, I did not want to know who he was. He was probably a student in the very first class about cyberspace that I taught, and I would have failed him, because I was furious about what he had done. The class was "The Law of Cyberspace"; version one of that class was at Yale.

I say version one because I had the extraordinary opportunity to teach that class at three extraordinary law schools—first at Yale, then at the University of

Chicago, and finally at Harvard. These were three very different places, with three very different student bodies, but one part of the course was the same in each place. Every year a "newsgroup" was associated with the class—an electronic bulletin board where students could post messages about questions raised in the course, or about anything at all. These postings began conversations—threads of discussion, one message posted after another, debating or questioning what the earlier message had said.

These newsgroups constituted what philosophers might call "dialogic communities." They were spaces where discussion could occur, but where what was said was preserved for others to read, as in CC. That was the dialogic part. The community was what was made over time as people got to know each other—both in this space and in real space. One year students in the class and students outside the class (who had been watching the .law.cyber discussions develop) had a party; another year the students outside the class were invited to attend one class. But over the three years, at three different schools, it was clear that three communities had been made. Each was born on a particular date, and each lived for at least a couple of months.

My story here comes from Yale. Yale is an odd sort of law school, though odd in a good way. It is small and filled with extremely bright people, many of whom do not really want to be lawyers. It fashions itself as a community, and everyone from the dean on down (not a "Yale" way to describe things) strives continuously to foster and sustain this sense of community among the students. To a large extent, it works—not in the sense that there is perpetual peace, but in the sense that people everywhere are aware of this sense of community. Some embrace it, others resist it, but resistance, like an embrace, says that something is there. One does not resist the community of people on a Greyhound bus.

One extraordinary feature of the Yale Law School is "the Wall." The Wall is a place where people can post comments about whatever they want to say. A letter can be posted about gay rights at Yale, or a protest about Yale's treatment of unionized workers. Political messages are posted as well as points about law. Each posting makes additional ones possible—either scribbled on the original post or appended underneath the post.

An extraordinary sign for any visitor, the Wall is located right at the center of the law school. In the middle of a fake Gothic structure is a stone space with scores of papers posted in random fashion. Around the posts stand wandering students, reading what others have said. This is Yale's speakers' corner, though the speakers are writers, and the writing is substantive. There is little to be gained on the Wall through rhetoric; to gain respect there, you must say something of substance.

One rule, however, governs this space. All postings must be signed; any posting without a signature is removed. Originally, no doubt, the rule meant that the posting must be signed by the person who wrote it. But because this is Yale, where no rule can exist without a thousand questions raised, a custom has emerged whereby an anonymous post can be signed by someone not its author ("Signed but not written by X"). That signature gives the post the pedigree it needs to survive on the Wall.

The reasons for this rule are clear, but so too are its problems. Let's say you want to criticize the dean for a decision he has made. The dean, however sweet, is a powerful person, and you might well prefer to post a message without your name attached to it. Or say you are a student with political views that make you an outsider. Posting a message with those views and your signature might draw the scorn of your classmates. Free speech is not speech without consequence, and scorn, or shame, or ostracism are likely consequences of lots of speech.

Anonymity, then, is a way around this dilemma. With anonymity, you can say what you want without fear. In some cases, for some people, the right to speak anonymously makes sense.

Still, a community might want to resist this right. Just as anonymity might give you the strength to state an unpopular view, it can also shield you if you post an irresponsible, or slanderous, or hurtful view. You might want to question the policies of the dean, or you might want falsely to accuse a fellow student of cheating. Both utterances benefit from anonymity, but the community has good reason to resist utterances like the second.

As far as I know, IBEX never said anything on the Wall. Instead, he spoke in the newsgroup associated with my class. By design, the newsgroup was open to anyone at Yale who wanted to speak. Unlike the Wall, however, the technology allowed users to call themselves whatever they wanted. "IBEX," of course, was a pseudonym. For purposes of the Wall, a pseudonym was just like anonymous speech—you did not have to use your real name. But in a newsgroup a pseudonymous posting is quite different from an anonymous posting. Over time you can come to know the character of a pseudonym. In the class that year, along with IBEX, we had SpeedRacer, MadMacs, CliffClaven, Aliens, blah, and Christopher Robbin. While members of the class might know who these participants were (we all knew who MadMacs was, but only a few of us knew SpeedRacer), each pseudonym had a character.

The character of IBEX was bad; this much was clear from the start. Before IBEX appeared, life in the space flourished. At first people were timid, but polite. Brave souls would post an idea or a joke, and conversation would continue around the idea or joke for a bit. After a couple of weeks the conversation would become quite intense. Patterns of exchange began. People had questions; others had answers. People stumbled as they spoke, but they were beginning, slowly, to speak.

Some things about how they spoke were immediately noticeable. First, women spoke more in this space than they did in class. Maybe not more in a statistically significant sense, but more.[42] Second, helpers quickly developed and differentiated from those who received their help. Soon a class developed online—a real class that identified itself as such and spoke as a class in a way that a teacher dreams of in real space, and in a way I had never known.

Why this happened I could not really say. Una Smith may have been a catalyst. I said that I taught this course three times. Each time (without my intervention at all) there was an Una Smith participating in the newsgroup. At Yale she was a real person, but after Yale I thought of her as a type. She was always a woman from outside the class; she was always extremely knowledgeable about the Net and about USENET; and she always wandered into my (virtual) class and began telling the others how they should behave. When someone violated a norm of the Net, Una would correct them. Often this instruction was not taken terribly well (these were, after all, law students). Soon the class would rally to defend the instructed and to challenge her to defend her rules. And of course, expert that she was, she usually had an answer that did defend the rules she had dictated. This exchange soon became a focus of the class. Una had drawn their anger, and the class gained cohesiveness as a result.

About a month and a half into the course, the group reached an apex of sorts. It became the best it would be. I remember the moment well. Early on a spring afternoon I noticed that someone had posted the first line of a poem. By the end of the day, without any coordination, the class had finished the poem. There had been rhythm to the exchanges; now there was rhyme. Things hummed in the newsgroup, and people were genuinely surprised about this space.

It was then that IBEX appeared. I think it was just after we had discussed anonymity in class, so maybe his later claims to have been serving a pedagogical role were true. But he appeared after one of our classes—appeared, it seemed, just to issue an attack on another member of the class. Not an attack on his ideas, but on him. So vicious and so extensive was this attack that when I read it, I didn't know quite how to understand it. Could it have been real?

Almost immediately, conversation in the group died. It just stopped. No one said anything, as if everyone were afraid that the monster that had entered our space would turn his fury on one of them next. Until, that is, the victim responded, with an answer that evinced the wounds of the attack. IBEX's words had cut. The victim was angry and hurt, and he attacked back.

But his salvo only inspired another round of viciousness, even more vile than the first. With this, other members of the class could not resist joining in. IBEX was attacked by a string of characters in the class as cowardly for hiding behind a pseudonym and as sick for what he had said. None of this had any effect. IBEX came back, again and again, with an ugliness that was as extreme as it was unrelenting.

The space had been changed. Conversation fell off, people drifted away. Some no doubt left because they were disgusted with what had happened; others did not want to be IBEX's next target. There was a brief period of life in the space as people rallied to attack IBEX. But as he came back again and again, each time more vicious than the last, most simply left. (One time IBEX came back to protest that he had been wronged; in the week before, he claimed, he had not posted anything, but someone wearing the white sheet of IBEX had posted in IBEX's name, so that he, the real IBEX, had been defamed. The class had little sympathy.)

But it was not just the online class that changed. As we met face to face each week, I felt the atmosphere bend. People felt the creature in the room, though no one could believe he was a student at the Yale Law School. This was their classmate, hiding behind a smile or a joke in real space, but vicious in cyberspace. And the very idea that this evil was hidden under a smile changed how people felt about smiles.

Some called this the "David Lynch effect," an allusion to the director who portrays the rot of society just under freshly painted façades. We felt in that class the rot of our community just under the surface of smiling and functional students. There was a (relatively tame) Jake Baker in our midst. The space had permitted behavior that destroyed community—community that the space itself had created. Community had been created in part through the ability to hide—to hide behind a benign pseudonym; to hide hesitation, or editing, in the writing; to hide your reaction; to hide that you were not paying attention. These anonymities had made the community what it was. But the same anonymity that created the community gave birth to IBEX as well, and thus took the community away.

SecondLi(f/v)e(s)

These four places that I have just described were all described in the first edition of this book, each in just about the same terms. They're old stories, and the lessons they teach are still precisely the lesson this chapter is meant to convey. But I don't mean to suggest that there's been no interesting progress in the cyberspaces that the Internet has inspired. The last five years have witnessed an explosion in cyberspaces, much more dramatic than anything I imagined when I first wrote this book.

In one sense, these spaces are nothing really new. They have fancy new technology that, because computers are faster and bandwidth is broader, functions much better than their earlier versions. But the MMOG space I described in Chapter 2 was inspired by real places.

What's changed, however, is size. As Julian Dibbell described it to me, the question is

> does size matter in these kinds of spaces? And I think it does. The text-based world is naturally limited in size. The limit is not so much text versus graphics as it is limited cultural accessibility versus a much broader accessibility. That makes for larger spaces.[43]

The result is "something socially richer in a lot of ways," "not so much the particular affordances of 3D graphic imagery, which will also someday look pretty crude."

Massively Multiple Online Role Playing Games (again, MMOGs, or MMORPGs) have become a whole industry. Literally millions spend hundreds, sometimes thousands of hours each year in these spaces along with literally billions of dollars to live these second lives. While living these second lives, of course, they are also living a life in real space. When they're playing the MMOG World of Warcraft, they are at the same time playing father or wife in real space. They have thus not left the real world to go to these other places. But they integrate the other places into their real world life, and the last five years has seen an explosion in the percentage of real-world life that is lived virtually.

These "games" can be divided roughly into two types. In one type, people "play" a game that has been defined by others. These are "role-playing games." Thus, World of Warcraft is a role-playing game in which people compete to gain wealth and status (making it not so different from real life). Grand Theft Auto is a game in which people engage in a kind of virtual crime. These games all have a structure to them, but they differ in the degree to which people can customize or create their own characters or environments. The vast majority of online games are role-playing games in this sense. One site that tracks these communities estimates 97 percent are role-playing games of some sort.[44]

The second type involves much more construction. These spaces provide communities in which people at a minimum socialize. In addition to socializing, there is creative and commercial activity. Depending upon the game, the mix among these activities differs substantially. But they all aim to create a virtual world that inspires a real community within itself. These games are an extension of the MOOs I described above. But they extend the virtual community of a MOO beyond those who feel comfortable manipulating text. These worlds are graphically real, even if they are virtual.

Of course, within both of these types of MMOGs, there is creativity. The differences between them are simply a matter of degree. And within both, there is commerce. Second Life—described more below—generates over "$4,000,000 U.S. in interpersonal transactions"[45] a month. Aggregated across games, as Edward Castronova describes, there is a great deal of commerce produced by these virtual worlds.

"The commerce flow generated by people buying and selling money and other virtual items (that is, magic wands, spaceships, armor) amounts to at least $30 million annually in the United States, and $100 million globally."[46]

And more interesting (and bizarre) is Castronova's estimate of the gross national product per capita produced in various virtual worlds. EverQuest, for example, has a GDP which is about half that of "the Caribbean Island Nation of Dominica."[47] And the GDP per capita of Norrath "was about the same as Bulgaria's and four times higher than China's or India's."[48]

For my purposes here, however, I want to focus on the second type of MMOG, and two of these in particular. The first was an early leader in this space—There. The second is a growing and extraordinary success—Second Life.

Second Life is, as its website describes, "a 3-D virtual world entirely built and owned by its residents." *3-D* in the sense that the experience seems three dimensional—the characters and the objects appear to be in three dimensions. A *virtual* world in the sense that the objects and people are rendered by computers. *Built* by its residents in the sense that Second Life merely provided a platform upon which its residents built the Second Life world. (And not just a few. On any given day, 15 percent of Second Life residents are editing the scripts that make Second Life run.[49] That platform originally rendered beautiful green fields. Residents acquired land in that world, and began building structures.) And *owned* by its residents in the sense that the stuff that the residents of Second Life build is theirs—both the "physical" thing itself (the car, or the surfboard, or the house), and any intellectual property right which might be embedded in that thing that they have built.

It is this last feature that contrasts most interestingly (for me at least) with the other MMOG that I mentioned, There. There was also a community site. But it was a radically different (and less successful) world from Second Life. It was to be centered around corporate franchises—Sony or Nike, for example, were expected to set up shop in There. People would also be allowed to create things in There, and when they sold or gave them away, There would get a percentage. The space itself came much more pre-fab, but there was significant opportunity for customization.

Its founders crafted the rhetoric of There at least around (at least their understanding of) the ideals of the United States. The exchange rate for There-bucks was 1787 to 1—1787 being the year the United States Constitution was written. And as the then-CEO of There explained to a class I was teaching, the values of the American republic informed the values of There.

My students were skeptical. And one fantastically bright student, Catherine Crump, gave the CEO a bit of a rough ride. She asked whether There would respect the principles of the First Amendment. "Of course," responded the CEO. "Would a citizen of There be allowed to put a sign on his land?" "Of course." "Would she be allowed to buy land next to, say, Nike?" "Of course." "Would she be allowed to put a sign up on her land next to Nike that says 'Nike uses sweatshop labor'?" "Umm. I'm not sure about that." So much for the First Amendment.

Or more relevantly to Second Life, Crump asked, "Who owns the IP [intellectual property] in the designs a citizen creates?" "There does." "Who owns the IP in the designs Nike creates?" "Of course, Nike does. How could it be any other way?" Well, it could be another way if you followed the principles of the American Constitution, Crump suggested, which said IP rights get vested in "authors or inventors," not in corporations.

There's real problem, however, was structural. It is the same problem of any planned or centralized economy. There was to be built by There, Inc. And therein was its problem. The structures of these virtual worlds are extraordinarily complex. The cost of building them is immense, and thus There, Inc. faced a huge capital cost in making There run.

Second Life (like all new nations) outsourced that cost of construction to its citizens. When you buy land in Second Life, you get an empty field or deserted island. You then have to buy, barter, or build to make it habitable. There's an economy to building it, and it can be hard work. But the things you build you can sell. And again, the designs you make are yours. More than 100,000 people now inhabit, and construct, Second Life. For them, the game is what it says.

These current rules, however, are the product of an evolution in Second Life. In the first public Alpha testing of the site that would become Second Life, there was no concept of land ownership. Everything was public. The ownership of land began with Beta testing, when all users could claim the public land at a price. When the land was claimed, the user could select whether others could create objects, scripts, or landmarks for the land. Later the options were extended.

In version 1.1, there was a fairly major change to the physics of land. Whereas before users were free to teleport anywhere, now, to avoid harassment, owners of land could decide whether others could "trespass" or not—either by setting a default to grant or deny access, or by adding a list of people who were free to visit. These restrictions, however, applied only to the first 15 meters above the property. Beyond that, anyone was free to fly, even if the owner didn't want them on the property.

Now this last restriction has an interesting parallel to the history of American law. As I describe in *Free Culture*,[50] property law in the American tradition considered the owner of land the owner of the space from the ground "an indefinite extent, upwards."[51] This created an obvious conflict when airplanes appeared. Did the pilot of an airplane trespass when he flew over your land?

The accommodation the law eventually drew was between flying very low and flying very high. It was not trespassing to fly very high over someone's land; it was a nuisance to fly very low over someone's land. So something like the solution that Second Life achieved was also achieved by the law.

But notice the important difference. In real space, the law means you can be penalized for violating the "high/low" rule. In Second Life, you simply can't violate the 15-meter rule. The rule is part of the code. The code controls how you are in Second Life. There isn't a choice about obeying the rule or not, any more than there's a choice about obeying gravity.

So code is law here. That code/law enforces its control directly. But obviously, this code (like law) changes. The key is to recognize that this change in the code is (unlike the laws of nature) crafted to reflect choices and values of the coders.

Consider another illustration of the same point. As I said, Second Life gives the creators of Intellectual Property in Second Life ownership of that property—both inside and outside Second Life.[52] (As one of the founders described, "Our lawyers shook their heads, but we decided the future of our company isn't tied up in our owning what our users create."[53]) That's the same with IP in real space: Unless you've signed your rights away to a corporation (don't!), when you create in real space, the law automatically gives you a copyright in your creativity. In both spaces, too, you have the right to give those rights away. I run a nonprofit called Creative Commons that makes it simple for creators to signal the freedoms they want to run with their creativity. In real space, when you use a Creative Commons license, you mark your content with the license you want. Users then know the freedoms they have. If a right is violated, it gets remedied through the law.

Second Life has taken this idea one step further. Creators in Second Life can mark their content with the license they want. But the wizards of this world are exploring the idea that the license they've selected could affect directly what others can do with that creativity. If content is marked with a Creative Commons license, then someone can take a picture of it without express permission. But if it is not marked with a license, then if you try to take a picture of it, the object will be invisible. Here again, the code expresses the law more effectively than the law in real space ever could.

The Internet

As I said, we can distinguish cyberspace from the Internet. But the point of this chapter, however clear with respect to cyberspace, is still true of the Internet. There are architectural features of the Internet that embed certain values. Those features can also change, and if they do, the values the Internet promotes will be different.

The most significant example of this is one I only mentioned in the first edition of this book, but which was at the center of *The Future of Ideas*. This is the "end-to-end" principle described by network architects Jerome Saltzer, David Clark, and David Reed in 1981.[54] The end-to-end ("e2e") principle is a design philosophy about how networks should be built. It counsels that a network should be kept as simple as possible and that the intelligence required in a network be vested in the edge, or ends of a network, at least so far as that's possible.

As I've already described, the Internet embodied this principle by keeping the functionality of TCP/IP focused quite narrowly—that is, on the single function best-efforts delivery of packets of data. What those packets do, or who they're meant for, is not a concern of the protocol. Just delivering packets is the end.

One consequence of this design, then, is that people can innovate for this network without any need to coordinate with any network owner. If you want to develop an application to deliver voice across IP, then all you need to do is to write the application to use the TCP/IP protocols to send data across the network in a way that will make your application run.

This design embeds a value that encourages innovation in applications for the network. It does so both because it minimizes the costs of developing new applications (you don't need the hassle of asking or clearing permission with anyone) and because it avoids strategic behavior by the network owner. Consider again the idea of developing a Voice-over-IP application. If the network is owned by the telephone companies, they would not be excited about an application that will cannibalize their telephone market. Thus, if permission were required before the VOIP application could be deployed, we might well expect the VOIP application not to be deployed—either because someone developed it, but it was blocked, or because smart developers knew it was a waste of time to develop it, because it would be blocked. As Susan Crawford describes, "The miraculous growth of the Internet has in large part come from the nondiscrimination against higher levels. . . . Innovators at the application layer have been able to assume the continued stable existence of the lower layers."[55]

The value here is innovation and competition. The network empowers the widest range of innovators—users of the network—and entitles all of them to innovate for this network. Any innovation can be deployed on the network (so long as it respects the TCP/IP protocols). If users of the network like the innovation, then the innovation is a success.

Simultaneously—at least so long as the e2e principle is respected—this design disables the potentially most powerful actor in the network, the network owner, from interfering with the opportunity for innovation within the network. The network owner might not like the stuff being developed, but e2e disables the opportunity to block that development.

In the same way that the original TCP/IP network could be effectively changed so that "gaps" in information about that network could be closed, the TCP/IP network could be changed to remove its e2e character. Indeed, the very tools that I described in Chapter 4 could have this effect. For example, a network owner could scan the packets that were traveling across its network and block any packet that didn't come from a known, or approved, application. To get on that list, application developers would have to contact the network owner and ask to be included on the list. That change to the way the Internet functions is completely technically possible. Indeed, versions of it are being pursued for both competitive and security reasons. That is, some networks, keen to control the kind of applications that run on the network for competitive reasons, could use this to block disfavored applications (again, think of telephone companies blocking VOIP). Others, keen to avoid viruses or other trouble on their network, could simply decide to block everything to make life simple. Either reason would produce the same result: that innovation on the Internet would be stifled.

As with the stories about "cyberspace," this case about the Internet also demonstrates the link between architecture and policy. End-to-end is a paradigm for technology that embeds values. Which architecture we encourage is a choice about which policy we encourage. This is true even in the context in which the Internet is not a "place"—even where, that is, it is "just" a medium.

HOW ARCHITECTURES MATTER AND SPACES DIFFER

The spaces I have described here are different. In some places there is community—a set of norms that are self-enforcing (by members of the community). Features such as visibility (as opposed to anonymity) and nontransience help create those norms; anonymity, transience, and diversity make it harder to create community.

In places where community is not fully self-enforcing, norms are supplemented by rules imposed either through code or by the relevant sovereign. These supplements may further some normative end, but at times they can be in tension with the goal of community building.

If we had to simplify this diversity of spaces by finding a dimension along which we could rank them, one such dimension might be each group's amenability to control. Some groups on this list can be controlled only through norms—.law.cyber, for example. The only technology for changing behavior there—given my commitment not to monitor and punish bad behavior—was the norms of the students in the law school class. Other groups are amenable to other technologies of control. Indeed, as we move from .law.cyber to CC to LambdaMOO to AOL to Second Life, the ability to use these other technologies of control increases, though, of course, that ability is constrained by competition. If the code makes the place no longer attractive, people will leave.

Thus, in CC and AOL, the architects could use technology to change behavior. But if the change is too far removed from what most members think the space is about, members may simply leave. The threat of that constraint turns upon the alternatives, of course. As blogs have flourished, a space like CC would have relatively little market power. AOL's market power is more complicated. There are many alternative ISPs, of course. But once you're a member of one, the costs of migrating are significant.

In LambdaMOO the story is even more complicated. Nothing really binds people to a particular MOO. (There are hundreds, and most are free.) But because characters in a MOO are earned rather than bought, and because this takes time and characters are not fungible, it becomes increasingly hard for members of a successful MOO to move elsewhere. They have the right to exit, but in the sense that Soviet citizens had the right to exit—namely, with none of the assets they had built in their particular world.

Finally, Second Life offers the potential for the most control. Code regulates experience in Second Life more than in any of the other four spaces, and the intimacy of experience in Second Life pulls people into the space and makes escape costly. Again, there are limits to the control, but the controls are

more finely articulated here than in any of the other contexts. And if Philip
Rosedale, the CEO of Second Life, is to be believed, the control through code
here will only become more subtly expressed. As he described to me:

> [O]ur feeling is ... that we should aggressively move into code anything we can,
> because of the enhanced scalability it gives us. And we should execute policy out-
> side of code only when absolutely necessary or unfeasible. There are things
> where we look at them and we say, "Well, we'll be able to do that in code some
> day, but for today, we're just going to do it by hand."[56]

REGULATING CODE TO REGULATE BETTER

I've surveyed a range of cyberspaces to make clear the elements of regulation
within each. One increasingly important element is code. In cyberspace in
particular, but across the Internet in general, code embeds values. It enables,
or not, certain control. And as has been the focus of this part, it is also a tool
of control—not of government control, at least in the cases I've surveyed—
but instead control to the end of whatever sovereign does the coding.

These stories suggest a technique, and once we see the idea, we'll recognize the technique in many different contexts of regulation. If Second Life can
use code to better control behavior, what about first-life? If AOL can use code
to better control fraud, what about America off-line? If the Internet can use
the design of e2e to better enable competition, what does that teach regulators
on the ground? How do these techniques of policy inform the practice of
policy makers?

The answer is that policy makers have done the same in real space for a
long time. Just as Chapter 5 described regulators using code to make behavior
more regulable, so too have regulators used code to directly control behavior.
Consider a few obvious examples:

Tapes

The most significant feature of digital media is that copies can be perfect.
Digital media is just data, and data is just a string of 1's and 0's. Computers
have complex algorithms to verify that when they've copied a string of data
they've copied that string precisely.

This feature thus creates a new risk for sellers of content. While the code
of analog copying technology meant that a copy was a degraded version of the
original, the code of digital technologies means that a copy could be identical

to the original. That means the threat to content providers from "copies" is greater in the digital world than in the analog world.

Digital Audio Technology (DAT) was the first technology to expose this risk. Like any digital recording, it can, in principle, copy content perfectly. Content providers were thus terrified that piracy from DAT tapes would destroy their industry, so they lobbied Congress effectively to add new laws to protect them from the digital threat.

Congress could have responded to their request in any number of ways. It could have used law to regulate behavior directly, by increasing the penalty for illegal copying. It could have funded a public ad campaign against illegal copying or funded programs in schools to discourage students from buying pirated editions of popular recordings. Congress could have taxed blank tapes and then transferred the revenue to owners of copyrighted material.[57] Or Congress could have tried to regulate DAT technology to weaken the threat that technology presented for copyright.

Congress chose the latter two. The Audio Home Recording Act both taxed blank tapes slightly and regulated the code of digital reproduction technologies directly. The Act requires producers of digital recording devices to install a chip in their systems that implements a code-based system to monitor the copies of any copy made on that machine.[58] The chip would allow a limited number of personal copies, but on copies of copies, the quality of the recording would be degraded. Congress in essence required that the code of digital copying be modified to restore the imperfections that were "natural" in the earlier code.

This again is Congress regulating code as a means of regulating behavior—mandating that multiple copies be imperfect as a way to minimize illegal copying. Like the telephone regulation, this regulation succeeds because there are relatively few manufacturers of DAT technology. Again, given a limited target, the government's regulation can be effective, and the effect of the government's regulation is to make more regulable the primary targeted behavior—copyright infringement.

Televisions

By the mid-1990s, parents' concern about the effect that violence on television has on their kids had caught the attention of Congress, and Congress responded through legislation. But given the state of First Amendment law, it would have been difficult for Congress to block violence on television directly. Thus, Congress sought a way to block violence on television indirectly. It sought to require that those broadcasting television content tag their content with labels that signaled the level of violence in the film, and it mandated that the television industry develop a technology to block content on the basis of those labels.

This was the "V-Chip," mandated as part of the Telecommunications Act of 1996.[59] The V-chip would facilitate the automatic blocking of television broadcasts, based on criteria of content that have not yet been completely determined. The crudest proposals involve something like the Motion Picture Association's movie rating system; the more sophisticated envision selections based on a much richer set of factors.

This again is Congress regulating code to affect a targeted behavior (providing violent programming) rather than regulating that behavior directly. The constraint on direct regulation here is similarly a regulability problem. But the lack of regulability in this context comes from constitutional limits, not the inability to track those being regulated by the technology. The constraint of the Constitution thus pushed Congress to require technology to empower parents. By giving parents more power to discriminate, Congress indirectly discourages an ill (exposure to violence) that it is constitutionally unable to regulate directly.[60]

Anti-Circumvention

Whatever problem the content industry had with DAT tapes, no doubt they look tiny compared with the problems the content industry has with digital content and the Internet. Although DAT makes perfect copies possible, it doesn't make distributing those perfect copies any easier. That honor fell to the Internet. Now digital technology not only assured perfect copies of the original, it also made it trivial to distribute those digital copies for free.

As I describe more in Chapter 10, one response to this "feature" of digital technologies is "digital rights management" technology. DRM technologies add code to digital content that disables the simple ability to copy or distribute that content—at least without the technical permission of the DRM technology itself.

Thus, the songs I've purchased and downloaded from Apple's iTunes music store are protected by Apple's "fairplay" DRM technology. That technology permits me to copy the song to a limited number of machines, but it restricts my ability to copy those songs broadly.

This restriction is effected through code. The "copy" function is produced through code; the DRM technology modifies, or qualifies, that "copy" functionality. It is thus a classic example of code being deployed to restore control over something that (different) code had disabled.

These systems of DRM are privately created. But in 1998, they got an important subsidy of protection from Congress. In the Digital Millennium Copyright Act, Congress banned the creation and distribution of technologies "produced for the purpose of circumventing a technological measure that effectively controls access" to a copyrighted work, or "primarily designed or produced for the purpose of circumventing protection afforded by a technological measure that effectively protects a right of a copyright owner."[61] By banning this code, Congress aimed to add support to the code content creators were distributing to protect their content. Thus, by directly regulating code, Congress indirectly regulated copyright infringement.

Since this enactment, there has been no end to trouble and litigation surrounding it. Beginning in 1999, the DVD-Copy Control Association began suing individuals and websites that facilitated access to a program, DeCSS, which could be used to decrypt data on DVDs.[62] In July 2001, 27-year-old Russian programmer Dmitry Sklyarov was arrested while giving a presentation in Las Vegas because the company he worked for in Russia had produced software that enabled people to circumvent the access protection technologies built into Adobe's eBook system.[63] Sklyarov spent six months in an American jail before he was permitted to return to his family in Russia.

The effect of this regulation is hard to measure. The Electronic Frontier Foundation has cataloged its view of the law's effect five years after the law was enacted.[64] And while the EFF's view may not be universal, there is a fairly universal surprise at the range of cases that have been brought under the statute. (I doubt the framers of the DMCA imagined that garage door companies would be suing to protect their automatic door openers from competition under the DMCA (they lost).[65])

Broadcast Flags

As broadcast television moves to digital television, copyright holders have become concerned about the risk they face in broadcasting copyrighted content. Unlike an ordinary television broadcast, the quality of a digital broadcast is perfect, so copies of digital broadcasts could likewise be perfect. And the spread of perfect copies of digital broadcasts on a free digital network (the Internet) terrifies copyright holders.

Their response is similar to the response with DAT technologies. First in the FCC, and now in Congress, copyright holders have pushed the government to mandate that any technology capable of reproducing digital broadcasts be architected to respect a "broadcast flag." If that flag was turned on, then the technology would be required to block any copy of that content. The content could be played, but it couldn't be reproduced. As Susan Crawford describes it,

> The broadcast flag rule, distilled to its essence, is a mandate that all consumer electronics manufacturers and information technology companies ensure that any device that touches digital television content "recognized and give effect to" the flag by protecting content against unauthorized onward distribution. The FCC claimed that the rule would protect digital television ("DTV") broadcasts from massive redistribution over the Internet.[66]

There is a lot to say about the broadcast flag, and if I were doing the saying, most of it would be bad.[67] But for our purposes, it is the form, not substance, of the broadcast flag that is relevant. This is the most direct example of a regulation of code designed to control primary behavior: law regulating code to make behavior better.

In each case, the government directs an intermediary that has some power over code to change that code to effect a change in behavior. Whether that change in code will effect a change in behavior depends upon the power of the particular application. If the application is a MOO, or an online discussion space like Counsel Connect, the power to control behavior is significantly limited. If the application is AOL or Second Life, the exit costs for a user could well be higher. The scope for effective regulation will thus be greater. And if the application is the Internet, or any digital technology produced or sold in the United States, then the power of the regulator is greater still. Code becomes law even if there remains a capacity to escape the regulation of that code.

These examples point to a general question about how regulation will function. That general point requires many significant qualifications. To understand the effect of code requirements on any regulatory policy will require, as Polk Wagner writes, an understanding that is "profoundly dynamic."[68] Part of that dynamic, of course, is resistance. Individuals can act to resist the force of code directly. Or individuals can act to resist the force of code through code. As Tim Wu has rightly described, code itself is not necessarily regulation enhancing—code can be used to foil regulation. A gun is a bit of code. It works wonders to destroy the peace. Circumvention technologies are code. They weaken rules reinforcing control. P2P filesharing protocols are code. They undermine the effectiveness of copyright regulations that restrict the freedom to distribute copyrighted works. Whether a particular regulation will be effective, then, requires consideration of these interactions, and any code-based resistance it might engender. As Wu puts it,

> The reason that code matters for law at all is its capability to define behavior on a mass scale. This capability can mean constraints on behavior, in which case code regulates. But it can also mean shaping behavior into legally advantageous forms.[69]

In this second sense, code functions "as an anti-regulatory mechanism: a tool to minimize the costs of law that certain groups will use to their advantage."[70]

More fundamentally, these complications suggest that a more general framework is needed. I've highlighted an interaction between technology, policy, and the law in this chapter. That interaction suggests a much broader model. In the next chapter, I describe that model. In the chapter following that, we will return to the dynamic of code regulation to consider one other important qualification.

SEVEN

what things regulate

JOHN STUART MILL WAS AN ENGLISHMAN. HE WAS ALSO ONE OF THE MOST influential political philosophers in America. His writings ranged from important work on logic to a still striking text about sexual equality, *The Subjection of Women*. But perhaps his most important continuing influence comes from a relatively short book titled *On Liberty*. Published in 1859, this powerful argument for individual liberty and diversity of thought represents an important view of liberal and libertarian thinking in the second half of the nineteenth century.

"Libertarian," however, has a specific meaning for us. For most, it associates with arguments against government.[1] Government, in the modern libertarian's view, is the threat to liberty; private action is not. Thus, the good libertarian is focused on reducing government's power. Curb the excesses of government, the libertarian says, and you will ensure freedom for your society.

Mill's view was not so narrow. He was a defender of liberty and an opponent of forces that suppressed it, but those forces were not confined to government. Liberty, in Mill's view, was threatened as much by norms as by government, as much by stigma and intolerance as by the threat of state punishment. His objective was to argue against these private forces of coercion. His work was a defense against liberty-suppressing norms, because, in England at that time, these were the real threat to liberty.

Mill's method is important, and it should be our own as well. It asks, What is the threat to liberty, and how can we resist it? It is not limited to asking, What is the threat to liberty from government? It understands that more than government can threaten liberty, and that sometimes this something more can be private rather than state action. Mill was not concerned with the source of the threat to liberty. His concern was with liberty.

Threats to liberty change. In England, norms may have been the threat to free speech in the late nineteenth century; I take it they are not as much a threat today. In the United States in the first two decades of the twentieth century, the threat to free speech was state suppression through criminal penalties for unpopular speech; the strong protections of the First Amendment now make that particular threat less significant.[2] The labor movement was founded on the idea that the market is sometimes a threat to liberty—not so much because of low wages, but because the market form of organization itself disables a certain kind of freedom.[3] In other societies, at other times, the market is a key to liberty, not the enemy.

Thus, rather than think of "liberty's enemy" in the abstract, we should focus upon a particular threat to liberty that might exist in a particular time and place. And this is especially true when we think about liberty in cyberspace. I believe that cyberspace creates a new threat to liberty, not new in the sense that no theorist had conceived of it before,[4] but new in the sense of newly urgent. We are coming to understand a newly powerful regulator in cyberspace. That regulator could be a significant threat to a wide range of liberties, and we don't yet understand how best to control it.

This regulator is what I call "code"—the instructions embedded in the software or hardware that makes cyberspace what it is. This code is the "built environment" of social life in cyberspace. It is its "architecture."[5] And if in the middle of the nineteenth century the threat to liberty was norms, and at the start of the twentieth it was state power, and during much of the middle twentieth it was the market, then my argument is that we must come to understand how in the twenty-first century it is a different regulator—code—that should be our current concern.

But not to the exclusion of other significant "regulators." My argument is not that there's only one threat to liberty, or that we should forget other, more traditional threats. It is instead that we must add one more increasingly salient threat to the list. And to see this new, salient threat, I believe we need a more general understanding of how regulation works—one that focuses on more than the single influence of any one force such as government, norms, or the market, and instead integrates these factors into a single account.

This chapter is a step toward that more general understanding.[6] It is an invitation to think beyond the threat to liberty from government power. It is a map for this more general understanding.

A DOT'S LIFE

There are many ways to think about "regulation." I want to think about it from the perspective of someone who is regulated, or, what is different, constrained. That someone regulated is represented by this (pathetic) dot—a creature (you or me) subject to different regulations that might have the effect of constraining (or as we'll see, enabling) the dot's behavior. By describing the various constraints that might bear on this individual, I hope to show you something about how these constraints function together.

Here then is the dot.

How is this dot "regulated"?

Let's start with something easy: smoking. If you want to smoke, what constraints do you face? What factors regulate your decision to smoke or not?

One constraint is legal. In some places at least, laws regulate smoking—if you are under eighteen, the law says that cigarettes cannot be sold to you. If you are under twenty-six, cigarettes cannot be sold to you unless the seller checks your ID. Laws also regulate where smoking is permitted—not in O'Hare Airport, on an airplane, or in an elevator, for instance. In these two ways at least, laws aim to direct smoking behavior. They operate as a kind of constraint on an individual who wants to smoke.

But laws are not the most significant constraints on smoking. Smokers in the United States certainly feel their freedom regulated, even if only rarely by the law. There are no smoking police, and smoking courts are still quite rare. Rather, smokers in America are regulated by norms. Norms say that one doesn't light a cigarette in a private car without first asking permission of the other passengers. They also say, however, that one needn't ask permission to smoke at a picnic. Norms say that others can ask you to stop smoking at a restaurant, or that you never smoke during a meal. These norms effect a certain constraint, and this constraint regulates smoking behavior.

Laws and norms are still not the only forces regulating smoking behavior. The market is also a constraint. The price of cigarettes is a constraint on your ability to smoke—change the price, and you change this constraint. Likewise with quality. If the market supplies a variety of cigarettes of widely varying quality and price, your ability to select the kind of cigarette you want increases; increasing choice here reduces constraint.

Finally, there are the constraints created by the technology of cigarettes, or by the technologies affecting their supply.[7] Nicotine-treated cigarettes are addictive and therefore create a greater constraint on smoking than untreated cigarettes. Smokeless cigarettes present less of a constraint because they can be smoked in more places. Cigarettes with a strong odor present more of a constraint because they can be smoked in fewer places. How the cigarette is, how it is designed, how it is built—in a word, its architecture—affects the constraints faced by a smoker.

Thus, four constraints regulate this pathetic dot—the law, social norms, the market, and architecture—and the "regulation" of this dot is the sum of these four constraints. Changes in any one will affect the regulation of the whole. Some constraints will support others; some may undermine others. Thus, "changes in technology [may] usher in changes in . . . norms,"[8] and the other way around. A complete view, therefore, must consider these four modalities together.

So think of the four together like this:

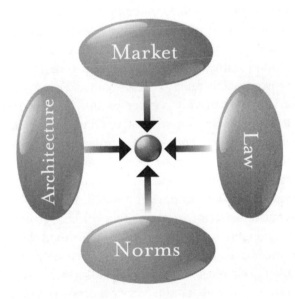

In this drawing, each oval represents one kind of constraint operating on our pathetic dot in the center. Each constraint imposes a different kind of cost on the dot for engaging in the relevant behavior—in this case, smoking. The cost from norms is different from the market cost, which is different from the cost from law and the cost from the (cancerous) architecture of cigarettes.

The constraints are distinct, yet they are plainly interdependent. Each can support or oppose the others. Technologies can undermine norms and laws; they can also support them. Some constraints make others possible; others make some impossible. Constraints work together, though they function differently and the effect of each is distinct. Norms constrain through the stigma that a community imposes; markets constrain through the price that they exact; architectures constrain through the physical burdens they impose; and law constrains through the punishment it threatens.

We can call each constraint a "regulator," and we can think of each as a distinct modality of regulation. Each modality has a complex nature, and the interaction among these four is also hard to describe. I've worked through this complexity more completely in the appendix. But for now, it is enough to see that they are linked and that, in a sense, they combine to produce the regulation to which our pathetic dot is subject in any given area.

We can use the same model to describe the regulation of behavior in cyberspace.[9]

Law regulates behavior in cyberspace. Copyright law, defamation law, and obscenity laws all continue to threaten ex post sanction for the violation of legal rights. How well law regulates, or how efficiently, is a different question: In some cases it does so more efficiently, in some cases less. But whether better or not, law continues to threaten a certain consequence if it is defied. Legislatures enact;[10] prosecutors threaten;[11] courts convict.[12]

Norms also regulate behavior in cyberspace. Talk about Democratic politics in the alt.knitting newsgroup, and you open yourself to flaming; "spoof" someone's identity in a MUD, and you may find yourself "toaded";[13] talk too much in a discussion list, and you are likely to be placed on a common bozo filter. In each case, a set of understandings constrain behavior, again through the threat of ex post sanctions imposed by a community.[14]

Markets regulate behavior in cyberspace. Pricing structures constrain access, and if they do not, busy signals do. (AOL learned this quite dramatically when it shifted from an hourly to a flat-rate pricing plan.)[15] Areas of the Web are beginning to charge for access, as online services have for some time. Advertisers reward popular sites; online services drop low-population forums. These behaviors are all a function of market constraints and market opportunity. They are all, in this sense, regulations of the market.

Finally, an analog for architecture regulates behavior in cyberspace—code. The software and hardware that make cyberspace what it is constitute a set of constraints on how you can behave. The substance of these constraints may vary, but they are experienced as conditions on your access to cyberspace. In some places (online services such as AOL, for instance) you must enter a password before you gain access; in other places you can enter whether identified or not.[16] In some places the transactions you engage in produce traces that link the transactions (the "mouse droppings") back to you; in other places this link is achieved only if you want it to be.[17] In some places you can choose to speak a language that only the recipient can hear (through encryption);[18] in other places encryption is not an option.[19] The code or software or architecture or protocols set these features, which are selected by code writers. They constrain some behavior by making other behavior possible or impossible. The code embeds certain values or makes certain values impossible. In this sense, it too is regulation, just as the architectures of real-space codes are regulations.

As in real space, then, these four modalities regulate cyberspace. The same balance exists. As William Mitchell puts it (though he omits the constraint of the market):

> Architecture, laws, and customs maintain and represent whatever balance has been struck in real space. As we construct and inhabit cyberspace communities, we will have to make and maintain similar bargains—though they will be embodied in software structures and electronic access controls rather than in architectural arrangements.[20]

Laws, norms, the market, and architectures interact to build the environment that "Netizens" know. The code writer, as Ethan Katsh puts it, is the "architect."[21]

But how can we "make and maintain" this balance between modalities? What tools do we have to achieve a different construction? How might the mix of real-space values be carried over to the world of cyberspace? How might the mix be changed if change is desired?

ON GOVERNMENTS AND WAYS TO REGULATE

I've described four constraints that I've said "regulate" an individual. But these separate constraints obviously don't simply exist as givens in a social life. They are neither found in nature nor fixed by God. Each can be changed, though the mechanics of changing them is complex. Law can have a significant role in this mechanics, and my aim in this section is to describe that role.

A simple example will suggest the more general point. Say the theft of car radios is a problem—not big in the scale of things, but a frequent and costly enough problem to make more regulation necessary. One response might be to increase the penalty for car radio theft to life in prison, so that the risk faced by thieves made it such that this crime did not pay. If radio thieves realized that they exposed themselves to a lifetime in prison each time they stole a radio, it might no longer make sense to them to steal radios. The constraint constituted by the threatened punishment of law would now be enough to stop the behavior we are trying to stop.

But changing the law is not the only possible technique. A second might be to change the radio's architecture. Imagine that radio manufacturers program radios to work only with a single car—a security code that electronically locks the radio to the car, so that, if the radio is removed, it will no longer work. This is a code constraint on the theft of radios; it makes the radio no longer effective once stolen. It too functions as a constraint on the radio's theft, and like the threatened punishment of life in prison, it could be effective in stopping the radio-stealing behavior.

Thus, the same constraint can be achieved through different means, and the different means cost different amounts. The threatened punishment of life in prison may be fiscally more costly than the change in the architecture of radios (depending on how many people actually continue to steal radios and how many are caught). From this fiscal perspective, it may be more efficient to change code than law. Fiscal efficiency may also align with the expressive content of law—a punishment so extreme would be barbaric for a crime so slight. Thus, the values may well track the efficient response. Code would be the best means to regulate.

The costs, however, need not align so well. Take the Supreme Court's hypothetical example of life in prison for a parking ticket.[22] It is likely that whatever code constraint might match this law constraint, the law constraint would be more efficient (if reducing parking violations were the only aim). There would be very few victims of this law before people conformed their behavior appropriately. But the "efficient result" would conflict with other values. If it is barbaric to incarcerate for life for the theft of a radio, it is all the more barbaric as a penalty for a parking violation. The regulator has a range of means to effect the desired constraint, but the values that these means entail need not align with their efficiency. The efficient answer may well be unjust—that is, it may conflict with values inherent in the norms, or law (constitution), of the society.

Law-talk typically ignores these other regulators and how law can affect their regulation. Many speak as if law must simply take the other three constraints as given and fashion itself to them.[23]

I say "as if" because today it takes only a second's thought to see that this narrowness is absurd. There were times when these other constraints were treated as fixed—when the constraints of norms were said to be immovable by governmental action,[24] or the market was thought to be essentially unregulable,[25] or the cost of changing real-space code was so high as to make the thought of using it for regulation absurd.[26] But we see now that these constraints are plastic.[27] They are, as law is, changeable, and subject to regulation.

The examples are obvious and many. Think first about the market: talk of a "free market" notwithstanding, there is no more heavily regulated aspect of our life.[28] The market is regulated by law not just in its elements—it is law that enforces contracts, establishes property, and regulates currency—but also in its effects. The law uses taxes to increase the market's constraint on certain behaviors and subsidies to reduce its constraint on others. We tax cigarettes in part to reduce their consumption, but we subsidize tobacco production to increase its supply. We tax alcohol to reduce its consumption. We subsidize child care to reduce the constraint the market puts on raising children. In many such ways the constraint of law is used to change the constraints of the market.

Law can also change the regulation of architecture. Think about the Americans with Disabilities Act (ADA).[29] Many of the "disabled" are cut off from access to much of the world. A building with only stairs is a building that is inaccessible to a person in a wheelchair; the stairs are a constraint on the disabled person's access to that building. But the ADA in part aims to change that constraint by requiring builders to change the design of buildings so that the disabled are not excluded. Here is a regulation of real-space code, by law, to change the constraint that real-space code creates.

Other examples are even better.

- Some of the power of the French Revolution derived from the architecture of Paris: The city's small and winding streets were easily barricaded, making it possible for revolutionaries to take control of the city with relatively little absolute strength. Louis Napoleon III understood this, and in 1853 he took steps to change it.[30] Paris was rebuilt, with wide boulevards and multiple passages, making it impossible for insurgents to take control of the city.
- Every schoolchild learns of L'Enfant's design to make an invasion of Washington difficult. But more interesting is the placement of the White House relative to the Capitol. The distance between them is one mile, and at the time it was a mile through difficult terrain (the mall was a swamp). The distance was a barrier meant to tilt the intercourse between Congress and the president by making it marginally more difficult for them to connect—and thereby more difficult for the executive to control the legislature.

- This same idea has influenced the placement of constitutional courts in Europe. Throughout Europe constitutional courts were placed in cities other than the capital. In Germany the court is in Karlsruhe rather than Berlin; in the Czech Republic it is in Brno rather than Prague. The reason again is tied to the constraint of geography: Placing constitutional courts far away from legislatures and executives was meant to minimize both the pressure the latter two bodies could place on the court and reduce the court's temptation to bow to it.

- The principle is not limited to high politics. Designers of parking garages or streets where children may play place speed bumps in the road so that drivers must slow down. These structures have the same purpose as a speed limit or a norm against driving too fast, but they operate by modifying architecture.

- Neither is the principle limited to virtuous regulation: Robert Moses built bridges on Long Island to block buses, so that African Americans, who depended primarily on public transportation, could not easily get to public beaches.[31] That was regulation through architecture, invidious yet familiar.

- Nor is it limited to governments. A major American airline noticed that passengers on early Monday morning flights were frustrated with the time it took to retrieve bags from the plane. They were much more annoyed than other passengers, even though it took no longer than average to retrieve the bags from these flights. The company began parking these flights at gates farther away from baggage claim, so that by the time the passengers arrived at baggage claim, their bags were there. Frustration with the baggage handling system was eliminated.

- A large hotel in an American city received many complaints about the slowness of its elevators. It installed mirrors next to the elevator doors. The complaints ended.

- Few are likely to recognize the leading regulation-through-architecture proponent of the 20th century—Ralph Nader. It is astonishing today to read his account of the struggle to get safety standards enforced upon auto makers. Nader's whole objective was to get the law to force car manufacturers to build safer cars. It is obvious today that the code of cars is an essential part of auto safety. Yet on this basic point, there was fundamental disagreement.[32]

- Neal Katyal has extensively considered the relationship of architecture to criminal law, from the deployment of street lights to the design of public spaces to maximize visibility.[33] The 2000 Sydney Olympics, for example, "self-consciously employed architecture to reduce crime."[34] And architects have begun to identify principles of design that can minimize crime—called "Crime Prevention Through Environmental Design."[35]

In each example, an architecture is changed so as to realize different behavior. The architecture effects that difference. As a sign above one of the portals at the 1933 Chicago World's Fair put it (though it was speaking of science): "Science Explores: Technology Executes: Man Conforms."[36]

Law can change social norms as well, though much of our constitutional jurisprudence seems dedicated to forgetting just how.[37] Education is the most obvious example. As Thurgood Marshall put it, "Education is not the teaching of the three R's. Education is the teaching of the overall citizenship, to learn to live together with fellow citizens, and above all to learn to obey the law."[38] Education is, in part at least, a process through which we indoctrinate children into certain norms of behavior—we teach them how to "say no" to sex and drugs. We try to build within them a sense of what is correct. This sense then regulates them to the law's end.

Plainly, the content of much of this education is regulated by law. Conservatives worry, for example, that by teaching sex education we change the norm of sexual abstinence. Whether that is correct or not, the law is certainly being used to change the norms of children. If conservatives are correct, the law is eliminating abstinence. If liberals are correct, the law is being used to instill a norm of safe sex. Either way, norms have their own constraint, and law is aiming to change that constraint.

To say that law plays a role is not to say that it always plays a positive role. The law can muck up norms as well as improve them, and I do not claim that the latter result is more common than the former.[39] The point is just to see the role, not to praise or criticize it.

In each case, the law chooses between direct and indirect regulation. The question is: Which means best advances the regulator's goal, subject to the constraints (whether normative or material) that the regulator must recognize? My argument is that any analysis of the strategies of regulation must take into account these different modalities. As Polk Wagner puts it, focusing on one additional modality:

> [J]ust as the choice of a legal rule will involve analytic trade offs between the familiar categories of property rules and liability rules, the incorporation of legal preemption rules in the cyberspace context will require a similar exercise along an additional dimension—the impact that the legal rule will have on corresponding software regulation (and thus the effect on the law-software interface).[40]

Or again, "legal policy proposals unsupported by predictions of technological response are deeply incomplete."[41] And the same can be said generally about the interaction between any modality and any policy proposal.

We can represent the point through a modification of the second figure:

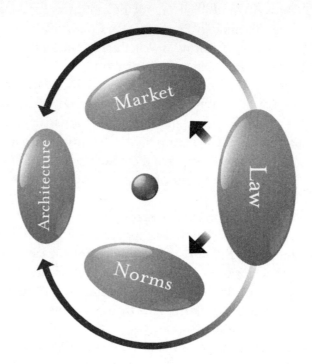

As Wagner rightly insists, again, the interaction among these modalities is dynamic, "requiring consideration of not only . . . legal adjustments, but also predicting the responsive effects such changes will stimulate."[42] The regulator seeks an "equilibrium," constantly considering trade-offs among modalities of regulation.

The point should be familiar, and the examples can be multiplied.

Seatbelts: The government may want citizens to wear seatbelts more often.[43] It could pass a law to require the wearing of seatbelts (law regulating behavior directly). Or it could fund public education campaigns to create a stigma against those who do not wear seatbelts (law regulating social norms as a means to regulating behavior). Or it could subsidize insurance companies to offer reduced rates to seatbelt wearers (law regulating the market as a way of regulating behavior). Finally, the law could mandate automatic seatbelts, or ignition-locking systems (changing the code of the automobile as a means of regulating belting behavior). Each action might be said to have some effect on seatbelt use; each has some cost. The question for the government is how to get the most seatbelt use for the least cost.

Discrimination against the disabled: The disabled bear the burden of significant social and physical barriers in daily life.[44] The government might decide to do something about those barriers. The traditional answer is law regulating behavior directly: a law barring discrimination on the basis of physical disability. But the law could do more. It could, for example, educate children in order to change social norms (regulating norms to regulate behavior). It could subsidize companies to hire the disabled (regulating the market to regulate behavior). It could regulate building codes to make buildings more accessible to the disabled (regulating "natural" or real-space codes to regulate behavior). Each of these regulations would have some effect on discrimination and would have a cost. The government would have to weigh the costs against the benefits and select the mode that regulates most effectively.

Drugs: The government is obsessed with reducing the consumption of illicit drugs. Its main strategy has been direct regulation of behavior through the threat of barbaric prison terms for violation of the drug laws. This policy has obvious costs and non-obvious benefits. But most interesting for our purposes are the non-obvious costs. As Tracey Meares persuasively argues, one effective structure for regulating the consumption of illegal drugs is the social structure of the community in which an individual lives.[45] These are what I've called social norm constraints: standards of appropriate behavior enforced by the sanctions of a community—whether through shame, exclusion, or force.

Just as government can act to strengthen these social norm constraints, it should be obvious that government can also act to weaken them.[46] One way to do this is by weakening the communities within which these norms operate. This, says Meares, is what the extreme sanctions of the criminal law do.[47] In their extremity and effect, they undermine the social structures that would support this social policy. This is an indirect effect of the direct regulation of law, and at some point this effect may overwhelm the effect of the law. We might call this the Laffer Curve for criminal law.

The net effect of these different constraints cannot be deduced a priori. The government acts in many ways to regulate the consumption of drugs. It supports extensive public education campaigns to stigmatize the consumption of drugs (regulating social norms to regulate behavior). It seizes drugs at the border, thereby reducing the supply, increasing the price, and presumably reducing demand (regulating the market to regulate behavior). And at times it has even (and grotesquely) regulated the "code" of drugs (by, for example, spraying marijuana fields with paraquat), making them more dangerous and thereby increasing the constraint on their consumption.[48] All of these together influence the consumption of drugs. But as advocates of legalization argue, they also influence the incidence of other criminal behavior as well. The policy maker must assess the net effect—whether on the whole these regulations reduce or increase social costs.

Abortion: One final example will complete the account. Since *Roe v. Wade*, the Court has recognized a woman's constitutional right to an abortion.[49] This right, however, has not stopped government from seeking to eliminate or reduce the number of abortions. Again, the government need not rely on direct regulation of abortion (which under Roe would be unconstitutional). It can instead use indirect means to the same end. In *Rust v. Sullivan*, the Court upheld the power of the government to bias the provision of family planning advice by forbidding doctors in "government-funded" clinics from mentioning abortion as a method of family planning.[50] This is a regulation of social norms (within the social structure of medical care) to regulate behavior. In *Maher v. Roe*, the Court upheld the right of the government to disable selectively medical funding for abortion.[51] This is the use of the market to regulate behavior. And in *Hodgson v. Minnesota*, the Court upheld the right of the state to force minor women to wait forty-eight hours before getting an abortion.[52] This is the use of real-space code (the constraints of time) to regulate access to abortion. In all these ways, *Roe* notwithstanding, the government can regulate the behavior of women wanting abortions.

In each of these examples, law functions in two very different ways.[53] When its operation is direct, it tells individuals how to behave and threatens punishment if they deviate from that behavior. When its operation is indirect, it modifies one of the other structures of constraint.[54] The regulator selects from among these various techniques according to the return from each—both in efficiency and in the values that each might express.

When we see regulation in this more general way, we can see more clearly how the unregulability of cyberspace is contingent. We get a stronger sense of how the state could intervene to make regulation work, and we should also get a sense of the increased dangers presented by this more expansive sense of regulation. In particular, we should have a stronger sense of the danger it presents to constitutional values. The next section considers one such threat.

THE PROBLEMS OF INDIRECTION

In 1985, after years of inaction, Congress passed the Low Level Radioactive Waste Policy Amendments Act to deal with the problem of nuclear waste. Someone needed to take and store nuclear waste.[55] After sufficient prodding by the government, a number of states formed a compact, which Congress then ratified, implementing a number of requirements and incentives for states to deal with the nuclear waste they produce.

The details of the overall plan are not important here. It is enough to focus on just one part. To induce states to follow federal guidelines for regulating nuclear waste, Congress gave them a choice: Either enact certain regulations or "take title" to the spent nuclear fuel. This was a "your money or your life" regulation, for the fuel to which the states would take title was not an asset but a great liability. In a very heavy-handed way, Congress was essentially forcing states to pass the regulations it wanted.

The Supreme Court struck down this part of the law. In effect, the Court held, Congress was commandeering the state legislatures to enact Congress's law. Congress itself, of course, had the power to enact those regulations directly. But it did not have the power to order states to enact laws. Indirection here was not allowed.

This case—*New York v. United States*—does not stand for the broad principle that government must regulate only directly, or even for the principle that indirect regulation generally is disfavored. The case was focused quite narrowly on the question of indirection as it involved the states. The most *New York* stands for is the idea that states, as independent sovereigns deserving of special constitutional respect, cannot be co-opted to the federal government's ends—that when the federal government has a program it wants to carry out, it must put its own name behind it.

But while *New York* doesn't establish a general constitutional principle, it does suggest why indirection should be a more general concern.

Indirection misdirects responsibility. When a government uses other structures of constraint to effect a constraint it could impose directly, it muddies the responsibility for that constraint and so undermines political accountability. If transparency is a value in constitutional government, indirection is its enemy. It confuses responsibility and hence confuses politics.[56]

Such misunderstandings are possible in other contexts as well. Think again about the case of *Rust*. The federal government helps to fund family planning clinics. ("Helps" fund, not completely funds.)[57] Before 1988 these clinics gave advice on a wide range of birth-related topics, including abortion. Doctors in family planning clinics would advise their patients about abortion whenever they felt such advice was proper.

The Reagan administration wanted to change that, so it ordered (the details of how are not important here) doctors in those clinics to not discuss abortion as a method of family planning with their patients. If asked, the doctors were to say, "The project does not consider abortion an appropriate method of family planning."[58]

The aim of this regulation was clear: to reduce the incidence of abortion. It did this by using doctors to steer patients away from abortion. A doctor has a great deal of power over a patient in a context like this, and the patient would most likely believe the doctor was recommending against abortion.

But notice the technique. The federal government could have stated its own position about abortion. It could have put up posters and billboards saying that abortion is wrong, or it could have used space in its clinics to advertise its view. But it chose instead to bury its policy choice in the words of doctors. It thereby could trade on the professional authority of the doctors to advance its own ends. It could regulate abortion indirectly by regulating the doctors directly.

Just as it tried to use the authority of the states to effect its ends in *New York,* the government trades on a misrepresentation in *Rust.* But worse than in the federalism context, the victim of the misrepresentation here does not even realize that the misrepresentation is a policy choice. The patient is unlikely to hear the doctor's statement as a political broadcast from the government; she is most likely to hear it as a medical opinion. Not only is there a confusion about who is responsible for the opinion expressed, but there is also confusion about whether it is an opinion at all.

Rust v. Sullivan is one of the great embarrassments of the Supreme Court—the case proving Justice Scalia's rule that any issue gets distorted once it gets near the question of abortion.[59] But my argument here doesn't depend upon whether *Rust* was right. My aim is to bring out a certain sensibility about regulation; *Rust* simply points the way.

Consider a third case. Until 1948 deeds could include covenants (promises) that the property covered by the deed could not be sold to people of a particular race. The purpose of these provisions was clear: to effect and preserve segregation. Their use was extensive. It was estimated, for example, that when *Shelley v Kraemer*[60] struck these provisions down as unconstitutional under the equal protection clause, 25 percent of the properties in south Chicago had been prohibited from sale to African Americans.[61]

As awful as such provisions were, they had a certain integrity. They clearly stated their purpose and were transparent about the values they affirmed. No one could pretend that the segregation they effected was somehow an accidental by-product of decisions made elsewhere. Although they were private covenants, they were enforced by the state and, indeed, derived their meaning from the state. They said: This society is racist.

When the Court struck these provisions down, however, the question became what would replace them. Few expected that the attitudes behind these covenants would suddenly disappear because of a single court judgment. So when the Court ended direct segregation, we should expect indirect segregation to emerge to replace it.

Sure enough, after 1948 local communities shifted their technique for preserving segregation. Rather than covenants, they used architecture. Communities were designed to "break the flow" of residents from one to another. Highways without easy crossings were placed between communities. Railroad tracks were used to divide. A thousand tiny inconveniences of architecture and zoning replaced the express preferences of covenants. Nothing formally prohibited integration, but informally, much did. [62]

Local governments thus did something very much like what the federal government did in *Rust* and tried to do in *New York:* No longer able to effect segregation directly, they used zoning laws—geographical architecture, or real-space code—to effect it indirectly. They built their communities and designed their streets to make it hard for integration to occur, and the tiny inconveniences of zoning regulations succeeded in keeping communities separate.

What is most significant is that now, even more than with *Rust,* it becomes very difficult to see the link between the regulation and its consequence. The continuing segregation of these communities is described as the product of "choice." Individuals choose to live in one neighborhood rather than another. In a strict sense, that is correct, but their choices are made in the face of costs that the state has imposed. It is easier to remain segregated, so people choose to do that. But it is only easier because government has moved mountains to make it that way.

Here the government is regulating indirectly by using the structures of real-space code to effect its ends, but this regulation, again, is not seen as regulation. Here the government gets an effect at no political cost. It gets the benefit of what would clearly be an illegal and controversial regulation without even having to admit any regulation exists.

In all three cases, the government is commandeering the power of another modality—another structure of constraint—to effect its own ends.[63] This in itself is not necessarily improper. There are plenty of examples that anyone would consider proper. A requirement that streets be well lit, for instance, is a regulation designed to reduce crime, and no one would think that regulation improper. Nor does all such regulation hide its pedigree. Think again about speed bumps–they are examples of indirect regulation. Like a winding road, they use the code of streets to keep down the speed of a car. But no one is fooled about the source of this regulation; no one believes the bumps are accidental.

Thus, the point is not against indirect regulation generally. The point is instead about transparency. The state has no right to hide its agenda. In a constitutional democracy its regulations should be public. And thus, one issue raised by the practice of indirect regulation is the general issue of publicity. Should the state be permitted to use nontransparent means when transparent means are available?

WHERE THIS LEADS

After I published an essay in the (then existing) *Industry Standard* arguing that "code is law,"[64] the following letter was sent to the editor:

> Typical for a Harvard Law Professor. . . . Lessig misses the entire forest while dancing among the trees. . . . While his riff on West Coast Code (from Silicon Valley Programmers) vs. East Coast Code (from government lawyers) is very cleverly crafted, it completely avoids the real difference between the two.
>
> The good professor seems to apply the word "regulation" equally to the efforts of private enterprises to control the behavior of their customers through market mechanisms and the efforts of government agencies to control the behavior of all citizens through force of law.
>
> So long as the creators and purveyors of West Coast Code (no matter how selfish, monopolistic, demonic or incompetent they may be) do not carry guns and badges, I will choose them over the enforcers of East Coast Code any time.[65]

Whether or not I've missed the "real difference" between code and law, the genius in this letter is that its author clearly sees the real similarity. The author (the president of an Internet-related business) understands that "private enterprises" try to "control the behavior of their customers," and he writes that they use "market mechanisms" to achieve that control. (Technically, I was speaking about architectures to achieve that effect, but never mind. Whether markets or architectures, the point is the same.) He therefore sees that there is "regulation" beyond law. He just has his favorite between the two (corporate executive that he is).

What this author sees is what we all must see to understand how cyberspace is regulated and to see how law might regulate cyberspace. I've argued in this chapter that government has a range of tools that it uses to regulate, and cyberspace expands that range. Indirectly, by regulating code writing, the government can achieve regulatory ends, often without suffering the political consequences that the same ends, pursued directly, would yield.

We should worry about this. We should worry about a regime that makes invisible regulation easier; we should worry about a regime that makes it easier to regulate. We should worry about the first because invisibility makes it hard to resist bad regulation; we should worry about the second because we don't yet—as I argue in Part III—have a sense of the values put at risk by the increasing scope of efficient regulation.

That's a lot of worries, no doubt. But before we go further with these worries, we could consider in more detail the contexts within which these worries become real.

EIGHT

the limits in open code

I'VE TOLD A STORY ABOUT HOW REGULATION WORKS, AND ABOUT THE INCREASING regulability of the Internet that we should expect. These are, as I described, changes in the architecture of the Net that will better enable government's control by making behavior more easily monitored—or at least more traceable. These changes will emerge even if government does nothing. They are the by-product of changes made to enable e-commerce. But they will be cemented if (or when) the government recognizes just how it could make the network its tool.

That was Part I. In this part, I've focused upon a different regulability—the kind of regulation that is effected through the architectures of the space within which one lives. As I argued in Chapter 5, there's nothing new about this modality of regulation: Governments have used architecture to regulate behavior forever. But what is new is its significance. As life moves onto the Net, more of life will be regulated through the self-conscious design of the space within which life happens. That's not necessarily a bad thing. If there were a code-based way to stop drunk drivers, I'd be all for it. But neither is this pervasive code-based regulation benign. Due to the manner in which it functions, regulation by code can interfere with the ordinary democratic process by which we hold regulators accountable.

The key criticism that I've identified so far is transparency. Code-based regulation—especially of people who are not themselves technically expert—risks making regulation invisible. Controls are imposed for particular policy reasons, but people experience these controls as nature. And that experience, I suggested, could weaken democratic resolve.

Now that's not saying much, at least about us. We are already a pretty apathetic political culture. And there's nothing about cyberspace to suggest things are going to be different. Indeed, as Castranova observes about virtual worlds: "How strange, then, that one does not find much democracy at all in synthetic worlds. Not a trace, in fact. Not a hint of a shadow of a trace. It's not there. The typical governance model in synthetic worlds consists of isolated moments of oppressive tyranny embedded in widespread anarchy."[1]

But if we could put aside our own skepticism about our democracy for a moment, and focus at least upon aspects of the Internet and cyberspace that we all agree matter fundamentally, then I think we will all recognize a point that, once recognized, seems obvious: If code regulates, then in at least some critical contexts, the kind of code that regulates is critically important.

By "kind" I mean to distinguish between two types of code: open and closed. By "open code" I mean code (both software and hardware) whose functionality is transparent at least to one knowledgeable about the technology. By "closed code," I mean code (both software and hardware) whose functionality is opaque. One can guess what closed code is doing; and with enough opportunity to test, one might well reverse engineer it. But from the technology itself, there is no reasonable way to discern what the functionality of the technology is.

The terms "open" and "closed" code will suggest to many a critically important debate about how software should be developed. What most call the "open source software movement," but which I, following Richard Stallman, call the "free software movement," argues (in my view at least) that there are fundamental values of freedom that demand that software be developed as free software. The opposite of free software, in this sense, is proprietary software, where the developer hides the functionality of the software by distributing digital objects that are opaque about the underlying design.

I will describe this debate more in the balance of this chapter. But importantly, the point I am making about "open" versus "closed" code is distinct from the point about how code gets created. I personally have very strong views about how code should be created. But whatever side you are on in the "free vs. proprietary software" debate in general, in at least the contexts I will identify here, you should be able to agree with me first, that open code is a constraint on state power, and second, that in at least some cases, code must, in the relevant sense, be "open."

To set the stage for this argument, I want to describe two contexts in which I will argue that we all should agree that the kind of code deployed matters. The balance of the chapter then makes that argument.

BYTES THAT SNIFF

In Chapter 2, I described technology that at the time was a bit of science fiction. In the five years since, that fiction has become even less fictional. In 1997, the government announced a project called Carnivore. Carnivore was to be a technology that sifted through e-mail traffic and collected just those e-mails written by or to a particular and named individual. The FBI intended to use this technology, pursuant to court orders, to gather evidence while investigating crimes.

In principle, there's lots to praise in the ideals of the Carnivore design. The protocols required a judge to approve this surveillance. The technology was intended to collect data only about the target of the investigation. No one else was to be burdened by the tool. No one else was to have their privacy compromised.

But whether the technology did what it was said to do depends upon its code. And that code was closed.[2] The contract the government let with the vendor that developed the Carnivore software did not require that the source for the software be made public. It instead permitted the vendor to keep the code secret.

Now it's easy to understand why the vendor wanted its code kept secret. In general, inviting others to look at your code is much like inviting them to your house for dinner: There's lots you need to do to make the place presentable. In this case in particular, the DOJ may have been concerned about security.[3] But substantively, however, the vendor might want to use components of the software in other software projects. If the code is public, the vendor might lose some advantage from that transparency. These advantages for the vendor mean that it would be more costly for the government to insist upon a technology that was delivered with its source code revealed. And so the question should be whether there's something the government gains from having the source code revealed.

And here's the obvious point: As the government quickly learned as it tried to sell the idea of Carnivore, the fact that its code was secret was costly. Much of the government's efforts were devoted to trying to build trust around its claim that Carnivore did just what it said it did. But the argument "I'm from the government, so trust me" doesn't have much weight. And thus, the efforts of the government to deploy this technology—again, a valuable technology if it did what it said it did—were hampered.

I don't know of any study that tries to evaluate the cost the government faced because of the skepticism about Carnivore versus the cost of developing Carnivore in an open way.[4] I would be surprised if the government's strategy made fiscal sense. But whether or not it was cheaper to develop closed rather than open code, it shouldn't be controversial that the government has an independent obligation to make its procedures—at least in the context of ordinary criminal prosecution—transparent. I don't mean that the investigator needs to reveal the things he thinks about when deciding which suspects to target. I mean instead the procedures for invading the privacy interests of ordinary citizens.

The only kind of code that can do that is "open code." And the small point I want to insist upon just now is that where transparency of government action matters, so too should the kind of code it uses. This is not the claim that all government code should be public. I believe there are legitimate areas within which the government can act secretly. More particularly, where transparency would interfere with the function itself, then there's a good argument against transparency. But there were very limited ways in which a possible criminal suspect could more effectively evade the surveillance of Carnivore just because its code was open. And thus, again, open code should, in my view, have been the norm.

MACHINES THAT COUNT

Before November 7, 2000, there was very little discussion among national policy makers about the technology of voting machines. For most (and I was within this majority), the question of voting technology seemed trivial. Certainly, there could have been faster technologies for tallying a vote. And there could have been better technologies to check for errors. But the idea that anything important hung upon these details in technology was not an idea that made the cover of the front page of the *New York Times*.

The 2000 presidential election changed all that. More specifically, Florida in 2000 changed all that. Not only did the Florida experience demonstrate the imperfection in traditional mechanical devices for tabulating votes (exhibit 1, the hanging chad), it also demonstrated the extraordinary inequality that having different technologies in different parts of the state would produce. As Justice Stevens described in his dissent in *Bush v. Gore,* almost 4 percent of punch-card ballots were disqualified, while only 1.43 percent of optical scan ballots were disqualified.[5] And as one study estimated, changing a single vote on each machine would have changed the outcome of the election.[6]

The 2004 election made things even worse. In the four years since the Florida debacle, a few companies had pushed to deploy new electronic voting machines. But these voting machines seemed to create more anxiety among voters than less. While most voters are not techies, everyone has a sense of the obvious queasiness that a totally electronic voting machine produces. You stand before a terminal and press buttons to indicate your vote. The machine confirms your vote and then reports the vote has been recorded. But how do you know? How could anyone know? And even if you're not conspiracy-theory-oriented enough to believe that every voting machine is fixed, how can anyone know that when these voting machines check in with the central server, the server records their votes accurately? What's to guarantee that the numbers won't be fudged?

The most extreme example of this anxiety was produced by the leading electronic voting company, Diebold. In 2003, Diebold had been caught fudging the numbers associated with tests of its voting technology. Memos leaked to the public showed that Diebold's management knew the machines were flawed and intentionally chose to hide that fact. (The company then sued students who had published these memos—for copyright infringement. The students won a countersuit against Diebold.)

That incident seemed only to harden Diebold in its ways. The company continued to refuse to reveal anything about the code that its machines ran. It refused to bid in contexts in which such transparency was required. And when you tie that refusal to its chairman's promise to "deliver Ohio" for President Bush in 2004, you have all the makings of a perfect trust storm. You control the machines; you won't show us how they work; and you promise a particular result in the election. Is there any doubt people would be suspicious?[7]

Now it turns out that it is a very hard question to know how electronic voting machines should be designed. In one of my own dumbest moments since turning 21, I told a colleague that there was no reason to have a conference about electronic voting since all the issues were "perfectly obvious." They're not perfectly obvious. In fact, they're very difficult. It seems obvious to some that, like an ATM, there should at least be a printed receipt. But if there's a printed receipt, that would make it simple for voters to sell their votes. Moreover, there's no reason the receipt needs to reflect what was counted. Nor does the receipt necessarily reflect what was transmitted to any central tabulating authority. The question of how best to design these systems turns out not to be obvious. And having uttered absolute garbage about this point before, I won't enter here into any consideration of how best this might be architected.

But however a system is architected, there is an independent point about the openness of the code that comprises the system. Again, the procedures used to tabulate votes must be transparent. In the nondigital world, those procedures were obvious. In the digital world, however they're architected, we need a way to ensure that the machine does what it is said it will do. One simple way to do that is either to open the code to those machines, or, at a minimum, require that that code be certified by independent inspectors. Many would prefer the latter to the former, just because transparency here might increase the chances of the code being hacked. My own intuition about that is different. But whether or not the code is completely open, requirements for certification are obvious. And for certification to function, the code for the technology must—in a limited sense at least—be open.

Both of these examples make a similar point. But that point, however, is not universal. There are times when code needs to be transparent, even if there are times when it does not. I'm not talking about all code for whatever purposes. I don't think Wal*Mart needs to reveal the code for calculating change at its check-out counters. I don't even think Yahoo! should have to reveal the code for its Instant Messaging service. But I do think we all should think that, in certain contexts at least, the transparency of open code should be a requirement.

This is a point that Phil Zimmermann taught by his practice more than 15 years ago. Zimmermann wrote and released to the Net a program called PGP (pretty good privacy). PGP provides cryptographic privacy and authentication. But Zimmermann recognized that it would not earn trust enough to provide these services well unless he made available the source code to the program. So from the beginning (except for a brief lapse when the program was owned by a company called NAI[8]) the source code has been available for anyone to review and verify. That publicity has built confidence in the code— a confidence that could never have been produced by mere command. In this case, open code served the purpose of the programmer, as his purpose was to build confidence and trust in a system that would support privacy and authentication. Open code worked.

The hard question is whether there's any claim to be made beyond this minimal one. That's the question for the balance of this chapter: How does open code affect regulability?

CODE ON THE NET

I've spent lots of time talking about "code." It's time to be a bit more specific about what "code" in the context of the Internet is, in what sense should we consider this code to be "open," and in what contexts its openness will matter.

As I've mentioned, the Internet is constructed by a set of protocols together referred to as TCP/IP. The TCP/IP suite includes a large number of protocols that feed different "layers" of the network. The standard model for describing layers of a network is the open systems interconnect (OSI) reference model. It describes seven network layers, each representing a "function performed when data is transferred between cooperating applications across" the network. But the TCP/IP suite is not as well articulated in that model. According to Craig Hunt, "most descriptions of TCP/IP define three to five functional levels in the protocol architecture." In my view, it is simplest to describe four functional layers in a TCP/IP architecture.[9] From the bottom of the stack up, we can call these the data link, network, transport, and application layers.[10]

Three layers constitute the essential plumbing of the Internet, hidden in the Net's walls. (The faucets work at the next layer; be patient.) At the very bottom, just above the physical layer of the Internet, in the data link layer, very few protocols operate, since that handles local network interactions exclusively. More protocols exist at the next layer up, the network layer, where the IP protocol is dominant. It routes data between hosts and across network links, determining which path the data should take. At the next layer up, the transport layer, two different protocols dominate—TCP and UDP. These negotiate the flow of data between two network hosts. (The difference between the two is reliability—UDP offers no reliability guarantee.)

The protocols together function as a kind of odd UPS. Data are passed from the application to the transport layer. There the data are placed in a (virtual) box and a (virtual) label is slapped on. That label ties the contents of the box to particular processes. (This is the work of the TCP or UDP protocols.) That box is then passed to the network layer, where the IP protocol puts the package into another package, with its own label. This label includes the origination and destination addresses. That box then can be further wrapped at the data link layer, depending on the specifics of the local network (whether, for example, it is an Ethernet network).

The whole process is thus a bizarre packaging game: A new box is added at each layer, and a new label on each box describes the process at that layer. At the other end, the packaging process is reversed: Like a Russian doll, each package is opened at the proper layer, until at the end the machine recovers the initial application data.

On top of these three layers is the application layer of the Internet. Here protocols "proliferate."[11] These include the most familiar network application protocols, such as FTP (file transfer protocol, a protocol for transferring files), SMTP (simple mail transport protocol, a protocol for transferring mail), and HTTP (hyper text transfer protocol, a protocol to publish and read hypertext documents across the Web). These are rules for how a client (your computer) will interact with a server (where the data are), or with another computer (in peer-to-peer services), and the other way around.[12]

These four layers of protocols are "the Internet." Building on simple blocks, the system makes possible an extraordinary range of interaction. It is perhaps not quite as amazing as nature—think of DNA—but it is built on the same principle: keep the elements simple, and the compounds will astound.

When I speak about regulating the code, I'm not talking about changing these core TCP/IP protocols. (Though in principle, of course, they could be regulated, and others have suggested that they should be.)[13] In my view these components of the network are fixed. If you required them to be different, you'd break the Internet. Thus rather than imagining the government changing the core, the question I want to consider is how the government might either (1) complement the core with technology that adds regulability, or (2) regulates applications that connect to the core. Both will be important, but my focus is on the code that plugs into the Internet. I will call that code the "application space" of the Internet. This includes all the code that implements TCP/IP protocols at the application layer—browsers, operating systems, encryption modules, Java, e-mail systems, P2P, whatever elements you want. The question for the balance of this chapter is: What is the character of that code that makes it susceptible to regulation?

A SHORT HISTORY OF CODE ON THE NET

In the beginning, of course, there were very few applications on the Net. The Net was no more than a protocol for exchanging data, and the original programs simply took advantage of this protocol. The file transfer protocol (FTP) was born early in the Net's history;[14] the electronic message protocol (SMTP) was born soon after. It was not long before a protocol to display directories in a graphical way (Gopher) was developed. And in 1991 the most famous of protocols—the hyper text transfer protocol (HTTP) and hyper text markup language (HTML)—gave birth to the World Wide Web.

Each protocol spawned many applications. Since no one had a monopoly on the protocol, no one had a monopoly on its implementation. There were many FTP applications and many e-mail servers. There were even a large number of browsers.[15] The protocols were open standards, gaining their blessing from standards bodies such as the Internet Engineering Task Force (IETF) and, later, the W3C. Once a protocol was specified, programmers could build programs that utilized it.

Much of the software implementing these protocols was "open," at least initially—that is, the source code for the software was available along with the object code.[16] This openness was responsible for much of the early Net's growth. Others could explore how a program was implemented and learn from that example how better to implement the protocol in the future.

The World Wide Web is the best example of this point. Again, the code that makes a web page appear as it does is called the hyper text markup language, or HTML.[17] With HTML, you can specify how a web page will appear and to what it will be linked.

The original HTML was proposed in 1990 by the CERN researchers Tim Berners-Lee and Robert Cailliau.[18] It was designed to make it easy to link documents at a research facility, but it quickly became obvious that documents on any machine on the Internet could be linked. Berners-Lee and Cailliau made both HTML and its companion HTTP freely available for anyone to take.

And take them people did, at first slowly, but then at an extraordinary rate. People started building web pages and linking them to others. HTML became one of the fastest-growing computer languages in the history of computing.

Why? One important reason was that HTML was always "open." Even today, on most browsers in distribution, you can always reveal the "source" of a web page and see what makes it tick. The source remains open: You can download it, copy it, and improve it as you wish. Copyright law may protect the source code of a web page, but in reality it protects it very imperfectly. HTML became as popular as it did primarily because it was so easy to copy. Anyone, at any time, could look under the hood of an HTML document and learn how the author produced it.

Openness—not property or contract but free code and access—created the boom that gave birth to the Internet that we now know. And it was this boom that then attracted the attention of commerce. With all this activity, commerce rightly reasoned, surely there was money to be made.

Historically the commercial model for producing software has been different.[19] Though the history began even as the open code movement continued, commercial software vendors were not about to produce "free" (what most call "open source") software. Commercial vendors produced software that was closed—that traveled without its source and was protected against modification both by the law and by its own code.

By the second half of the 1990s—marked most famously by Microsoft's Windows 95, which came bundled Internet-savvy—commercial software vendors began producing "application space" code. This code was increasingly connected to the Net—it increasingly became code "on" the Internet. But for the most part, the code remained closed.

That began to change, however, around the turn of the century. Especially in the context of peer-to-peer services, technologies emerged that were dominant and "open." More importantly, the protocols these technologies depended upon were unregulated. Thus, for example, the protocol that the peer-to-peer client Grokster used to share content on the Internet is itself an open standard that anyone can use. Many commercial entities tried to use that standard, at least until the Supreme Court's decision in *Grokster*. But even if that decision inspires every commercial entity to abandon the StreamCast network, noncommercial implementations of the protocol will still exist.

The same mix between open and closed exists in both browsers and blogging software. Firefox is the more popular current implementation of the Mozilla technology—the technology that originally drove the Netscape browser. It competes with Microsoft's Internet Explorer and a handful of other commercial browsers. Likewise, WordPress is an open-source blogging tool that competes with a handful of other proprietary blogging tools.

This recent growth in open code builds upon a long tradition. Part of the motivation for that tradition is ideological, or values based. Richard Stallman is the inspiration here. In 1984, Stallman began the Free Software Foundation with the aim of fueling the growth of free software. A MacArthur Fellow who gave up his career to commit himself to the cause, Stallman has devoted the last twenty years of his life to free software. That work began with the GNU project, which sought to develop a free operating system. By 1991, the GNU project had just about everything it needed, except a kernel. That final challenge was taken up by an undergraduate at the University of Helsinki. That year, Linus Torvalds posted on the Internet the kernel of an operating system. He invited the world to extend and experiment with it.

People took up the challenge, and slowly, through the early 1990s, marrying the GNU project with Torvald's kernel, they built an operating system—GNU/Linux. By 1998, it had become apparent to all that GNU/Linux was going to be an important competitor to the Microsoft operating system. Microsoft may have imagined in 1995 that by 2000 there would be no other server operating system available except Windows NT, but when 2000 came around, there was GNU/Linux, presenting a serious threat to Microsoft in the server market. Now in 2007, Linux-based web servers continue to gain market share at the expense of Microsoft systems.

GNU/Linux is amazing in many ways. It is amazing first because it is theoretically imperfect but practically superior. Linus Torvalds rejected what computer science told him was the ideal operating system design,[20] and instead built an operating system that was designed for a single processor (an Intel 386) and not cross-platform-compatible. Its creative development, and the energy it inspired, slowly turned GNU/Linux into an extraordinarily powerful system. As of this writing, GNU/Linux has been ported to at least eighteen different computer architecture platforms—from the original Intel processors, to Apple's PowerPC chip, to Sun SPARC chips, and mobile devices using ARM processors.[21] Creative hackers have even ported Linux to squeeze onto Apple's iPod and old Atari systems. Although initially designed to speak only one language, GNU/Linux has become the lingua franca of free software operating systems.

What makes a system open is a commitment among its developers to keep its core code public—to keep the hood of the car unlocked. That commitment is not just a wish; Stallman encoded it in a license that sets the terms that control the future use of most free software. This is the Free Software Foundation's General Public License (GPL), which requires that any code licensed with GPL (as GNU/Linux is) keep its source free. GNU/Linux was developed by an extraordinary collection of hackers worldwide only because its code was open for others to work on.

Its code, in other words, sits in the commons.[22] Anyone can take it and use it as she wishes. Anyone can take it and come to understand how it works. The code of GNU/Linux is like a research program whose results are always published for others to see. Everything is public; anyone, without having to seek the permission of anyone else, may join the project.

This project has been wildly more successful than anyone ever imagined. In 1992, most would have said that it was impossible to build a free operating system from volunteers around the world. In 2002, no one could doubt it anymore. But if the impossible could become possible, then no doubt it could become impossible again. And certain trends in computing technology may create precisely this threat.

For example, consider the way Active Server Pages (ASP) code works on the network. When you go to an ASP page on the Internet, the server runs a program—a script to give you access to a database, for example, or a program to generate new data you need. ASPs are increasingly popular ways to provide program functionality. You use it all the time when you are on the Internet.

But the code that runs ASPs is not technically "distributed." Thus, even if the code is produced using GPL'd code, there's no GPL obligation to release it to anyone. Therefore, as more and more of the infrastructure of networked life becomes governed by ASP, less and less will be effectively set free by free license.

"Trusted Computing" creates another threat to the open code ecology. Launched as a response to virus and security threats within a networked environment, the key technical feature of "trusted computing" is that the platform blocks programs that are not cryptographically signed or verified by the plat-form. For example, if you want to run a program on your computer, your computer would first verify that the program is certified by one of the author-ities recognized by the computer operating system, and "incorporat[ing] hardware and software . . . security standards approved by the content providers themselves."[23] If it isn't, the program wouldn't run.

In principle, of course, if the cost of certifying a program were tiny, this limitation might be unproblematic. But the fear is that this restriction will operate to effectively block open code projects. It is not easy for a certifying authority to actually know what a program does; that means certifying authorities won't be keen to certify programs they can't trust. And that in turn will effect a significant discrimination against open code.

REGULATING OPEN CODE

Open code projects—whether free software or open source software projects—share the feature that the knowledge necessary to replicate the project is intended always to be available to others. There is no effort, through law or technology, for the developer of an open code project to make that development exclusive. And, more importantly, the capacity to replicate and redirect the evolution of a project provided in its most efficient form is also always preserved.

How does this fact affect the regulability of code?

In Chapter 5, I sketched examples of government regulating code. But think again about those examples: How does such regulation work?

Consider two. The government tells the telephone company something about how its networks are to be designed, and the government tells television manufacturers what kinds of chips TVs are to have. Why do these regulations work?

The answer in each case is obvious. The code is regulable only because the code writers can be controlled. If the state tells the phone company to do some-thing, the phone company is not likely to resist. Resistance would bring punish-ment; punishment is expensive; phone companies, like all other companies, want to reduce the cost of doing business. If the state's regulation is rational (that is, effective), it will set the cost of disobeying the state above any possible benefit. If the target of regulation is a rational actor within the reach of the state, then the regulation is likely to have its intended effect. CALEA's regulation of the network architecture for telephones is an obvious example of this (see Chapter 5).

An unmovable, and unmoving, target of regulation, then, is a good start toward regulability. And this statement has an interesting corollary: Regulable code is closed code. Think again about telephone networks. When the government induces the telephone networks to modify their network software, users have no choice about whether to adopt this modification or not. You pick up the phone, you get the dial tone the phone company gives you. No one I know hacks the telephone company's code to build a different network design. The same with the V-chip—I doubt that many people would risk destroying their television by pulling out the chip, and I am certain that no one re-burns the chip to build in a different filtering technology.

In both cases the government's regulation works because when the target of the regulation complies, customers can do little but accept it.

Open code is different. We can see something of the difference in a story told by Netscape's former legal counsel, Peter Harter, about Netscape and the French.[24]

In 1996, Netscape released a protocol (SSL v3.0) to facilitate secure electronic commerce on the Web. The essence of its function is to permit secure exchange between a browser and a server. The French were not happy with the security that SSL gave; they wanted to be able to crack SSL transactions. So they requested that Netscape modify SSL to enable their spying.

There are plenty of constraints on Netscape's ability to modify SSL—not the least of which being that Netscape has given SSL over to the public, in the form of a public standard. But assume for a second that it had not. Assume Netscape really did control the standards for SSL and in theory could modify the code to enable French spying. Would that mean that Netscape could comply with the French demand?

No. Technically, it could comply by modifying the code of Netscape Communicator and then posting a new module that enabled hacking by a government. But because Netscape (or more generally, the Mozilla project) is open source, anyone is free to build a competing module that would replace the Frenchified SSL module. That module would compete with other modules. The module that wins would be the one users wanted. Users don't typically want a module that enables spying by a government.

The point is simple, but its implication is profound. To the extent that code is open code, the power of government is constrained. Government can demand, government can threaten, but when the target of its regulation is plastic, it cannot rely on its target remaining as it wants.

Say you are a Soviet propagandist, and you want to get people to read lots of information about Papa Stalin. So you declare that every book published in the Soviet Union must have a chapter devoted to Stalin. How likely is it that such books will actually affect what people read?

Books are open code: They hide nothing; they reveal their source—they are their source! A user or adopter of a book always has the choice to read only the chapters she wants. If it is a book on electronics, then the reader can certainly choose not to read the chapter on Stalin. There is very little the state can do to modify the reader's power in this respect.

The same idea liberates open code. The government's rules are rules only to the extent that they impose restrictions that adopters would want. The government may coordinate standards (like "drive on the right"), but it certainly cannot impose standards that constrain users in ways they do not want to be constrained. This architecture, then, is an important check on the government's regulatory power. Open code means open control—there is control, but the user is aware of it.[25]

Closed code functions differently. With closed code, users cannot easily modify the control that the code comes packaged with. Hackers and very sophisticated programmers may be able to do so, but most users would not know which parts were required and which parts were not. Or more precisely, users would not be able to see the parts required and the parts not required because the source code does not come bundled with closed code. Closed code is the propagandist's best strategy—not a separate chapter that the user can ignore, but a persistent and unrecognized influence that tilts the story in the direction the propagandist wants.

So far I've played fast and loose with the idea of a "user." While some "users" of Firefox could change its code if they didn't like the way it functioned, the vast majority could not. For most of us, it is just as feasible to change the way Microsoft Word functions as it is to change the way GNU/Linux operates.

But the difference here is that there is—and legally can be—a community of developers who modify open code, but there is not—or legally cannot be—a community of developers who modify closed code, at least without the owner's permission. That culture of developers is the critical mechanism that creates the independence within open code. Without that culture, there'd be little real difference between the regulability of open and closed code.

This in turn implies a different sort of limit on this limit on the regulability of code. Communities of developers are likely to enable some types of deviations from rules imposed by governments. For example, they're quite likely to resist the kind of regulation by the French to enable the cracking of financial safety. They're less likely to disable virus protection or spam filters.

WHERE THIS LEADS

My argument so far has taken a simple path. In answer to those who say that the Net cannot be regulated, I've argued that whether it can be regulated depends on its architecture. Some architectures would be regulable, others would not. I have then argued that government could take a role in deciding whether an architecture would be regulable or not. The government could take steps to transform an architecture from unregulable to regulable, both indirectly (by making behavior more traceable) and directly (by using code to directly effect the control the government wants).

The final step in this progression of regulability is a constraint that is only now becoming significant. Government's power to regulate code, to make behavior within the code regulable, depends in part on the character of the code. Open code is less regulable than closed code; to the extent that code becomes open, government's power is reduced.

Take for example the most prominent recent controversy in the area of copyright—peer-to-peer filesharing. As I've described, P2P filesharing is an application that runs on the network. Filesharing networks like StreamCast are simply protocols that P2P applications run. All these protocols are open; anyone can build to them. And because the technology for building to them is widely available, whether or not a particular company builds to them doesn't affect whether they will be built to—but demand does.

Thus, imagine for the moment that the recording industry is successful in driving out of business every business that supports P2P filesharing. The industry won't be successful in driving P2P out of existence. This is because open code has enabled noncommercial actors to sustain the infrastructure of P2P sharing, without the commercial infrastructure.

This is not, obviously, an absolute claim. I am discussing relative, not absolute, regulability. Even with open code, if the government threatens punishments that are severe enough, it will induce a certain compliance. And even with open code, the techniques of identity, tied to code that has been certified as compliant, will still give government plenty of power. Thus, much of the argument from Part I survives this point about open code—if the world becomes certificate-rich, regulability still increases. The same conclusion follows if more code were burned into hardware rather than left to exist as software. Then, even if the code were open, it would not be modifiable.[26]

But when designing an architecture for cyberspace, the margins matter. The values of a given space are not only the values of speech, autonomy, access, or privacy. They may also be values of limited control. As John Perry Barlow puts it, they are the values of a certain bug being programmed into the architecture of the Net—a bug that inhibits the power of government to control the Net perfectly, even if it does not disable that power entirely.

For some, the objective is to build code that disables any possible governmental control. That is not my objective. I certainly believe that government must be constrained, and I endorse the constraints that open code imposes, but it is not my objective to disable government generally. As I've argued already, and as the next part makes plain, some values can be achieved only if government intervenes. Government has a role, even if not as substantial a role as it would wish. We need to understand this role, as well as how our values might be advanced in the context of the Web.

One constraint seems clear in this account. As I argue more extensively later in the book, even if open code does not disable government's power to regulate completely, it certainly changes that power. On the margin, open code reduces the reward from burying regulation in the hidden spaces of code. It functions as a kind of Freedom of Information Act for network regulation. As with ordinary law, open code requires that lawmaking be public, and thus that lawmaking be transparent. In a sense that George Soros ought to understand, open code is a foundation to an open society.

Even this is an important—some might say an essential—check on the power of government. But whether or not one is for transparency generally, my aim so far is just to map out the links. Regulability is conditional on the character of the code, and open code changes that character. It is a limit on government's power to regulate—not necessarily by defeating the power to regulate, but by changing it.

PART THREE

latent ambiguities

The story so far has focused on regulation—both the changing regulability of behavior in cyberspace (it is increasing) and the distinctive way in which behavior in cyberspace will be regulated (through code).

In this Part, I apply the analysis drawn so far to three areas of social and political life that will be affected by these changes—intellectual property, privacy, and free speech.

In each of these areas, I will identify values that are relevant. I will then ask how those values translate to life online. In some cases, the values carry over quite directly, but, in others, they produce what I called in Chapter 2 a "latent ambiguity." That ambiguity forces us to choose between two very different conceptions of the value at stake. My aim is not to make that choice, but instead simply to throw at least two options into relief.

I have another objective in each chapter as well. In my view, the most important lesson about law in cyberspace is the need for law to account for the regulatory effect of code. Just as the wise regulator accounts for the way the market interacts with legal regulation, so too the wise regulator must account for the ways in which technology interacts with legal regulation. That interaction is often counterintuitive. But unless a regulator takes this interactive effect into account, the regulation—whether to control behavior or to protect certain liberties—will fail.

To know what values are relevant, however, we need a method for carrying values into a new context. I begin this part with an account of that method. The values I will describe are part of our tradition, and they need to be interpreted and made real in this context. Thus, I begin this part with one approach that the law has developed for recognizing and respecting these values. This is the interpretive practice I call "translation." A translator practices a fidelity to earlier commitments to value. Latent ambiguities are those instances where fidelity runs out. We have nothing to be faithful to, because the choices we now face are choices that our forbears did not.[1]

NINE

translation

AT THE HEIGHT OF A PREVIOUS WAR ON DRUGS—PROHIBITION, IN THE LATE 1920s—the federal government began using a technique of police work that startled many but proved quite effective: wiretapping.[1] Life had just begun to move onto the wires, and, in an effort to take advantage of the evidence that this new medium might yield, the government began to tap phones without warrants.

Because law enforcement officials themselves were conflicted about the ethics of wiretapping, taps were used sparingly. Nonetheless, for threats perceived to be extremely grave, the technique was deployed. Illegal alcohol, the obsession of the age, was just such a threat.

The most famous of these taps led to the 1928 Supreme Court case *Olmstead v. United States*. The government was investigating one of the largest illegal liquor import, distribution, and sales organizations in the nation. As part of the investigation, the government began to tap the telephones used by dealers and their agents. These were private phones, but the taps were always secured without trespassing on the property of the targets.[2] Instead, the taps were placed on the wires in places where the government had rightful access to the phone lines.

Using these taps, the government recorded many hours of conversations (775 typewritten pages, according to Justice Louis Brandeis),[3] and it used these recordings to convict the defendants in the case. The defendants challenged the use of these recordings, claiming that the government had violated the Constitution in securing them. The Fourth Amendment protects "persons, houses, papers, and effects, against unreasonable searches and seizures," and this wiretapping, the defendants argued, was a violation of their right to be protected from unreasonable searches.

Under then-existing law, it was plain that to enter the apartments of alleged bootlegger Roy Olmstead and his associates and search them (at least while they were gone), the government investigators would have needed a warrant, that is, they would have needed the approval of a judge or magistrate before invading the defendants' privacy. This is what the Fourth Amendment had come to mean—that certain places (persons, houses, papers, and effects) were protected by presumptively requiring a warrant before they could be invaded.[4] Here there had been no warrant, and hence, as the defendants argued, the search had been illegal. The evidence had to be excluded.

We might pause to ask why. If we read the text of the Fourth Amendment carefully, it is hard to see just where a warrant is required:

(a) The right of the people to be secure in their persons, houses, papers, and effects, against unreasonable searches and seizures, shall not be violated, and

(b) no Warrants shall issue, but upon probable cause, supported by Oath or affirmation, and particularly describing the place to be searched, and the persons or things to be seized.

The Fourth Amendment is really two commands. (I've added "a" and "b" to help make the point.) The first says that a certain right ("the right of the People to be secure") shall not be violated; the second limits the conditions under which a warrant shall be issued. But the text of the amendment does not state a relationship between the first part and the second part. And it certainly does not say that a search is unreasonable if it is not supported by a warrant. So why the "warrant requirement"?[5]

To make sense of the amendment, we must go back to its framing. At that time, the legal protection against the invasion of privacy was trespass law. If someone entered your property and rifled through your stuff, that person violated your common law rights against trespass. You could sue that person for trespass, whether he was a police officer or private citizen. The threat of such suits gave the police an incentive not to invade your privacy.[6]

Even without a warrant, however, a trespassing police officer might have a number of defenses. These boil down to whether the search was "reasonable." But there were two important facts about this reasonableness. First, the determination of reasonableness was made by a jury. Neighbors and peers of the officer judged whether his behavior had been proper. Second, in some cases reasonableness was found as a matter of law—that is, the judge would instruct the jury to find that the search had been reasonable. (For example, when the officer found contraband on the property of the defendant, whether there was sufficient suspicion before the search or not, the search was reasonable.)[7]

This regime created obvious risks for an officer before he searched some-one's property. If he searched and found nothing, or if a jury thought later that his search had not been reasonable, then he paid for his illegal behavior by being held personally liable for the rights he had violated.

But the regime also offered insurance against this liability—the warrant. If the officer secured a warrant from a judge before he made his search, the warrant immunized him against trespass liability. If he then found no contra-band or his search turned out to be unreasonable, he still had a defense to a suit.

Creating incentives was one aim of the original system. The law gave an officer an incentive to obtain a warrant before he searched; if he was uncer-tain, or wanted to avoid all risk of liability, he could first check his judgment by asking a judge. But if the officer was sure, or wanted to hazard the gamble, then not getting a warrant did not make the search automatically unreason-able. He was at risk of increased liability, but his liability was all that was at stake.

The weak link in this system was the judge. If judges were too lax, then warrants would be too easy to get,[8] and weak judges were a concern for the framers. Under British rule judges had been appointed by the Crown, and by the time of the Revolution, the Crown was the enemy. Having seen much abuse of the power to issue warrants, the framers were not keen to give judges control in determining whether the government's searches were reasonable.

In particular (as I described in Chapter 2), the framers had in mind some famous cases in which judges and the executive had issued "general warrants" giving government officers the power to search generally for objects of contra-band.[9] In modern terms, these were "fishing expeditions." Because the officers had warrants, they could not be sued; because the judges were largely immune from suit, they could not be sued. Because no one could be sued, there was a temptation for abuse. The framers wanted to avoid just such judge-made abuse. If there was to be immunity, it would come from a jury, or from a suc-cessful search.

This is the origin of clause (b) of the Fourth Amendment. The framers required that judges, when issuing warrants, name particularly "the place to be searched, and the persons or things to be seized," so that judges would not be able to issue warrants of general power. The immunity of the warrant would be limited to particular people and places, and only when probable cause existed to issue the warrant.

This constitutional regime was designed to balance the people's interests in privacy against the legitimate need for the government to search. The offi-cer had an incentive to get a warrant (to avoid the risk of personal liability);

the judge had a rule that restricted the conditions under which he could issue a warrant; and together these structures limited official invasions of privacy to cases that presented a strong reason to invade.

That much is background. But notice what follows.

The original regime presupposed a great deal. Most obviously, it presupposed a common-law system of trespass law—it was the threat of legal liability from trespass law that created the incentives for officers to seek warrants in the first place. This presupposition placed property at the core of the Constitution's original protections.

Equally important, the regime presupposed much about the technology of the time. The Fourth Amendment focuses on trespass because that was the primary mode of searching at the time. If it had been possible simply to view the contents of a house without going inside, the restrictions of the Fourth Amendment would have made little sense. But the protections of the amendment did make sense as a way to draw the balance between government's power to search and the people's right to privacy given the regime of trespass law and privacy-invading technologies that prevailed at the end of the eighteenth century.

Presuppositions—what is taken for granted or considered undebatable— change.[10] How do we respond when such presuppositions change? How do we read a text written against a background of certain presuppositions when those presuppositions no longer apply?

For Americans, or for any nation with a constitution some two hundred years old, this is the central problem for constitutional interpretation. What if state governments, for example, were simply to abolish rights against trespass? Would the amendment be read any differently?[11] What if technologies for searching were to change so dramatically that no one would ever need to enter another's property to know what is kept there? Should the amendment then be read differently?

The history of the Supreme Court's treatment of such questions lacks a perfectly clear pattern, but we can identify two distinct strategies competing for the Court's attention. One strategy is focused on what the framers or founders would have done—the strategy of one-step originalism. The second strategy aims at finding a current reading of the original Constitution that preserves its original meaning in the present context—a strategy that I call translation.

Both strategies are present in the *Olmstead* wiretapping case. When the government tapped the phones of the defendants without any warrant, the Court had to decide whether the use of this kind of evidence was permissible or consistent with the principles of the Fourth Amendment. The defendants said: The government must get a warrant to tap phones. The government said: The Fourth Amendment simply does not apply.

The government's argument was quite simple. The amendment presupposed that the government would be trespassing to search, and it was regulating the conditions under which officers could trespass. But because wiretapping is an invasion of privacy without a trespass, the government is able to tap the defendants' phones without ever entering their property; the amendment therefore does not apply. It simply does not reach to protect invasions that are invasions without trespass.

The Supreme Court agreed. In an opinion written by Chief Justice (and former President) William Howard Taft, the Court followed the government.

The amendment does not forbid what was done here. There was no searching. There was no seizure. The evidence was secured only by the use of the sense of hearing and that only. The language of the amendment cannot be extended and expanded to include telephone wires reaching to the whole world from the defendant's house or office.[12]

This conclusion was received with surprise and shock. Already much of life had moved to the wires. People were beginning to understand what it meant to have intimate contact "online"; they counted on the telephone system to protect their intimate secrets. Indeed, telephone companies, having strongly fought the authority that the government claimed, pledged not to assist the government except as required by law.[13] This resistance notwithstanding, the Court concluded that the Constitution did not interfere with invasions of this sort. It would not have done so when the Constitution was written; it did not do so at the time when the case was decided.

But the dissent written by Justice Brandeis (there was also a dissent by Justices Holmes, Stone, and Butler) had a different view. As with Taft's opinion, the focus was fidelity. But his fidelity was quite differently conceived.

Brandeis acknowledged that the Fourth Amendment, as originally written, applied only to trespass.[14] But it did so, he argued, because when it was written trespass was the technology for invading privacy. That was the framers' presupposition, but that presupposition had now changed. Given this change, Brandeis argued, it was the Court's responsibility to read the amendment in a way that preserved its meaning, changed circumstances notwithstanding. The aim must be to translate the original protections into a context in which the technology for invading privacy had changed.[15] This would be done, Brandeis argued, by applying the Fourth Amendment's protection to invasions that were not themselves trespasses.

These two opinions mark two different modes of constitutional interpretation. Taft finds fidelity by simply repeating what the framers did; Brandeis finds fidelity by finding the current equivalent to what the framers did. If we followed Taft, Brandeis argued, we would defeat the protections for privacy that the framers originally set; if we followed Brandeis, Taft implied, we would be adding something to the Constitution that the framers had not written.

Partisans on both sides claimed that the opinion of the other would have "changed" the meaning of the Constitution. But whose opinion, the Court's or Justice Brandeis's, would really "change" the meaning of the Fourth Amendment?

To answer this question, we must first ask: Change relative to what? What is the baseline against which this change is a change? Certainly Brandeis would have agreed that in 1791 any finding by the Court that the amendment reached beyond trespass would have been improper. But when something presupposed by the original amendment has changed, is it clear that the Court's proper response is to act as if nothing has changed at all?

Brandeis's method accounted for the changed presupposition. He offered a reading that changed the scope of the amendment in order to maintain the amendment's protection of privacy. Taft, on the other hand, offered a reading that maintained the scope of the amendment but changed its protection of privacy. Each reading kept something constant; each also changed something. The question is: Which reading preserved what fidelity demands should be preserved?

We might better see the point through a somewhat stylized re-creation. Imagine that we could quantify privacy; we could thus describe the change in the quantity of privacy that any change in technology might bring. (Robert Post has given an absolutely persuasive argument about why privacy is not quantifiable, but my purposes here are simply illustrative.[16]) Imagine that in 1791 protecting against physical trespass protected 90 percent of personal privacy. The government could still stand on the street and listen through open windows, but the invasion presented by that threat was small, all things considered. For the most part, a regime that protected against trespass also protected privacy.

When telephones came along, however, this protection changed. A lot of private information was put out across the phone lines. Now, if tapping was not trespass, much less of private life was protected from government snooping. Rather than 90 percent being protected by the amendment, only 50 percent was protected.

Brandeis wanted to read the amendment so that it protected the 90 percent it originally protected—even though doing so required that it protect against more than simple trespass. He wanted to read it differently, we could say, so that it protected the same.

This form of argument is common in our constitutional history, and it is central to the best in our constitutional tradition.[17] It is an argument that responds to changed circumstances by proposing a reading that neutralizes those changes and preserves an original meaning. It is an argument invoked by justices on both the right and the left,[18] and it is a way to keep life in a constitutional provision—to make certain that changes in the world do not change the meaning of the Constitution's text. It is an argument, we can say, that aims at translating the protections that the Fourth Amendment gave in 1791 into the same set of protections at any time later in our history. It acknowledges that to do this the Court may have to read the amendment differently, but it is not reading the amendment differently to improve the amendment or to add to its protections. It is reading the amendment differently to accommodate the changes in protection that have resulted from changes in technology. It is translation to preserve meaning.

If there is a justice who deserves cyberspace's praise, if there is a Supreme Court opinion that should be the model for cyber activists in the future, if there is a first chapter in the fight to protect cyberspace, it is this justice, this opinion, and this case. Brandeis gave us a model for reading the Constitution to preserve its meaning, and its values, across time and context. It is a method that recognizes what has changed and accommodates that change to preserve something of what the framers originally gave us. It is a method that translates the Constitution's meaning across fundamentally different contexts—whether they are as temporally distant as we are from the framers or as distant as cyberspace is from real space.

But it was Taft's opinion that became law and his narrow view of the Fourth Amendment that prevailed. It took forty years for the Supreme Court to embrace Brandeis's picture of the Fourth Amendment—40 years before *Olmstead* was overruled. The case overruling it was *Katz v. United States*.[19]

Charles Katz was suspected of transmitting gambling information to clients in other states by telephone. Federal agents recorded his half of several of his telephone calls by attaching an eavesdropping device to the outside of a public phone booth where he made his calls. Katz was convicted on the basis of this evidence, and the court of appeals upheld the conviction on the basis of *Olmstead*.

Harvard Law School Professor Laurence Tribe was involved in the case at the beginning of his legal career:

> As a [law] clerk to Supreme Court Justice Potter Stewart, I found myself working on a case involving the government's electronic surveillance of a suspected criminal in the form of a tiny device attached to the outside of a public telephone booth. Because

the invasion of the suspect's privacy was accomplished without physical trespass into a "constitutionally protected area," the Federal Government argued, relying upon *Olmstead,* that there had been no "search" or "seizure" and therefore the Fourth Amendment "right of the people to be secure in their persons, houses, papers, and effects, against unreasonable searches and seizures" simply did not apply.

At first, there were only four votes to overrule *Olmstead* and to hold the Fourth Amendment applicable to wiretapping and electronic eavesdropping. I'm proud to say that, as a 26-year-old kid, I had at least a little bit to do with changing that number from four to seven—and with the argument, formally adopted by a seven-Justice majority in December 1967, that the Fourth Amendment "protects people, not places" [389 US at 351]. In that decision, *Katz v. United States,* the Supreme Court finally repudiated *Olmstead* and the many decisions that had relied upon it, reasoning that, given the role of electronic telecommunications in modern life, the [First Amendment] purposes of protecting free speech as well as the [Fourth Amendment] purposes of protecting privacy require treating as a "search" any invasion of a person's confidential telephone communications, with or without physical trespass.[20]

The Court in *Katz* followed Brandeis rather than Taft. It sought a reading of the Fourth Amendment that made sense of the amendment in a changed context. In the framers' context of 1791, protecting against trespass to property was an effective way to protect against trespass to privacy, but in the *Katz* context of the 1960s it was not. In the 1960s much of intimate life was conducted in places where property rules did not reach (in the "ether," for example, of the AT&T telephone network). And so a regime that made privacy hang on property did not protect privacy to the same degree that the framers had intended. Justice Stewart in *Katz* sought to remedy that by linking the Fourth Amendment to a more direct protection of privacy.

The link was the idea of "a reasonable expectation of privacy." The core value, Stewart wrote, was the protection of "people, not places."[21] Hence, the core technique should be to protect people where they have a reasonable expectation of privacy. Where this is the case, the government cannot invade that space without satisfying the requirements of the Fourth Amendment.

There is much to admire in Stewart's opinion, at least to the extent that he is willing to fashion tools for preserving the Constitution's meaning in changed circumstances—or again, to the extent that he attempts to translate the protections of the Fourth Amendment into a modern context. There is also much to question.[22] But we can put those questions aside for the moment and focus on one feature of the problem that is fairly uncontentious.

While lines will be hard to draw, it is at least fairly clear that the framers made a conscious choice to protect privacy. This was not an issue off the table of their original debate or a question they did not notice. And this is not the "right to privacy" that conservatives complain about in the context of the right to abortion. This is the right to be free from state intrusion into the "sanctity" of a private home. State-enforced threats to individual privacy were at the center of the movement that led to the republic. Brandeis and Stewart simply aimed to effect that choice in contexts where the earlier structure had grown ineffectual.

Translations like these are fairly straightforward. The original values chosen are fairly clear; the way in which contexts undermine the original application is easily grasped; and the readings that would restore the original values are fairly obvious. Of course, such cases often require a certain interpretive courage—a willingness to preserve interpretive fidelity by changing an interpretive practice. But at least the direction is clear, even if the means are a bit unseemly.[23]

These are the easy cases. They are even easier when we are not trying to carry values from some distant past into the future but instead are simply carrying values from one context into another. When we know what values we want to preserve, we need only be creative about how to preserve them.

Cyberspace will present many such easy cases. When courts confront them, they should follow the example of Brandeis: They should translate, and they should push the Supreme Court to do likewise. Where circumstances have changed to nullify the protections of some original right, the Court should adopt a reading of the Constitution that restores that right.

But some cases will not be so easy. Sometimes translation will not be an option, and sometimes the values that translation would track are values we no longer want to preserve. Sometimes we cannot tell which values translation would select. This was the problem in Chapter 2 with the worm, which made the point about latent ambiguities. Changing contexts sometimes reveals an ambiguity latent in the original context. We must then choose between two different values, either of which could be said to be consistent with the original value. Since either way could be said to be right, we cannot say that the original context (whether now or two hundred years ago) decided the case.

Professor Tribe describes an example in a founding article in the law of cyberspace, "The Constitution in Cyberspace."[24] Tribe sketches a method of reading the Constitution in cyberspace that aims to make the Constitution "technologically neutral." The objective is to adopt readings (or perhaps even an amendment) that make it plain that changes in technology are not to change the Constitution's meaning. We must always adopt readings of the Constitution that preserve its original values. When dealing with cyberspace, judges are to be translators: Different technologies are the different languages, and the aim is to find a reading of the Constitution that preserves its meaning from one world's technology to another.[25]

This is fidelity as translation. This kind of translation speaks as if it is just carrying over something that has already been said. It hides the creativity in its act; it feigns a certain polite or respectful deference. This way of reading the Constitution insists that the important political decisions have already been made and all that is required is a kind of technical adjustment. It aims to keep the piano in tune as it is moved from one concert hall to another.

But Tribe then offers an example that may make this method seem empty. The question is about the meaning of the confrontation clause of the Sixth Amendment—the defendant's right in a criminal trial "to be confronted with the witnesses against him." How, Tribe asks, should we read this clause today?

At the time of the founding, he argues, the technology of confrontation was simple—confrontation was two-way. If a witness confronted the accused, the accused, of necessity, confronted the witness. This was a necessity given to us by the technology of the time. But today it is possible for confrontation to be one-way—the witness confronts the accused, but the accused need not confront the witness. The question then is whether the confrontation clause requires one-way or two-way confrontation.[26]

Let us grant that Tribe's descriptions of the available technologies are correct and that the framers embraced the only confrontation clause that their technology permitted. The real question comes in step two. Now that technology allows two possibilities—one-way or two-way confrontation—which does the Constitution require?

The Court's answer in its 1990 decision in *Maryland v. Craig* was clear: The Constitution requires only one-way confrontation. A confrontation clause regime that permits only one-way confrontation, at least when there are strong interests in not requiring two, is a fair translation of the original clause.[27]

As a matter of political choice, I certainly like this answer. But I do not see its source. It seems to me that this is a question the framers did not decide, and a question that if presented to them might well have divided them. Given the technology of 1791, they did not have to decide between one-way and two-way confrontation; given the conflict of values at stake, it is not obvious how they would have decided it. Thus, to speak as if there were an answer here that the framers gave us is a bit misleading. The framers gave no answer here, and, in my view, no answer can be drawn from what they said.

Like the worm in Chapter 2, the confrontation clause presents a latent ambiguity.[28] Constitutional law in cyberspace will reveal many more such latent ambiguities. And these ambiguities offer us a choice: How will we go on?

Choices are not terrible. It is not a disaster if we must make a decision—as long as we are capable of it. But here is the nub of the problem as I see it. As I argue in more detail in Part IV, given the current attitudes of our courts, and our legal culture generally, constitutional choices are costly. We are bad at making them; we are not likely to get better at it soon.

When there is no answer about how to proceed—when the translation leaves open a question—we have two sorts of responses in constitutional practice. One response is passive: The court simply lets the legislature decide. This is the response that Justice Scalia presses in the context of the Fourteenth Amendment. On matters that, to the framers, were "undebatable," the Constitution does not speak.[29] In this case, only the legislature can engage and press questions of constitutional value and thus say what the Constitution will continue to mean.

The second response is more active: The court finds a way to articulate constitutional values that were not present at the founding. The courts help spur a conversation about these fundamental values—or at least add their voice to this conversation—to focus a debate that may ultimately be resolved elsewhere. The first response is a way of doing nothing; the second is a way of exciting a dialogue about constitutional values as a means to confronting and resolving new questions.[30]

My fear about cyberspace is that we will respond in the first way—that the courts, the institutions most responsible for articulating constitutional values, will stand back while issues of constitutional import are legislatively determined. My sense is that they will step back because they feel (as the balance of this book argues) that these are new questions that cyberspace has raised. Their newness will make them feel political, and when a question feels political, courts step away from resolving it.

I fear this not because I fear legislatures, but because in our day constitutional discourse at the level of the legislature is a very thin sort of discourse. The philosopher Bernard Williams has argued that because the Supreme Court has taken so central a role in the articulation of constitutional values, legislatures no longer do.[31] Whether Williams is correct or not, this much is clear: The constitutional discourse of our present Congress is far below the level at which it must be to address the questions about constitutional values that will be raised by cyberspace.

How we could reach beyond this thinness of discourse is unclear. Constitutional thought has been the domain of lawyers and judges for too long. We have been trapped by a mode of reasoning that pretends that all the important questions have already been answered, that our job now is simply to translate them for modern times. As a result, we do not quite know how to proceed when we think the answers are not already there. As nations across the world struggle to express and embrace constitutional values, we, with the oldest written constitutional tradition, have lost the practice of embracing, articulating, and deciding on constitutional values.

I return to this problem in Chapter 15. For now, my point is simply descriptive. Translation is one way to deal with the choices that cyberspace presents. It is one way of finding equivalence across contexts. But in the four applications that follow, I press the question: Is the past enough? Are there choices the framers did not address? Are they choices that we must make?[32]

TEN

intellectual property

HAROLD REEVES IS AMONG THE BEST RESEARCH ASSISTANTS I HAVE HAD. (BUT ALAS, the law has now lost him—he's become a priest!). Early into his second year at the University of Chicago Law School, he came to me with an idea he had for a student "comment"—an article that would be published in the law review.[1] The topic was trespass law in cyberspace—whether and how the law should protect owners of space in cyberspace from the kinds of intrusions that trespass law protects against in real space. His initial idea was simple: There should be no trespass law in cyberspace.[2] The law should grant "owners" of space in cyberspace no legal protection against invasion; they should be forced to fend for themselves.

Reeves's idea was a bit nutty, and in the end, I think, wrong.[3] But it contained an insight that was quite brilliant, and that should be central to thinking about law in cyberspace.

The idea—much more briefly and much less elegantly than Reeves has put it—is this: The question that law should ask is, What means would bring about the most efficient set of protections for property interests in cyberspace? Two sorts of protections are possible. One is the traditional protection of law—the law defines a space where others should not enter and punishes people who enter nonetheless. The other protection is a fence, a technological device (a bit of code) that (among other things) blocks the unwanted from entering. In real space, of course, we have both—law, in the form of trespass law, and fences that supplement that law. Both cost money, and the return from each is not necessarily the same. From a social perspective, we would want the mix that provides optimal protection at the lowest cost. (In economics-speak, we would want a mix such that the marginal cost of an additional unit of protection is equivalent to the marginal benefit.)

The implication of this idea in real space is that it sometimes makes sense to shift the burden of protection to citizens rather than to the state. If, for example, a farmer wants to store some valuable seed on a remote part of his farm, it is better for him to bear the cost of fencing in the seed than to require the police to patrol the area more consistently or to increase the punishment for those they catch. The question is always one of balance between the costs and benefits of private protection and state protection.

Reeves's insight about cyberspace follows the same line. The optimal protection for spaces in cyberspace is a mix between public law and private fences. The question to ask in determining the mix is which protection, on the margin, costs less. Reeves argues that the costs of law in this context are extremely high—in part because of the costs of enforcement, but also because it is hard for the law to distinguish between legitimate and illegitimate uses of cyberspaces. There are many "agents" that might "use" the space of cyberspace. Web spiders, which gather data for web search engines; browsers, who are searching across the Net for stuff to see; hackers (of the good sort) who are testing the locks of spaces to see that they are locked; and hackers (of the bad sort) who are breaking and entering to steal. It is hard, ex ante, for the law to know which agent is using the space legitimately and which is not. Legitimacy depends on the intention of the person granting access.

So that led Reeves to his idea: Since the intent of the "owner" is so crucial here, and since the fences of cyberspace can be made to reflect that intent cheaply, it is best to put all the incentive on the owner to define access as he wishes. The right to browse should be the norm, and the burden to lock doors should be placed on the owner.[4]

Now put Reeves's argument aside, and think for a second about something that will seem completely different but is very much the same idea. Think about "theft" and the protections that we have against it.

- I have a stack of firewood behind my house. No one steals it. If I left my bike out overnight, it would be gone.
- A friend told me that, in a favorite beach town, the city used to find it impossible to plant flowers—they would immediately be picked. But now, he proudly reports, after a long "community spirit" campaign, the flowers are no longer picked.
- There are special laws about the theft of automobiles, planes, and boats. There are no special laws about the theft of skyscrapers. Cars, planes, and boats need protection. Skyscrapers pretty much take care of themselves.

Many things protect property against theft—differently. The market protects my firewood (it is cheaper to buy your own than it is to haul mine away); the market is a special threat to my bike (which if taken is easily sold). Norms sometimes protect flowers in a park; sometimes they do not. Nature sometimes conspires with thieves (cars, planes, and boats) and sometimes against them (skyscrapers).

These protections are not fixed. I could lock my bike and thereby use real-space code to make it harder to steal. There could be a shortage of firewood; demand would increase, making it harder to protect. Public campaigns about civic beauty might stop flower theft; selecting a distinctive flower might do the same. Sophisticated locks might make stolen cars useless; sophisticated bank fraud might make skyscrapers vulnerable. The point is not that protections are given, or unchangeable, but that they are multiplied and their modalities different.

Property is protected by the sum of the different protections that law, norms, the market, and real-space code yield. This is the implication of the argument made in Chapter 7. From the point of view of the state, we need law only when the other three modalities leave property vulnerable. From the point of view of the citizen, real-space code (such as locks) is needed when laws and norms alone do not protect enough. Understanding how property is protected means understanding how these different protections work together.

Reeves's idea and these reflections on firewood and skyscrapers point to the different ways that law might protect "property" and suggest the range of kinds of property that law might try to protect. They also invite a question that has been asked by Justice Stephen Breyer and many others: Should law protect some kinds of property—in particular, intellectual property—at all?[5]

Among the kinds of property law might protect, my focus in this chapter will be on the property protected by copyright.[6] Of all the different types of property, this type is said to be the most vulnerable to the changes that cyberspace will bring. Many believe that intellectual property cannot be protected in cyberspace. And in the terms that I've sketched, we can begin to see why one might think this, but we will soon see that this thought must be wrong.

ON THE REPORTS OF COPYRIGHT'S DEMISE

Roughly put, copyright gives a copyright holder certain exclusive rights over the work, including, most famously, the exclusive right to copy the work. I have a copyright in this book. That means, among other rights, and subject to some important exceptions, you cannot copy this book without my permission. The right is protected to the extent that laws (and norms) support it, and it is threatened to the extent that technology makes it easy to copy. Strengthen the law while holding technology constant, and the right is stronger. Proliferate copying technology while holding the law constant, and the right is weaker.

In this sense, copyright has always been at war with technology. Before the printing press, there was not much need to protect an author's interest in his creative work. Copying was so expensive that nature itself protected that interest. But as the cost of copying decreased, and the spread of technologies for copying increased, the threat to the author's control increased. As each generation has delivered a technology better than the last, the ability of the copyright holder to protect her intellectual property has been weakened.

Until recently, the law's response to these changes has been measured and gradual. When technologies to record and reproduce sound emerged at the turn of the last century, composers were threatened by them. The law responded by giving composers a new, but limited, right to profit from recordings. When radio began broadcasting music, the composers were held to be entitled to compensation for the public performance of their work, but performers were not compensated for the "performance" of their recordings. Congress decided not to remedy that problem. When cable television started rebroadcasting television broadcasts, the copyright holders in the original broadcasts complained their work was being exploited without compensation. Congress responded by granting the copyright holders a new, but limited, right to profit from the rebroadcasts. When the VCR made it simple to record copyrighted content from off the air, copyright holders cried "piracy." Congress decided not to respond to that complaint. Sometimes the change in technology inspired Congress to create new rights, and sometimes not. But throughout this history, new technologies have been embraced as they have enabled the spread of culture.

During the same period, norms about copyrighted content also evolved. But the single, defining feature of these norms can perhaps be summarized like this: that a consumer could do with the copyrighted content that he legally owned anything he wanted to do, without ever triggering the law of copyright. This norm was true almost by definition until 1909, since before then, the law didn't regulate "copies." Any use the consumer made of copyrighted content was therefore highly unlikely to trigger any of the exclusive rights of copyright. After 1909, though the law technically regulated "copies," the technologies to make copies were broadly available. There was a struggle about Xerox machines, which forced a bit of reform,[7] but the first real conflict that copyright law had with consumers happened when cassette tapes made it easy to copy recorded music. Some of that copying was for the purpose of making a "mixed tape," and some was simply for the purpose of avoiding the need to buy the original recording. After many years of debate, Congress decided not to legislate a ban on home taping. Instead, in the Audio Home Recording Act, Congress signaled fairly clear exemptions from copyright for such consumer activity. These changes reinforced the norm among consumers that they were legally free to do whatever they wanted with copyrighted work. Given the technologies most consumers had access to, the stuff they wanted to do either did not trigger copyright (e.g., resell their books to a used bookstore), or if it did, the law was modified to protect it (e.g., cassette tapes).

Against the background of these gradual changes in the law, along with the practical norm that, in the main, the law didn't reach consumers, the changes of digital technology were a considerable shock. First, from the perspective of technology, digital technologies, unlike their analog sister, enabled perfect copies of an original work. The return from copying was therefore greater. Second, also from the perspective of technology, the digital technology of the Internet enabled content to be freely (and effectively anonymously) distributed across the Internet. The availability of copies was therefore greater. Third, from the perspective of norms, consumers who had internalized the norm that they could do with "their content" whatever they wanted used these new digital tools to make "their content" available widely on the Internet. Companies such as Napster helped fuel this behavior, but the practice existed both before and after Napster. And fourth, from the perspective of law, because the base technology of the Internet didn't reveal anything about the nature of the content being shared on the Internet, or about who was doing the sharing, there was little the law could do to stop this massive "sharing" of content. Thus fifth, and from the perspective of copyright holders, digital technologies and the Internet were the perfect storm for their business model: If they made money by controlling the distribution of "copies" of copyrighted content, you could well understand why they viewed the Internet as a grave threat.

Very quickly, and quite early on, the content industry responded to this threat. Their first line of defense was a more aggressive regime of regulation. Because, the predictions of cyberspace mavens notwithstanding, not everyone was willing to concede that copyright law was dead. Intellectual property lawyers and interest groups pushed early on to have law shore up the protections of intellectual property that cyberspace seemed certain to erase.

LAW TO THE RESCUE

The initial response to this push was a White Paper produced by the Commerce Department in 1995. The paper outlined a series of modifications aimed, it said, at restoring "balance" in intellectual property law. Entitled "Intellectual Property and the National Information Infrastructure," the report sought to restate existing intellectual property law in terms that anyone could understand, as well as to recommend changes in the law in response to the changes the Net would bring. But as scholars quickly pointed out, the first part was a bust.[8] The report no more "restated" existing law than Soviet historians "retold" stories of Stalin's administration. The restatement had a tilt, very definitely in the direction of increased intellectual property protection, but it pretended that its tilt was the natural lay of the land.

For our purposes, however, it is the recommendations that were most significant. The government proposed four responses to the threat presented by cyberspace. In the terms of Chapter 7, these responses should be familiar.

The first response was traditional. The government proposed changes in the law of copyright to "clarify" the rights that it was to protect.[9] These changes were intended to better define the rights granted under intellectual property law and to further support these rights with clarified (and possibly greater) legal penalties for their violation.

The second response addressed norms, specifically copying norms. The report recommended increased educational efforts, both in schools and among the general public, about the nature of intellectual property and the importance of protecting it. In the terms of Chapter 7, this is the use of law to change norms so that norms will better support the protection of intellectual property. It is an indirect regulation of behavior by direct regulation of norms.

The third and fourth responses mixed technology and the market. The report called for legal support—through financial subsidies and special legal protection—of "copyright management schemes." These "schemes" were simply technologies that would make it easier to control access to and use of copyrighted material. We will explore these "schemes" at some length later in this chapter, but I mention them now as another example of indirect regulation—using the market to subsidize the development of a certain software tool, and using law to regulate the properties of other software tools. Copyright management systems would be supported by government funding and by the threat of criminal sanctions for anyone deploying software to crack them.[10]

Congress followed the recommendations of the 1995 White Paper in some respects. The most important was the enactment of the Digital Millennium Copyright Act in 1998. That statute implemented directly the recommendation that "technological protection measures" be protected by law. Code that someone implements to control either access to or use of a copyrighted work got special legal protection under the DMCA: Circumvention of that code, subject to a few important exceptions, constituted a violation of the law.

We will return to the DMCA later. The point just now, however, is to recognize something important about the presumption underlying the White Paper. The 1995 package of proposals was a scattershot of techniques—some changes in law, some support for changing norms, and lots of support for changing the code of cyberspace to make it better able to protect intellectual property. Perhaps nothing better than this could have been expected in 1995—the law promised a balance of responses to deal with the shifting balance brought on by cyberspace.

Balance is attractive, and moderation seems right. But something is missing from this approach. The White Paper proceeds as if the problem of protecting intellectual property in cyberspace was just like the problem of protecting intellectual property in real space. It proceeds as if the four constraints would operate in the same proportions as in real space, as if nothing fundamental had changed.

But something fundamental has changed: the role that code plays in the protection of intellectual property. Code can, and increasingly will, displace law as the primary defense of intellectual property in cyberspace. Private fences, not public law.

The White Paper did not see this. Built into its scattershot of ideas is one that is crucial to its approach but fundamentally incorrect—the idea that the nature of cyberspace is anarchy. The White Paper promises to strengthen law in every area it can. But it approaches the question like a ship battening down for a storm: Whatever happens, the threat to copyright is real, damage will be done, and the best we can do is ride it out.

This is fundamentally wrong. We are not entering a time when copyright is more threatened than it is in real space. We are instead entering a time when copyright is more effectively protected than at any time since Gutenberg. The power to regulate access to and use of copyrighted material is about to be perfected. Whatever the mavens of the mid-1990s may have thought, cyberspace is about to give holders of copyrighted property the biggest gift of protection they have ever known.

In such an age, the real question for law is not, how can law aid in that protection? but rather, is the protection too great? The mavens were right when they predicted that cyberspace will teach us that everything we thought about copyright was wrong.[11] But the lesson in the future will be that copyright is protected far too well. The problem will center not on copy-right but on copy-duty—the duty of owners of protected property to make that property accessible.

That's a big claim. To see it, however, and to see the consequences it entails, we need consider three examples. The first is a vision of a researcher from Xerox PARC (appropriately enough), Mark Stefik, and his idea of "trusted systems."[12] The second is an implication of a world dominated by trusted systems. The third is an unreckoned cost to the path we are now on to "protect intellectual property." The examples will throw into relief the threat that these changes present for values that our tradition considers fundamental. They should force us to make a choice about those values, and about their place in our future.

THE PROMISE FOR INTELLECTUAL PROPERTY IN CYBERSPACE

It all depends on whether you really understand the idea of trusted systems. If you don't understand them, then this whole approach to commerce and digital publishing is utterly unthinkable. If you do understand them, then it all follows easily.

Ralph Merkle, quoted in Stefik, "Letting Loose the Light" (1996)

In what we can call the first generation of digital technologies, content owners were unable to control who copied what. If you have a copy of a copyrighted photo rendered in a graphics file, you could make unlimited copies of that file with no effect on the original. When you make the one-hundredth copy, nothing would indicate that it was the one-hundredth copy rather than the first. And as we've described again and again, in the original code of the Internet, there was nothing to regulate how or to whom copyrighted content was distributed. The function of "copying" as it was developed by the coders who built it, either in computers or networks, aimed at "copying"—not at "copying" with specified permissions.

This character to the function "copy" was not unique to cyberspace. We have seen a technology that presented the same problem, and I've already described how a solution was subsequently built into the technology.[13] Digital Audio Tape (DAT) technology was thought to be a threat to copyright owners. A number of solutions to this threat were proposed. Some people argued for higher penalties for illegal copying of tapes (direct regulation by law). Some, such as Richard Stallman, argued for a tax on blank tapes, with the proceeds compensating copyright holders (indirect regulation of the market by law). Some argued for better education to stop illegal copies of tapes (indirect regulation of norms by law). But some argued for a change in the code of DAT machines that would block unlimited perfect copying.

The tax and code regulators won. In late 1992, as a compromise between the technology and content industries, Congress passed the Audio Home Recording Act. The act first imposed a tax on both recorders and blank DAT media, with the revenues to be used to compensate copyright holders for the expected copyright infringement enabled by the technology. But more interestingly, the Act required manufacturers of DAT technology to include a Serial Copy Management System, which would limit the ability of DAT technology to copy. That limit was effected through a code inserted in copies made using DAT technology. From an original, the technology would always permit a copy. But from a copy made on a DAT recorder, no further digital copy could be made. (An analog copy could be made, thus degrading the quality of the copy, but not a perfect digital copy.) The technology was thus designed to break the "copy" function under certain conditions, so as to indirectly protect copyright owners. The net effect of these two changes was to minimize any harm from the technology, as well as to limit the functionality of the technology where it would be expected that functionality would encourage the violation of copyright. (Many think the net effect of this regulation also killed DAT technology.)

Something like the same idea animated Stefik's vision.[14] He was not keen to make the quality of copies decrease. Rather, his objective was to make it possible to track and control the copies of digital content that are made.[15]

Think of the proposal like this. Today, when you buy a book, you may do any number of things with it. You can read it once or one hundred times. You can lend it to a friend. You can photocopy pages in it or scan it into your computer. You can burn it, use it as a paperweight, or sell it. You can store it on your shelf and never once open it.

Some of these things you can do because the law gives you the right to do them—you can sell the book, for example, because the copyright law explicitly limits the copyright owner's right to control your use of the physical book after the "first sale." Other things you can do because there is no effective way to stop you. A book seller might sell you the book at one price if you promise to read it once, and at a different price if you want to read it one hundred times, but there is no way for the seller to know whether you have obeyed the contract. In principle, the seller could sell a police officer with each book to follow you around and make sure you use the book as you promised, but the costs of this control would plainly exceed any benefit.

But what if each of these rights could be controlled, and each unbundled and sold separately? What if, that is, the software itself could regulate whether you read the book once or one hundred times; whether you could cut and paste from it or simply read it without copying; whether you could send it as an attached document to a friend or simply keep it on your machine; whether you could delete it or not; whether you could use it in another work, for another purpose, or not; or whether you could simply have it on your shelf or have it and use it as well?

Stefik describes a network that makes such unbundling of rights possible. He describes an architecture that would allow owners of copyrighted materials to sell access to those materials on the terms they want and would enforce those contracts.

The details of the system are not important here (it builds on the encryption architecture I described in Chapter 4),[16] but its general idea is easy enough to describe. As the Net is now, basic functions like copying and access are crudely regulated in an all-or-nothing fashion. You generally have the right to copy or not, to gain access or not.

But a more sophisticated system of rights could be built into the Net— not into a different Net, but on top of the existing Net. This system would function by discriminating in the intercourse it has with other systems. A system that controlled access in this more fine-grained way would grant access to its resources only to another system that controlled access in the same way. A hierarchy of systems would develop, and copyrighted material would be traded only among systems that properly controlled access.

In such a world, then, you could get access, say, to the *New York Times* and pay a different price depending on how much of it you read. The *Times* could determine how much you read, whether you could copy portions of the newspaper, whether you could save it on your hard disk, and so on. But if the code you used to access the *Times* site did not enable the control the *Times* demanded, then the *Times* would not let you onto its site at all. In short, systems would exchange information only with others that could be trusted, and the protocols of trust would be built into the architectures of the systems.

Stefik calls this "trusted systems," and the name evokes a helpful analog. Think of bonded couriers. Sometimes you want to mail a letter with something particularly valuable in it. You could simply give it to the post office, but the post office is not a terribly reliable system; it has relatively little control over its employees, and theft and loss are not uncommon. So instead of going to the post office, you could give your letter to a bonded courier. Bonded couriers are insured, and the insurance is a cost that constrains them to be reliable. This reputation then makes it possible for senders of valuable material to be assured about using their services. As Stefik writes:

> with trusted systems, a substantial part of the enforcement of a digital contract
> is carried out by the trusted system. [T]he consumer does not have the option of

disregarding a digital contract by, for example, making unauthorized copies of a work. A trusted system refuses to exercise a right that is not sanctioned by the digital contract.[17]

This is what a structure of trusted systems does for owners of intellectual property. It is a bonded courier that takes the thing of value and controls access to and use of it according to the orders given by the principal.

Imagine for a moment that such a structure emerged generally in cyberspace. How would we then think about copyright law?

An important point about copyright law is that, though designed in part to protect authors, the control it was designed to create was never to be perfect. As the Supreme Court noted, copyright "protection has never accorded the copyright owner complete control over all possible uses of his work."[18] Thus, the law grants only particular exclusive rights, and those rights are subject to important limitations, such as "fair use," limited terms, and the first sale doctrine. The law threatened to punish violators of copyright laws—and it was this threat that induced a fairly high proportion of people to comply—but the law was never designed to simply do the author's bidding. It had public purposes as well as the author's interest in mind.

Trusted systems provide authors with the same sort of protection. Because authors can restrict unauthorized use of their material, they can extract money in exchange for access. Trusted systems thus achieve what copyright law aims to, but they can achieve this protection without the law doing the restricting. It permits a much more fine-grained control over access to and use of protected material than the law permits, and it can do so without the aid of the law.

What copyright seeks to do using the threat of law and the push of norms, trusted systems do through the code. Copyright orders others to respect the rights of the copyright holder before using his property; trusted systems give access only if rights are respected in the first place. The controls needed to regulate this access are built into the systems, and no users (except hackers) have a choice about whether to obey them. The code complements the law by codifying the rules, making them more efficient.

Trusted systems in this sense are a privatized alternative to copyright law. They need not be exclusive; there is no reason not to use both law and trusted systems. Nevertheless, the code is effectively doing the work that the law was designed to do. It implements the law's protection, through code, far more effectively than the law did.

What could be wrong with this? We do not worry when people put double bolts on their doors to supplement the work of the neighborhood cop. We do not worry when they lock their cars and take their keys. It is not an offense to protect yourself rather than rely on the state. Indeed, in some contexts it is a virtue. Andrew Jackson's mother, for example, told him, "Never tell a lie, nor take what is not your own, nor sue anybody for slander, assault and battery. Always settle them cases yourself."[19] Self-sufficiency is strength and going to the law a sign of weakness.

There are two steps to answering this question. The first rehearses a familiar but forgotten point about the nature of "property"; the second makes a less familiar, but central, point about the nature of intellectual property. Together they suggest why perfect control is not the control that law has given owners of intellectual property. And together they suggest the potential problem that copyright law in cyberspace will create.

THE LIMITS ON THE PROTECTION OF PROPERTY

The realists in American legal history (circa 1890–1930) were scholars who (in part) emphasized the role of the state in what was called "private law."[20] At the time they wrote, it was the "private" in private law that got all the emphasis. Forgotten was the "law," as if "property" and "contract" existed independent of the state.

The realists' aim was to undermine this view. Contract and property law, they argued, gave private parties power.[21] If you breach a contract with me, I can have the court order the sheriff to force you to pay; the contract gives me access to the state power of the sheriff. If your contract with your employer says that it may dismiss you for being late, then the police can be called in to eject you if you refuse to leave. If your lease forbids you to have cats, then the landlord can use the power of the courts to evict you if you do not get rid of the cats. These are all instances where contract and property, however grounded in private action, give a private person an entitlement to the state.

No doubt this power is justified in many cases; to call it "law" is not to call it unjust. The greatest prosperity in history has been created by a system in which private parties can order their lives freely through contract and property. But whether justified in the main or not, the realists argued that the contours of this "law" should be architected to benefit society.[22]

This is not communism. It is not an attack on private property, and it is not to say that the state creates wealth (put your Ayn Rand away). These are claims about the relationship between private law and public law, and they should be uncontroversial.

Private law creates private rights to the extent that these private rights serve some collective good. If a private right is harmful to a collective good, then the state has no reason to create it. The state's interests are general, not particular. It has a reason to create rights when those rights serve a common, rather than particular, end.

The institution of private property is an application of this point. The state has an interest in defining rights to private property because private property helps produce a general, and powerful, prosperity. It is a system for ordering economic relations that greatly benefits all members of society. No other system that we have yet devised better orders economic relations. No other system, some believe, could.[23]

But even with ordinary property—your car, or your house—property rights are never absolute. There is no property that does not have to yield at some point to the interests of the state. Your land may be taken to build a highway, your car seized to carry an accident victim to the hospital, your driveway crossed by the postman, your house inspected by health inspectors. In countless ways, the system of property we call "private property" is a system that balances exclusive control by the individual against certain common state ends. When the latter conflict with the former, it is the former that yields.

This balance, the realists argued, is a feature of all property. But it is an especially important feature of intellectual property. The balance of rights with intellectual property differs from the balance with ordinary real or personal property. "Information," as Boyle puts it, "is different."[24] And a very obvious feature of intellectual property shows why.

When property law gives me the exclusive right to use my house, there's a very good reason for it. If you used my house while I did, I would have less to use. When the law gives me an exclusive right to my apple, that too makes sense. If you eat my apple, then I cannot. Your use of my property ordinarily interferes with my use of my property. Your consumption reduces mine.

The law has a good reason, then, to give me an exclusive right over my personal and real property. If it did not, I would have little reason to work to produce it. Or if I did work to produce it, I would then spend a great deal of my time trying to keep you away. It is better for everyone, the argument goes, if I have an exclusive right to my (rightly acquired) property, because then I have an incentive to produce it and not waste all my time trying to defend it.[25]

Things are different with intellectual property. If you "take" my idea, I still have it. If I tell you an idea, you have not deprived me of it.[26] An unavoidable feature of intellectual property is that its consumption, as the economists like to put it, is "nonrivalrous." Your consumption does not lessen mine. If I write a song, you can sing it without making it impossible for me to sing it. If I write a book, you can read a copy of it (please do) without disabling me from reading another copy of it. Ideas, at their core, can be shared with no reduction in the amount the "owner" can consume. This difference is fundamental, and it has been understood since the founding.

Jefferson put it better than I:

> If nature has made any one thing less susceptible than all others of exclusive property, it is the action of the thinking power called an idea, which an individual may exclusively possess as long as he keeps it to himself; but the moment it is divulged, it forces itself into the possession of every one, and the receiver cannot dispossess himself of it. Its peculiar character, too, is that no one possesses the less, because every other possess the whole of it. He who receives an idea from me, receives instruction himself without lessening mine; as he who lites his taper at mine, receives light without darkening me. That ideas should freely spread from one to another over the globe, for the moral and mutual instruction of man, and improvement of his condition, seems to have been peculiarly and benevolently designed by nature, when she made them, like fire, expansible over all space, without lessening their density at any point, and like the air in which we breathe, move, and have our physical being, incapable of confinement or exclusive appropriation. Inventions then cannot, in nature, be a subject of property.[27]

Technically, Jefferson presents two concepts: One is the possibility of excluding others from using or getting access to an idea, which he defines as "action of the thinking power . . . which an individual may exclusively possess as long as he keeps it to himself." This is the question whether ideas are "excludable"; Jefferson affirms that an idea is "excludable" until "the moment it is divulged."

The other concept is whether my use of a divulged idea lessens your use of the same idea. This is the question of whether divulged ideas are "rivalrous."[28] Again, Jefferson suggests that, once they are divulged, ideas are not "rivalrous." Jefferson believes that the act of divulging/sharing has made ideas both nonexcludable and nonrivalrous, and that there is little that man can do to change this fact.[29]

In fact, shared ideas are both nonexcludable and nonrivalrous. I can exclude people from my secret ideas or writings—I can keep them secret, or build fences to keep people out. How easily, or how effectively, I can do so is a technical question. It depends on the architecture of protection that a given context provides. But given the proper technology, there is no doubt that I can keep people out. What I cannot do is to exclude people from my shared ideas or writings simply because they are not my secrets anymore.

My shared ideas are "nonrivalrous" goods, too. No technology (that we know of) will erase an idea from your head as it passes into my head. My knowing what you know does not lessen your knowing the same thing. That fact is a given in the world, and it makes intellectual property different. Unlike apples, and unlike houses, once shared, ideas are something I can take from you without diminishing what you have.

It does not follow, however, that there is no need for property rights over expressions or inventions.[30] Just because you can have what I have without lessening what I have does not mean that the state has no reason to create rights over ideas, or over the expression of ideas.

If a novelist cannot stop you from copying (rather than buying) her book, then she may have very little incentive to produce more books. She may have as much as she had before you took the work she produced, but if you take it without paying, she has no monetary incentive to produce more.

Now, of course, the incentives an author faces are quite complex, and it is not possible to make simple generalizations.[31] But generalizations do not have to be perfect to make a point: Even if some authors write for free, it is still the case that the law needs some intellectual property rights. If the law did not protect authorship at all, there would be fewer authors. The law has a reason to protect the rights of authors, at least insofar as doing so gives them an incentive to produce. With ordinary property, the law must both create an incentive to produce and protect the right of possession; with intellectual property, the law need only create the incentive to produce.

This is the difference between these two very different kinds of property, and this difference fundamentally affects the nature of intellectual property law. While we protect real and personal property to protect the owner from harm and give the owner an incentive, we protect intellectual property to ensure that we create a sufficient incentive to produce it. "Sufficient incentive," however, is something less than "perfect control." And in turn we can say that the ideal protections of intellectual property law are something less than the ideal protections for ordinary or real property.

This difference between the nature of intellectual property and ordinary property was recognized by our Constitution, which in article I, section 8, clause 8, gives Congress the power "to promote the Progress of Science and useful Arts, by securing for limited Times to Authors and Inventors the exclusive Right to their respective Writings and Discoveries."

Note the special structure of this clause. First, it sets forth the precise reason for the power—to promote the progress of science and useful arts. It is for those reasons, and those reasons only, that Congress may grant an exclusive right. And second, note the special temporality of this right: "for limited Times." The Constitution does not allow Congress to grant authors and inventors permanent exclusive rights to their writings and discoveries, only limited rights. (Though apparently those limited times can be extended.[32]) It does not give Congress the power to give them a perpetual "property" in their writings and discoveries, only an exclusive right over them for a limited time.

The Constitution's protection for intellectual property then is fundamentally different from its protection of ordinary property. I've said that all property is granted subject to the limit of the public good. But even so, if the government decided to nationalize all property after a fifteen-year term of ownership, the Constitution would require it to compensate the owners. By contrast, if Congress set the copyright term at fifteen years, there would be no claim that the government pay compensation after the fifteen years were up. Intellectual property rights are a monopoly that the state gives to producers of intellectual property in exchange for their production of it. After a limited time, the product of their work becomes the public's to use as it wants. This is Communism at the core of our Constitution's protection of intellectual property. This "property" is not property in the ordinary sense of that term.

And this is true for reasons better than tradition as well. Economists have long understood that granting property rights over information is dangerous (to say the least).[33] This is not because of leftist leanings among economists; it is because economists are consequentialists, and their objective in granting any property right is simply to facilitate production. But there is no way to know, in principle, whether increasing or decreasing the rights granted under intellectual property law will lead to an increase in the production of intellectual property. The reasons are complex, but the point is not: Increasing intellectual property's protection is not guaranteed to "promote the progress of science and useful arts"—indeed, often doing so will stifle it.

The balance that intellectual property law traditionally strikes is between the protections granted the author and the public use or access granted everyone else. The aim is to give the author sufficient incentive to produce. Built into the law of intellectual property are limits on the power of the author to control use of the ideas she has created.[34]

A classic example of these limits and of this public use dimension is the right of "fair use." Fair use is the right to use copyrighted material, regardless of the wishes of the owner of that material. A copyright gives the owner certain rights; fair use is a limitation on those rights. It gives you the right to criticize this book, cut sections from it, and reproduce them in an article attacking me. In these ways and in others, you have the right to use this book independent of how I say it should be used.

Fair use does not necessarily work against the author's interest—or more accurately, fair use does not necessarily work against the interests of authors as a class. When fair use protects the right of reviewers to criticize books without the permission of authors, then more critics criticize. And the more criticism there is, the better the information is about what books people should buy. The better the information is about what to buy, the more people will buy it. Authors as a whole benefit from the system of fair use, even if particular authors do not.

The law of copyright is filled with such rules. Another is the "first sale" doctrine. If you buy this book, you can sell it to someone else free of any constraint I might impose on you.[35] This doctrine differs from the tradition in, for example, Europe, where there are "moral rights" that give the creator power over subsequent use.[36] I've already mentioned another example—limited term. The creator cannot extend the term for which the law will provide protection (even if Congress can); that is fixed by the statute and runs out when the statute runs out.

Taken together, these rules give the creator significant—but not perfect—control over the use of what he produces. They give the public some access, but not complete access. They are balanced differently from the balance the law strikes for ordinary property—by design. They are constitutionally structured to help build an intellectual and cultural commons.

The law strikes this balance. It is not a balance that would exist in nature. Without the law, and before cyberspace, authors would have very little protection; with the law, they have significant, but not perfect, protection. The law gives authors something they otherwise would not have in exchange for limits on their rights, secured to benefit the intellectual commons as a whole.

PRIVATE SUBSTITUTES FOR PUBLIC LAW

So copyright law strikes a balance between control and access. What about that balance when code is the law? Should we expect that any of the limits will remain? Should we expect code to mirror the limits that the law imposes? Fair use? Limited term? Would private code build these "bugs" into its protections?

The point should be obvious: When intellectual property is protected by code, nothing requires that the same balance be struck. Nothing requires the owner to grant the right of fair use. She might allow individuals to browse for free, as a bookstore does, but she might not. Whether she grants this right depends on whether it profits her. Fair use becomes contingent upon private gain. More importantly, it becomes contingent upon the private gain of authors individually rather than authors as a class.

Thus, as privatized law, trusted systems regulate in the same domain that copyright law regulates. But unlike copyright law, they do not guarantee the same limits on copyright's protection. Trusted systems give the producer maximum control over the uses of copyrighted work—admittedly at a cheaper cost, thus perhaps permitting many more authors to publish. But they give authors almost perfect control in an area in which the law did not. Code thus displaces the balance that copyright law strikes by displacing the limits the law imposes. As Daniel Benloliel puts it,

> [D]ecentralized content providers are . . . privatizing the enforcement authority with strict technological standards, under which individuals would be banned from access and use of particular digital content in a way that might override legitimate fair use.[37]

So far my description simply sets law against code: the law of copyright either complemented by, or in conflict with, private code. You may not yet be convinced that we should consider this a conflict, because it has always been the case that one can exercise more control over a copyrighted work than the law gives you the right to exercise over the copyright. For example, if you own a painting that is in the public domain, there's no requirement for you to let anyone see it. You could lock it in your bedroom and never let anyone see it ever. In a sense, you've thus deprived the world of the value of this painting being in the "public domain." But no one has ever thought that this interaction between the law of trespass and copyright has created any important conflict. So why should anyone be troubled if copyright owners use code to lock up their content beyond the balance the law of copyright strikes?

If this is where you're stuck, then let me add one more part to the story. As I mentioned above, the DMCA contains an anti-circumvention provision. That part of the law forbids the circumvention of some technical protection measures; it forbids the development of tools to circumvent technical protection as well. Most important, it forbids these circumventions regardless of the purpose of the circumvention. Thus, if the underlying use you would make of a copyrighted work—if you could get access to it—is a "fair use," the DMCA still makes it an offense to circumvent technical protections to get access to it. Thus one part of the law of copyright grants "fair use," while another part of copyright removes at least some fair use liberty where the fair use has been removed by technical means.[38]

But so what, the skeptic will ask. What the law gives, the law can take away, can't it?

No it can't, and that's the point. As the Supreme Court has indicated, copyright law is consistent with the First Amendment only because of certain important limitations built into the law. Removing those limitations would then raise important First Amendment questions. Thus, when the law acts with code to remove the law's protection for fair use, this should raise an important question—at least for those concerned about maintaining the balance that copyright law strikes.

But maybe this conflict is just temporary. Couldn't the code be changed to protect fair use?

The answer to that hopeful (and again, hopeful because my main point is about whether incentives to protect fair use exist) question is no, not directly. Fair use inherently requires a judgment about purpose, or intent. That judgment is beyond the ken of even the best computers. Indirectly, however, fair use could be protected. A system that allowed an individual to unlock the trusted system if he claimed the use was fair (perhaps marking the used work with a tag to make it possible to trace the use back to the user) could protect fair use. Or as Stefik describes, a system that granted users a "fair use license," allowing them to unlock the content and use insurance backing the license to pay for any misuse, might also protect fair use.[39] But these alternatives again rely on structures beyond code. With the code itself, there is no way adequately to police fair use.

Some will respond that I am late to the party: Copyright law is already being displaced, if not by code then by the private law of contract. Through the use of click-wrap, or shrink-wrap, licenses, authors are increasingly demanding that purchasers, or licensees, waive rights that copyright law gave them. If copyright law gives the right to reverse-engineer, then these contracts might extract a promise not to reverse-engineer. If copyright law gives the right to dispose of the book however the purchaser wants after the first sale, then a contract might require that the user waive that right. And if these terms in the contract attached to every copyright work are enforceable merely by being "attached" and "knowable," then already we have the ability through contract law to rewrite the balance that copyright law creates.

I agree that this race to privatize copyright law through contract is already far along, fueled in particular by decisions such as Judge Frank Easterbrook's in *ProCD v. Zeidenberg*. But contracts are not as bad as code. Contracts are a form of law. If a term of a contract is inconsistent with a value of copyright law, you can refuse to obey it and let the other side get a court to enforce it. In some cases, courts have expressly refused to follow a contract term precisely because it is inconsistent with a copyright law value.[40] The ultimate power of a contract depends upon the decision by a court to enforce the contract or not. Although courts today are relatively eager to find ways to enforce these contracts, there is at least hope that if the other side makes its case very clear, courts could shift direction again.[41] As Stefik writes, trusted systems "differ from an ordinary contract in critical ways."

> [I]n an ordinary contract, compliance is not automatic; it is the responsibility of the agreeing parties. There may be provisions for monitoring and checking on compliance, but the actual responsibility for acting in accordance with the terms falls on the parties. In addition, enforcement of the contract is ultimately the province of the courts.[42]

The same is not true of code. Whatever problems there are when contracts replace copyright law, the problems are worse when code displaces copyright law. Again—where do we challenge the code? When the software protects without relying in the end on the state, where can we challenge the nature of the protection? Where can we demand balance when the code takes it away?

I don't mean to enter the extremely contentious debate about whether this change in control is good or appropriate. I've said too much about that elsewhere.[43] For our purposes here, the point is simply to recognize a significant change. Code now makes possible increasingly perfect control over how culture is spread. Regulations have "been fairly consistent . . . on the side of expanding the power of the owners to control the use of their products."[44] And these regulations invite a demand for perfect control over how culture is spread.

The rise of contracts qualifying copyright law and the rise of code qualifying copyright law raise a question that the law of copyright has not had to answer before. We have never had to choose whether authors should be permitted perfectly to control the use of their intellectual property independent of the law, for such control was not possible. The balance struck by the law was the best that authors could get. But now, code gives authors a better deal. The question for legal policy is whether this better deal makes public sense.

Here we confront the first latent ambiguity within the law of copyright. There are those who would say that copyright law already decides this question—whether against code-based control, or for it. But in my view, this is a choice the law has yet to make. I have my own views about how the law should decide the question. But what technology has done is force us to see a choice that was not made before. See the choice, and then make it.

Put most directly: There has always been a set of uses of copyrighted work that was unregulated by the law of copyright. Even within the boundary of uses that were regulated by the law of copyright, "fair use" kept some uses free. The core question is why? Were these transactions left free because it was too costly to meter them? Or were these transactions left free because keeping them free was an important public value tied to copyright?

This is a question the law never had to resolve, though there is support for both views.[45] Now the technology forces us to resolve it. The question, then, is how.

A nice parallel to this problem exists in one part of constitutional law. The framers gave Congress the power to regulate interstate commerce and commerce that affects interstate commerce.[46] At the founding, that was a lot of commerce, but because of the inefficiencies of the market, not all of it. Thus, the states had a domain of commerce that they alone could regulate.[47]

Over time, however, the scope of interstate commerce has changed so that much less commerce is now within the exclusive domain of the states. This change has produced two sorts of responses. One is to find other ways to give states domains of exclusive regulatory authority. The justification for this response is the claim that these changes in interstate commerce are destroying the framers' vision about state power.

The other response is to concede the increasing scope of federal authority, but to deny that it is inconsistent with the framing balance.[48] Certainly, at the founding, some commerce was not interstate and did not affect interstate commerce. But that does not mean that the framers intended that there must always be such a space. They tied the scope of federal power to a moving target; if the target moves completely to the side of federal power, then that is what we should embrace.[49]

In both contexts, the change is the same. We start in a place where balance is given to us by the mix of frictions within a particular regulatory domain: Fair use is a balance given to us because it is too expensive to meter all use; state power over commerce is given to us because not all commerce affects interstate commerce. When new technology disturbs the balance, we must decide whether the original intent was that there be a balance, or that the scope of one side of each balance should faithfully track the index to which it was originally tied. Both contexts, in short, present ambiguity.

Many observers (myself included) have strong feelings one way or the other. We believe this latent ambiguity is not an ambiguity at all. In the context of federal power, we believe either that the states were meant to keep a domain of exclusive authority[50] or that the federal government was to have whatever power affected interstate commerce.[51] In the context of fair use, we believe that either fair use is to be a minimum of public use, guaranteed regardless of the technology,[52] or that it is just an efficient compromise in response to an inefficient technology, to be removed as soon as efficiency can be achieved.

But in both cases, this may make the problem too easy. The best answer in both contexts may be that the question was unresolved at the framing: Perhaps no one thought of the matter, and hence there is no answer to the question of what they would have intended if some central presupposition had changed. And if there was no original answer, we must decide the question by our own lights. As Stefik says of trusted systems—and, we might expect, of the implications of trusted systems—"It is a tool never imagined by the creators of copyright law, or by those who believe laws governing intellectual property cannot be enforced."[53]

The loss of fair use is a consequence of the perfection of trusted systems. Whether you consider it a problem or not depends on your view of the value of fair use. If you consider it a public value that should exist regardless of the technological regime, then the emergence of this perfection should trouble you. From your perspective, there was a value latent in the imperfection of the old system that has now been erased.

But even if you do not think that the loss of fair use is a problem, trusted systems threaten other values latent in the imperfection of the real world. Consider a second.

THE ANONYMITY THAT IMPERFECTION ALLOWS

I was a student at an English university for a number of years. In the college I attended, there was a "buttery"—a shop inside the college that basically sold alcohol. During the first week I was there I had to buy a large amount of Scotch (a series of unimaginative gifts, as I remember). About a week after I made these purchases, I received a summons from my tutor to come talk with him in his office. When I arrived, the tutor asked me about my purchases. This was, to his mind, an excessive amount of alcohol, and he wanted to know whether I had a good reason for buying it.

Needless to say, I was shocked at the question. Of course, technically, I had made a purchase at the college, and I had not hidden my name when I did so (indeed, I had charged it on my college account), so, formally, I had revealed my alcohol purchases to the college and its agents. Still, it shocked me that this information would be monitored by college authorities and then checked up on. I could see why they did it, and I could see the good that might come from it. It just never would have occurred to me that these data would be used in this way.

If this was an invasion, of course, it was a small one. Later it was easy for me to hide my binges simply by buying from a local store rather than the college buttery. (Though I later learned that the local store rented its space from the college, so who knows what deal they had struck?) And in any case,

I was not being punished. The college was just concerned. But the example suggests a more general point: We reveal to the world a certain class of data about ourselves that we ordinarily expect the world not to use. What happens when they use it?

Trusted systems depend on such data—they depend on the ability to know how people use the property that is being protected. To set prices most efficiently, the system ideally should know as much about individuals and their reading habits as possible. It needs to know this data because it needs an efficient way to track use and so to charge for it.[54]

But this tracking involves a certain invasion. We live now in a world where we think about what we read in just the way that I thought about what I bought as a student in England—we do not expect that anyone is keeping track. We would be shocked if we learned that the library was keeping tabs on the books that people checked out and then using this data in some monitoring way.

Such tracking, however, is just what trusted systems require. And so the question becomes: Should there be a right against this kind of monitoring? The question is parallel to the question of fair use. In a world where this monitoring could not effectively occur, there was, of course, no such right against it. But now that monitoring can occur, we must ask whether the latent right to read anonymously, given to us before by imperfections in technologies, should be a legally protected right.

Julie Cohen argues that it should, and we can see quite directly how her argument proceeds.[55] Whatever its source, it is a value in this world that we can explore intellectually on our own. It is a value that we can read anonymously, without fear that others will know or watch or change their behavior based on what we read. This is an element of intellectual freedom; it is a part of what makes us as we are.[56]

But this element is potentially erased by trusted systems. These systems need to monitor, and this monitoring destroys anonymity. We need to decide whether, and how, to preserve values from today in a context of trusted systems.

This could first be a question of translation: namely, how should changes in technology be accommodated to preserve values from an earlier context in a new context? It is the same question that Brandeis asked about wiretapping.[57] It is the question the Court answers in scores of contexts all the time. It is fundamentally a question about preserving values when contexts change.

In the context of both fair use and reading, Cohen has a consistent answer to this question of translation. She argues that there is a right to resist, or "hack," trusted systems to the extent that they infringe on traditional fair use. (Others have called this the "Cohen Theorem.") As for reading, she argues that

copyright management schemes must protect a right to read anonymously—
that if they monitor, they must be constructed so that they preserve
anonymity. The strategy is the same: Cohen identifies a value yielded by an
old architecture but now threatened by a new architecture, and then argues in
favor of an affirmative right to protect the original value.

But here again we might view the question more ambiguously. I share
Cohen's view, but the argument on the other side is not silly. If it's permissible
to use technology to make copyrighted works available, why isn't it permissible to gather data about who uses what works? That data gathering is not
part of the copyright itself; it is a byproduct of the technology. And as our tradition has never had this technical capacity before, it is hard to say a choice
was made about it in the past.

PERMISSION CULTURE VS. FREE

I've already described the limits copyright law places on itself. These limits, as
I argued, reflect important values. They express the balance that copyright law
aims to be.

But what is too often missed in this discussion of balance is any sense of
perspective. We focus on the gradual shifts in the law but miss the profound
sense in which the significance of the law has changed.

This change is produced by the unintended interaction between the architecture of digital technologies and the architecture of the law.

Copyright law at its core regulates "copies." In the analog world, there
were very few contexts in which one produced "copies." As Jessica Litman
described more than a decade ago,

> At the turn of the century, U.S. copyright law was technical, inconsistent, and
> difficult to understand, but it didn't apply to very many people or very many
> things. If one were an author or publisher of books, maps, charts, paintings,
> sculpture, photographs or sheet music, a playwright or producer of plays, or a
> printer, the copyright law bore on one's business. Booksellers, piano-roll and
> phonograph record publishers, motion picture producers, musicians, scholars,
> members of Congress, and ordinary consumers could go about their business
> without ever encountering a copyright problem.[58]

Thus there were many ways in which you could use creative work in the
analog world without producing a copy.

Digital technology, at its core, makes copies. Copies are to digital life as
breathing is to our physical life. There is no way to use any content in a digital

context without that use producing a copy. When you read a book stored on your computer, you make a copy (at least in the RAM memory to page through the book). When you do anything with digital content, you technically produce a copy.

This technical fact about digital technologies, tied to the technical architecture of the law, produces a profound shift in the scope or reach of the law of copyright that too many simply miss: While in the analog world, life was sans copyright law; in the digital world, life is subject to copyright law. Every single act triggers the law of copyright. Every single use is either subject to a license or illegal, unless deemed to be "fair use." The emergence of digital technologies has thus radically increased the domain of copyright law—from regulating a tiny portion of human life, to regulating absolutely every bit of life on a computer.

Now if all you think about is protecting the distribution of professionally created culture, this might not concern you much. If you're trying to stop "piracy," then a regime that says every use requires permission is a regime that gives you a fairly broad range of tools for stamping out piracy.

But though you wouldn't notice this listening to the debates surrounding copyright law just now, in fact, protecting the distribution of professionally created culture is not the only, or even, I suggest, the most important part of culture. And indeed, from a historical perspective, top-down, professionally produced culture is but a tiny part of what makes any culture sing. The 20th century may have been an exception to this rule, but no Congress voted to make professional culture the only legal culture within our society.

Standing alongside professional culture is amateur culture—where amateur doesn't mean inferior or without talent, but instead culture created by people who produce not for the money, but for the love of what they do. From this perspective, there is amateur culture everywhere—from your dinner table, where your father or sister tell jokes that take off from the latest political scandal or the latest *Daily Show;* from your basement, where your brother and his three best friends are causing permanent damage to their eardrums as they try to become the next Rolling Stones; from your neighbors who gather each Thursday and Sunday to sing in a church choir; from your neighborhood schools, where kids and teachers create art or music in the course of learning about our culture; from the kids at your neighborhood school, who tear their pants or wear their shirts in some odd way, all as a way to express and make culture.

This amateur culture has always been with us, even if it is to us today, as Dan Hunter and Greg Lastowska put it, "hidden."[59] It is precisely how the imagination of kids develops;[60] it is how culture has always developed. As Siva Vaidhyanathan writes,

> widespread democratic cultural production (peer-to-peer production, one might say) . . . merely echoes how cultural texts have flowed through and been revised by discursive communities everywhere for centuries. Texts often undergo a process similar to a game of "telephone," through which a text is substantially—sometimes almost unintentionally—distorted through many small revisions. . . . Such radical textual revisions have occurred in other contexts and have helped build political critiques, if not movements. For instance, historian Lawrence Levine (1988) has documented how working-class players and audiences in nineteenth-century America adapted and revised the works of William Shakespeare to their local contexts, concerns and ideologies. And historian Eric Lott (1993) has shown how *Uncle Tom's Cabin* was reworked by working-class white communities to aid the cause of racial dominance instead of the Christian liberationist message the book was intended to serve.[61]

Importantly, too, this kind of cultural remix has historically been free of regulation. No one would think that as you tell a joke around your dinner table, or sing songs with your friends, or practice to become the next Rolling Stones, you need a lawyer standing next to you, clearing the rights to "use" the culture as you make your creative remix. The law of copyright, historically, has been focused on commercial life. It has left the noncommercial, or beyond commercial, creativity free of legal regulation.

All this has now changed, and digital technologies are responsible. First, and most important, digital technologies have radically expanded the scope of this amateur culture. Now the clever remix of some political event or the latest song by your favorite band are not just something you can share with your friends. Digital technologies have made it simple to capture and share this creativity with the world. The single most important difference between the Internet circa 1999 and the Internet circa today is the explosion of user-generated creativity—from blogs, to podcasts, to videocasts, to mashups, the Internet today is a space of extraordinary creativity.

Second, digital technologies have democratized creativity. Technology has given a wide range of potential creators the capacity to become real. "People are waking from their consumerist coma," one commentator describes.[62] As DJ Danger Mouse put it at the Web 2.0 conference in 2004,

> Mashing is so easy. It takes years to learn how to play the guitar and write your own songs. It takes a few weeks of practice with a turntable to make people

dance and smile. It takes a few hours to crank out something good with some software. So with such a low barrier to entry, everyone jumps in and starts immediately being creative.[63]

But third, and directly relevant to the story of this chapter, to the extent this creativity finds its expression on the Net, it is now subject to the regulation of copyright law. To the extent it uses others' creativity, it needs the permission of others. To the extent it builds upon the creativity of others, it needs to be sure that that creativity can be built upon legally. A whole system of regulation has now been grafted upon an economy of creativity that until now has never known regulation. Amateur culture, or bottom up culture, or the culture that lives outside of commercial transactions—all of this is subject to regulation in a way that 30 years ago it was not.

A recent example of this conflict makes the point very concisely. There's a genre of digital creativity called Anime Music Videos (AMVs). AMVs are remixes of anime cartoons and music. Kids spend hundreds, sometimes thousands of hours reediting the anime cartoons to match them perfectly to music. The result is, in a word, extraordinary. It is among the most creative uses of digital technology that I have seen.

While this genre of creativity is not small, it's also not huge. Basically one site dominates activity around AMVs. That site has more than 500,000 members, and some 30,000 creators upload AMV content to the site.

In November 2005, one prominent record label, Wind-Up Records, informed this website that it wanted all Wind-Up Records artists removed from the site. That was some 3,000 videos, representing at least 250,000 hours of volunteer work by creators across the world—work that would have just one real effect: to promote the underlying artists' work.

From the perspective of the law as it is, this is an easy case. What the kids are doing is making a derivative work of the anime; they are distributing full copies of the underlying music; and they are synchronizing the music to video—all without the permission of the copyright owners.

But from the perspective of culture, this should be a very hard case. The creativity demonstrated by this work is extraordinary. I can't show you that creativity in a book, but the notes point you to an example that you can see.[64] It is noncommercial, amateur creative work—precisely the sort that has never been subject to the regulation of the law, but which now, because it is living in digital context, is monitored, and regulated, by the law.

Here again, I have strong feelings about what the right answer should be. But we should recognize the latent ambiguity this conflict presents:

Because of the changes in digital technology, it is now possible for the law to regulate every single use of creative work in a digital environment. As life increasingly moves into a digital environment, this means that the law will regulate more and more of the use of culture.

Is this consistent with our values?

The answer again could be found first by trying to translate framing values into the current context. From that perspective, it would be extraordinarily difficult to imagine that the framing vision would have included the level of legal regulation that the current regime entails.

Again, that conclusion could be questioned by recognizing that the possibility of such extensive regulation didn't exist, and so the choice about whether such extensive regulation should be allowed wasn't made. That choice, when made, should recognize that while there is extensive and new regulation of amateur culture, that regulation creates new wealth for professional culture. There's a choice to be made about which form of culture we should protect. That choice has not yet been made directly. It is one more choice we have yet to make.

THE PROBLEMS THAT PERFECTION MAKES

These three examples reveal a common pattern—one that will reach far beyond copyright. At one time we enjoyed a certain kind of liberty. But that liberty was not directly chosen; it was a liberty resulting from the high costs of control.[65] That was the conclusion we drew about fair use—that when the cost of control was high, the space for fair use was great. So too with anonymous reading: We read anonymously in real space not so much because laws protect that right as because the cost of tracking what we read is so great. And it was the same with amateur culture: That flourished free of regulation because regulation could not easily reach it.

When costs of control fall, however, liberty is threatened. That threat requires a choice—do we allow the erosion of an earlier liberty, or do we erect other limits to re-create that original liberty?

The law of intellectual property is the first example of this general point. As the architecture of the Internet changes, it will allow for a greater protection of intellectual property than real-space architectures allowed; this greater protection will force a choice on us that we do not need to make in real space. Should the architecture allow perfect control over intellectual property, or should we build into the architecture an incompleteness that guarantees a certain aspect of public use or a certain space for individual freedom?

Ignoring these questions will not make them go away. Pretending that the framers answered them is no solution either. In this context (and this is just the first) we will need to make a judgment about which values the architecture will protect.

CHOICES

I've argued that cyberspace will open up three important choices in the context of intellectual property: whether to allow intellectual property in effect to become completely propertized (for that is what a perfect code regime for protecting intellectual property would do); and whether to allow this regime to erase the anonymity latent in less efficient architectures of control; and whether to allow the expansion of intellectual property to drive out amateur culture. These choices were not made by our framers. They are for us to make now.

I have a view, in this context as in the following three, about how we should exercise that choice. But I am a lawyer. Lawyers are taught to point elsewhere—to the framers, to the United Nations charter, to an act of Congress—when arguing about how things ought to be. Having said that there is no such authority here, I feel as if I ought to be silent.

Cowardly, not silent, however, is how others might see it. They say that I should say what I think. So in each of these three applications (intellectual property, privacy, and free speech), I will offer my view about how these choices should be made. But I do this under some duress and encourage you to simply ignore what I believe. It will be short, and summary, and easy to discard. It is the balance of the book—and, most importantly, the claim that we have a choice to make—that I really want to stick.

Anonymity

Cohen, it seems to me, is plainly right about anonymity, and the Cohen Theorem is inspirational. However efficient the alternative may be, we should certainly architect cyberspaces to ensure anonymity—or more precisely, pseudonymity—first. If the code is going to monitor what I do, then at least it should not know that it is "I" that it is monitoring. I am less troubled if it knows that "14AH342BD7" read such and such; I am deeply troubled if that number is tied back to my name.

Cohen is right for a second reason as well: All of the good that comes from monitoring could be achieved while protecting privacy. It may take a bit more coding to build in routines for breaking traceability; it may take more planning to ensure that privacy is protected. But if those rules are embedded up front, the cost would not be terribly high. It is far cheaper to architect privacy protections now rather than retrofit for them later.

The Commons

By "the Commons" I mean a resource that anyone within a relevant community can use without seeking the permission of anyone else. Such permission may not be required because the resource is not subject to any legal control (it is, in other words, in the public domain). Or it may not be required because permission to use the resource has already been granted. In either case, to use or to build upon this resource requires nothing more than access to the resource itself.[66]

In this sense, the questions about the scope and reach of copyright law ask whether our future will protect the intellectual commons that it did in the past. Again, it did so in the past because the friction of control was too great. But now that that friction is gone, will we preserve or destroy the commons that used to exist?

My view is that it ought to be preserved.

We can architect cyberspace to preserve a commons or not. (Jefferson thought that nature had already done the architecting, but Jefferson wrote before there was code.) We should choose to architect it with a commons. Our past had a commons that could not be designed away; that commons gave our culture great value. What value the commons of the future could bring us is something we are just beginning to see. Intellectual property scholars saw it—long before cyberspace came along—and laid the groundwork for much of the argument we need to have now.[67] The greatest work in the law of cyberspace has been written in the field of intellectual property. In a wide range of contexts, these scholars have made a powerful case for the substantive value of an intellectual commons.[68]

James Boyle puts the case most dramatically in his extraordinary book *Shamans, Software, and Spleens.*[69] Drawing together both cyberspace and non-cyberspace questions, he spells out the challenge we face in an information society—particularly the political challenge.[70] Elsewhere he identifies our need for an "environmental movement" in information policy—a rhetoric that gets people to see the broad range of values put at risk by this movement to propertize all information. Boyle's work has inspired many others to push a similar agenda of freedom.[71]

That freedom would limit the law's regulation over the use and reuse of culture. It would resist perfect control over use; it would free a wide range of reuse. It would build through affirmative protections for freedom the liberty that friction gave us before. It would do so because it believes in the values this freedom stands for, and it would demonstrate the value in that freedom by enabling the communities that freedom would itself enable.

But this freedom could be constructed either through changes in the law or voluntarily. That is, the law could be rebalanced to encourage the freedom thought important, or this property could be redeployed to effect the freedom thought important.

The second strategy was the technique of the Free Software Movement, described in Chapter 8. Using copyright law, Stallman deployed a software license that both preserved the four freedoms of free software, and also required that those modifying and distributing free software distribute the modifications freely. This license thus effects a software commons, since the software is available to all to use, and this software commons has become a critical raw material fueling the digital age.

More recently, Stallman's idea has been copied by others seeking to rebuild a commons in cyberspace. The Wikipedia project, for example, has built—to the astonishment of most—an extraordinary online encyclopedia solely through the volunteer efforts of thousands, contributing essays and edits in a public wiki. The product of that work is now protected perpetually (yes, I know, only for a "limited time," but don't correct *me* about that little detail) through a copyright license that, like the GPL, requires any modification to be distributed freely as well. (More on Wikipedia in Chapter 12.)

And so too has Creative Commons used private law to build an effective public commons. Again, following Stallman, Creative Commons offers copyright holders a simple way to mark their creative work with the freedoms they intend it to carry. That mark is a license which reserves to the author some rights, while dedicating to the public rights that otherwise would have been held privately. As these licenses are nonexclusive and public, they too effectively build a commons of creative resources that anyone can build upon.

Though I have spent a great deal of my time helping to build the Creative Commons, I still believe private action alone is not enough. Yet there is value in learning something from what this private action produces, as its lesson may help policy makers recraft copyright law in the future.

ELEVEN

privacy

THE CONCLUSION OF PART 1 WAS THAT CODE COULD ENABLE A MORE REGULABLE cyberspace; the conclusion of Part 2 was that code would become an increasingly important regulator in that more regulable space. Both conclusions were central to the story of the previous chapter. Contrary to the early panic by copyright holders, the Internet will become a space where intellectual property can be more easily protected. As I've described, that protection will be effected through code.

Privacy is a surprisingly similar story. Indeed, as Jonathan Zittrain argued in an essay published in the *Stanford Law Review*,[1] the problems of privacy and copyright are exactly the same. With both, there's a bit of "our" data that "we've" lost control over. In the case of copyright, it is the data constituting a copy of our copyrighted work; in the case of privacy, it is the data representing some fact about us. In both cases, the Internet has produced this loss of control: with copyright, because the technology enables perfect and free copies of content; with privacy, as we'll see in this chapter, because the technology enables perpetual and cheap monitoring of behavior. In both cases, the question policy makers should ask is what mix of law and technology might restore the proper level of control. That level must balance private and public interests: With copyright, the balance is as I described in the last chapter; with privacy, it is as we'll explore in this chapter.

The big difference between copyright and privacy, however, is the political economy that seeks a solution to each problem. With copyright, the interests threatened are powerful and well organized; with privacy, the interests threatened are diffuse and disorganized. With copyright, the values on the other side of protection (the commons, or the public domain) are neither compelling nor well understood. With privacy, the values on the other side of protection (security, the war against terrorism) *are* compelling and well understood. The result of these differences, as any political theorist would then predict, is that over the past ten years, while we've seen a lot of legislative and technical changes to solve the problems facing copyright, we've seen very few that would solve the problems of privacy.

Yet as with copyright, we could restrike the balance protecting privacy. There are both changes in law and changes in technology that could produce a much more private (and secure) digital environment. Whether we will realize these changes depends upon recognizing both the dynamics to regulation in cyberspace and the importance of the value that privacy is.

We will think about three aspects of privacy, and how cyberspace has changed each of them. Two of these three will be the focus of this chapter, but I begin with the third to help orient the balance.

PRIVACY IN PRIVATE

The traditional question of "privacy" was the limit the law placed upon the ability of others to penetrate your private space. What right does the government have to enter your home, or search your papers? What protection does the law of trespass provide against others beyond the government snooping into your private stuff? This is one meaning of Brandeis's slogan, "the right to be left alone."[2] From the perspective of the law, it is the set of legal restrictions on the power of others to invade a protected space.

Those legal restrictions were complemented by physical barriers. The law of trespass may well say it's illegal to enter my house at night, but that doesn't mean I won't lock my doors or bolt my windows. Here again, the protection one enjoys is the sum of the protections provided by the four modalities of regulation. Law supplements the protections of technology, the protections built into norms, and the protections from the costliness of illegal penetration.

Digital technologies have changed these protections. The cost of parabolic microphone technology has dropped dramatically; that means it's easier for me to listen to your conversation through your window. On the other hand, the cost of security technologies to monitor intrusion has also fallen dramatically. The net of these changes is difficult to reckon, but the core value is not rendered ambiguous by this difficulty. The expectation of privacy in what is reasonably understood to be "private" spaces remains unchallenged by new technologies. This sort of privacy doesn't present a "latent ambiguity."

PRIVACY IN PUBLIC: SURVEILLANCE

A second kind of privacy will seem at first oxymoronic—privacy in public. What kind of protection is there against gathering data about me while I'm on a public street, or boarding an airplane?

The traditional answer was simple: None. By stepping into the public, you relinquished any rights to hide or control what others came to know about you. The facts that you transmitted about yourself were as "free as the air to common use."[3] The law provided no legal protection against the use of data gathered in public contexts.

But as we've seen again and again, just because the law of privacy didn't protect you it doesn't follow that you weren't protected. Facts about you while you are in public, even if not legally protected, are effectively protected by the high cost of gathering or using those facts. Friction is thus privacy's best friend.

To see the protection that this friction creates, however, we must distinguish between two dimensions along which privacy might be compromised.

There is a part of anyone's life that is *monitored,* and there is a part that can be *searched.* The monitored is that part of one's daily existence that others see or notice and can respond to, if response is appropriate. As I walk down the street, my behavior is monitored. If I walked down the street in a small village in western China, my behavior would be monitored quite extensively. This monitoring in both cases would be transitory. People would notice, for example, if I were walking with an elephant or in a dress, but if there were nothing special about my walk, if I simply blended into the crowd, then I might be noticed for the moment but forgotten soon after—more quickly in San Francisco, perhaps, than in China.

The *searchable* is the part of your life that leaves, or is, a record. Scribblings in your diary are a record of your thoughts. Stuff in your house is a record of what you possess. The recordings on your telephone answering machine are a record of who called and what they said. Your hard drive is you. These parts of your life are not ephemeral. They instead remain to be reviewed—at least if technology and the law permit.

These two dimensions can interact, depending upon the technology in each. My every action in a small village may be monitored by my neighbors. That monitoring produces a record—in their memories. But given the nature of the recording technology, it is fairly costly for the government to search that record. Police officers need to poll the neighbors; they need to triangulate on the inevitably incomplete accounts to figure out what parts are true, and what parts are not. That's a familiar process, but it has its limits. It might be easy to poll the neighbors to learn information to help locate a lost person, but if the government asked questions about the political views of a neighbor, we might expect (hope?) there would be resistance to that. Thus, in principle, the data are there. In practice, they are costly to extract.

Digital technologies change this balance—radically. They not only make more behavior monitorable; they also make more behavior searchable. The same technologies that gather data now gather it in a way that makes it searchable. Thus, increasingly life becomes a village composed of parallel processors, accessible at any time to reconstruct events or track behavior.

Consider some familiar examples:

The Internet

In Part I, I described the anonymity the Internet originally provided. But let's be clear about something important: That relative anonymity of the "old days" is now effectively gone. Everywhere you go on the Internet, the fact that IP address xxx.xxx.xxx.xxx went there is recorded. Everywhere you go where you've allowed a cookie to be deposited, the fact that the machine carrying that cookie went there is recorded—as well as all the data associated with that cookie. They know you from your mouse droppings. And as businesses and advertisers work more closely together, the span of data that can be aggregated about you becomes endless.

Consider a hypothetical that is completely technically possible under the existing architectures of the Net. You go to a web page of a company you trust, and you give that company every bit of your private data—your name, address, social security number, favorite magazines and TV shows, etc. That company gives you a cookie. You then go to another site, one you don't trust. You decide not to give that site any personal data. But there's no way for you to know whether these companies are cooperating about the data they collect. Its perfectly possible they synchronize the cookies data they create. And thus, there's no technical reason why once you've given your data once, it isn't known by a wide range of sites that you visit.

In the section that follows, we'll consider more extensively how we should think about privacy in any data I've affirmatively provided others, such as my name, address, or social security number. But for the moment, just focus upon the identity data they've collected as I move around in "public." Unless you've taken extraordinary steps—installing privacy software on your computer, or disabling cookies, etc.—there's no reason you should expect that the fact that you visited certain sites, or ran certain searches, isn't knowable by someone. It is. The layers of technology designed to identify "the customer" have produced endless layers of data that can be traced back to you.

Searches

In January 2006, Google surprised the government by doing what no other search company had done: It told the government "no." The Justice Department had launched a study of pornography on the Net as a way to defend Congress's latest regulation of pornography. It thus wanted data about how often, and in what form, people search for porn on the Internet. It asked Google to provide 1,000,000 random searches from its database over a specified period. Google—unlike Yahoo! and MSN—refused.

I suspect that when most first heard about this, they asked themselves an obvious question—Google keeps search requests? It does. Curiosity is monitored, producing a searchable database of the curious. As a way to figure out better how to do its job, Google—and every other search engine[4]—keeps a copy of every search it's asked to make. More disturbingly, Google links that search to a specific IP address, and, if possible, to a Google users' account. Thus, in the bowels of Google's database, there is a list of all searches made by you when you were logged into your gmail account, sitting, waiting, for someone to ask to see it.

The government did ask. And in the normal course of things, the government's request would be totally ordinary. It is unquestioned that the government gets to ask those with relevant evidence to provide it for an ongoing civil or criminal investigation (there are limits, but none really significant). Google has evidence; the government would ordinarily have the right to get it.

Moreover, the government in this case explicitly promised it would not use this evidence for anything more than evaluating patterns of consumption around porn. In particular, it promised it wouldn't trace any particularly suspicious searches. It would ignore that evidence—which ordinarily it would be free to use for whatever purpose it chose—just so it could get access to aggregate data about searches for porn.

So what's the problem this example illustrates?

Before search engines, no one had any records of curiosity; there was no list of questions asked. Now there is. People obsessively pepper search engines with questions about everything. The vast majority of these are totally benign ("mushrooms AND ragout"). Some of them show something less benign about the searcher ("erotic pictures AND children"). Now there's a list of all these questions, with some providing evidence of at least criminal intent.

The government's interest in that list will increase. At first, its demands will seem quite harmless—so what if it counts the number of times people ask Google to point them to erotic pictures? Then, when not so harmless, the demands will link to very harmful behavior—searches that suggest terrorism, or abuse. Who could argue against revealing that? Finally, when not so harmless, and when the crime is not so harmful, the demands will simply insist this is an efficient way to enforce the law. "If you don't like the law, change it. But until you do, let us enforce it." The progression is obvious, inevitable, and irresistible.

E-mail

Electronic mail is a text-based message stored in digital form. It is like a transcribed telephone call. When sent from one person to another, e-mail is copied and transmitted from machine to machine; it sits on these different machines until removed either by routines—decisions by machines—or by people.

The content of many e-mail messages is like the content of an ordinary telephone call—unplanned, unthinking, the ordinary chatter of friends. But unlike a telephone call, this content is saved in a searchable form. Companies now invest millions in technologies that scan the conversations of employees that before were effectively private. Both in real time and in retrospect, the content of conversations can become known. On the theory that they "own the computer,"[5] employers increasingly snoop in the e-mail of employees, looking for stuff they deem improper.[6]

In principle, such monitoring and searching are possible with telephone calls or letters. In practice, these communications are not monitored. To monitor telephones or regular mail requires time and money—that is, human intervention. And this cost means that most won't do it. Here again, the costs of control yield a certain kind of freedom.

Controlling employees (or spouses) is one important new use of e-mail technologies. Another is the better delivery of advertisement. Google is again the leader here with its new Gmail service. Gmail can advertise to you as you read your e-mail. But the advance is that the advertisement is triggered by the content of the e-mail. Imagine a television that shifted its advertisement as it heard what you were talking about on the phone. The content of the e-mail—and perhaps the content of your inbox generally—helps determine what is shown to you.

To make this system work well, Google needs you to keep lots of data on its servers. Thus the only thing within Gmail that is difficult to do—and it is really really difficult—is to delete content from a Google Gmail account.

Gmail lets you delete one screen at a time. But when you have 20,000 e-mails in your inbox, who has time? Would it be difficult for Gmail to enable a "delete all" function? Of course not. This is Google! Thus, through the clever use of architecture, Google assures more data is kept, and that data then becomes a resource for other purposes. If you ever get involved in a lawsuit, the first question of the lawyer from the other side should be—do you have a Gmail account? Because, if you do, your life sits open for review.

V-mail

If e-mail becomes a permanent record, why not v-mail? Voice mail systems archive messages and record the communication attributes of the conversations. As technologies for voice recognition improve, so does the ability to search voice records. As voice mail systems shift to digital systems, archiving content on central servers rather than $50 devices connected to the phone at home, they become practical search resources. In principle, every night the government could scan all the stored voice recordings at every telephone company in the nation. This search would impose no burden on the user; it could be targeted on and limited to specific topics, and it could operate in the background without anyone ever knowing.

Voice

And why stop with recordings? According to one report, the NSA monitors over 650 million telephone conversations *a day*.[7] That monitoring is automatic. It used to be of foreigners only, but now apparently the system monitors an extraordinary range of communication, searching for that bit or clue that triggers investigative concern. The system produces something akin to a weather report as well as particularized indicators. There are, for example, measures of "chatter" that may signal a storm.

This monitoring, like each of the examples before, creates no burden for those using a telephone. Those using the phone don't know something is listening on the other end. Instead, the system works quietly in the background, searching this monitored communication in real time.

Video

In each of the examples so far, someone has chosen to use a technology, and that technology has made their privacy vulnerable. The change is produced as that technology evolves to make it simpler to monitor and search behavior.

But the same evolution is happening outside networks as well. Indeed, it is happening in the quintessentially public place—the streets, or in public venues. This monitoring is the production of the current version of video technology. Originally, video cameras were a relatively benign form of monitoring. Because the product of their monitoring relied solely upon human interpretation, there were relatively few contexts in which it paid to have someone watch. And where someone wasn't watching in real time, then the use of these technologies is to trace bad behavior after it happens. Few seem upset when a convenience store video camera makes it possible to identify the criminal who has murdered the attendant.

Digital technology has changed the video, however. It is now a tool of intelligence, not just a tool to record. In London, as I've described, cameras are spread through the city to monitor which cars drive in the city. This is because nonresidents must pay a special tax to drive in "congestion zones." The cameras record and interpret license places, and then determine whether the right tax was paid for that car. The objective of the system was to minimize congestion in London. Its consequence is a database of every car that enters London, tied to a particular time and location.

But the more ambitious use of video surveillance is human face recognition. While the technology received some very bad press when first introduced in Tampa,[8] the government continues to encourage companies to develop the capacity to identify who someone is while that someone is in a traditionally anonymous place. As one vendor advertises, "[f]ace recognition technology is the least intrusive and fastest biometric technology. . . . There is no intrusion or delay, and in most cases the subjects are entirely unaware of the process. They do not feel 'under surveillance' or that their privacy has been invaded."[9]

These technologies aren't yet reliable. But they continue to be funded by both private investors and the government. Indeed, the government runs evaluation tests bi-annually to rate the reliability of the technologies.[10] There must at least be someone who expects that someday it will possible to use a camera to identify who is in a crowd, or who boarded a train.

Body Parts

Criminals leave evidence behind, both because they're usually not terribly rational and because it's extremely hard not to. And technology is only making it harder not to. With DNA technology, it becomes increasingly difficult for a criminal to avoid leaving his mark, and increasingly easy for law enforcement to identify with extremely high confidence whether X did Y.

Some nations have begun to capitalize on this new advantage. And again, Britain is in the lead.[11] Beginning in 1995, the British government started collecting DNA samples to include in a national registry. The program was initially promoted as a way to fight terrorism. But in a decade, its use has become much less discriminating.

In December 2005, while riding public transportation in London, I read the following on a public announcement poster:

> Abuse, Assault, Arrest: Our staff are here to help you. Spitting on DLR staff is classified as an assault and is a criminal offence. Saliva Recovery Kits are now held on every train and will be used to identify offenders against the national DNA database.

And why not? Spitting may be harmless. But it is insulting. And if the tools exist to identify the perpetrator of the insult, why not use them?

In all these cases, technologies designed either without monitoring as their aim or with just limited monitoring as their capacity have now become expert technologies for monitoring. The aggregate of these technologies produces an extraordinary range of searchable data. And, more importantly, as these technologies mature, there will be essentially no way for anyone living within ordinary society to escape this monitoring. Monitoring to produce searchable data will become the default architecture for public space, as standard as street lights. From the simple ability to trace back to an individual, to the more troubling ability to know what that individual is doing or likes at any particular moment, the maturing data infrastructure produces a panopticon beyond anything Bentham ever imagined.

"Orwell" is the word you're looking for. And while I believe that analogies to Orwell are just about always useless, let's make one comparison here nonetheless. While the ends of the government in *1984* were certainly vastly more evil than anything our government would ever pursue, it is interesting to note just how inefficient, relative to the current range of technologies, Orwell's technologies were. The central device was a "telescreen" that both broadcasted content and monitored behavior on the other side. But the great virtue of the telescreen was that you knew what it, in principle, could see. Winston knew where to hide, because the perspective of the telescreen was transparent.[12] It was easy to know what it couldn't see, and hence easy to know where to do the stuff you didn't want it to see.

That's not the world we live in today. You can't know whether your search on the Internet is being monitored. You don't know whether a camera is trying to identify who you are. Your telephone doesn't make funny clicks as the

NSA listens in. Your e-mail doesn't report when some bot has searched it. The technologies of today have none of the integrity of the technologies of *1984*. None are decent enough to let you know when your life is being recorded.

There's a second difference as well. The great flaw to the design of *1984* was in imagining just how it was that behavior was being monitored. There were no computers in the story. The monitoring was done by gaggles of guards watching banks of televisions. But that monitoring produced no simple way for the guards to connect their intelligence. There was no search across the brains of the guards. Sure, a guard might notice that you're talking to someone you shouldn't be talking to or that you've entered a part of a city you shouldn't be in. But there was no single guard who had a complete picture of the life of Winston.

Again, that "imperfection" can now be eliminated. We can monitor everything and search the product of that monitoring. Even Orwell couldn't imagine that.

I've surveyed a range of technologies to identify a common form. In each, the individual acts in a context that is technically public. I don't mean it should be treated by the law as "public" in the sense that privacy should not be protected there. I'm not addressing that question yet. I mean only that the individual is putting his words or image in a context that he doesn't control. Walking down 5th Avenue is the clearest example. Sending a letter is another. In both cases, the individual has put himself in a stream of activity that he doesn't control.

The question for us, then, is what limits there should be—in the name of "privacy"—on the ability to surveil these activities. But even that question puts the matter too broadly. By "surveil," I don't mean surveillance generally. I mean the very specific kind of surveillance the examples above evince. I mean what we could call "digital surveillance."

"Digital surveillance" is the process by which some form of human activity is analyzed by a computer according to some specified rule. The rule might say "flag all e-mail talking about Al Qaeda." Or it might say "flag all e-mail praising Governor Dean." Again, at this point I'm not focused upon the normative or legal question of whether such surveillance should be allowed. At this point, we're just working through definitions. In each of the cases above, the critical feature in each is that a computer is sorting data for some follow-up review by some human. The sophistication of the search is a technical question, but there's no doubt that its accuracy is improving substantially.

So should this form of monitoring be allowed?

I find when I ask this question framed precisely like this that there are two polar opposite reactions. On the one hand, friends of privacy say that there's nothing new here. There's no difference between the police reading your mail, and the police's computer reading your e-mail. In both cases, a legitimate and reasonable expectation of privacy has been breached. In both cases, the law should protect against that breach.

On the other hand, friends of security insist there is a fundamental difference. As Judge Richard Posner wrote in the *Washington Post,* in an article defending the Bush Administration's (extensive[13]) surveillance of domestic communications, "[m]achine collection and processing of data cannot, as such, invade privacy." Why? Because it is a machine that is processing the data. Machines don't gossip. They don't care about your affair with your co-worker. They don't punish you for your political opinions. They're just logic machines that act based upon conditions. Indeed, as Judge Posner argues, "[t]his initial sifting, far from invading privacy (a computer is not a sentient being), keeps most private data from being read by any intelligence officer." We're better off having machines read our e-mail, Posner suggests, both because of the security gain, and because the alternative snoop—an intelligence officer—would be much more nosey.

But it would go too far to suggest there isn't some cost to this system. If we lived in a world where our every communication was monitored (if?), that would certainly challenge the sense that we were "left alone." We would be left alone in the sense a toddler is left in a playroom—with parents listening carefully from the next room. There would certainly be something distinctively different about the world of perpetual monitoring, and that difference must be reckoned in any account of whether this sort of surveillance should be allowed.

We should also account for the "best intentions" phenomenon. Systems of surveillance are instituted for one reason; they get used for another. Jeff Rosen has cataloged the abuses of the surveillance culture that Britain has become:[14] Video cameras used to leer at women or for sensational news stories. Or in the United States, the massive surveillance for the purpose of tracking "terrorists" was also used to track domestic environmental and antiwar groups.[15]

But let's frame the question in its most compelling form. Imagine a system of digital surveillance in which the algorithm was known and verifiable: We knew, that is, exactly what was being searched for; we trusted that's all that was being searched for. That surveillance was broad and indiscriminate. But before anything could be done on the basis of the results from that surveillance, a court would have to act. So the machine would spit out bits of data implicating X in some targeted crime, and a court would decide whether that data sufficed either to justify an arrest or a more traditional search. And finally, to make the system as protective as we can, the only evidence that could be used from this surveillance would be evidence directed against the crimes being surveilled for. So for example, if you're looking for terrorists, you don't use the evidence to prosecute for tax evasion. I'm not saying what the targeted crimes are; all I'm saying is that we don't use the traditional rule that allows all evidence gathered legally to be usable for any legal end.

Would such a system violate the protections of the Fourth Amendment? Should it?

The answer to this question depends upon your conception of the value protected by the Fourth Amendment. As I described in Chapter 6, that amendment was targeted against indiscriminate searches and "general warrants"—that is, searches that were not particularized to any particular individual and the immunity that was granted to those engaging in that search. But those searches, like any search at that time, imposed burdens on the person being searched. If you viewed the value the Fourth Amendment protected as the protection from the unjustified burden of this indiscriminate search, then this digital surveillance would seem to raise no significant problems. As framed above, they produce no burden at all unless sufficient evidence is discovered to induce a court to authorize a search.

But it may be that we understand the Fourth Amendment to protect a kind of dignity. Even if a search does not burden anyone, or even if one doesn't notice the search at all, this conception of privacy holds that the very idea of a search is an offense to dignity. That dignity interest is only matched if the state has a good reason to search *before* it searches. From this perspective, a search without justification harms your dignity whether it interferes with your life or not.

I saw these two conceptions of privacy play out against each other in a tragically common encounter in Washington, D.C. A friend and I had arranged a "police ride-along"—riding with District police during their ordinary patrol. The neighborhood we patrolled was among the poorest in the city, and around 11:00 P.M. a report came in that a car alarm had been tripped in a location close to ours. When we arrived near the scene, at least five police officers were attempting to hold three youths; three of the officers were holding the suspects flat against the wall, with their legs spread and their faces pressed against the brick.

These three were "suspects"—they were near a car alarm when it went off—and yet, from the looks of things, you would have thought they had been caught holding the Hope diamond.

And then an extraordinary disruption broke out. To the surprise of every-one, and to my terror (for this seemed a tinder box, and what I am about to describe seemed the match), one of the three youths, no older than seventeen, turned around in a fit of anger and started screaming at the cops. "Every time anything happens in this neighborhood, I get thrown against the wall, and a gun pushed against my head. I've never done anything illegal, but I'm con-stantly being pushed around by cops with guns."

His friend then turned around and tried to calm him down. "Cool it, man, they're just trying to do their job. It'll be over in a minute, and every-thing will be cool."

"I'm not going to cool it. Why the fuck do I have to live this way? I am not a criminal. I don't deserve to be treated like this. Someday one of these guns is going to go off by accident—and then I'll be a fucking statistic. What then?"

At this point the cops intervened, three of them flipping the indignant youth around against the wall, his face again flat against the brick. "This will be over in a minute. If you check out, you'll be free to go. Just relax."

In the voice of rage of the first youth was the outrage of dignity denied. Whether reasonable or not, whether minimally intrusive or not, there was something insulting about this experience—all the more insulting when repeated, one imagines, over and over again. As Justice Scalia has written, wondering whether the framers of the Constitution would have considered constitutional the police practice known as a "Terry stop"—stopping and frisking any individual whenever the police have a reasonable suspicion—"I frankly doubt . . . whether the fiercely proud men who adopted our Fourth Amendment would have allowed themselves to be subjected, on mere suspi-cion of being armed and dangerous, to such indignity."[16]

And yet again, there is the argument of minimal intrusion. If privacy is a protection against unjustified and excessive disruption, then this was no inva-sion of privacy. As the second youth argued, the intrusion was minimal; it would pass quickly (as it did—five minutes later, after their identification checked out, we had left); and it was reasonably related to some legitimate end. Privacy here is simply the protection against unreasonable and burden-some intrusions, and this search, the second youth argued, was not so unrea-sonable and burdensome as to justify the fit of anger (which also risked a much greater danger).

From this perspective, the harm in digital surveillance is even harder to reckon. I'm certain there are those who feel an indignity at the very idea that records about them are being reviewed by computers. But most would recog-nize a very different dignity at stake here. Unlike those unfortunate kids against the wall, there is no real interference here at all. Very much as with those kids, if nothing is found, nothing will happen. So what is the indignity? How is it expressed?

A third conception of privacy is about neither preserving dignity nor minimizing intrusion. It is instead substantive—privacy as a way to constrain the power of the state to regulate. Here the work of William Stuntz is a guide.[17] Stuntz argues that the real purpose of the Fourth and Fifth Amendments is to make some types of regulation too difficult by making the evidence needed to prosecute such violations effectively impossible to gather.

This is a hard idea for us to imagine. In our world, the sources of evidence are many—credit card records, telephone records, video cameras at 7-Elevens—so it's hard for us to imagine any crime that there wouldn't be some evidence to prosecute. But put yourself back two hundred years when the only real evidence was testimony and things, and the rules of evidence forbade the defendant from testifying at all. Imagine in that context the state wanted to punish you for "sedition." The only good evidence of sedition would be your writings or your own testimony about your thoughts. If those two sources were eliminated, then it would be practically impossible to prosecute sedition successfully.

As Stuntz argues, this is just what the Fourth and Fifth Amendments do. Combined, they make collecting the evidence for a crime like sedition impossible, thereby making it useless for the state to try to prosecute it. And not just sedition—as Stuntz argues, the effect of the Fourth, Fifth, and Sixth Amendments was to restrict the scope of regulation that was practically possible. As he writes: "Just as a law banning the use of contraceptives would tend to encourage bedroom searches, so also would a ban on bedroom searches tend to discourage laws prohibiting contraceptives."[18]

But were not such searches already restricted by, for example, the First Amendment? Would not a law punishing seditious libel have been unconstitutional in any case? In fact, that was not at all clear at the founding; indeed, it was so unclear that in 1798 Congress passed the Alien and Sedition Acts, which in effect punished sedition quite directly.[19] Many thought these laws unconstitutional, but the Fourth and Fifth Amendments would have been effective limits on their enforcement, whether the substantive laws were constitutional or not.

In this conception, privacy is meant as a substantive limit on government's power.[20] Understood this way, privacy does more than protect dignity or limit intrusion; privacy limits what government can do.

If this were the conception of privacy, then digital surveillance could well accommodate it. If there were certain crimes that it was inappropriate to prosecute, we could remove them from the search algorithm. It would be hard to identify what crimes constitutionally must be removed from the algo-rithm—the First Amendment clearly banishes sedition from the list already. Maybe the rule simply tracks constitutional limitation.

Now the key is to recognize that, in principle, these three distinct concep-tions of privacy could yield different results depending on the case. A search, for example, might not be intrusive but might offend dignity. In that case, we would have to choose a conception of privacy that we believed best captured the Constitution's protection.

At the time of the founding, however, these different conceptions of pri-vacy would not, for the most part, have yielded different conclusions. Any search that reached beyond the substantive limits of the amendment, or beyond the limits of dignity, would also have been a disturbance. Half of the framers could have held the dignity conception and half the utility concep-tion, but because every search would have involved a violation of both, all the framers could have endorsed the protections of the Fourth Amendment.

Today, however, that's not true. Today these three conceptions could yield very different results. The utility conception could permit efficient searches that are forbidden by the dignity and substantive conceptions. The correct translation (as Brandeis employed the term in the Olmstead wiretapping case) depends on selecting the proper conception to translate.

In this sense, our original protections were the product of what Cass Sun-stein calls an "incompletely theorized agreement."[21] Given the technology of the time, there was no reason to work out which theory underlay the consti-tutional text; all three were consistent with existing technology. But as the technology has changed, the original context has been challenged. Now that technologies such as the worm can search without disturbing, there is a con-flict about what the Fourth Amendment protects.

This conflict is the other side of Sunstein's incompletely theorized agree-ment. We might say that in any incompletely theorized agreement ambiguities will be latent, and we can describe contexts where these latencies emerge. The latent ambiguities about the protection of privacy, for example, are being ren-dered patent by the evolution of technology. And this in turn forces us to choose.

Some will once again try to suggest that the choice has been made—by our Constitution, in our past. This is the rhetoric of much of our constitu-tional jurisprudence, but it is not very helpful here. I do not think the framers worked out what the amendment would protect in a world where perfectly noninvasive searches could be conducted. They did not establish a constitu-tion to apply in all possible worlds; they established a constitution for their world. When their world differs from ours in a way that reveals a choice they did not have to make, then we need to make that choice.

PRIVACY IN PUBLIC: DATA

The story I've told so far is about limits on government: What power should the government have to surveil our activities, at least when those activities are in public? That's the special question raised by cyberspace: What limits on "digital surveillance" should there be? There are, of course, many other more traditional questions that are also important. But my focus was "digital surveillance."

In this part, I consider a third privacy question that is closely related, but very distinct. This is the question of what presumptive controls we should have over the data that we reveal to others. The issue here is not primarily the control of the government. The question is thus beyond the ordinary reach of the Fourth Amendment. Instead, the target of this control is private actors who have either gathered data about me as they've observed me, or collected data from me.

Again, let's take this from the perspective of real space first. If I hire a private detective to follow you around, I've not violated anyone's rights. If I compile a list of places you've been, there's nothing to stop me from selling that list. You might think this intrusive. You might think it outrageous that the law would allow this to happen. But again, the law traditionally didn't worry much about this kind of invasion because the costs of such surveillance were so high. Celebrities and the famous may wish the rules were different, but for most of us, for most of our history, there was no need for the law to intervene.

The same point could be made about the data I turned over to businesses or others in the days before the Internet. There was nothing in the law to limit what these entities did with that data. They could sell it to mailing list companies or brokers; they could use it however they wanted. Again, the practical cost of doing things with such data was high, so there wasn't that much done with this data. And, more importantly, the invasiveness of any such use of data was relatively low. Junk mail was the main product, and junk mail in physical space is not a significant burden.

But here, as with "digital surveillance," things have changed dramatically. Just a couple stories will give us a taste of the change:

- In the beginning of 2006, the *Chicago Sun-Times* reported[22] that there were websites selling the records of telephone calls made from cell phones. A blog, AmericaBlog, demonstrated the fact by purchasing the cell phone records of General Wesley Clark. For around $120, the blog was able to prove what most would have thought impossible: that anyone with a credit card could find

something so personal as the list (and frequency and duration) of people someone calls on a cell phone.

This conduct was so outrageous that no one really stood up to defend it.
But the defense isn't hard to construct. Wesley Clark "voluntarily" dialed the
numbers on his cell phone. He thus voluntarily turned that data over to the cell
phone company. Because the cell phone company could sell data, it made it easier for the company to keep prices low(er). Clark benefited from those lower
prices. So what's his complaint?

• A number of years ago I received a letter from AT&T. It was addressed to an old
girlfriend, but the letter had not been forwarded. The address was my then-
current apartment. AT&T wanted to offer her a new credit card. They were a bit
late: She and I had broken up eight years before. Since then, she had moved to
Texas, and I had moved to Chicago, to Washington, back to Chicago, on to New
Haven, back to Chicago, and finally to Boston, where I had moved twice. My
peripateticism, however, did not deter AT&T. With great faith in my constancy,
it believed that a woman I had not even seen in many years was living with me
in this apartment.

How did AT&T maintain such a belief? Well, floating about in cyberspace is
lots of data about me. It has been collected from me ever since I began using
credit cards, telephones, and who knows what else. The system continuously
tries to update and refine this extraordinary data set—that is, it profiles who I
am and, using that profile, determines how it will interact with me.

These are just the tip of the iceberg. Everything you do on the Net produces data. That data is, in aggregate, extremely valuable, more valuable to
commerce than it is to the government. The government (in normal times)
really cares only that you obey some select set of laws. But commerce is keen
to figure out how you want to spend your money, and data does that. With
massive amounts of data about what you do and what you say, it becomes
increasingly possible to market to you in a direct and effective way. Google
Gmail processes the data in your e-mail to see what it should try to sell. Amazon watches what you browse to see what special "Gold Box" offers it can
make. There's an endless list of entities that want to know more about you to
better serve (at least) their interests. What limits, or restrictions, ought there
to be on them?

We should begin with an obvious point that might help direct an answer.
There's a big difference between (1) collecting data about X to suss out a
crime or a criminal, (2) collecting data about X that will be sold to Y simply
to reveal facts about X (such as his cell phone calls), and (3) collecting data
about X to better market to X. (1) and (2) make X worse off, though if we

believe the crime is properly a crime, then with (1), X is not worse off relative to where he should be. (3) in principle could make you better off—it facilitates advertising that is better targeted and better designed to encourage voluntary transactions. I say "in principle" because even though it's possible that the ads are better targeted, there are also more of them. On balance, X might be worse off with the flood of well-targeted offers than with a few less well-targeted offers. But despite that possibility, the motive of (3) is different from (1) and (2), and that might well affect how we should respond.

So let's begin with the focus on (3): What is the harm from this sort of "invasion"? Arguments rage on both sides of this question.

The "no harm" side assumes that the balance of privacy is struck at the line where you reveal information about yourself to the public. Sure, information kept behind closed doors or written in a private diary should be protected by the law. But when you go out in public, when you make transactions there or send material there, you give up any right to privacy. Others now have the right to collect data about your public behavior and do with it what suits them.

Why is that idea not troubling to these theorists? The reasons are many:

- First, the harm is actually not very great. You get a discount card at your local grocery store; the store then collects data about what you buy. With that data, the store may market different goods to you or figure out how better to price its products; it may even decide that it should offer different mixes of discounts to better serve customers. These responses, the argument goes, are the likely ones, because the store's business is only to sell groceries more efficiently.
- Second, it is an unfair burden to force others to ignore what you show them. If data about you are not usable by others, then it is as if you were requiring others to discard what you have deposited on their land. If you do not like others using information about you, do not put it in their hands.
- Third, these data actually do some good. I do not know why Nike thinks I am a good person to tell about their latest sneakers, and I do not know why Keds does not know to call. In both cases, I suspect the reason is bad data about me. I would love it if Nike knew enough to leave me alone. And if these data were better collected and sorted, it would.
- Finally, in general, companies don't spend money collecting these data to actually learn anything about you. They want to learn about people *like* you. They want to know your type. In principle, they would be happy to know your type even if they could not then learn who you are. What the merchants want is a way to discriminate—only in the sense of being able to tell the difference between sorts of people.

The other side of this argument, however, also has a point. It begins, again, by noticing the values that were originally protected by the imperfection of monitoring technology. This imperfection helped preserve important substantive values; one such value is the benefit of innocence. At any given time, there are innocent facts about you that may appear, in a particular context or to a particular set, guilty. Peter Lewis, in a *New York Times* article called "Forget Big Brother," puts the point well:

> Surveillance cameras followed the attractive young blond woman through the lobby of the midtown Manhattan hotel, kept a glassy eye on her as she rode the elevator up to the 23rd floor and peered discreetly down the hall as she knocked at the door to my room. I have not seen the videotapes, but I can imagine the digital readout superimposed on the scenes, noting the exact time of the encounter. That would come in handy if someone were to question later why this woman, who is not my wife, was visiting my hotel room during a recent business trip. The cameras later saw us heading off to dinner and to the theater—a middle aged, married man from Texas with his arm around a pretty East Village woman young enough to be his daughter.

"As a matter of fact," Lewis writes, "she is my daughter."[23]

One lesson of the story is the burden of these monitored facts. The burden is on you, the monitored, first to establish your innocence, and second to assure all who might see these ambiguous facts that you are innocent. Both processes, however, are imperfect; say what you want, doubts will remain. There are always some who will not believe your plea of innocence.

Modern monitoring only exacerbates this problem. Your life becomes an ever-increasing record; your actions are forever held in storage, open to being revealed at any time, and therefore at any time demanding a justification.

A second value follows directly from this modern capacity for archiving data. We all desire to live in separate communities, or among or within separate normative spaces. Privacy, or the ability to control data about yourself, supports this desire. It enables these multiple communities and disables the power of one dominant community to norm others into oblivion. Think, for example, about a gay man in an intolerant small town.

The point comes through most clearly when contrasted with an argument advanced by David Brin.[24] Brin argues against this concern with privacy—at least if privacy is defined as the need to block the production and distribution of data about others. He argues against it because he believes that such an end is impossible; the genie is out of the bottle. Better, he suggests, to find ways to ensure that this data-gathering ability is generally available. The solution to your spying on me is not to block your spying, but to let me spy on you—to hold you accountable, perhaps for spying, perhaps for whatever else you might be doing.

There are two replies to this argument. One asks: Why do we have to choose? Why can't we both control spying and build in checks on the distribution of spying techniques?

The other reply is more fundamental. Brin assumes that this counter spying would be useful to hold others "accountable." But according to whose norms? "Accountable" is a benign term only so long as we have confidence in the community doing the accounting. When we live in multiple communities, accountability becomes a way for one community to impose its view of propriety on another. Because we do not live in a single community, we do not live by a single set of values. And perfect accountability can only undermine this mix of values.

The imperfection in present monitoring enables this multiplication of normative communities. The ability to get along without perfect recording enables a diversity that perfect knowledge would erase.

A third value arises from a concern about profiling. If you search within Google for "mortgage" in a web search engine, advertising for mortgages appears on your computer screen. The same for sex and for cars. Advertising is linked to the search you submit. Data is collected, but not just about the search. Different sites collect just about every bit of personal information about you that they can.[25] And when you link from the Google search to a web page, the search you just performed is passed along to the next site.

Data collection is the dominant activity of commercial websites. Some 92 percent of them collect personal data from web users, which they then aggregate, sort, and use.[26] Oscar Gandy calls this the "panoptic sort"—a vast structure for collecting data and discriminating on the basis of that data—and it is this discrimination, he says, that ought to concern us.[27]

But why should it concern us? Put aside an important class of problems— the misuse of the data—and focus instead on its ordinary use. As I said earlier, the main effect is simply to make the market work more smoothly: Interests and products are matched to people in a way that is better targeted and less intrusive than what we have today. Imagine a world where advertisers could tell which venues paid and which did not; where it was inefficient to advertise with billboards and on broadcasts; where most advertising was targeted and specific. Advertising would be more likely to go to those people for whom it would be useful information. Or so the argument goes. This is discrimination, no doubt, but not the discrimination of Jim Crow. It is the wonderful sort of discrimination that spares me Nike ads.

But beyond a perhaps fleeting concern about how such data affect the individual, profiling raises a more sustained collective concern about how it might affect a community.

That concern is manipulation. You might be skeptical about the power of television advertising to control people's desires: Television is so obvious, the motives so clear. But what happens when the motive is not so obvious? When options just seem to appear right when you happen to want them? When the system seems to know what you want better and earlier than you do, how can you know where these desires really come from?

Whether this possibility is a realistic one, or whether it should be a concern, are hard and open questions. Steven Johnson argues quite effectively that in fact these agents of choice will facilitate a much greater range and diversity—even, in part, chaos—of choice.[28] But there's another possibility as well—profiles will begin to normalize the population from which the norm is drawn. The observing will affect the observed. The system watches what you do; it fits you into a pattern; the pattern is then fed back to you in the form of options set by the pattern; the options reinforce the pattern; the cycle begins again.

A second concern is about equality. Profiling raises a question that was latent in the market until quite recently. For much of the nineteenth century in the United States economic thought was animated by an ideal of equality. In the civil space individuals were held to be equal. They could purchase and sell equally; they could approach others on equal terms. Facts about individuals might be known, and some of these facts might disqualify them from some economic transactions—your prior bankruptcy, for example, might inhibit your ability to make transactions in the future. But in the main, there were spaces of relative anonymity, and economic transactions could occur within them.[29]

Over time this space of equality has been displaced by economic zonings that aim at segregation.[30] They are laws, that is, that promote distinctions based on social or economic criteria.[31] The most telling example is zoning itself. It was not until this century that local law was used to put people into segregated spaces.[32] At first, this law was racially based, but when racially based zoning was struck down, the techniques of zoning shifted.[33]

It is interesting to recall just how contentious this use of law was.[34] To many, rich and poor alike, it was an affront to the American ideal of equality to make where you live depend on how much money you had. It always does, of course, when property is something you must buy. But zoning laws add the support of law to the segregation imposed by the market. The effect is to recreate in law, and therefore in society, distinctions among people.

There was a time when we would have defined our country as a place that aimed to erase these distinctions. The historian Gordon Wood describes this goal as an important element of the revolution that gave birth to the United States.[35] The enemy was social and legal hierarchy; the aim was a society of equality. The revolution was an attack on hierarchies of social rank and the special privileges they might obtain.

All social hierarchies require information before they can make discriminations of rank. Having enough information about people required, historically, fairly stable social orders. Making fine class distinctions—knowing, for instance, whether a well-dressed young man was the gentleman he claimed to be or only a dressed-up tradesman—required knowledge of local fashions, accents, customs, and manners. Only where there was relatively little mobility could these systems of hierarchy be imposed.

As mobility increased, then, these hierarchical systems were challenged. Beyond the extremes of the very rich and very poor, the ability to make subtle distinctions of rank disappeared as the mobility and fluidity of society made them too difficult to track.

Profiling changes all this. An efficient and effective system for monitoring makes it possible once again to make these subtle distinctions of rank. Collecting data cheaply and efficiently will take us back to the past. Think about frequent flyer miles. Everyone sees the obvious feature of frequent flyer miles—the free trips for people who fly frequently. This rebate program is quite harmless on its own. The more interesting part is the power it gives to airlines to discriminate in their services.

When a frequent flyer makes a reservation, the reservation carries with it a customer profile. This profile might include information about which seat she prefers or whether she likes vegetarian food. It also tells the reservation clerk how often this person flies. Some airlines would then discriminate on the basis of this information. The most obvious way is through seat location—frequent flyers get better seats. But such information might also affect how food is allocated on the flight—the frequent flyers with the most miles get first choice; those with the fewest may get no choice.

In the scheme of social justice, of course, this is small potatoes. But my point is more general. Frequent flyer systems permit the re-creation of systems of status. They supply information about individuals that organizations might value, and use, in dispensing services.[36] They make discrimination possible because they restore information that mobility destroyed. They are ways of defeating one benefit of anonymity—the benefit of equality.

Economists will argue that in many contexts this ability to discriminate—in effect, to offer goods at different prices to different people—is overall a benefit.[37] On average, people are better off if price discrimination occurs than if it does not. So we are better off, these economists might say, if we facilitate such discrimination when we can.

But these values are just one side of the equation. Weighed against them are the values of equality. For us they may seem remote, but we should not assume that because they are remote now they were always remote.

Take tipping: As benign (if annoying) as you might consider the practice of tipping, there was a time at the turn of the century when the very idea was an insult. It offended a free citizen's dignity. As Viviana Zelizer describes it:

> In the early 1900s, as tipping became increasingly popular, it provoked great moral and social controversy. In fact, there were nationwide efforts, some successful, by state legislatures to abolish tipping by turning it into a punishable misdemeanor. In countless newspaper editorials and magazine articles, in etiquette books, and even in court, tips were closely scrutinized with a mix of curiosity, amusement, and ambivalence—and often open hostility. When in 1907, the government officially sanctioned tipping by allowing commissioned officers and enlisted men of the United States Navy to include tips as an item in their travel expense vouchers, the decision was denounced as an illegitimate endorsement of graft. Periodically, there were calls to organize anti-tipping leagues.[38]

There is a conception of equality that would be corrupted by the efficiency that profiling embraces. That conception is a value to be weighed against efficiency. Although I believe this value is relatively weak in American life, who am I to say? The important point is not about what is strong or weak, but about the tension or conflict that lay dormant until revealed by the emerging technology of profiling.

The pattern should be familiar by now, because we have seen the change elsewhere. Once again, the code changes, throwing into relief a conflict of values. Whereas before there was relative equality because the information that enabled discrimination was too costly to acquire, now it pays to discriminate. The difference—what makes it pay—is the emergence of a code. The code changes, the behavior changes, and a value latent in the prior regime is displaced.

We could react by hobbling the code, thus preserving this world. We could create constitutional or statutory restrictions that prevent a move to the new world. Or we could find ways to reconcile this emerging world with the values we think are fundamental.

SOLUTIONS

I've identified two distinct threats to the values of privacy that the Internet will create. The first is the threat from "digital surveillance"—the growing capacity of the government (among others) to "spy" on your activities "in public." From Internet access, to e-mail, to telephone calls, to walking on the street, digital technology is opening up the opportunity for increasingly perfect burdenless searches.

The second threat comes from the increasing aggregation of data by private (among other) entities. These data are gathered not so much to "spy" as to facilitate commerce. Some of that commerce exploits the source of the data (Wesley Clark's cell phone numbers). Some of that commerce tries to facilitate commerce with the source of that data (targeted ads).

Against these two different risks, we can imagine four types of responses, each mapping one of the modalities that I described in Chapter 7:

- Law: Legal regulation could be crafted to respond to these threats. We'll consider some of these later, but the general form should be clear enough. The law could direct the President not to surveil American citizens without reasonable suspicion, for example. (Whether the President follows the law is a separate question.) Or the law could ban the sale of data gathered from customers without express permission of the customers. In either case, the law threatens sanctions to change behavior directly. The aim of the law could either be to enhance the power of individuals to control data about them, or to disable such power (for example, by making certain privacy-related transactions illegal).
- Norms: Norms could be used to respond to these threats. Norms among commercial entities, for example, could help build trust around certain privacy protective practices.
- Markets: In ways that will become clearer below, the market could be used to protect the privacy of individuals.
- Architecture/Code: Technology could be used to protect privacy. Such technologies are often referred to as "Privacy Enhancing Technologies." These are technologies designed to give the user more technical control over data associated with him or her.

As I've argued again and again, there is no single solution to policy problems on the Internet. Every solution requires a mix of at least two modalities. And in the balance of this chapter, my aim is to describe a mix for each of these two threats to privacy.

No doubt this mix will be controversial to some. But my aim is not so much to push any particular mix of settings on these modality dials, as it is to demonstrate a certain approach. I don't insist on the particular solutions I propose, but I do insist that solutions in the context of cyberspace are the product of such a mix.

Surveillance

The government surveils as much as it can in its fight against whatever its current fight is about. When that surveillance is human—wiretapping, or the like—then traditional legal limits ought to apply. Those limits impose costs (and thus, using the market, reduce the incidence to those most significant); they assure at least some review. And, perhaps most importantly, they build within law enforcement a norm respecting procedure.

When that surveillance is digital, however, then it is my view that a different set of restrictions should apply. The law should sanction "digital surveillance" if, *but only if*, a number of conditions apply:

1. The purpose of the search enabled in the algorithm is described.
2. The function of the algorithm is reviewed.
3. The purpose and the function match is certified.
4. No action—including a subsequent search—can be taken against any individual on the basis of the algorithm without judicial review.
5. With very limited exceptions, no action against any individual can be pursued for matters outside the purpose described. Thus, if you're looking for evidence of drug dealing, you can't use any evidence discovered for prosecuting credit card fraud.

That describes the legal restrictions applied against the government in order to enhance privacy. If these are satisfied, then in my view such digital surveillance should not conflict with the Fourth Amendment. In addition to these, there are privacy enhancing technologies (PETs) that should be broadly available to individuals as well. These technologies enable individuals to achieve anonymity in their transactions online. Many companies and activist groups help spread these technologies across the network.

Anonymity in this sense simply means non-traceability. Tools that enable this sort of non-traceability make it possible for an individual to send a message without the content of that message being traced to the sender. If implemented properly, there is absolutely no technical way to trace that message. That kind of anonymity is essential to certain kinds of communication.

It is my view that, at least so long as political repression remains a central feature of too many world governments, free governments should recognize a protected legal right to these technologies. I acknowledge that view is controversial. A less extreme view would acknowledge the differences between the digital world and real world,[39] and guarantee a right to pseudonymous communication but not anonymous communication. In this sense, a pseudonymous transaction doesn't obviously or directly link to an individual without court intervention. But it contains an effective fingerprint that would allow the proper authority, under the proper circumstances, to trace the communication back to its originator.

In this regime, the important question is who is the authority, and what process is required to get access to the identification. In my view, the authority must be the government. The government must subject its demand for revealing the identity of an individual to judicial process. And the executive should never hold the technical capacity to make that link on its own.

Again, no one will like this balance. Friends of privacy will be furious with any endorsement of surveillance. But I share Judge Posner's view that a sophisticated surveillance technology might actually increase effective privacy, if it decreases the instances in which humans intrude on other humans. Likewise, friends of security will be appalled at the idea that anyone would endorse technologies of anonymity. "Do you know how hard it is to crack a drug lord's encrypted e-mail communication?" one asked me.

The answer is no, I don't have a real sense. But I care less about enabling the war on drugs than I do about enabling democracies to flourish. Technologies that enable the latter will enable the former. Or to be less cowardly, technologies that enable Aung San Suu Kyi to continue to push for democracy in Burma will enable Al Qaeda to continue to wage its terrorist war against the United States. I acknowledge that. I accept that might lead others to a less extreme position. But I would urge the compromise in favor of surveillance to go no further than protected pseudonymity.

Control of Data

The problem of controlling the spread or misuse of data is more complex and ambiguous. There are uses of personal data that many would object to. But many is not all. There are some who are perfectly happy to reveal certain data to certain entities, and there are many more who would become happy if they could trust that their data was properly used.

Here again, the solution mixes modalities. But this time, we begin with the technology.[40]

As I described extensively in Chapter 4, there is an emerging push to build an Identity Layer onto the Internet. In my view, we should view this Identity Layer as a PET (private enhancing technology): It would enable individuals to more effectively control the data about them that they reveal. It would also enable individuals to have a trustable pseudonymous identity that websites and others should be happy to accept. Thus, with this technology, if a site needs to know I am over 18, or an American citizen, or authorized to access a university library, the technology can certify this data without revealing anything else. Of all the changes to information practices that we could imagine, this would be the most significant in reducing the extent of redundant or unnecessary data flowing in the ether of the network.

A second PET to enable greater control over the use of data would be a protocol called the Platform for Privacy Preferences (or P3P for short).[41] P3P would enable a *machine-readable* expression of the privacy preferences of an individual. It would enable an automatic way for an individual to recognize when a site does not comply with his privacy preferences. If you surf to a site that expresses its privacy policy using P3P, and its policy is inconsistent with your preferences, then depending upon the implementation, either the site or you are made aware of the problem created by this conflict. The technology thus could make clear a conflict in preferences. And recognizing that conflict is the first step to protecting preferences.

The critical part of this strategy is to make these choices machine-readable. If you Google "privacy policy," you'll get close to 2.5 *billion* hits on the Web. And if you click through to the vast majority of them (not that you could do that in this lifetime), you will find that they are among the most incomprehensible legal texts around (and that's saying a lot). These policies are the product of pre-Internet thinking about how to deal with a policy problem. The government was pushed to "solve" the problem of Internet privacy. Its solution was to require "privacy policies" be posted everywhere. But does anybody read these policies? And if they do, do they remember them from one site to another? Do you know the difference between Amazon's policies and Google's?

The mistake of the government was in not requiring that those policies also be understandable by a computer. Because if we had 2.5 billion sites with both a human readable and machine readable statement of privacy policies, then we would have the infrastructure necessary to encourage the development of this PET, P3P. But because the government could not think beyond its traditional manner of legislating—because it didn't think to require changes in code as well as legal texts—we don't have that infrastructure now. But, in my view, it is critical.

These technologies standing alone, however, do nothing to solve the problem of privacy on the Net. It is absolutely clear that to complement these technologies, we need legal regulation. But this regulation is of three very different sorts. The first kind is substantive—laws that set the boundaries of privacy protection. The second kind is procedural—laws that mandate fair procedures for dealing with privacy practices. And the third is enabling—laws that make enforceable agreements between individuals and corporations about how privacy is to be respected.

(1) Limits on Choice

One kind of legislation is designed to limit individual freedom. Just as labor law bans certain labor contracts, or consumer law forbids certain credit arrangements, this kind of privacy law would restrict the freedom of individuals to give up certain aspects of their privacy. The motivation for this limitation could either be substantive or procedural—substantive in that it reflects a substantive judgment about choices individuals should not make, or procedural in that it reflects the view that systematically, when faced with this choice, individuals will choose in ways that they regret. In either case, the role of this type of privacy regulation is to block transactions deemed to weaken privacy within a community.

(2) The Process to Protect Privacy

The most significant normative structure around privacy practices was framed more than thirty years ago by the HEW (Health, Education, Welfare) Advisory Committee on Automated Data Systems. This report set out five principles that were to define the "Code of Fair Information Practices."[42] These principles require:

1. There must be no personal data record-keeping systems whose very existence is secret.
2. There must be a way for a person to find out what information about the person is in a record and how it is used.
3. There must be a way for a person to prevent information about the person that was obtained for one purpose from being used or made available for other purposes without the person's consent.
4. There must be a way for a person to correct or amend a record of identifiable information about the person.

5. Any organization creating, maintaining, using, or disseminating records of identifiable personal data must assure the reliability of the data for their intended use and must take precautions to prevent misuses of the data.

These principles express important substantive values—for example, that data not be reused beyond an original consent, or that systems for gathering data be reliable—but they don't interfere with an individual's choice to release his or her own data for specified purposes. They are in this sense individual autonomy enhancing, and their spirit has guided the relatively thin and ad hoc range of privacy legislation that has been enacted both nationally and at the state level.[43]

(3) Rules to Enable Choice About Privacy

The real challenge for privacy, however, is how to enable a meaningful choice in the digital age. And in this respect, the technique of the American government so far—namely, to require text-based privacy policy statements—is a perfect example of how not to act. Cluttering the web with incomprehensible words will not empower consumers to make useful choices as they surf the Web. If anything, it drives consumers away from even attempting to understand what rights they give away as they move from site to site.

P3P would help in this respect, but only if (1) there were a strong push to spread the technology across all areas of the web and (2) the representations made within the P3P infrastructure were enforceable. Both elements require legal action to be effected.

In the first edition of this book, I offered a strategy that would, in my view, achieve both (1) and (2): namely, by protecting personal data through a property right. As with copyright, a privacy property right would create strong incentives in those who want to use that property to secure the appropriate consent. That content could then be channeled (through legislation) through appropriate technologies. But without that consent, the user of the privacy property would be a privacy pirate. Indeed, many of the same tools that could protect copyright in this sense could also be used to protect privacy.

This solution also recognizes what I believe is an important feature of privacy—that people value privacy differently.[44] It also respects those different values. It may be extremely important to me not to have my telephone number easily available; you might not care at all. And as the law's presumptive preference is to use a legal device that gives individuals the freedom to be different—meaning the freedom to have and have respected wildly different subjective values—that suggests the device we use here is property. A property

system is designed precisely to permit differences in value to be respected by the law. If you won't sell your Chevy Nova for anything less than $10,000, then the law will support you.

The opposite legal entitlement in the American legal tradition is called a "liability rule."[45] A liability rule also protects an entitlement, but its protection is less individual. If you have a resource protected by a liability rule, then I can take that resource so long as I pay a state-determined price. That price may be more or less than you value it at. But the point is, I have the right to take that resource, regardless.

An example from copyright law might make the point more clearly. A derivative right is the right to build upon a copyrighted work. A traditional example is a translation, or a movie based on a book. The law of copyright gives the copyright owner a property right over that derivative right. Thus, if you want to make a movie out of John Grisham's latest novel, you have to pay whatever Grisham says. If you don't, and you make the movie, you've violated Grisham's rights.

The same is not true with the derivative rights that composers have. If a songwriter authorizes someone to record his song, then anyone else has a right to record that song, so long as they follow certain procedures and pay a specified rate. Thus, while Grisham can choose to give only one filmmaker the right to make a film based on his novel, the Beatles must allow anyone to record a song a member of the Beatles composed, so long as that person pays. The derivative right for novels is thus protected by a property rule; the derivative right for recordings by a liability rule.

The law has all sorts of reasons for imposing a liability rule rather than a property rule. But the general principle is that we should use a property rule, at least where the "transaction costs" of negotiating are low, and where there is no contradicting public value.[46] And it is my view that, with a technology like P3P, we could lower transaction costs enough to make a property rule work. That property rule in turn would reinforce whatever diversity people had about views about their privacy—permitting some to choose to waive their rights and others to hold firm.

There was one more reason I pushed for a property right. In my view, the protection of privacy would be stronger if people conceived of the right as a property right. People need to take ownership of this right, and protect it, and propertizing is the traditional tool we use to identify and enable protection. If we could see one fraction of the passion defending privacy that we see defending copyright, we might make progress in protecting privacy.

But my proposal for a property right was resoundingly rejected by critics whose views I respect.[47] I don't agree with the core of these criticisms. For the reasons powerfully marshaled by Neil Richards, I especially don't agree with the claim that there would be a First Amendment problem with propertizing privacy.[48] In any case, William McGeveran suggested an alternative that reached essentially the same end that I sought, without raising any of the concerns that most animated the critics.[49]

The alternative simply specifies that a representation made by a website through the P3P protocol be considered a binding offer, which, if accepted by someone using the website, becomes an enforceable contract.[50] That rule, tied to a requirement that privacy policies be expressed in a machine-readable form such as P3P, would both (1) spread P3P and (2) make P3P assertions effectively law. This would still be weaker than a property rule, for reasons I will leave to the notes.[51] And it may well encourage the shrink-wrap culture, which raises its own problems. But for my purposes here, this solution is a useful compromise.

To illustrate again the dynamic of cyberlaw: We use law (a requirement of policies expressed in a certain way, and a contract presumption about those expressions) to encourage a certain kind of technology (P3P), so that that technology enables individuals to better achieve in cyberspace what they want. It is LAW helping CODE to perfect privacy POLICY.

This is not to say, of course, that we have no protections for privacy. As we have seen throughout, there are other laws besides federal, and other regulators besides the law. At times these other regulators may protect privacy better than law does, but where they don't, then in my view law is needed.

PRIVACY COMPARED

The reader who was dissatisfied with my argument in the last chapter is likely to begin asking pointed questions. "Didn't you reject in the last chapter the very regime you are endorsing here? Didn't you reject an architecture that would facilitate perfect sale of intellectual property? Isn't that what you've created here?"

The charge is accurate enough. I have endorsed an architecture here that is essentially the same architecture I questioned for intellectual property. Both are regimes for trading information; both make information "like" "real" property. But with copyright, I argued against a fully privatized property regime; with privacy, I am arguing in favor of it. What gives?

The difference is in the underlying values that inform, or that should inform, information in each context. In the context of intellectual property, our bias should be for freedom. Who knows what "information wants";[52] whatever it wants, we should read the bargain that the law strikes with holders of intellectual property as narrowly as we can. We should take a grudging attitude to property rights in intellectual property; we should support them only as much as necessary to build and support information regimes.

But (at least some kinds of) information about individuals should be treated differently. You do not strike a deal with the law about personal or private information. The law does not offer you a monopoly right in exchange for your publication of these facts. That is what is distinct about privacy: Individuals should be able to control information about themselves. We should be eager to help them protect that information by giving them the structures and the rights to do so. We value, or want, our peace. And thus, a regime that allows us such peace by giving us control over private information is a regime consonant with public values. It is a regime that public authorities should support.

There is a second, perhaps more helpful, way of making the same point. Intellectual property, once created, is non-diminishable. The more people who use it, the more society benefits. The bias in intellectual property is thus, properly, towards sharing and freedom. Privacy, on the other hand, is diminishable. The more people who are given license to tread on a person's privacy, the less that privacy exists. In this way, privacy is more like real property than it is like intellectual property. No single person's trespass may destroy it, but each incremental trespass diminishes its value by some amount.

This conclusion is subject to important qualifications, only two of which I will describe here.

The first is that nothing in my regime would give individuals final or complete control over the kinds of data they can sell, or the kinds of privacy they can buy. The P3P regime would in principle enable upstream control of privacy rights as well as individual control. If we lived, for example, in a regime that identified individuals based on jurisdiction, then transactions with the P3P regime could be limited based on the rules for particular jurisdictions.

Second, there is no reason such a regime would have to protect all kinds of private data, and nothing in the scheme so far tells us what should and should not be considered "private" information. There may be facts about yourself that you are not permitted to hide; more important, there may be claims about yourself that you are not permitted to make ("I am a lawyer," or, "Call me, I'm a doctor"). You should not be permitted to engage in fraud or to do harm to others. This limitation is an analog to fair use in intellectual property—a limit to the space that privacy may protect.

I started this chapter by claiming that with privacy the cat is already out of the bag. We already have architectures that deny individuals control over what others know about them; the question is what we can do in response.

My response has been: Look to the code, Luke. We must build into the architecture a capacity to enable choice—not choice by humans but by machines. The architecture must enable machine-to-machine negotiations about privacy so that individuals can instruct their machines about the privacy they want to protect.

But how will we get there? How can this architecture be erected? Individuals may want cyberspace to protect their privacy, but what would push cyberspace to build in the necessary architectures?

Not the market. The power of commerce is not behind any such change. Here, the invisible hand would really be invisible. Collective action must be taken to bend the architectures toward this goal, and collective action is just what politics is for. Laissez-faire will not cut it.

TWELVE

free speech

THE RIGHT TO FREE SPEECH IS NOT THE RIGHT TO SPEAK FOR FREE. IT IS NOT THE right to free access to television, or the right that people will not hate you for what you have to say. Strictly speaking—legally speaking—the right to free speech in the United States means the right to be free from punishment by the government in retaliation for at least some (probably most) speech. You cannot be jailed for criticizing the President, though you can be jailed for threatening him; you cannot be fined for promoting segregation, though you will be shunned if you do. You cannot be stopped from speaking in a public place, though you can be stopped from speaking with an FM transmitter. Speech in the United States is protected—in a complex, and at times convoluted, way—but its constitutional protection is a protection against the government.

Nevertheless, a constitutional account of free speech that thought only of government would be radically incomplete. Two societies could have the same "First Amendment"—the same protections against government's wrath—but if within one dissenters are tolerated while in the other they are shunned, the two societies would be very different free-speech societies. More than government constrains speech, and more than government protects it. A complete account of this—and any—right must consider the full range of burdens and protections.

Consider, for example, the "rights" of the disabled to protection against discrimination as each of the four modalities of Chapter 7 construct them. The law protects the disabled. Social norms don't. The market provides goods to help the disabled, but they bear the full cost of that help. And until the law intervened, architecture did little to help the disabled integrate into society (think about stairs). The net of these four modalities describes the protection, or "rights," that in any particular context the disabled have. Law might intervene

233

to strengthen that protection—for example, by regulating architectures so they better integrate the disabled. But for any given "right," we can use this mix of modalities to describe how well (or not) that "right" is protected.

In the terms of Chapter 7, then, these are modalities of both regulation and protection. That is, they can function both as constraints on behavior and as protections against other constraints. The following figure captures the point.

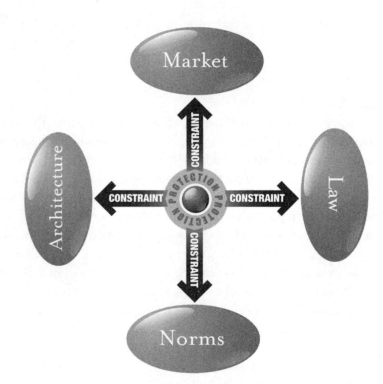

In the center is the object regulated—the pathetic dot from Chapter 7. Surrounding the individual now is a shield of protection, the net of law/norms/market/architecture that limits the constraints these modalities would otherwise place on the individual. I have not separated the four in the sphere of the shield because obviously there is no direct match between the modality of constraint and the modality of protection. When law as protector conflicts with law as constraint, constitutional law overrides ordinary law.

These modalities function together. Some might undercut others, meaning that the sum of protections might seem to be less significant than the parts. The "right" to promote the decriminalization of drugs in the present context of the war on drugs is an example. The law protects your right to advocate the decriminalization of drugs. The state cannot lock you up if, like George Soros, you start a campaign for the decriminalization of marijuana or if, like the Nobel Prize–winning economist Milton Friedman or the federal judge Richard Posner, you write articles suggesting it. If the First Amendment means anything, it means that the state cannot criminalize speech about law reform.

But that legal protection does not mean that I would suffer no consequences for promoting legalization of drugs. My hometown neighbors would be appalled at the idea, and some no doubt would shun me. Nor would the market necessarily support me. It is essentially impossible to buy time on television for a speech advocating such a reform. Television stations have the right to select their ads (within some limits); mine would most likely be deemed too controversial.[1] Stations also have the FCC—an active combatant in the war on drugs—looking over their shoulders. And even if I were permitted to advertise, I am not George Soros. I do not have millions to spend on such a campaign. I might manage a few off-hour spots on a local station, but I could not afford, for instance, a campaign on the networks during prime time.

Finally, architecture wouldn't protect my speech very well either. In the United States at least, there are few places where you can stand before the public and address them about some matter of public import without most people thinking you a nut or a nuisance. There is no speakers' corner in every city; most towns have no town meeting. "America offline," in this sense, is very much like America Online—not designed to give individuals access to a wide audience to address public matters. Only professionals get to address Americans on public issues—politicians, scholars, celebrities, journalists, and activists, most of whom are confined to single issues. The rest of us have a choice—listen, or be dispatched to the gulag of social lunacy.

Thus, the effective protection for controversial speech is more conditional than a view of the law alone would suggest. Put differently, when more than law is reckoned, the right to be a dissenter is less protected than it could be.

Let's take this example now to cyberspace. How is the "right" to promote the legalization of drugs in cyberspace protected? Here too, of course, the law protects my right of advocacy—at least in the United States. But it is quite possible that my speech would be illegal elsewhere and that perhaps I could be prosecuted for uttering such speech in cyberspace "in" another country. Speech promoting the Nazi Party, for example, is legal in the United States but not in Germany.[2] Uttering such speech in cyberspace may make one liable in German space as well.

The law therefore is an imperfect protection. Do norms help to protect speech? With the relative anonymity of cyberspace and its growing size, norms do not function well there. Even in cyberspaces where people know each other well, they are likely to be more tolerant of dissident views when they know (or believe, or hope) the dissident lives thousands of miles away.

The market also provides a major protection to speech in cyberspace—relative to real space, market constraints on speech in cyberspace are tiny. Recall how easily Jake Baker became a publisher, with a potential readership greater than the readership of all law books (like this one) published in the last decade. Look at the more than 50 million blogs that now enable millions to express their view of whatever. The low cost of publishing means publishing is no longer a barrier to speaking. As Eben Moglen asks, "Will there be an unpublished poet in the 21st Century?"

But on top of this list of protectors of speech in cyberspace is (once again) architecture. Relative anonymity, decentralized distribution, multiple points of access, no necessary tie to geography, no simple system to identify content, tools of encryption[3]—all these features and consequences of the Internet protocol make it difficult to control speech in cyberspace. The architecture of cyberspace is the real protector of speech there; it is the real "First Amendment in cyberspace," and this First Amendment is no local ordinance.[4]

Just think about what this means. For over 60 years the United States has been the exporter of a certain political ideology, at its core a conception of free speech. Many have criticized this conception: Some found it too extreme, others not extreme enough. Repressive regimes—China, North Korea—rejected it directly; tolerant regimes—France, Hungary—complained of cultural decay; egalitarian regimes—the Scandinavian countries—puzzled over how we could think of ourselves as free when only the rich can speak and pornography is repressed.

This debate has gone on at the political level for a long time. And yet, as if under cover of night, we have now wired these nations with an architecture of communication that builds within their borders a far stronger First Amendment than our ideology ever advanced. Nations wake up to find that their telephone lines are tools of free expression, that e-mail carries news of their repression far beyond their borders, that images are no longer the monopoly of state-run television stations but can be transmitted from a simple modem. We have exported to the world, through the architecture of the Internet, a First Amendment more extreme in code than our own First Amendment in law.

This chapter is about the regulation of speech and the protection of speech in cyberspace—and therefore also in real space. My aim is to obsess about the relationship between architecture and the freedom it makes possible, and about the significance of law in the construction of that architecture. It is to get you to see how this freedom is built—the constitutional politics in the architectures of cyberspace.

I say "politics" because this building is not over. As I have argued (over and over again), there is no single architecture for cyberspace; there is no given or necessary structure to its design. The first-generation Internet might well have breached walls of control. But there is no reason to believe that architects of the second generation will do so, or not to expect a second generation to rebuild control. There is no reason to think, in other words, that this initial flash of freedom will not be short-lived. And there is certainly no justification for acting as if it will not.

We can already see the beginnings of this reconstruction. The architecture is being remade to re-regulate what real-space architecture before made regulable. Already the Net is changing from free to controlled space.

Some of these steps to re-regulate are inevitable; some shift back is unavoidable. Before the change is complete, however, we must understand the freedoms the Net now provides and determine which freedoms we mean to preserve.

And not just preserve. The architecture of the Internet, as it is right now, is perhaps the most important model of free speech since the founding. This model has implications far beyond e-mail and web pages. Two hundred years after the framers ratified the Constitution, the Net has taught us what the First Amendment means. If we take this meaning seriously, then the First Amendment will require a fairly radical restructuring of the architectures of speech off the Net as well.[5]

But all of that is getting ahead of the story. In the balance of this chapter, I address four distinct free speech in cyberspace questions. With each, I want to consider how "free speech" is regulated.

These stories do not all have the same constitutional significance. But they all illustrate the dynamic at the core of the argument of this book—how technology interacts with law to create policy.

THE REGULATORS OF SPEECH: PUBLICATION

Floyd Abrams is one of America's leading First Amendment lawyers. In 1971 he was a young partner at the law firm of Cahill, Gordon.[6] Late in the evening of Monday, June 14, he received a call from James Goodale, in-house counsel for the *New York Times*. Goodale asked Abrams, together with Alexander Bickel, a Yale Law School professor, to defend the *New York Times* in a lawsuit that was to be filed the very next day.

The *New York Times* had just refused the government's request that it cease all publication of what we now know as the "Pentagon Papers" and return the source documents to the Department of Defense.[7] These papers, mostly from the Pentagon's "History of U.S. Decision Making Process on Vietnam Policy," evaluated U.S. policy during the Vietnam War.[8] Their evaluation was very negative, and their conclusions were devastating. The papers made the government look extremely bad and made the war seem unwinnable.

The papers had been given to the *New York Times* by someone who did think the war was unwinnable; who had worked in the Pentagon and helped write the report; someone who was not anti-war at first but, over time, had come to see the impossibility that the Vietnam War was.

This someone was Daniel Ellsberg. Ellsberg smuggled one of the 15 copies of the papers from a safe at the RAND Corporation to an offsite photocopier. There, he and a colleague, Anthony Russo, photocopied the papers over a period of several weeks.[9] Ellsberg tried without success to make the papers public by having them read into the Congressional Record. He eventually contacted the *New York Times* reporter Neil Sheehan in the hope that the *Times* would publish them. Ellsberg knew that this was a criminal act, but for him the war itself was a criminal act; his aim was to let the American people see just what kind of a crime it was.

For two and a half months the *Times* editors pored over the papers, working to verify their authenticity and accuracy. After an extensive review, the editors determined that they were authentic and resolved to publish the first of a ten-part series of excerpts and stories on Sunday, June 13, 1971.[10]

On Monday afternoon, one day after the first installment appeared, Attorney General John Mitchell sent a telegraph to the *New York Times* stating:

> I respectfully request that you publish no further information of this character and advise me that you have made arrangements for the return of these documents to the Department of Defense.[11]

When the *Times* failed to comply, the government filed papers to enjoin the paper from continuing to publish stories and excerpts from the documents.[12]

The government's claims were simple: These papers contained government secrets; they were stolen from the possession of the government; to publish them would put many American soldiers at risk and embarrass the United States in the eyes of the world. This concern about embarrassment was more than mere vanity: Embarrassment, the government argued, would weaken our bargaining position in the efforts to negotiate a peace. Because of the harm that would come from further publication, the Court should step in to stop it.

The argument was not unprecedented. Past courts had stopped the publication of life-threatening texts, especially in the context of war. As the Supreme Court said in *Near v. Minnesota,* for example, "no one would question but that a government might prevent actual obstruction to its recruiting service or the publication of the sailing dates of transports or the number and location of troops."[13]

Yet the question was not easily resolved. Standing against precedent was an increasingly clear command: If the First Amendment meant anything, it meant that the government generally cannot exercise the power of prior restraint.[14] "Prior restraint" is when the government gets a court to stop publication of some material, rather than punish the publisher later for what was illegally published. Such a power is thought to present much greater risks to a system of free speech.[15] Attorney General Mitchell was asking the Court to exercise this power of prior restraint.

The Court struggled with the question, but resolved it quickly. It struggled because the costs seemed so high,[16] but when it resolved the question, it did so quite squarely against the government. In the Court's reading, the Constitution gave the *New York Times* the right to publish without the threat of prior restraint.

The *Pentagon Papers* is a First Amendment classic—a striking reminder of how powerful a constitution can be. But even classics get old. And in a speech that Abrams gave around the time the first edition to this book was published, Abrams asked an incredible question: Is the case really important anymore? Or has technology rendered this protection of the First Amendment unnecessary?

Abrams's question was motivated by an obvious point: For the government to succeed in a claim that a printing should be stopped, it must show "irreparable harm"—harm so significant and irreversible that the Court must intervene to prevent it.[17] But that showing depends on the publication not occurring—if the Pentagon Papers had already been published by the *Chicago Tribune,* the government could have claimed no compelling interest to stop its publication in the *New York Times.* When the cat is already out of the bag, preventing further publication does not return the cat to the bag.

This point is made clear in a case that came after *New York Times*—a case that could have been invented by a law professor. In the late 1970s, the *Progressive* commissioned an article by Howard Morland about the workings of an H-bomb. The *Progressive* first submitted the manuscript to the Department of Energy, and the government in turn brought an injunction to block its publication. The government's claim was compelling: to give to the world the secrets of how to build a bomb would make it possible for any terrorist to annihilate any city. On March 26, 1979, Judge Robert Warren of the Western District of Wisconsin agreed and issued a temporary restraining order enjoining the *Progressive* from publishing the article.[18]

Unlike the Pentagon Papers case, this case didn't race to the Supreme Court. Instead, it stewed, no doubt in part because the district judge hearing the case understood the great risk this publication presented. The judge did stop the publication while he thought through the case. He thought for two and a half months. The publishers went to the Court of Appeals, and to the Supreme Court, asking each to hurry the thinking along. No court intervened.

Until Chuck Hansen, a computer programmer, ran a "Design Your Own H-Bomb" contest and circulated an eighteen-page letter in which he detailed his understanding of how an H-Bomb works. On September 16, 1979, the *Press-Connection* of Madison, Wisconsin, published the letter. The next day the government moved to withdraw its case, conceding that it was now moot. The compelling interest of the government ended once the secret was out.[19]

Note what this sequence implies. There is a need for the constitutional protection that the Pentagon Papers case represents only because there is a real constraint on publishing. Publishing requires a publisher, and a publisher can be punished by the state. But if the essence or facts of the publication are published elsewhere first, then the need for constitutional protection disappears. Once the piece is published, there is no further legal justification for suppressing it.

So, Abrams asks, would the case be important today? Is the constitutional protection of the Pentagon Papers case still essential?

Surprisingly, Floyd Abrams suggests not.[20] Today there's a way to ensure that the government never has a compelling interest in asking a court to suppress publication. If the *New York Times* wanted to publish the Pentagon Papers today, it could ensure that the papers had been previously published simply by leaking them to a USENET newsgroup, or one of a million blogs. More quickly than its own newspaper is distributed, the papers would then be published in millions of places across the world. The need for the constitutional protection would be erased, because the architecture of the system gives anyone the power to publish quickly and anonymously.

Thus the architecture of the Net, Abrams suggested, eliminates the need for the constitutional protection. Even better, Abrams went on, the Net protects against prior restraint just as the Constitution did—by ensuring that strong controls on information can no longer be achieved. The Net does what publication of the Pentagon Papers was designed to do—ensure that the truth does not remain hidden.

But there's a second side to this story.

On July 17, 1996, TWA Flight 800 fell from the sky ten miles off the southern coast of Center Moriches, New York. Two hundred and thirty people were killed. Immediately after the accident the United States launched the (then) largest investigation of an airplane crash in the history of the National Transportation Safety Board (NTSB), spending $27 million to discover the cause of the crash, which eventually was determined to have been a mechanical failure.[21]

This was not, however, the view of the Internet. From the beginning, stories circulated about "friendly fire"—missiles that were seen to hit the airplane. Dozens of eyewitnesses reported that they saw a streaking light shoot toward the plane just before it went down. There were stories about missile tests conducted by the Navy seventy miles from the crash site.[22] The Net claimed that there was a cover-up by the U.S. government to hide its involvement in one of the worst civil air disasters in American history.

The government denied these reports. Yet the more the government denied them, the more contrary "evidence" appeared on the Net.[23] And then, as a final straw in the story, there was a report, purportedly by a government insider, claiming that indeed there was a conspiracy—because evidence suggested that friendly fire had shot down TWA 800.[24]

The former press secretary to President John F. Kennedy believed this report. In a speech in France, Pierre Salinger announced that his government was hiding the facts of the case, and that he had the proof.

I remember this event well. I was talking to a colleague just after I heard Salinger's report. I recounted Salinger's report to this colleague, a leading constitutional scholar from one of the top American law schools. We both were at a loss about what to believe. There were cross-cutting intuitions about credibility. Salinger was no nut, but the story was certainly loony.

Salinger, it turns out, had been caught by the Net. He had been tricked by the flip side of the point Floyd Abrams has made. In a world where everyone can publish, it is very hard to know what to believe. Publishers are also editors, and editors make decisions about what to publish—decisions that ordinarily are driven at least in part by the question, is it true? Statements cannot verify themselves. We cannot always tell, from a sentence reporting a fact about the world, whether that sentence is true.[25] So in addition to our own experience and knowledge of the world, we must rely on structures of reputation that build credibility. When something is published, we associate the claim with the publisher. If the *New York Times* says that aliens have kidnapped the President, it is viewed differently from a story with the identical words published in the *National Enquirer*.

When a new technology comes along, however, we are likely to lose our bearings. This is nothing new. It is said that the word phony comes from the birth of the telephone—the phony was the con artist who used the phone to trick people who were familiar with face-to-face communication only. We should expect the same uncertainty in cyberspace, and expect that it too, at first, will shake expectations of credibility.

Abrams's argument then depends on a feature of the Net that we cannot take for granted. If there were credibility on the Net, the importance of the Pentagon Papers case would indeed be diminished. But if speech on the Net lacks credibility, the protections of the Constitution again become important.

"Credibility," however, is not a quality that is legislated or coded. It comes from institutions of trust that help the reader separate reliable from unreliable sources. Flight 800 thus raises an important question: How can we reestablish credibility in this space so that it is not lost to the loons?[26]

In the first edition of this book, that question could only be answered hypothetically. But in the time since, we've begun to see an answer to this question emerge. And the word at the center of that answer is: Blog.

At this writing, there are more than 50 million weblogs on the Internet. There's no single way to describe what these blogs are. They differ dramatically, and probably most of what gets written there is just crap. But it is wrong to judge a dynamic by a snapshot. And the structure of authority that this dynamic is building is something very new.

At their best, blogs are instances of amateur journalism—where "amateur," again, means not second rate or inferior, but one who does what he does for the love of the work and not the money. These journalists write about the world—some from a political perspective, some from the point of view of a particular interest. But they all triangulate across a range of other writers to produce an argument, or a report, that adds something new. The ethic of this space is linking—of pointing, and commenting. And while this linking is not "fair and balanced," it does produce a vigorous exchange of ideas.

These blogs are ranked. Services such as Technorati constantly count the blog space, watching who links to whom, and which blogs produce the greatest credibility. And these rankings contribute to an economy of ideas that builds a discipline around them. Bloggers get authority from the citation others give them; that authority attracts attention. It is a new reputation system, established not by editors or CEOs of media companies, but by an extraordinarily diverse range of contributors.

And in the end, these amateur journalists have an effect. When TWA flight 800 fell from the sky, there were theories about conspiracies that filtered through no structure of credibility. Today, there are more structures of credibility. So when Dan Rather produced a letter on CBS's *60 Minutes* purporting to establish a certain fraud by the President, it took the blogosphere 24 hours to establish this media company's evidence was faked. More incredibly, it took CBS almost two weeks to acknowledge what blogs had established.[27] The collaborative work of the blogs uncovered the truth, and in the process embarrassed a very powerful media company. But by contrast to the behavior of that media company, they demonstrated something important about how the Net had matured.

This collaboration comes with no guarantees, except the guarantee of a process. The most extraordinary collaborative process in the context of content is Wikipedia. Wikipedia is a free online encyclopedia, created solely by volunteers. Launched at the beginning of 2001, these (literally thousands of) volunteers have now created over 2 million articles. There are nine major language versions (not including the Klingon version), with about half of the total articles in English.

The aim of the Wikipedia is neutrality. The contributors edit, and reedit, to frame a piece neutrally. Sometimes that effort fails—particularly controversial topics can't help but attract fierce conflict. But in the main, the work is an unbelievable success. With nothing more than the effort of volunteers, the most used, and perhaps the most useful encyclopedia ever written has been created through millions of uncoordinated instances of collaboration.

Wikipedia, however, can't guarantee its results. It can't guarantee that, at any particular moment, there won't be errors in its entries. But of course, no one can make that guarantee. Indeed, in one study that randomly collected entries from Wikipedia and from *Encyclopedia Britannica,* there were just as many errors in *Britannica* as in Wikipedia.[28]

But Wikipedia is open to a certain kind of risk that *Britannica* is not—maliciousness. In May 2005, the entry to an article about John Seigenthaler Sr. was defaced by a prankster. Because not many people were monitoring the entry, it took four months before the error was noticed and corrected. Seigenthaler wasn't happy about this. He, understandably, complained that it was the architecture of Wikipedia that was to blame.

Wikipedia's architecture could be different. But the lesson here is not its failures. It is instead the extraordinary surprise of Wikipedia's success. There

is an unprecedented collaboration of people from around the world working to converge upon truth across a wide range of topics. That, in a sense, is
what science does as well. It uses a different kind of "peer review" to police
its results. That "peer review" is no guarantee either—South Koreans, for
example, were quite convinced that one of their leading scientists, Hwang
Woo-Suk, had discovered a technique to clone human stem cells. They
believed it because peer-reviewed journals had reported it. But whether
right to believe it or not, the journals were wrong. Woo-Suk was a fraud, and
he hadn't cloned stem cells, or anything else worth the attention of the
world.

Blogs don't coordinate any collaborative process to truth in the way
Wikipedia does. In a sense, the votes for any particular position at any particular moment are always uncounted, while at every moment they are always
tallied on Wikipedia. But even if they're untallied, readers of blogs learn to triangulate on the truth. Just as with witnesses at an accident (though better,
since these witnesses have reputations), the reader constructs what must be
true from a range of views. Cass Sunstein rightly worries that the norms
among bloggers have not evolved enough to include internal diversity of citation.[29] That may well be true. But whatever the normal reading practice is for
ordinary issues, the diversity of the blogosphere gives readers an extremely
wide range of views to consider when any major issue—such as that which
stung Salinger—emerges. When tied to the maturing reputation system that
constantly tempers influence, this means that it is easier to balance extreme
views with the correction that many voices can build.

A credibility can thus emerge, that, while not perfect, is at least differently
encumbered. NBC News must worry about its bottom line, because its reporting increasingly responds to it. Blogs don't have a bottom line. They are—in
the main—amateurs. Reputation constrains both, and the competition
between the two forms of journalism has increasingly improved each. We
have a richer environment for free speech today than five years ago—a commercial press tempered by blogs regulated by a technology of reputation that
guides the reader as much as the writer.

Errors will remain. Everyone has a favorite example—mine is the ridiculous story about Al Gore claiming to have "invented the Internet." The story
originated with a CNN interview on March 9, 1999. In that interview, in
response to a question about what was different about Gore over Bradley,
Gore said the following:

> During my service in the United States Congress, I took the initiative in creating
> the Internet. I took the initiative in moving forward a whole range of initiatives

that have proven to be important to our country's economic growth and environmental protection, improvements in our educational system.[30]

As is clear from the context, Gore is stating not that he invented the technology of the Internet, but that he "took the initiative in moving forward a whole range of initiatives" that have been important to the country. But the story was retold as the claim that Gore "invented the Internet." That's how the Internet journalist Declan McCullagh repeated it two weeks later: "[T]he vice president offered up a whopper of a tall tale in which he claimed to have invented the Internet." That characterization—plainly false—stuck. In a 2003 study of the media's handling of the story, Chip Health and Jonathan Bendor conclude, "We show that the false version of Gore's statement dominated the true one in mainstream political discourse by a wide margin. This is a clear failure in the marketplace of ideas, which we document in detail."[31]

The only redeeming part of this story is that it's simple to document the falsity—because of the Internet. Seth Finkelstein, a programmer and anti-censorware activist, has created a page on the Internet collecting the original interview and the subsequent reports about it.[32] His is the model of the very best the Internet could be. That virtue, however, didn't carry too far beyond the Internet.

REGULATIONS OF SPEECH: SPAM AND PORN

For all our talk about loving free speech, most of us, deep down, wouldn't mind a bit of healthy speech regulation, at least in some contexts. Or at least, more of us would be eager for speech regulation today than would have been in 1996. This change is because of two categories of speech that have become the bane of existence to many on the Net: spam and porn.

By "spam" I mean unsolicited commercial e-mail sent in bulk. "Unsolicited," in the sense that there's no relationship between the sender and recipient; "commercial" in a sense that excludes political e-mail; "e-mail" in the sense not restricted to e-mail, but that includes every medium of interaction in cyberspace (including blogs); and "bulk" meaning many (you pick the number) missives sent at once.

By "porn," I mean not obscenity and not child porn, but what the United States Supreme Court calls sexually explicit speech that is "harmful to minors."[33] This is the category of legally permitted erotic speech—for adults, at least, not for kids. Obscenity and child porn are permitted to no one.

These two types of speech—porn and spam—are very different, but they are similar in the structure of regulation that each demands. Neither kind of speech should be banned by regulation: There are some who are happy to receive spam; there are some who are constitutionally entitled to access porn. But for both kinds of speech, there is a class of individuals who would like the power to block access to each: most of us with respect to spam; parents with respect to porn. This is a desire for a kind of "speech regulation." The question is how, or whether, the law can support it.

I'm all for this form of speech regulation, properly architected. "But how," anti-regulation sorts might ask, "can you so easily embrace the idea of regulation? Have you forgotten the important values of free speech?"

But if the lovers of this form of speech regulation have been reading carefully, they have a quick answer to this charge of censorship. It is clear, upon reflection, that in the sense of Chapter 7, spam and porn have always been regulated in real space. The only question for cyberspace is whether the same effect of those real space regulations can be achieved in cyberspace.

Real-Space Regulations: Spam and Porn

Think first about spam in real space. In the sense of Chapter 7, spam, in real space, is regulated extensively. We can understand that regulation through the four modalities.

First law: Regulations against fraud and misrepresentation constrain the games bulk mailers can play in real space. Contests are heavily regulated (just read the disclaimers on the Publishers' Clearing House Sweepstakes).

Second, norms regulate bulk mail in real space. There's a sense of what is appropriate to advertise for; advertisement outside that range is almost self-defeating.

Third, markets regulate bulk mail in real space. The cost of real space mail is high, meaning the returns must be significant before it pays to send bulk mail. That radically reduces the range of bulk mail that gets sent in real space.

And finally, architecture regulates bulk mail in real space. We get our mail just once a day, and it's fairly simple to segregate bulk from real. It's also simple to dump the bulk without ever even opening it. The burdens of real-space spam are thus not terribly great.

These factors together restrict the spread of spam in real space. There is less of it than the spammers would like, even if there is more than the rest of us like. These four constraints thus regulate what gets made.

A similar story can be told about porn.

Pornography, in real space, is regulated extensively—again not obscenity and not child porn, but what the Supreme Court calls sexually explicit speech that is "harmful to minors." Obscenity and child porn are regulated too, but their regulation is different: Obscenity and child porn are banned for all people in real space (United States); porn is banned only for children.

We can also understand porn's regulation by considering the four modalities of regulation. All four are directed to a common end: to keep porn away from kids while (sometimes) ensuring adults' access to it.

First, laws do this. Laws in many jurisdictions require that porn not be sold to kids.[34] Since at least 1968, when the Supreme Court decided *Ginsberg v. New York*,[35] such regulation has been consistently upheld. States can require vendors of porn to sell it only to adults; they can also require vendors to check the ID of buyers.

But not only laws channel. Social norms do as well. Norms restrict the sale of porn generally—society for the most part sneers at consumers of porn, and this sneer undoubtedly inhibits its sale. Norms also support the policy of keeping porn away from kids. Porn dealers likely don't like to think of themselves as people who corrupt. Selling porn to kids is universally seen as corrupting, and this is an important constraint on dealers, as on anyone else.

The market, too, keeps porn away from kids. Porn in real space costs money. Kids do not have much money. Because sellers discriminate on the basis of who can pay, they thus help to discourage children from buying porn.

But then regulations of law, market, and norms all presuppose another regulation that makes the first three possible: the regulation of real-space architecture. In real space it is hard to hide that you are a child. He can try, but without any likely success. Thus, because a kid cannot hide his age, and because porn is largely sold face to face, the architectures of real space make it relatively cheap for laws and norms to be effective.

This constellation of regulations in real space has the effect of controlling, to an important degree, the distribution of porn to kids. The regulation is not perfect—any child who really wants the stuff can get it—but regulation does not need to be perfect to be effective. It is enough that these regulations make porn generally unavailable.

Cyberspace Regulations: Spam and Porn

Spam and porn are regulated differently in cyberspace. That is, these same four modalities constrain or enable spam and porn differently in cyberspace.

Let's begin with porn this time. The first difference is the market. In real space porn costs money, but in cyberspace it need not—at least not much. If you want to distribute one million pictures of "the girl next door" in real space, it is not unreasonable to say that distribution will cost close to $1 million. In cyberspace distribution is practically free. So long as you have access to cyberspace and a scanner, you can scan a picture of "the girl next door" and then distribute the digital image across USENET to many more than one million people for just the cost of an Internet connection.

With the costs of production so low, a much greater supply of porn is produced for cyberspace than for real space. And indeed, a whole category of porn exists in cyberspace that doesn't in real space—amateur porn, or porn produced for noncommercial purposes. That category of supply simply couldn't survive in real space.

And then there is demand. Porn in cyberspace can be accessed—often and in many places—for free. Thousands of commercial sites make porn available for free, as a tease to draw in customers. Even more porn is distributed in noncommercial contexts, such as USENET, or free porn websites. Again, this low price translates into much greater demand.

Much of this supply and demand is for a market that, at least in the United States, is constitutionally protected. Adults have a constitutional right in the United States to access porn, in the sense that the government can do nothing that burdens (perhaps unreasonably burdens) access to porn. But there is another market for porn in the United States that is not constitutionally protected. Governments have the right in the United States to block access by kids to porn.

As we saw in the previous section, for that regulation to work, however, there needs to be a relatively simple way to know who is a kid. But as we've seen throughout this book, this is an architectural feature that cyberspace doesn't have. It's not that kids in cyberspace can easily hide that they are kids. In cyberspace, there is no fact to disguise. You enter without an identity and you identify only what you want—and even that can't be authenticated with any real confidence. Thus, a kid in cyberspace need not disclose that he is a kid. And therefore he need not suffer the discriminations applied to a child in real space. No one needs to know that Jon is Jonny; therefore, the architecture does not produce the minimal information necessary to make regulation work.

The consequence is that regulations that seek selectively to block access to kids in cyberspace don't work, and they don't work for reasons that are very different from the reasons they might not work well in real space. In real space, no doubt, there are sellers who want to break the law or who are not typically motivated to obey it. But in cyberspace, even if the seller wants to obey the law, the law can't be obeyed. The architecture of cyberspace doesn't provide the tools to enable the law to be followed.

A similar story can be told about spam: Spam is an economic activity. People send it to make money. The frictions of real space significantly throttle that desire. The costs of sending spam in real space mean that only projects expecting a significant return get sent. As I said, even then, laws and norms add another layer of restriction. But the most significant constraint is cost.

But the efficiency of communication in cyberspace means that the cost of sending spam is radically cheaper, which radically increases the quantity of spam that it is rational to send. Even if you make only a .01% profit, if the cost of sending the spam is close to zero, you still make money.

Thus, as with porn, a different architectural constraint means a radically different regulation of behavior. Both porn and spam are reasonably regulated in real space; in cyberspace, this difference in architecture means neither is effectively regulated at all.

And thus the question that began this section: Is there a way to "regulate" spam and porn to at least the same level of regulation that both face in real space?

Regulating Net-Porn

Of all the possible speech regulations on the Net (putting copyright to one side for the moment), the United States Congress has been most eager to regulate porn. That eagerness, however, has not yet translated into success. Congress has passed two pieces of major legislation. The first was struck down completely. The second continues to be battered down in its struggle through the courts.

The first statute was the product of a scare. Just about the time the Net was coming into the popular consciousness, a particularly seedy aspect of the Net came into view first. This was porn on the Net. This concern became widespread in the United States early in 1995.[36] Its source was an extraordinary rise in the number of ordinary users of the Net, and therefore a rise in use by kids and an even more extraordinary rise in the availability of what many call porn on the Net. An extremely controversial (and deeply flawed) study published in the *Georgetown University Law Review* reported that the Net was awash in porn.[37] *Time* ran a cover story about its availability.[38] Senators and congressmen were bombarded with demands to do something to regulate "cybersmut."

Congress responded in 1996 with the Communications Decency Act (CDA). A law of extraordinary stupidity, the CDA practically impaled itself on the First Amendment. The law made it a felony to transmit "indecent" material on the Net to a minor or to a place where a minor could observe it. But it gave speakers on the Net a defense—if they took good-faith, "reasonable, effective" steps to screen out children, then they could speak "indecently."[39]

There were at least three problems with the CDA, any one of which should have doomed it to well-deserved extinction.[40] The first was the scope of the speech it addressed: "Indecency" is not a category of speech that Congress has the power to regulate (at least not outside the context of broadcasting.)[41] As I have already described, Congress can regulate speech that is "harmful to minors," or *Ginsberg* speech, but that is very different from speech called "indecent." Thus, the first strike against the statute was that it reached too far.

Strike two was vagueness. The form of the allowable defenses was clear: So long as there was an architecture for screening out kids, the speech would be permitted. But the architectures that existed at the time for screening out children were relatively crude, and in some cases quite expensive. It was unclear whether, to satisfy the statute, they had to be extremely effective or just reasonably effective given the state of the technology. If the former, then the defenses were no defense at all, because an extremely effective block was extremely expensive; the cost of a reasonably effective block would not have been so high.

Strike three was the government's own doing. In arguing its case before the Supreme Court in 1997, the government did little either to narrow the scope of the speech being regulated or to expand the scope of the defenses. It stuck with the hopelessly vague, overbroad definition Congress had given it, and it displayed a poor understanding of how the technology might have provided a defense. As the Court considered the case, there seemed to be no way that an identification system could satisfy the statute without creating an undue burden on Internet speakers.

Congress responded quickly by passing a second statute aimed at protecting kids from porn. This was the Child Online Protection Act (COPA) of 1998.[42] This statute was better tailored to the constitutional requirements. It aimed at regulating speech that was harmful to minors. It allowed commercial websites to provide such speech so long as the website verified the viewer's age. Yet in June 2003, the Supreme Court enjoined enforcement of the statute.[43]

Both statutes respond to a legitimate and important concern. Parents certainly have the right to protect their kids from this form of speech, and it is perfectly understandable that Congress would want to help parents secure this protection.

But both statutes by Congress are unconstitutional—not, as some suggest, because there is no way that Congress could help parents. Instead both are unconstitutional because the particular way that Congress has tried to help parents puts more of a burden on legitimate speech (for adults that is) than is necessary.

In my view, however, there is a perfectly constitutional statute that Congress could pass that would have an important effect on protecting kids from porn.

To see what that statute looks like, we need to step back a bit from the CDA and COPA to identify what the legitimate objectives of this speech regulation would be.

Ginsberg[44] established that there is a class of speech that adults have a right to but that children do not. States can regulate that class to ensure that such speech is channeled to the proper user and blocked from the improper user.

Conceptually, for such a regulation can work, two questions must be answered:

1. Is the speaker uttering "regulable" speech—meaning speech "harmful to minors"?
2. Is the listener entitled to consume this speech—meaning is he a minor?

And with the answers to these questions, the logic of this regulation is:

> IF
> (speech == regulable)
> AND
> (listener == minor)
> THEN
> block access.

Now between the listener and the speaker, clearly the speaker is in a better position to answer question #1. The listener can't know whether the speech is harmful to minors until the listener encounters the speech. If the listener is a minor, then it is too late. And between the listener and the speaker, clearly the listener is in a better position to answer question #2. On the Internet especially, it is extremely burdensome for the speaker to certify the age of the listener. It is the listener who knows his age most cheaply.

The CDA and COPA placed the burden of answering question #1 on the speaker, and #2 on both the speaker and the listener. A speaker had to determine whether his speech was regulable, and a speaker and a listener had to cooperate to verify the age of the listener. If the speaker didn't, and the listener was a minor, then the speaker was guilty of a felony.

Real-space law also assigns the burden in exactly the same way. If you want to sell porn in New York, you both need to determine whether the content you're selling is "harmful to minors," and you need to determine whether the person you're selling to is a minor. But real space is importantly different from cyberspace, at least in the high cost of answering question #2: In real space, the answer is almost automatic (again, it's hard for a kid to hide that he's a kid). And where the answer is not automatic, there's a cheap system of identification (a driver's license, for example). But in cyberspace, any mandatory system of identification constitutes a burden both for the speaker and the listener. Even under COPA, a speaker has to bear the burden of a credit card system, and the listener has to trust a pornographer with his credit card just to get access to constitutionally protected speech.

There's another feature of the CDA/COPA laws that seems necessary but isn't: They both place the burden of their regulation upon everyone, including those who have a constitutional right to listen. They require, that is, everyone to show an ID when it is only kids who can constitutionally be blocked.

So compare then the burdens of the CDA/COPA to a different regulatory scheme: one that placed the burden of question #1 (whether the content is harmful to minors) on the speaker and placed the burden of question #2 (whether the listener is a minor) on the listener.

One version of this scheme is simple, obviously ineffective and unfair to the speaker: A requirement that a website blocks access with a page that says "The content on this page is harmful to minors. Click here if you are a minor." This scheme places the burden of age identification on the kid. But obviously, it would have zero effect in actually blocking a kid. And, less obviously, this scheme would be unfair to speakers. A speaker may well have content that constitutes material "harmful to minors," but not everyone who offers such material should be labeled a pornographer. This transparent block is stigmatizing to some, and if a less burdensome system were possible, that stigma should also render regulation supporting this unconstitutional.

So what's an alternative for this scheme that might actually work?

I'm going to demonstrate such a system with a particular example. Once you see the example, the general point will be easier to see as well.

Everyone knows the Apple Macintosh. It, like every modern operating system, now allows users to specify "accounts" on a particular machine. I've set one up for my son, Willem (he's only three, but I want to be prepared). When I set up Willem's account, I set it up with "parental controls." That means I get to specify precisely what programs he gets to use, and what access he has to the Internet. The "parental controls" make it (effectively) impossible to change these specifications. You need the administrator's password to do that, and if that's kept secret, then the universe the kid gets to through the computer is the universe defined by the access the parent selects.

Imagine one of the programs I could select was a browser with a function we could call "kids-mode-browsing" (KMB). That browser would be programmed to watch on any web page for a particular mark. Let's call that mark the "harmful to minors" mark, or <H2M> for short. That mark, or in the language of the Web, tag, would bracket any content the speaker believes is harmful to minors, and the KMB browser would then not display any content bracketed with this <H2M> tag. So, for example, a web page marked up "Blah blah blah <H2M>block this</H2M> blah blah blah" would appear on a KMB screen as: "Blah blah blah blah blah blah."

So, if the world of the World Wide Web was marked with <H2M> tags, and if browser manufacturers built this <H2M>-filtering function into their browsers, then parents would be able to configure their machines so their kids didn't get access to any content marked <H2M>. The policy objective of enabling parental control would be achieved with a minimal burden on constitutionally entitled speakers.

How can we get (much of the) world of the Web to mark its harmful to minors content with <H2M> tags?

This is the role for government. Unlike the CDA or COPA, the regulation required to make this system work—to the extent it works, and more on that below—is simply that speakers mark their content. Speakers would not be required to block access; speakers would not be required to verify age. All the speaker would be required to do is to tag content deemed harmful to minors with the proper tag.

This tag, moreover, would not be a public marking that a website was a porn site. This proposal is not like the (idiotic, imho) proposals that we create a .sex or .xxx domain for the Internet. People shouldn't have to locate to a red-light district just to have adult material on their site. The <H2M> tag instead would be hidden from the ordinary user—unless that user looks for it, or wants to block that content him or herself.

Once the government enacts this law, then browser manufacturers would have an incentive to build this (very simple) filtering technology into their browsers. Indeed, given the open-source Mozilla browser technology—to which anyone could add anything they wanted—the costs of building this modified browser are extremely low. And once the government enacts this law, and browser manufacturers build a browser that recognizes this tag, then parents have would have as strong a reason to adopt platforms that enable them to control where their kids go on the Internet.

Thus, in this solution, the LAW creates an incentive (through penalties for noncompliance) for sites with "harmful to minors" material to change their ARCHITECTURE (by adding <H2M> tags) which creates a MARKET for browser manufacturers (new markets) to add filtering to their code, so that parents can protect their kids. The only burden created by this solution is on the speaker; this solution does not burden the rightful consumer of porn at all. To that consumer, there is no change in the way the Web is experienced, because without a browser that looks for the <H2M> tag, the tag is invisible to the consumer.

But isn't that burden on the speaker unconstitutional? It's hard to see why it would be, if it is constitutional in real space to tell a speaker he must filter kids from his content "harmful to minors." No doubt there's a burden. But the question isn't whether there's a burden. The constitutional question is whether there is a less burdensome way to achieve this important state interest.

But what about foreign sites? Americans can't regulate what happens in Russia. Actually, that's less true than you think. As we'll see in the next chapter, there's much that the U.S. government can do and does to effectively control what other countries do.

Still, you might worry that sites in other countries won't obey American law because it's not likely we'll send in the Marines to take out a noncomplying website. That's certainly true. But to the extent that a parent is concerned about this, as I already described, there is a market already to enable geographic filtering of content. The same browser that filters on <H2M> could in principle subscribe to an IP mapping service to enable access to American sites only.

But won't kids get around this restriction? Sure, of course some will. But the measure of success for legislation (as opposed to missile tracking software) is not 100 percent. The question the legislature asks is whether the law will make things better off.[45] To substantially block access to <H2M> content would be a significant improvement, and that would be enough to make the law make sense.

But why not simply rely upon filters that parents and libraries install on their computers? Voluntary filters don't require any new laws, and they therefore don't require any state-sponsored censorship to achieve their ends.

It is this view that I want to work hardest to dislodge, because built within it are all the mistakes that a pre-cyberlaw understanding brings to the question of regulation in cyberspace.

First, consider the word "censorship." What this regulation would do is give parents the opportunity to exercise an important choice. Enabling parents to do this has been deemed a compelling state interest. The kids who can't get access to this content because their parents exercised this choice might call it "censorship," but that isn't a very useful application of the term. If there is a legitimate reason to block this form of access, that's speech regulation. There's no reason to call it names.

Second, consider the preference for "voluntary filters." If voluntary filters were to achieve the very same end (blocking H2M speech and only H2M speech), I'd be all for them. But they don't. As the ACLU quite powerfully described (shortly after winning the case that struck down the CDA partly on the grounds that private filters were a less restrictive means than government regulation):

> The ashes of the CDA were barely smoldering when the White House called a summit meeting to encourage Internet users to self-rate their speech and to urge industry leaders to develop and deploy the tools for blocking "inappropriate speech." The meeting was "voluntary," of course: the White House claimed it wasn't holding anyone's feet to the fire. [But] the ACLU and others . . . were genuinely alarmed by the tenor of the White House summit and the unabashed enthusiasm for technological fixes that will make it easier to block or render invisible controversial speech. . . . [I]t was not any one proposal or announcement that caused our alarm; rather, it was the failure to examine the longer-term implications for the Internet of rating and blocking schemes.[46]

The ACLU's concern is the obvious one: The filters that the market has created not only filter much more broadly than the legitimate interest the state has here—blocking <H2M> speech—they also do so in a totally non-transparent way. There have been many horror stories of sites being included in filters for all the wrong reasons (including for simply criticizing the filter).[47] And when you are wrongfully blocked by a filter, there's not much you can do. The filter is just a particularly effective recommendation list. You can't sue Zagat's just because they steer customers to your competitors.

My point is not that we should ban filters, or that parents shouldn't be allowed to block more than H2M speech. My point is that if we rely upon private action alone, more speech will be blocked than if the government acted wisely and efficiently.

And that frames my final criticism: As I've argued from the start, our focus should be on the liberty to speak, not just on the government's role in restricting speech. Thus, between two "solutions" to a particular speech problem, one that involves the government and suppresses speech narrowly, and one that doesn't involve the government but suppresses speech broadly, constitutional values should tilt us to favor the former. First Amendment values (even if not the First Amendment directly) should lead to favoring a speech regulation system that is thin and accountable, and in which the government's action or inaction leads only to the suppression of speech the government has a legitimate interest in suppressing. Or, put differently, the fact that the government is involved should not *necessarily* disqualify a solution as a proper, rights-protective solution.

The private filters the market has produced so far are both expensive and over-inclusive. They block content that is beyond the state's interest in regulating speech. They are effectively subsidized because there is no less restrictive alternative.

Publicly required filters (which are what the <H2M> tag effectively enables) are narrowly targeted on the legitimate state interest. And if there is a dispute about that tag—if for example, a prosecutor says a website with information about breast cancer must tag the information with an <H2M> tag—then the website at least has the opportunity to fight that. If that filtering were in private software, there would be no opportunity to fight it through legal means. All that free speech activists could then do is write powerful, but largely invisible, articles like the ACLU's famous plea.

It has taken key civil rights organizations too long to recognize this private threat to free-speech values. The tradition of civil rights is focused directly on government action alone. I would be the last to say that there's not great danger from government misbehavior. But there is also danger to free speech from private misbehavior. An obsessive refusal to even consider the one threat against the other does not serve the values promoted by the First Amendment.

But then what about public filtering technologies, like PICS? Wouldn't PICS be a solution that avoided the "secret list problem" you identified?

PICS is an acronym for the World Wide Web Consortium's Platform for Internet Content Selection. We have already seen a relative (actually, a child) of PICS in the chapter about privacy: P3P. Like PICS, is a protocol for rating and filtering content on the Net. In the context of privacy, the content was made up of assertions about privacy practices, and the regime was designed to help individuals negotiate those practices.

With online speech the idea is much the same. PICS divides the problem of filtering into two parts—labeling (rating content) and then filtering (blocking content on the basis of the rating). The idea was that software authors would compete to write software that could filter according to the ratings; content providers and rating organizations would compete to rate content. Users would then pick their filtering software and rating system. If you wanted the ratings of the Christian Right, for example, you could select its rating system; if I wanted the ratings of the Atheist Left, I could select that. By picking our raters, we would pick the content we wanted the software to filter.

This regime requires a few assumptions. First, software manufacturers would have to write the code necessary to filter the material. (This has already been done in some major browsers). Second, rating organizations would actively have to rate the Net. This, of course, would be no simple task; organizations have not risen to the challenge of billions of web pages. Third, organizations that rated the Net in a way that allowed for a simple translation from one rating system to another would have a competitive advantage over other raters. They could, for example, sell a rating system to the government of Taiwan and then easily develop a slightly different rating system for the "government" of IBM.

If all three assumptions held true, any number of ratings could be applied to the Net. As envisioned by its authors, PICS would be neutral among ratings and neutral among filters; the system would simply provide a language with which content on the Net could be rated, and with which decisions about how to use that rated material could be made from machine to machine.[48]

Neutrality sounds like a good thing. It sounds like an idea that policymakers should embrace. Your speech is not my speech; we are both free to speak and listen as we want. We should establish regimes that protect that freedom, and PICS seems to be just such a regime.

But PICS contains more "neutrality" than we might like. PICS is not just horizontally neutral—allowing individuals to choose from a range of rating systems the one he or she wants; PICS is also vertically neutral—allowing the filter to be imposed at any level in the distributional chain. Most people who first endorsed the system imagined the PICS filter sitting on a user's computer, filtering according to the desires of that individual. But nothing in the design of PICS prevents organizations that provide access to the Net from filtering content as well. Filtering can occur at any level in the distributional chain— the user, the company through which the user gains access, the ISP, or even the jurisdiction within which the user lives. Nothing in the design of PICS, that is, requires that such filters announce themselves. Filtering in an architecture like PICS can be invisible. Indeed, in some of its implementations invisibility is part of its design.[49]

This should set off alarms for those keen to protect First Amendment values—even though the protocol is totally private. As a (perhaps) unintended consequence, the PICS regime not only enables nontransparent filtering but, by producing a market in filtering technology, engenders filters for much more than *Ginsberg* speech. That, of course, was the ACLU's legitimate complaint against the original CDA. But here the market, whose tastes are the tastes of the community, facilitates the filtering. Built into the filter are the norms of a community, which are broader than the narrow filter of *Ginsberg*. The filtering system can expand as broadly as the users want, or as far upstream as sources want.

The H2M+KMB solution alternative is much narrower. It enables a kind of private zoning of speech. But there would be no incentive for speakers to block out listeners; the incentive of a speaker is to have more, not fewer, listeners. The only requirements to filter out listeners would be those that may constitutionally be imposed—*Ginsberg* speech requirements. Since they would be imposed by the state, these requirements could be tested against the Constitution, and if the state were found to have reached too far, it could be checked.

The difference between these two solutions, then, is in the generalizability of the regimes. The filtering regime would establish an architecture that could be used to filter any kind of speech, and the desires for filtering then could be expected to reach beyond a constitutional minimum; the zoning regime would establish an architecture for blocking that would not have this more general purpose.

Which regime should we prefer?

Notice the values implicit in each regime. Both are general solutions to particular problems. The filtering regime does not limit itself to *Ginsberg* speech; it can be used to rate, and filter, any Internet content. And the zoning regime, in principle, is not limited to zoning only for *Ginsberg* speech. The <H2M> kids-ID zoning solution could be used to advance other child protective schemes. Thus, both have applications far beyond the specifics of porn on the Net.

At least in principle. We should be asking, however, what incentives are there to extend the solution beyond the problem. And what resistance is there to such extensions?

Here we begin to see the important difference between the two regimes. When your access is blocked because of a certificate you are holding, you want to know why. When you are told you cannot enter a certain site, the claim to exclude is checked at least by the person being excluded. Sometimes the exclusion is justified, but when it is not, it can be challenged. Zoning, then, builds into itself a system for its own limitation. A site cannot block someone from the site without that individual knowing it.[50]

Filtering is different. If you cannot see the content, you cannot know what is being blocked. Content could be filtered by a PICS filter somewhere upstream and you would not necessarily know this was happening. Nothing in the PICS design requires truth in blocking in the way that the zoning solution does. Thus, upstream filtering becomes easier, less transparent, and less costly with PICS.

This effect is even clearer if we take apart the components of the filtering process. Recall the two elements of filtering solutions—labeling content, and then blocking based on that labeling. We might well argue that the labeling is the more dangerous of the two elements. If content is labeled, then it is possible to monitor who gets what without even blocking access. That might well raise greater concerns than blocking, since blocking at least puts the user on notice.

These possibilities should trouble us only if we have reason to question the value of filtering generally, and upstream filtering in particular. I believe we do. But I must confess that my concern grows out of yet another latent ambiguity in our constitutional past.

There is undeniable value in filtering. We all filter out much more than we process, and in general it is better if we can select our filters rather than have others select them for us. If I read the *New York Times* rather than the *Wall Street Journal*, I am selecting a filter according to my understanding of the values of both newspapers. Obviously, in any particular case, there cannot be a problem with this.

But there is also a value in confronting the unfiltered. We individually may want to avoid issues of poverty or of inequality, and so we might prefer to tune those facts out of our universe. But it would be terrible from the standpoint of society if citizens could simply tune out problems that were not theirs, because those same citizens have to select leaders to manage these very problems.[51]

In real space we do not have to worry about this problem too much because filtering is usually imperfect. However much I'd like to ignore homelessness, I cannot go to my bank without confronting homeless people on the street; however much I'd like to ignore inequality, I cannot drive to the airport without passing through neighborhoods that remind me of how unequal a nation the United States is. All sorts of issues I'd rather not think about force themselves on me. They demand my attention in real space, regardless of my filtering choices.

Of course, this is not true for everyone. The very rich can cut themselves off from what they do not want to see. Think of the butler on a 19th-century English estate, answering the door and sending away those he thinks should not trouble his master. Those people lived perfectly filtered lives. And so do some today.

But most of us do not. We must confront the problems of others and think about issues that affect our society. This exposure makes us better citizens.[52] We can better deliberate and vote on issues that affect others if we have some sense of the problems they face.

What happens, then, if the imperfections of filtering disappear? What happens if everyone can, in effect, have a butler? Would such a world be consistent with the values of the First Amendment?

Some believe that it would not be. Cass Sunstein, for example, has argued quite forcefully that the framers embraced what he calls a "Madisonian" conception of the First Amendment.[53] This Madisonian conception rejects the notion that the mix of speech we see should solely be a function of individual choice.[54] It insists, Sunstein claims, on ensuring that we are exposed to the range of issues we need to understand if we are to function as citizens. It therefore would reject any architecture that makes consumer choice trump. Choice is not a bad circumstance in the Madisonian scheme, but it is not the end of the matter. Ithiel de Sola Pool makes a very similar point:

> What will it mean if audiences are increasingly fractionated into small groups with special interests? What will it mean if the agenda of national fads and concerns is no longer effectively set by a few mass media to which everyone is exposed? Such a trend raises for society the reverse problems from those posed by mass conformism. The cohesion and effective functioning of a democratic society depends upon some sort of public agora in which everyone participates and where all deal with a common agenda of problems, however much they may argue over the solutions.[55]

On the other side are scholars such as Geoffrey Stone, who insists just as strongly that no such paternalistic ideal is found anywhere in the conception of free speech embraced by our framers.[56] The amendment, he says, is merely concerned with banning state control of private choice. Since enabling private choice is no problem under this regime, neither is perfect filtering.

This conflict among brilliant University of Chicago law professors reveals another latent ambiguity, and, as with other such ambiguity, I do not think we get far by appealing to Madison. To use Sunstein against Sunstein, the framers' First Amendment was an incompletely theorized agreement, and it is better simply to confess that it did not cover the case of perfect filtering. The framers couldn't imagine a PICS-enabled world; they certainly didn't agree upon the scope of the First Amendment in such a world. If we are to support one regime over another, we must do so by asserting the values we want to embrace rather than claiming they have already been embraced.

So what values should we choose? In my view, we should not opt for perfect filtering.[57] We should not design for the most efficient system of censoring—or at least, we should not do this in a way that allows invisible upstream filtering. Nor should we opt for perfect filtering so long as the tendency worldwide is to overfilter speech. If there is speech the government has an interest in controlling, then let that control be obvious to the users. A political response is possible only when regulation is transparent.

Thus, my vote is for the regime that is least transformative of important public values. A zoning regime that enables children to self-identify is less transformative than a filtering regime that in effect requires all speech to be labeled. A zoning regime is not only less transformative but less enabling (of other regulation)—it requires the smallest change to the existing architecture of the Net and does not easily generalize to a far more significant regulation.

I would opt for a zoning regime even if it required a law and the filtering solution required only private choice. If the state is pushing for a change in the mix of law and architecture, I do not care that it is pushing with law in one context and with norms in the other. From my perspective, the question is the result, not the means—does the regime produced by these changes protect free speech values?

Others are obsessed with this distinction between law and private action. They view regulation by the state as universally suspect and regulation by private actors as beyond the scope of constitutional review. And, to their credit, most constitutional law is on their side.

But as I've hinted before, and defend more below, I do not think we should get caught up in the lines that lawyers draw. Our question should be the values we want cyberspace to protect. The lawyers will figure out how.

The annoying skeptic who keeps noting my "inconsistencies" will like to pester me again at this point. In the last chapter, I embraced an architecture for privacy that is in essence the architecture of PICS. P3P, like PICS, would enable machine-to-machine negotiation about content. The content of P3P is rules about privacy practices, and with PICS it is rules about content. But how, the skeptic asks, can I oppose one yet favor the other?

The answer is the same as before: The values of speech are different from the values of privacy; the control we want to vest over speech is less than the control we want to vest over privacy. For the same reasons that we disable some of the control over intellectual property, we should disable some of the control over speech. A little bit of messiness or friction in the context of speech is a value, not a cost.

But are these values different just because I say they are? No. They are only different if *we* say they are different. In real space we treat them as different. My core argument is that we choose how we want to treat them in cyber-space.

Regulating Spam

Spam is perhaps the most theorized problem on the Net. There are scores of books addressing how best to deal with the problem. Many of these are filled with ingenious technical ideas for ferreting out spam, from advanced Bayesian filter techniques to massive redesigns of the e-mail system.

But what is most astonishing to me as a lawyer (and depressing to me as the author of *Code*) is that practically all of these works ignore one important tool with which the problem of spam could be addressed: the law. It's not that they weigh the value of the law relative to, for example, Bayesian filters or the latest in heuristic techniques, and conclude it is less valuable than these other techniques. It's that they presume the value of the law is zero—as if spam were a kind of bird flu which lived its own life totally independently of what humans might want or think.

This is an extraordinary omission in what is, in effect, a regulatory strategy. As I have argued throughout this book, the key to good policy in cyberspace is a proper mix of modalities, not a single silver bullet. The idea that code alone could fix the problem of spam is silly—code can always be coded around, and, unless the circumventers are not otherwise incentivized, they will code around it. The law is a tool to change incentives, and it should be a tool used here as well.

Most think the law can't play a role here because they think spammers will be better at evading the law than they are at evading spam filters. But this thinking ignores one important fact about spam. "Spam" is not a virus. Or at least, when talking about "spam," I'm not talking about viruses. My target in this part is communication that aims at inducing a commercial transaction. Many of these transactions are ridiculous—drugs to stop aging, or instant weight loss pills. Some of these transactions are quite legitimate—special sales of overstocked products, or invitations to apply for credit cards. But all of these transactions aim in the end to get something from you: Money. And crucially, if they aim to get money from you, then there must be someone to whom you are giving your money. That someone should be the target of regulation.

So what should that regulation be?

The aim here, as with porn, should be to regulate to the end of assuring what we could call "consensual communication." That is, the only purpose of the regulation should be to block nonconsensual communication, and enable consensual communication. I don't believe that purpose is valid in every speech context. But in this context—private e-mail, or blogs, with limited bandwidth resources, with the costs of the speech born by the listener—it is completely appropriate to regulate to enable individuals to block commercial communications that they don't want to receive.

So how could that be done?

Today, the only modality that has any meaningful effect upon the supply of spam is code. Technologists have demonstrated extraordinary talent in devising techniques to block spam. These techniques are of two sorts—one which is triggered by the content of the message, and one which is triggered by the behavior of the sender.

The technique that is focused upon content is an array of filtering technologies designed to figure out what the meaning of the message is. As Jonathan Zdziarski describes, these techniques have improved dramatically. While early heuristic filtering techniques had error rates around 1 in 10, current Bayesian techniques promise up to 99.5%–99.95% accuracy.[58]

But the single most important problem with these techniques is the arms race that they produce.[59] Spammers have access to the same filters that network administrators use to block spam—at least if the filters are heuristic.[60] They can therefore play with the message content until it can defeat the filter. That then requires filter writers to change the filters. Some do it well; some don't. The consequence is that the filters are often over and under inclusive—blocking much more than they should or not blocking enough.

The second code-based technique for blocking spam focuses upon the e-mail practices of the sender—meaning not the person sending the e-mail, but the "server" that is forwarding the message to the recipient. A large number of network vigilantes—by which I mean people acting for the good in the world without legal regulation—have established lists of good and bad e-mail servers. These blacklists are compiled by examining the apparent rules the e-mail server uses in deciding whether to send e-mail. Those servers that don't obey the vigilante's rules end up on a blacklist, and people subscribing to these blacklists then block any e-mail from those servers.

This system would be fantastic if there were agreement about how best to avoid "misuse" of servers. But there isn't any such agreement. There are instead good faith differences among good people about how best to control spam.[61] These differences, however, get quashed by the power of the boycott. Indeed, in a network, a boycott is especially powerful. If 5 out of 100 recipients of your e-mail can't receive it because of the rules your network administrator adopts for your e-mail server, you can be sure the server's rules—however sensible—will be changed. And often, there's no appeal of the decision to be included on a blacklist. Like the private filtering technologies for porn, there's no likely legal remedy for wrongful inclusion on a blacklist. So many types of e-mail services can't effectively function because they don't obey the rules of the blacklists.

Now if either or both of these techniques were actually working to stop spam, I would accept them. I'm particularly troubled by the process-less blocking of blacklists, and I have personally suffered significant embarrassment and costs when e-mail that wasn't spam was treated as spam. Yet these costs might be acceptable if the system in general worked.

But it doesn't. The quantity of spam continues to increase. The Raducatu Group "predicts that by 2007, 70% of all e-mail will be spam."[62] And while there is evidence that the rate of growth in spam is slowing, there's no good evidence the pollution of spam is abating.[63] The only federal legislative response, the CAN-SPAM Act, while preempting many innovative state solutions, is not having any significant effect.[64]

Not only are these techniques not blocking spam, they are also blocking legitimate bulk e-mail that isn't—at least from my perspective[65]—spam. The most important example is political e-mail. One great virtue of e-mail was that it would lower the costs of social and political communication. That in turn would widen the opportunity for political speech. But spam-blocking technologies have now emerged as a tax on these important forms of social speech. They have effectively removed a significant promise the Internet originally offered.

Thus, both because regulation through code alone has failed, and because it is actually doing harm to at least one important value that the network originally served, we should consider alternatives to code regulation alone. And, once again, the question is, what mix of modalities would best achieve the legitimate regulatory end?

Begin with the problem: Why is spam so difficult to manage? The simple reason is that it comes unlabeled. There's no simple way to know that the e-mail you've received is spam without opening the e-mail.

That's no accident. Spammers know that if you knew an e-mail was spam, you wouldn't open it. So they do everything possible to make you think the e-mail you're receiving is not spam.

Imagine for a moment that we could fix this problem. Imagine a law that required spam to be labeled, and imagine that law worked. I know this is extremely difficult to imagine, but bear with me for a moment. What would happen if every spam e-mail came with a specified label in its subject line— something like [ADV] in the subject line.[66]

Well, we know what would happen initially. Everyone (or most of us) would either tell our e-mail client or ask our e-mail service to block all e-mail with [ADV] in the subject line. It would be glorious moment in e-mail history, a return to the days before spam.

But the ultimate results of a regulation are not always its initial results. And it's quite clear with this sort of regulation, initial results would be temporary. If there's value in unsolicited missives to e-mail inboxes, then this initial block would be an incentive to find different ways into an inbox. And we can imagine any number of different ways:

1. Senders could get recipients to opt-into receiving such e-mail. The opt-in would change the e-mail from unsolicited to solicited. It would no longer be spam.
2. Senders could add other tags to the subject line. For example, if this spam were travel spam, the tags could be [ADV][Travel]. Then recipients could modify their filter to block all ADV traffic except Travel e-mails.
3. Senders could begin to pay recipients for receiving e-mails. As some have proposed, the e-mail could come with an attachment worth a penny, or something more. Recipients could select to block all ADVs except those carrying cash.

The key to each of these modified results is that the recipient is now receiving commercial e-mail by choice, not by trick. This evolution from the initial regulation thus encourages more communication, but only by encouraging consensual communication. Nonconsensual communication—assuming again the regulation was obeyed—would be (largely) eliminated.

So in one page, I've solved the problem of spam—assuming, that is, that the labeling rule is obeyed. But that, of course, is an impossible assumption. What spammer would comply with this regulation, given the initial effect is to radically shrink his market?

To answer this question, begin by returning to the obvious point about spam, as opposed to viruses or other malware. Spammers are in the business to make money. Money-seekers turn out to be relatively easy creatures to regulate. If the target of regulation is in it for the money, then you can control his behavior by changing his incentives. If ignoring a regulation costs more than obeying it, then spammers (on balance) will obey it. Obeying it may mean changing spamming behavior, or it may mean getting a different job. Either way, change the economic incentives, and you change spamming behavior.

So how can you change the incentives of spammers through law? What reason is there to believe any spammer would pay attention to the law?

People ask that question because they realize quite reasonably that governments don't spend much time prosecuting spammers. Governments have better things to do (or so they think). So even a law that criminalized spam is not likely to scare many spammers.

But what we need here is the kind of creativity in the adaptation of the law that coders evince when they build fantastically sophisticated filters for spam. If law as applied by the government is not likely to change the incentives of spammers, we should find law that is applied in a way that spammers would fear.

One such innovation would be a well-regulated bounty system. The law would require spam to be marked with a label. That's the only requirement. But the penalty for not marking the spam with a label is either state prosecution, or prosecution through a bounty system. The FTC would set a number that it estimates would recruit a sufficient number of bounty hunters. Those bounty hunters would then be entitled to the bounty if they're the first, or within the first five, to identify a responsible party associated with a noncomplying e-mail.

But how would a bounty hunter do that? Well, the first thing the bounty hunter would do is determine whether the regulation has been complied with. One part of that answer is simple; the other part, more complex. Whether a label is attached is simple. Whether the e-mail is commercial e-mail will turn upon a more complex judgment.

Once the bounty hunter is convinced the regulation has been breached, he or she must then identify a responsible party. And the key here is to follow an idea Senator John McCain introduced into the only spam legislation Congress has passed to date, the CAN-SPAM Act. That idea is to hold responsible either the person sending the e-mail, or the entity for which the spam is an advertisement.

In 99 percent of the cases, it will be almost impossible to identify the person sending the spam. The techniques used by spammers to hide that information are extremely sophisticated.[67]

But the entity for which the spam is an advertisement is a different matter. Again, if the spam is going to work, there must be someone to whom I can give my money. If it is too difficult to give someone my money, then the spam won't return the money it needs to pay.

So how can I track the entity for which the spam is an advertisement?

Here the credit card market would enter to help. Imagine a credit card— call it the "bounty hunters' credit card"—that when verified, was always declined. But when that credit card was used, a special flag was attached to the transaction, and the credit card holder would get a report about the entity that attempted the charge. The sole purpose of this card would be to ferret out and identify misbehavior. Credit card companies could charge something special for this card or charge for each use. They should certainly charge to make it worthwhile for them. But with these credit cards in hand, bounty hunters could produce useable records about to whom money was intended to be sent. And with that data, the bounty hunter could make his claim for the bounty.

But what's to stop some malicious sort from setting someone else up? Let's say I hate my competitor, Ajax Cleaners. So I hire a spammer to send out spam to everyone in California, promoting a special deal at Ajax Cleaners. I set up an account so Ajax received the money, and then I use my bounty credit card to nail Ajax. I show up at the FTC to collect my bounty; the FTC issues a substantial fine to Ajax. Ajax goes out of business.

This is a substantial concern with any bounty system. But it too can be dealt with through a careful reckoning of incentives. First, and obviously, the regulation should make such fraud punishable by death. (Ok, not death, but by a significant punishment). And second, any person or company charged with a violation of this spam statute could assert, under oath, that it did not hire or direct any entity to send spam on its behalf. If such an assertion is made, then the company would not be liable for any penalty. But the assertion would include a very substantial penalty if it is proven false—a penalty that would include forfeiture of both personal and corporate assets. A company signing such an oath once would likely be given the benefit of the doubt. But a company or individual signing such an oath more than once would be a target for investigation by the government. And by this stage, the exposure that the spammers would be facing would be enough to make spamming a business that no longer pays.

Here again, then, the solution is a mixed modality strategy. A LAW creates the incentive for a certain change in the CODE of spam (it now comes labeled). That law is enforced through a complex set of MARKET and NORM-based incentives—both the incentive to be a bounty hunter, which is both financial and normative (people really think spammers are acting badly), as well as the incentive to produce bounty credit cards. If done right, the mix of these modalities would change the incentives spammers face. And, if done right, the change could be enough to drive most spammers into different businesses.

Of course there are limits to this strategy. It won't work well with foreign sites. Nor with spammers who have ideological (or pathological) interests. But these spammers could then be the target of the code-based solutions that I described at the start. Once the vast majority of commercially rational spam is eliminated, the outside cases can be dealt with more directly.

This has been a long section, but it makes a couple important points. The first is a point about perspective: to say whether a regulation "abridg[es] the freedom of speech, or of the press" we need a baseline for comparison. The regulations I describe in this section are designed to restore the effective regulation of real space. In that sense, in my view, they don't "abridge" speech.

Second, these examples show how doing nothing can be worse for free-speech values than regulating speech. The consequence of no legal regulation to channel porn is an explosion of bad code regulation to deal with porn. The consequence of no effective legal regulation to deal with spam is an explosion of bad code that has broken e-mail. No law, in other words, sometimes produces bad code. Polk Wagner makes the same point: "[l]aw and software together define the regulatory condition. Less law does not necessarily mean more freedom."[68] As code and law are both regulators (even if different sorts of regulators) we should be avoiding bad regulation of whatever sort.

Third, these examples evince the mixed modality strategy that regulating cyberspace always is. There is no silver bullet—whether East Coast code or West Coast code. There is instead a mix of techniques—modalities that must be balanced to achieve a particular regulatory end. That mix must reckon the interaction among regulators. The question, as Polk Wagner describes it, is for an equilibrium. But the law has an important role in tweaking that mix to assure the balance that advances a particular policy.

Here, by regulating smartly, we could avoid the destructive code-based regulation that would fill the regulatory gap. That would, in turn, advance free speech interests.

THE REGULATIONS OF SPEECH: FREE CULTURE

The third context in which to consider the special relevance of cyberspace to free speech follows directly from Chapter 10. As I describe there, the interaction between the architecture of copyright law and the architecture of digital networks produces an explosion of creativity within reach of copyright never contemplated by any legislature.

The elements in that change are simple. Copyright law regulates, at a minimum, "copies." Digital networks function by making "copies": There's no way to use a work in a digital environment without making a copy. Thus, every single use of creative work in a digital environment triggers, in theory at least, copyright.

This is a radical change from life in real space. In real space, there are any number of ways to "use" a creative work without triggering the law of copyright. When you retell a joke to friends, the law of copyright is not invoked—no "copy" is made, and to friends, no public performance occurs. When you loan a friend your book, the law of copyright is not triggered. When you read a book, the law of copyright would never take notice. Practically every single ordinary use of culture in real space is free of the regulation of copyright. Copyright targets abnormal uses—such as "publishing" or public performances.

The gap between normal and abnormal uses began to close as the technologies for "copying" were democratized. Xerox created the first blip; cassette tape recorders were close behind. But even these technologies were the exception, never the rule. They raised copyright questions, but they didn't inject copyright into the center of ordinary life.

Digital technologies have. As more and more of ordinary life moves onto the Internet, more and more of ordinary life is subject to copyright. The functional equivalent to activities from real space that were essentially unregulated is now subject to copyright's rule in cyberspace. Creativity activity that never needed to grapple with copyright regulation must now, to be legal, clear a whole host of hurdles, some of which, because of the insanely inefficient property system that copyright is, are technically impossible. A significant portion of creative activity has now moved from a free culture to a permission culture. And the question for the values of free speech is whether that expanded regulation should be allowed to occur unchecked.

Again, I have my own (overly strong) views about the matter.[69] I continue to be astonished that a Court so keen to avoid "rais[ing] the costs of being a producer of sexual materials troubling to the majority"[70] is apparently oblivious to the way copyright law raises the costs of being a producer of creative and critical speech.

But for our purposes here, we should simply note once again a latent ambiguity in our constitutional tradition. As the Supreme Court has held, the First Amendment imposes important limitations on the scope of copyright. Among those are at least the requirements that copyright not regulate "ideas," and that copyright be subject to "fair use."

But these "traditional First Amendment safeguards" were developed in a context in which copyright was the exception, not the rule. We don't yet have a tradition in which every single use of creative work is subject to copyright's reach. Digital technologies have produced that world. But most of the rest of the world has not yet woken up to it.

So what should First Amendment values be in this world? One view is that the First Amendment should have no role in this world—beyond the minimal protections of the "idea/expression" distinction and the requirement of "fair use." In this view, the scope of Congress's regulation of creative activities is, subject to these minimal conditions, plenary. Any creative act reduced to a tangible form could be subject to the monopoly right of copyright. And as every creative act in digital context is reduced to a tangible form, this view means that everything in the digital world could be made subject to copyright.

The opposite view rejects this unlimited scope for copyright. While the monopoly right of copyright makes sense in certain commercial contexts, or more broadly, makes sense where it is necessary to "promote . . . progress," there is no legitimate reason to burden the vast majority of creative expression with the burdens of copyright law. That a kid making a video book report needs to clear permissions with the author of the book, or that friends making a mashup of a favorite artist can't do so unless the label has granted them permission, extends the reach of copyright beyond any legitimate purpose.

But between these two views, it is plain that the Framers never made a choice. They were never confronted with the option that copyright could (efficiently) control every single use of a creative work. Any control possible in 1790 would have been radically too burdensome. And while I have my bets about how they would vote, given their strong antipathy to monopolies and the very restrictive IP clause they enacted, that's nothing more than a bet. If there's a choice to be made here, it is a choice they didn't make. It is instead a choice that we must make: Whether the values of free speech restrict this radical increase in the scope of copyright's regulation.

THE REGULATORS OF SPEECH: DISTRIBUTION

So far my arguments about architecture have been about architectures in cyberspace. In this final story, I blur the borders a bit. I want to use the architecture of cyberspace to show something important about the regulation of broadcasting.

The Federal Communications Commission regulates speech. If I wanted to broadcast a political speech on FM radio at a frequency of 98.6 MHz in San Francisco, the FCC would have me prosecuted.[71] To speak on 98.6 in San Francisco, I need a license, because to speak using these radio frequencies without a license is a crime. It is a crime despite the fact that the Constitution says, "Congress shall make no law . . . abridging the freedom of speech, or of the press." What gives?

The answer rests on a deeply held assumption at the core of our jurisprudence governing broadcasting technologies: Only a fixed amount of "spectrum" is available for broadcasting, and the only way to facilitate broadcasting using that spectrum is to allocate slices of it to users, who are then the ones entitled to use their allocated spectrum within a particular geographical region. Without allocation, there would be chaos, the assumption goes. And chaos would kill broadcasting.

This view first came on the constitutional scene after Congress passed the Radio Act of 1927.[72] In 1926 Secretary of Commerce Herbert Hoover gave up the practice of controlling broadcasting after a number of circuit courts held that he did not have the power to do so. If he did not have the power, he said, then the invisible hand would have to govern. But Hoover was no real friend of the invisible hand. He predicted what would happen when he withdrew federal jurisdiction—chaos—and some suggest his aim was to help bring about just what he predicted. Stations would override other stations, he said; broadcasting would be a mess. When some confusion did arise, Hoover used this to justify new federal regulation. [73]

Congress then rode to the rescue by authorizing the FCC to regulate spectrum in a massively invasive way. Only the licensed could speak; what they said would be controlled by their license; they had to speak in the public interest; they had to share their resource with their opponents. In short, Congress said, broadcasting had to be regulated in the same way the Soviet Union regulated wheat.[74] We had no choice. As Justice Felix Frankfurter said in upholding the regime, such sovietism was compelled by the "nature" of radio.[75]

From the beginning, however, there have been skeptics of this view. Not skeptics about the idea that spectrum must be regulated, but about the manner by which it is regulated. Is it really necessary to have a central agency allocate what in effect are property rights? As these skeptics argued, the common law had done just fine before the federal government entered. It could also do fine if the government simply made spectrum a kind of tradable property right. Ronald Coase was most famous for pushing for a regime in which spectrum was auctioned rather than licensed.[76] And Coase's idea caught on—fifty years later. In the United States, the FCC now auctions huge chunks of the broadcasting spectrum. Just this year, it is positioning itself to sell prime real estate spectrum—the part that used to broadcast UHF television.

Now under either scenario—either when the FCC allocates spectrum or when it allocates property rights to spectrum—there is a role for the government. That role is most extensive when the FCC allocates spectrum: Then the FCC must decide who should get what. When spectrum is property, the FCC need only enforce the boundaries that the property right establishes. It is, in a way, a less troubling form of government action than the government deciding who it likes best.

Both forms of government regulation, however, produce a "press" (at least the press that uses spectrum) that is very different from the "press" at the founding. In 1791, the "press" was not the *New York Times* or the *Wall Street Journal*. It was not comprised of large organizations of private interests, with millions of readers associated with each organization. Rather, the press was much like the Internet today. The cost of a printing press was low, the readership was slight, the government subsidized its distribution, and anyone (within reason) could become a publisher. An extraordinary number did.[77]

Spectrum licenses and spectrum property, however, produce a very different market. The cost of securing either becomes a barrier to entry. It would be like a rule requiring a "newspaper license" in order to publish a newspaper. If that license was expensive, then fewer could publish.[78]

Of course, under our First Amendment it would be impossible to imagine the government licensing newspapers (at least if that license was expensive and targeted at the press). That's because we all have a strong intuition that we want competition to determine which newspapers can operate, not artificial governmental barriers. And we all intuitively know that there's no need for the government to "rationalize" the newspaper market. People are capable of choosing among competing newspapers without any help from the government.

So what if the same were true about spectrum? Most of us haven't any clue about how what we call "spectrum" works. The weird sounds and unstable reception of our FM and AM radios make us think some kind of special magic happens between the station and receiver. Without that magic, radio waves would "interfere" with each other. Some special coordination is thought necessary to avoid such "collision" and the inevitable chaos that would result. Radio waves, in this view, are delicate invisible airplanes, which need careful air traffic controllers to make sure disaster doesn't strike.

But what most of us think we know about radio is wrong. Radio waves aren't butterflies. They don't need the protection of the federal bureaucrats to do their work. And as technology that is totally familiar to everyone using the Internet demonstrates, there is in fact very little reason for *either* spectrum-licenses *or* spectrum-property. The invisible hand, here, can do all the work.

To get a clue about how, consider two contexts, at least one of which everyone is familiar with. No doubt, radio waves are different from sound waves. But for our purposes here, the following analogy works.

Imagine you're at a party. There are 50 people in the room, and each of them is talking. Each is therefore producing sound waves. But though these many speakers produce different sound waves, we don't have any trouble listening to the person speaking next to us. So long as no one starts shouting, we can manage to hear quite well. More generally, a party (at least early in the evening) is comprised of smart speakers and listeners who coordinate their speaking so that most everyone in the room can communicate without any real trouble.

Radios could function similarly—if the receiver and transmitter were analogously intelligent. Rather than the dumb receivers that ordinary FM or AM radio relies upon, smart radios could figure out what to listen to and communicate with just as people at a party learn to focus on the conversation they're having.

The best evidence of this is the second example I offer to dislodge the common understanding of how spectrum works. This example is called "WiFi." WiFi is the popular name of a particular set of protocols that together enable computers to "share" bands of unlicensed spectrum. The most popular of these bands are in the 2.5 GHz and 5 GHz range. WiFi enables a large number of computers to use that spectrum to communicate.

Most of the readers of this book have no doubt come across WiFi technology. I see it every day I teach: a room full of students, each with a laptop, the vast majority on the Internet—doing who knows what. The protocols within each machine enable them all to "share" a narrow band of spectrum. There is no government or regulator that tells which machine when it can speak, any more than we need the government to make sure that people can communicate at cocktail parties.

These examples are of course small and limited. But there is literally a whole industry now devoted to spreading the lesson of this technology as broadly as possible. Some theorists believe the most efficient use of all spectrum would build upon these models—using ultra-wide-band technologies to maximize the capacity of radio spectrum. But even those who are skeptical of spectrum utopia are coming to see that our assumptions about how spectrum must be allocated are driven by ignorance about how spectrum actually works.

The clearest example of this false assumption is the set of intuitions we're likely to have about the necessary limitations in spectrum utilization. These assumptions are reinforced by the idea of spectrum-property. The image we're likely to have is of a resource that can be overgrazed. Too many users can clog the channels, just as too many cattle can overgraze a field.

Congestion is certainly a possible consequence of spectrum usage. But the critical point to recognize—and again, a point that echoes throughout this book—is that the possibility congestion depends upon the design. WiFi networks can certainly become congested. But a different architecture for "sharing" spectrum need not. Indeed, under this design, more users don't deplete capacity—they increase it.[79]

The key to making this system possible is for every receiver to become a node in the spectrum architecture. Users then wouldn't be just consumers of someone else's broadcast. Instead, receivers are now also broadcasters. Just as peer-to-peer technologies such as BitTorrent harness the bandwidth of users to share the cost of distributing content, users within a certain mesh-network architecture for spectrum could actually increase the spectrum capacity of the network. Under this design, then, the more who use the spectrum, the more spectrum there is for others to use—producing not a tragedy of the commons, but a comedy of the commons.

The basic architecture of this mesh system imagines every computer in the system is both a receiver and a transmitter. Of course, in one sense, that's what these machines already are—a computer attached to a WiFi network both receives transmissions from and sends transmissions to the broadcasting node. But that architecture is a 1-to-many broadcasting architecture. The mesh architecture is something different. In a mesh architecture, each radio can send packets of data to any other radio within the mesh. Or, put differently, each is a node in the network. And with every new node, the capacity of the network could increase. In a sense, this is precisely the architecture of much of the Internet. Machines have addresses; they collect packets addressed to that machine from the Net.[80] Your machine shares the Net with every other machine, but the Net has a protocol about sharing this commons. Once this protocol is agreed on, no further regulation is required.

We don't have go too deep into the technology to recognize the question that I mean this section to pose: If technology makes it possible for radios to share the spectrum—without either spectrum-licenses or spectrum-property—then what justification does the government have for imposing either burden on the use of spectrum? Or, to link it back to the beginning of this section, if spectrum users could share spectrum without any coordination by the government, why is it any more justified to impose a property system on spectrum than it is for the government to charge newspapers for the right to publish?

No doubt, the architecture that enables sharing is not totally free of government regulation. The government may well require that only certified devices be used in this network (as the FCC already does with any device that can radiate within a range of spectrum). It may push the technology to the capacity, increasing mesh architecture. It may even reasonably impose nuisance-like limits on the power of any transmitter. But beyond these simple regulations, the government would not try to limit who could use the spectrum. It would not ban the use of spectrum for people who hadn't either paid or been licensed.

So here we have two architectures for spectrum—one where spectrum is allocated, and one where spectrum (like the market for newspapers) is shared. Which is more consistent with the First Amendment's design?

Here, finally, we have an example of a translation that works. We have a choice between an architecture that is the functional equivalent of the architecture of the American framing and an architecture equivalent to the Soviet framing. One architecture distributes power and facilitates speech; the other concentrates power and raises the price of speech. Between these two, the American framers made a choice. The state was not to be in the business of licensing speakers either directly or indirectly. Yet that is just the business that the current rule for spectrum allocation allows.

A faithful reading of the framers' Constitution, my colleague Yochai Ben-kler and I have argued,[81] would strike down the regime of spectrum alloca-tion.[82] A faithful reading would reject an architecture that so strongly concentrates power. The model for speech that the framers embraced was the model of the Internet—distributed, noncentralized, fully free and diverse. Of course, we should choose whether we want a faithful reading—translation does not provide its own normative support. But if fidelity is our aim, this is its answer.

SPEECH LESSONS

What I described at the start of the book as modalities of constraint I have redescribed in this chapter as modalities of protection. While modalities of constraint can be used as swords against the individual (powers), modalities of protection can be used as shields (rights).

In principle we might think about how the four modalities protect speech, but I have focused here on architectures. Which architectures protect what speech? How does changing an architecture change the kind of speech being protected?

I have not tried to be comprehensive. But I have pushed for a view that addresses the relationship between architectures and speech globally and uses constitutional values to think not just about what is permitted given a partic-ular architecture, but also about which architectures are permitted. Our real-space constitution should inform the values of our cyberspace constitution. At the least, it should constrain the state in its efforts to architect cyberspace in ways that are inconsistent with those values.

THIRTEEN

interlude

LET'S PAUSE FOR A MOMENT AND LOOK BACK OVER THESE THREE CHAPTERS. THERE is a pattern to the problems they present—a way of understanding how all three problems are the same.

In one sense, each has asked: How much control should we allow over information, and by whom should this control be exercised? There is a battle between code that protects intellectual property and fair use; there is a battle between code that might make a market for privacy and the right to report facts about individuals regardless of that market; there is a battle between code that enables perfect filtering of speech and architectures that ensure some messiness about who gets what. Each case calls for a balance of control.

My vote in each context may seem to vary. With respect to intellectual property, I argue against code that tracks reading and in favor of code that guarantees a large space for an intellectual commons. In the context of privacy, I argue in favor of code that enables individual choice—both to encrypt and to express preferences about what personal data is collected by others. Code would enable that choice; law could inspire that code. In the context of free speech, however, I argue against code that would perfectly filter speech—it is too dangerous, I claim, to allow perfect choice there. Better choice, of course, is better, so code that would empower better systems of reputation is good, as is code that would widen the legitimate range of broadcasting.

The aim in all three contexts is to work against centralized structures of choice. In the context of filtering, however, the aim is to work against structures that are too individualized as well.

You may ask whether these choices are consistent. I think they are, but it's not important that you agree. You may believe that a different balance makes sense—more control for intellectual property or filtering perhaps, and less for privacy. My real interest is in conveying the necessity of such balancing and of the values implicit in the claim that we will always require a balance. Always there is a competition between the public and private; always the rights of the private must be balanced against the interests of the public. Always a choice must be made about how far each side will be allowed to reach. These questions are inherent to public law: How will a particular constellation of constitutional values be reckoned? How will a balance be struck in particular factual contexts?

I have argued this point while neglecting to specify who is responsible for any given imbalance. There are those who would say that there is too much filtering, or not enough privacy, or too much control over intellectual property, but these are not public concerns unless the government is responsible for these imbalances. Constitutional value in the United States extends only so far as state action extends. And I have not shown just how state action extends to these contexts.

I do not intend to. In my view, our tradition reveals at least an ambiguity about how far constitutional values are to extend. In a world where only governments are regulators, keeping the Constitution's authority limited to state action makes some sense. But when the modalities of regulation are multiplied, there is no reason to ignore the reach of constitutional values. Our framers made no choice about this; there is no reason why regulation through code cannot be informed by constitutional values. No argument has been made for why this part of our life should be cut off from the limitations and protections traditionally provided by the Constitution.

Code strikes the balance between individual and collective rights that I have highlighted so far. In the next chapter, a different balance is struck—one again made salient by code. However, this time the balance is not between the state and the individual but between the state and the implicit regulations of the architectures of cyberspace. Now the threat is to a traditional sovereignty. How do we translate that tradition to fit a world where code is law?

PART FOUR

competing sovereigns

Sovereigns take themselves very seriously—especially sovereigns in cyberspace. Each has a strong sense of its own domain, and sometimes that sense translates into dominance in other domains. As more move online, the claims of one sovereign to control speech or behavior will increasingly conflict with the claims others sovereigns. That conflict will prove to be the most important generative fact for the Internet to be.

I approach the question of this conflict in two steps. The first chapter in this Part addresses the question of sovereignty independently of the question of conflict. What does sovereignty mean? How is it manifest? The next chapter then focuses upon the particular dynamic that the conflict among sovereigns will create. That conflict, I argue, will press the architecture of the Internet to a certain familiar form.

F O U R T E E N

s o v e r e i g n t y

VIETNAM IS A COMMUNIST NATION. IT IS ONE OF THE FEW REMAINING COMMUNIST states, and, of course, its communism is nothing like the communism that gave birth to the Cold War. But nonetheless, it is a sovereign nation that still links its identity to Marx and Lenin (through Chairman Ho).

The United States is not a Communist nation. Defeated by Vietnam, but a victor in the Cold War, we are a nation that in large part defines itself in opposition to the ideology of Marx and Lenin. Vietnam sets the state in service of the withering of the state as its ideal; the United States sets the withered state in the service of liberty as its ideal. Control is the model of communism; freedom is the model of the United States.

Or so we are to think.

I confess a certain fascination with Communist states. In the early 1980s I wandered through every European Communist state that would let me in. In the early 1990s, I worked with constitutionalists in Georgia as they drafted their constitution. And in 1996, I spent much of the summer wandering through Vietnam. Alone and e-mail-free, I tried to understand this place that in my childhood fell victim to my nation's exported struggle with the Cold War.

Though I've been to many different places around the world, I've never been to a place more spectacular. One is always overwhelmed by forgiveness, and an American can't help being overwhelmed by this nation's warmth and welcome. Perhaps had we "won" the war forgiveness would not be so forthcoming. But it apparently comes easily to those who did win.

I wasn't there, however, to understand forgiveness. I wanted to learn something about how the place ran. I wanted to understand how this state exercises control over its citizens; how it continues to regulate; how it qualifies as one of the last remaining Communist states. So I spent time talking to lawyers, businessmen, and managers of the emerging Net in Vietnam ("Net-Nam"). Very quickly, a surprising picture emerged.

Though the ideology of a Communist state admits very little limitation on the power of the state; though the Vietnamese state sets as its ideal a common good rather than the good of individuals or individual liberty; though on paper there is no "liberty" in Vietnam in the sense that we in the West like to imagine it—though all this is true, I could not escape the feeling that people in Vietnam, in their day-to-day existence, are far less "regulated" than people in the United States. Not all people, of course: Political opponents undoubtedly feel the power of the state quite forcefully. But I sensed that ordinary people in their ordinary lives, many running small shops, had no conception of the control that government can exercise; no experience of having their wages reported to a central bureaucracy once a quarter; no understanding of what it is like to live under the (relative) efficiency of the regulation we have here. Life there is remarkably free from governmental control. It was hard to imagine how it would have been different had Nixon won the war. Pornography was banned and hippies were harassed, but in the main, people and business got on with very little direct or effective regulation by government.

This fact (if you'll allow random observations of an untrained anthropologist to count as fact) is not hard to understand. The "law" on the books in Vietnam may or may not be a stricter or more extensive regulator than the "law" in the United States. But the architecture of life in Vietnam clearly makes any real regulation by the state impossible. There is no infrastructure of control—there is barely any infrastructure at all. Whatever the regulations of the state may be, there is no architecture that could make them effective. Even if there is more regulation there than here (and frankly I doubt that there is), Vietnam has an effective "freedom."

This makes perfect sense. The power to regulate is a function of architecture as much as of ideology; architectures enable regulation as well as constrain it. To understand the power a government might have, we must understand the architectures within which it governs.

The preceding chapters have all been about this very point. We can have an idea of sovereign power—the power of the sovereign to regulate or control behavior—but the significance of that power gets realized in a particular context. The state's power may be "absolute," but if the architecture does not support regulation, the state's effective power is quite slight. On the other hand, the state's power may be limited, but if the architectures of control are very efficient, this limited power can be extraordinarily extensive. To understand a state's power to regulate we must ask: How well does its infrastructure support regulation?

This is the question we should ask about cyberspace, as a first step to understanding sovereignty there. What power do sovereigns have to regulate life in cyberspace? How do the modalities of regulation help or limit that power?

We'll consider this question in three parts, two of which are the subject of this chapter. First, what is the nature of the sovereignty in cyberspace? How is it different from the sovereignty of France? Second, what limits the sovereignty of cyberspace? And third, the subject the next section, how will sovereigns interact in the regulation of cyberspace, not so much to control behavior there as to control the effects of that behavior here? How will they compete?

THE SOVEREIGN OF THE SPACE: RULES

When you enter the world of MMOG Second Life as a new character, the rules of Second Life are explained to you. Some of these rules are the techniques you will need to get around in Second Life—how to move, or how to fly. Some of the rules are normative commands that tell you what you can and can't do.

It is impossible when confronting this introduction not to notice that these constraints are constructed. God didn't make Second Life. No one is confused about whether he or she did. Nor is it likely that one entering this space wouldn't notice that one important dimension to that construction is construction through code. That you can fly is a choice of the coders. Where you can fly is a choice of the coders. That when you bump into someone, a warning box is displaced is a choice of the coders. That you can turn off IM conversations from people you don't want to hear from is a choice of the coders. No one mistakes that there are *choices* made here. Everyone recognizes that a critical part of the cyberspace world is made through code. As Second Life's CEO, Philip Rosedale, put it to me: "What is God in a virtual world? Your only God is the code."[1]

Now, as I've said from the start, we should distinguish between richly controlling spaces and thinly controlling spaces. Spaces like Second Life richly control the life of people playing there. Indeed, the whole objective of playing there is create the impression that one is *there*. These, again, are the sorts of places I call cyberspace.

Cyberspace is very different from life on a bill-paying website, or on a site holding your e-mail. Code controls these, too. But the control, or sovereignty, of those sites is distinct from the control of Second Life. In Second Life, or in what I've defined to be cyberspace generally, the control is ubiquitous; on a bill-paying website, or on what I've called the Internet, the control is passing, transitory.

Interestingly, there is an important dynamic shift that we've already identified, more in thinly controlling spaces than thick. This is the preference for code controls where code controls are possible.

Think again about the bill-paying website. It is of course against the law to access someone's bank account and transfer funds from that account without the authorization of the account owner. But no bank would ever simply rely upon the law to enforce that rule. Every bank adds a complex set of code to authenticate who you are when you enter a bill-paying website. Where a policy objective can be coded, then the only limit on that coding is the marginal cost of code versus the marginal benefit of the added control.

But in a thickly controlling environment such as Second Life, there's a limit to the use of code to guide social behavior. Sometimes, in other words, better code can weaken community. As Second Life's Rosedale put it,

> In some ways the difficulty of Second Life is a benefit because you have to be taught. And that Act of being taught is such a huge win for both the teacher and the student. . . . [We] have this sort of mentoring going on that is such a psychologically appealing relationship—one which the real world doesn't give us very much.[2]

A second way in which better code can weaken community is even more important. As Second Life is, it doesn't enable people easily to segregate. As Rosedale described,

> In Second Life, there's basically not any zoning. What this means is that neighbor disputes are frequent. But from the standpoint of learning, this is actually a real positive. I've gotten e-mail from people that says, "Well, I didn't get along with my neighbors, and as a result, I learned very rapidly a great deal about how to resolve disputes. How to be a good neighbor." . . . [I]n the real world . . . there so much law . . . that you don't actually have to talk to your neighbors. [Instead] there's simply a law that says you can or can't do [something.] . . . There's an opportunity to communicate and interact [in the virtual world] in a way that the real world offers only under very rare circumstances.[3]

The code thus doesn't simply make all problems go away. It doesn't remove the need for neighbors to work stuff out. And in this way, the code helps build community. The practice of interaction builds bonds that would not be built if the code produced the same results, automatically. Optimal design leaves certain problems to the players to work out—not because the solution couldn't be coded, but also because coding a solution would have collateral costs.

Nonetheless, it is still the sovereign in these virtual spaces that chooses one modality over another. The trade-off is complicated. Perfect efficiency of results is not always perfectly efficient. But still the choice of means remains.

THE SOVEREIGN OF THE SPACE: CHOOSING RULES

But how is that choice made? Or more directly, what about democracy? In real space, the rule is that sovereigns are legitimate only if democratic. We barely tolerate (most) nondemocratic regimes. The general norm for real space life is that ultimately, the people rule.

But the single most interesting nondevelopment in cyberspace is that, again, as Castronova puts it, "one does not find much democracy at all in synthetic worlds."[4] The one real exception is a world called "A Tale in the Desert."[5] Democracy has not broken out across cyberspace, or on the Internet. Instead, democracy is a rare exception to a fairly strong rule—that the "owner" of the space is the sovereign. And in Castronova's view, the owner is not ordinarily a very good sovereign:

> In sum, none of the worlds, to my knowledge, has ever evolved institutions of good government. Anarchy reigns in all worlds.[6]

This isn't to say that aggregated views don't matter in cyberspace. Indeed, they are crucial to central aspects of the Internet as it is just now. A kind of voting—as manifested through links—guides search engines. Technorati, as I've already described, relies upon the same to rank blogs. And important sites, such as Slashdot, routinely use rankings or votes of editors to determine which comments will rise to the top.

These are all democracy-like. But they are not democracy. Democracy is the practice of the people choosing the rules that will govern a particular place. And with the exception of Wikipedia, and "A Tale in the Desert," there are very few major Internet or cyberspace institutions that run by the rule of the people.

So what explains this democracy gap? And should we expect it to change?

Our history of self-government has a particular form, with two importantly contingent features. Before our founding, life was geographically based—a nation was a society located in a physical space, with a single sovereign allegiance. As we'll consider more extensively in the chapter that follows, the conceptual revolution of the American Republic was that citizens could have two sovereigns—more precisely, that they (as the ultimate sovereign) could vest their sovereign power in two different delegates. Their state government was one delegate, the federal government was another; individuals living in a single geographic location could thus be citizens of both governments. That was the idea of the founding document, and the Fourteenth Amendment made it explicit: "All persons born or naturalized in the United States, and subject to the jurisdiction thereof, are citizens of the United States and of the State wherein they reside."

Citizenship in this sense did not always mean a right to contribute to the self-government of whatever community you were a citizen of.[7] Even today there are citizens that have no right to vote—e.g., children. But for those recognized as members of civil and political society, citizenship is an entitlement: It is a right to participate in the governing of the political community of which they are members. As a citizen of the United States, I have the right to vote in U.S. elections; as a citizen of California, I have the right to vote in California elections. I have both rights at the same time.

At this level, the link between entitlement and geography makes sense. But as mobility has increased, the at-one-time obvious link between geography and citizenship has become less and less obvious. I live in San Francisco, but I work in Palo Alto. The rules give me full participation rights in San Francisco but none in Palo Alto. Why does this make sense?

Political theorists have noted this problem for some time.[8] Scholars such as Richard Ford and Lani Guinier have developed powerful alternative conceptions of self-government that would enable a kind of self-government not tied directly to geography. With one such alternative, voters choose (within limits) the community where their votes count. Thus if I felt participating in the future of Palo Alto was more important than participating in the future of San Francisco, I would have the right to vote in Palo Alto though I lived in San Francisco.

These complications are magnified when we consider the link between geography and cyberspace. Even if I should have the right to vote in the community where I work, should I have the right to vote in the community where I play? Why would real-space citizens need to have any control over cyberplaces or their architectures? You might spend most of your life in a mall, but no one would say you have a right to control the mall's architecture. Or you might like to visit Disney World every weekend, but it would be odd to claim that you therefore have a right to regulate Disney World. Why isn't cyberspace more like a mall or a theme park than like the district in which you live and vote?

Your relationship to a mall, or to Disney World, is the relationship of consumer to merchant. If you don't like two-all-beef-patties-special-sauce-lettuce-cheese-pickles-onions-on-a-sesa-me-seed-bun, then you can go to Burger King; McDonald's has no duty to let you vote on how it makes its hamburgers. If you don't like the local mall, you can go to another. The power you have over these institutions is your ability to exit. They compete for your attention, your custom, and your loyalty; if they compete well, you will give them your custom; if they don't, you will go somewhere else. That competition is crucial in disciplining these institutions. What makes them work well is this competition among these potential sources for your custom.

This merchant-sovereign part of our life is important. It is where we spend most of our time, and most people are more satisfied with this part of their lives than they are with the part within which they get to vote. In this sense, all these places are sovereigns; they all impose rules on us. But our recourse with respect to merchant-sovereigns is simply to take our business elsewhere.

But the merchant-sovereign part of our life is not exclusive. There are also citizen-sovereign parts of our life. There are no states that get to say to their citizens: "You have no right to vote here; if you don't like it, leave." Our role in relation to our governments is that of a stakeholder with a voice. We have a right—if the government is to be called democratic—to participate in its structuring.

And this is true not just with governments. It would be an odd university that gave its faculty no right to vote on issues central to the university (though it is an odd corporation that gives its employees a right to vote on issues related to employment). It would be an odd social club that did not give members some control over its functions—though again, there are such clubs, just as there are nondemocratic governments. Even the church allows its members to determine a great deal of how members are governed. In these institutions, we are members, not consumers—or, not just consumers. These institutions give consumers control over the rules that will govern them. In this sense, these institutions are citizen-sovereignties.

As a descriptive matter, then, cyberspace is not yet dominated (or even broadly populated) by citizen-sovereignties. The sovereignties we see so far are all merchant-sovereignties. And this is even more clearly true with the Internet. To the extent sites are sovereign, they are merchant-sovereigns. Our relationship to them is the same as our relationship to McDonald's.

Some theorists have tried to collapse these two different models into one. Some have tried to carry the member model into every sphere of social life—the workplace, the mall, the local pub.[9] Others have tried to carry the consumer model into every sphere of social life—followers of Charles Tiebout, for example, have tried to explain competition among governments along the lines of the choices we make among toothpastes.[10] But even if we cannot articulate perfectly the justifications for treating these choices differently, it would be a mistake to collapse these different spheres into one. It would be hell to have to vote on the design of toothpaste, and tyranny if our only recourse against a government we didn't like was to move to a different land.

But then is it a problem that cyberspace is comprised of just merchant-sovereignties? The first defense for merchant-sovereignties is developed in the writings of David Post and his sometime coauthor David Johnson.[11] Post's article "Anarchy, State, and the Internet" best sets the stage. Communities in cyberspace, Post argues, are governed by "rule-sets." We can understand these rule-sets to be the requirements, whether embedded in the architecture or promulgated in a set of rules, that constrain behavior in a particular place. The world of cyberspace, he argues, is comprised by these rule-sets. Individuals will choose to enter one rule-set or another. As rule-sets compete for our attention, the world of cyberspace will come to be defined by this competition of merchant-sovereigns for customers.

Post's account again is descriptively accurate. It is also, Post argues, normatively recommended. Sovereigns should be understand as a firm's market power is understood in antitrust law. By "market power" antitrust lawyers and economists mean a firm's ability to raise prices profitably. In a perfectly competitive market, a firm with no market power is the one that cannot raise its prices because it would lose so much in sales as to make the increase not worth it.[12] The firm that does have market power can raise prices and see its profits increase. The firm with market power also has the ability to force consumers to accept a price for a good that is higher than the price in a competitive market.

We might imagine an analogous constraint operating on government. Sovereigns, like firms, can get away with only so much. As they become more repressive, or as they regulate more harshly, other sovereigns, or other rule-sets, become competitors. At some point it is easier for citizens to leave than to put up with the burdens of regulation,[13] or easier to evade the law than to comply with it.

Because such moves are costly in real space, sovereigns, at least in the short run, can get away with a lot. But in cyberspace, moving is not so hard. If you do not like the rule-set of your MMOGs, you can change games. If you do not like the amount of advertising on one Internet portal, then in two seconds you can change your default portal. Life in cyberspace is about joining without ever leaving your home. If the group you join does not treat you as you want to be treated, you can leave. Because competitive pressure is greater in cyberspace, governments and other propagators of rule-sets must behave like firms in a competitive market.

This is an important and interesting conception of governance. Important because it describes governance in cyberspace; interesting because it perhaps shows the purpose and limits of citizen-sovereignty in real space. It argues for a world of volunteers, one where rules are not imposed but selected. It is a world that minimizes the unconcented-to-power of any particular government, by making governments competitors for citizens. It is government like McDonald's or Coca-Cola—eager to please, fearful of revolt.

There are reasons, however, to be skeptical about this view. First, consider the claim that exit costs are lower in cyberspace than in real space. When you switch to a different ISP or Internet portal, you no doubt confront a different set of "rules," and these rules no doubt compete for your attention. This is just like going from one restaurant or shopping mall to another. There are competing rule-sets; they are among several factors you consider in choosing an ISP; and to the extent that there is easy movement among these rule-sets, this movement is undoubtedly a competition among them. Some ISPs, of course, try to make this movement difficult. If you've been a member of AOL for ten years, and you decide you want to switch, AOL doesn't make that change easy by providing, for example, a simple ability to forward your e-mail. But as people recognize this restriction imposed by AOL, they'll choose other ISPs. If the competition is real, the rule-set will compete.

Communities, however, are different. Consider the "competition" among, say, MMOGs. You join an MMOG and spend months building a character in that community. You also collect assets—buildings you've built, or weapons you've acquired. Both resources are a kind of capital. The set of relationships you've developed are the social capital; all the stuff you have is the physical capital.

If you then become dissatisfied with life in your chosen MMOGs, you can leave. But leaving is costly. You can't transfer the social capital you've built, and, depending upon the game, you may not be able to transfer the physical capital either. Like choosing to join a different frequent flyer program, the choice to join a different MMOG is a decision to waste certain assets. And that fact will weaken the competition among these rule-sets.

I don't mean to overstate the point. Indeed, as markets have developed for selling assets within MMOGs, and the nature of the games has become standardized, some argue that it is becoming much easier to move from one game to another. In real space you also can't easily transfer social capital from one community to another. Friends are not fungible, even if they can give you connections at your new home. But physical assets in real space are transferable. I can sell what I don't want and move what I do. Always. In MMOGs, not always.

Paradoxically, then, we might say that it may be harder to change communities in cyberspace than it is in real space. It is harder because you must give up everything in a move from one cyber-community to another, whereas in real space you can bring much of it with you.[14] Communities in cyberspace may in the short run have more power over their citizens (regarding social capital) than real-space communities do.

This means that the picture of competing rule-sets in cyberspace is more complex than Post suggests. The pressure on competition is potentially greater in turn. That might motivate a desire in cyberspace communities to shift toward citizen-sovereignty, but, again, there's not much evidence of that shift yet.

There is a second, more fundamental skepticism. Even if we could construct cyberspace on the model of the market—so that we relate to spaces in cyberspace the way we relate to toothpaste in real space—there are strong reasons not to. As life moves online, and more and more citizens from states X, Y, and Z come to interact in cyberspaces A, B, and C, these cyberspaces may well need to develop the kind of responsibility and attention that develops (ideally) within a democracy. Or, put differently, if cyberspace wants to be considered its own legitimate sovereign, and thus deserving of some measure of independence and respect, it must become more clearly a citizen-sovereignty.

This same dynamic happens in real space. There are many institutions that are not "sovereign" in the sense that they control how people live, but are "sovereign" in the sense that within the institution, they control how people behave. Universities, social clubs, churches, and corporations are the obvious examples of institutions that gain a kind of autonomy from ordinary government. This autonomy can be thick or thin. And my suggestion is that it gets thicker the more the institution reflects values of citizen-sovereignty.

This kind of sovereignty is expressed in the law through doctrines of immunity. A corporation has certain immunities, but that depends upon it fitting a particular corporate form. Churches have a certain immunity, but it is increasingly challenged as its governance becomes more alien.

Communities in cyberspace will earn a similar immunity more quickly if they reflect citizen-sovereign values rather than merchant-sovereign values. The more responsible the communities become, the more likely real-space governments will defer to their norms through doctrines like immunity.

This maturation—if it is that—is obviously a long way down the road. It depends upon an increasing self-recognition by members of these cyberspace communities that they are, in a sense, separate, or complementary communities. It depends upon an increasing recognition among noncommunity members that there's something distinctive about these communities. Some are optimistic that this will happen. As Dan Hunter and Greg Lastowka write:

> Courts will need to recognize that virtual worlds are jurisdictions separate from our own, with their own distinctive community norms, laws, and rights. While cyborg inhabitants will demand that these rights be recognized by real-world courts and virtual-world wizards, they will need to arrive at these rights themselves within the context of the virtual worlds.[15]

We've seen something similar to this progression in our own history. There was a time when the United States was really "these united States," a time when the dominant political reality was local and there were real differences of culture and values between New York and Virginia. Despite these differences, in 1789 these states united to establish a relatively thin national government. This government was to be minimal and limited; it had a number of narrow, strictly articulated purposes, beyond which it was not to go.

These limits made sense in the limited community that the United States was. At the time there was very little that the states shared as a nation. They shared a history of defeating the strongest army in the world and a purpose of growing across an almost endless continent,[16] but they did not share a social or political life. Life was local, exchange was relatively rare, and in such a world limited national government made sense.

Nevertheless, there were national questions to be articulated and resolved. Slavery, for example, was a mark on our country as a whole, even though the practice was limited to a few states. There had been arguments at the founding about whether slavery should be left to local regulation. But the Constitution was founded on a compromise about that question. Congress was not permitted to address the question of the "importation" of slaves until 1808.[17] After that, it could, and people, increasingly, said that it should. Slavery continued, however, to be a stain on the moral standing of our nation. Congress could eliminate it in the territories at least, and some argued that it should do so in the southern states as well.

Opponents to this call for Congress to cleanse our nation of slavery were of two sorts. One type supported the institution of slavery and believed it was central to southern life. They are not my focus here. My focus is a second type—those who, with perfect integrity and candor, argued that slavery was a local issue, not a national issue; that the framers had understood it not to be a national issue; and that the national government should let it alone.

However true that claim might have been in 1791 or 1828, it became less plausible over time. As the nation became socially and economically more integrated, the plausibility of saying "I am a Virginian first" declined, and the significance of being a citizen of the nation as a whole increased.[18]

This change came about not through some political decision but as a result of a changing economic and social reality. Our sense of being members of a national community increased until, at a certain stage, it became impossible to deny our national citizenship. A war produced that recognition. The Fourteenth Amendment wrote it into the Constitution; economic and social intercourse made it completely real. And as this change took hold, the claim that issues like slavery were local became absurd.

The very same process is happening to us now, internationally, and cyberspace is making an important contribution. It has been slowly gaining momentum, of course, since the end of World War II, but the Internet has wildly accelerated the pace. Ordinary citizens are connected internationally and can make international transactions as never before. The presence of a community that is beyond any individual state is increasingly undeniable.

As this international community develops in cyberspace, its citizens will find it increasingly difficult to stand neutral in this international space. Just as a principled sort of citizen in 1791 might have said that slavery in Virginia was irrelevant to a citizen in Maine, so in 1991 the control of speech in Singapore may have been irrelevant to a citizen of the United States. But just as the claim about slavery's local relevance became implausible in the course of the nineteenth century, the claim about speech on the Net will become equally implausible in the 21st century. Cyberspace is an international community; there are constitutional questions for it to answer; and we cannot simply stand back from this international space and say that these questions are local issues.

At least, we could not say that once we effectively invaded this international space with the Internet of 1995. We put into the world an architecture that facilitated extraordinarily free speech and extraordinary privacy; that enabled secure communications through a protocol that permitted encryption; and that encouraged free communications through a protocol that resisted censorship. That was the speech architecture that the Net gave the world—that we gave the world.

Now we are changing that architecture. We are enabling commerce in a way we did not before; we are contemplating the regulation of encryption; we are facilitating identity and content control. We are remaking the values of the Net, and the question is: Can we commit ourselves to neutrality in this reconstruction of the architecture of the Net?

I don't think that we can. Or should. Or will. We can no more stand neutral on the question of whether the Net should enable centralized control of speech than Americans could stand neutral on the question of slavery in 1861. We should understand that we are part of a worldwide political battle; that we have views about what rights should be guaranteed to all humans, regardless of their nationality; and that we should be ready to press these views in this new political space opened up by the Net.

I am not arguing for world government. Indeed, the impossibility of such an idea is the focus of much of the next chapter. My argument instead is that we must take responsibility for the politics we are building into this architecture, for this architecture is a sovereign governing the community that lives in that space. We must consider the politics of the architectures of the life there.

I have argued that we should understand the code in cyberspace to be its own sort of regulatory regime, and that this code can sometimes be in competition with the law's regulatory regime. For example, we saw how copyright law could be inconsistent with the regulatory regime of trusted systems. My argument is that we should understand these to be two regulatory regimes in competition with each other. We need a way to choose between them. We need a way to decide which should prevail.

As this system of regulation by code develops, it will contain its own norms, which it will express in its structures or in the rules it imposes. If the predictions of law and economics are correct, these norms will no doubt be efficient, and they may well be just. But to the extent that justice does not track efficiency, they will be efficient and unjust. The question will then be: How do we react to this gap?

There is an important pattern in this competition between code and law. Law, at least as it regulates international relations, is the product of extended negotiations. Countries must come to an agreement about how law will regulate and about any norms that they will impose on private ordering. As their work relates to cyberspace in particular, this agreement is quite significant. It will require the nations of the world to come to a common understanding about this space and to develop a common strategy for dealing with its regulation.

F I F T E E N

competition among sovereigns

CONFLICTS

Here are two stories about the power of sovereignty, one you're likely to have heard of, and the other not.

1. Protecting the French

The French don't like Nazis (and resist your French-bashing urge to add "anymore" to that sentence; remember, but for the French, we likely would not have a nation). French law doesn't let the Nazis fight back. As in Germany, it is a crime in France to promote the Nazi party and sell Nazi paraphernalia. The French are vigilant that this virus of an ideology not revive itself in Europe.

French law is different from American law in this respect. The First Amendment would block any viewpoint-based limitation on political propaganda. The state could no more block the sale of Nazi paraphernalia than it could block the sale of Republican buttons. Free speech means that the viewpoint of a political relic can't determine whether the relic is sold.

Yahoo! is an American company. In 1999, Yahoo! opened a French branch, and, at Yahoo! France, Yahoo! opened an auction site.[1] Like eBay, this site permitted individuals to list items for auction. Like eBay, the site ran the auction and helped facilitate the ultimate sale of the items auctioned.

Very soon after the site opened, and contrary to French law, Nazi paraphernalia began to appear on the Yahoo! auction sites available for sale in

France. Some in France were not happy. In 2000, a lawsuit was filed against Yahoo!, demanding Yahoo either remove the Nazi paraphernalia from its site or block access to the Nazi paraphernalia.[2]

This in turn made Yahoo! unhappy. This was the Internet, Yahoo! insisted. It is a global medium. There was no way to block French citizens from the Yahoo! sites. And it would be absurd if the rules of one country became the rules of the world. There would be a race to the bottom (or top, depending upon your perspective) if every country could force every website in the world to comply with its own law. France should just accept that in the world of the Internet, the rule of France won't be absolute. As the Ninth Circuit Court of Appeals summarized Yahoo!'s argument, "Yahoo! wants a decision providing broad First Amendment protection for speech . . . on the Internet that might violate the laws . . . of other countries."[3]

French Judge Jean-Jacques Gomez didn't agree with Yahoo! In an opinion issued in May 2000, the judge required Yahoo! either to remove the Nazi paraphernalia or to block French citizens.[4] In a second order issued in November, the French court directed Yahoo! to comply within three months, or pay 100,000 French francs per day of the delay.[5]

The Internet was outraged. Thousands of websites criticized the French Court's decision, and hundreds of newspapers followed suit. France was destroying "free speech" on the Internet by forcing its rule on anyone who used the Internet anywhere. As the Cato Institute's Adam Thierer commented,

> Thankfully, Americans take free speech a bit more seriously than the Brits, the French, the Germans and rest of the world. And, yes, America could become the guardian of free speech worldwide by offering the protection of the First Amendment over the Net to millions of people who have been denied the right to speak freely in their own countries.[6]

2. Protecting Hollywood

In 2000, a serial entrepreneur, Bill Craig, launched a Toronto-based service for the World Wide Web called iCraveTV. iCraveTV was designed to stream ordinary television across the Internet. Under Canadian law, at least as interpreted at the time,[7] iCraveTV believed it didn't need permission to stream broadcast television across the Internet. Under Canadian law, so long as the broadcast itself wasn't changed, you could use any technology to extend the reach of the broadcast.[8] So Craig bought his servers, fired up the streams, and with a much-hyped launch, sat back to wait for the customers to come. And come they did, by the millions. Craig's service was an instant success. It seemed lots more than Craig craved TV.

Not long after Craig's launch, however, he began to discover that not everyone loved Craig's idea. In particular, U.S. copyright holders were not too keen on the free TV that Craig had created. While one was free in Canada to rebroadcast television across the Internet, one wasn't in the United States. United States copyright law heavily regulates the right to rebroadcast, and Craig had not satisfied U.S rules.

iCraveTV did take some steps to keep U.S. residents out. But no one could really have expected these steps would work. At first, iCraveTV simply warned people that only Canadians were to use the site. Later iCraveTV added an area-code block to its site—you needed to specify your area code to get in; if the area code was not Canadian, you couldn't get in. But it's not hard to find a Canadian area code (for example, the telephone number of iCraveTV itself prominently displayed on iCraveTV's website.)

But Craig didn't think it was his job to police the infringing behavior of Americans. It didn't violate the law for anyone to stream TV in Canada. Why did he need to worry about whether it violated the law in the U.S.?

A posse of American lawyers quickly convinced Craig that he needed to worry. In a lawsuit filed in Pittsburgh, the National Football League (and a few other parties) charged iCraveTV with copyright infringement in the United States. Whether or not it was legal in Canada to stream TV across the Internet, it was not legal in the United States. Thus, to the extent Americans could get access to this Canadian site, they were violating American law. And to the extent this Canadian site made it possible for Americans to access this Canadian site, it was violating American law. The NFL thus demanded that the Pittsburgh court shut this Canadian server down.

The U.S. District Court Judge, Donald Ziegler, conducted an extensive fact-finding proceeding. On February 8, 2000, the Court issued an injunction shutting iCraveTV down. The Court gave iCraveTV 90 days to demonstrate that it had the technology to block U.S. residents. iCraveTV promised that, using some of the IP technologies described in Chapter 4, it could block 98 percent of American citizens. But 98 percent wasn't good enough for the Court. If any American could access the iCraveTV site, iCraveTV was violating U.S. law.

iCraveTV couldn't promise 100 percent success. Unlike Judge Gomez's decision about France, however, there was no outrage on the Net following this decision. There weren't thousands of websites criticizing it, or even a handful of editorials questioning it. Indeed, almost nobody noticed.

Reciprocal Blindness

The Yahoo! France case and the iCraveTV case raise the same funda-mental issue. In each, there is a behavior that is legal in one country (selling Nazi paraphernalia for the United States, streaming free TV across the Inter-net for Canada), and illegal in another country (selling Nazi paraphernalia in France; streaming free TV in the United States). In both cases, the judge in the country whose laws were being violated exercised his power to stop the violation (Judge Gomez ordering Yahoo! either to remove the Nazi material or to block it from France; Judge Ziegler ordering iCraveTV to either remove broadcast television from its site or block it from Americans). But in one case, this result was vilified as "censorship" while in the other, it was barely noticed.

This is reciprocal blindness. We see a fault in others that we can't see in ourselves. To an American, blocking the speech of Nazis is "censorship." And it adds insult to injury to demand that such speech be censored in the United States—where it is legal—just because it is not legal in France.

But why isn't it "censorship" to block free TV in Canada just because it is illegal in the United States? In both cases, speech legal in one country is being blocked in that country by a court in a second. The United States blocks Canadians from getting free TV just because free TV is illegal in the United States. The French blocks Americans from getting Nazi paraphernalia on the Yahoo! auction site just because that paraphernalia is illegal in France.

Indeed, in one important respect, the iCraveTV case is worse than the Yahoo! case. In the Yahoo! case, the Court considered evidence about whether Yahoo! could take technical measures to block French citizens.[9] As Joel Reiden-berg emphasizes,[10] its trigger for liability was the conclusion that there were reasonable technical means for blocking French citizens from the Nazi mate-rial. Those means weren't perfect, but the Court estimated that over 90 percent of French users could be identified.[11] But in the iCraveTV case, the technical means, though promised to be 98 percent effective, were deemed not enough. The restriction of the American court was thus greater than the restriction of French court.

Americans don't have any monopoly on blindness. And I don't pick this case to pick on Americans. Instead, this brace of cases teaches a general lesson. There will be no nation that has no speech that it wishes to regulate on the Internet. Every nation will have something it wants to control. Those things, however, will be different, nation to nation. The French will want to regulate Nazi speech; the Americans will want to regulate porn; the Germans will want to regulate both; the Swedes will want to regulate neither.

This chapter is about these overlapping desires for control. How will the Internet accommodate this mix? Whose rules will apply? Is there a way to avoid either anarchy or total regulation? Will the most restrictive regimes determine the freedom left for the rest of us?

In my view, we've seen enough to see how the story will unfold. I describe that unfolding in the balance of this chapter. But first, we should be clear about the reason why this regulation of cyberspace will occur. We should all recognize the interest the government has here and just how strong, or weak, that interest is. And, more importantly, we should recognize how the architecture of the network has changed to make securing that interest possible. As Jack Goldsmith and Tim Wu write,

> Yahoo!'s arguments were premised on the 1990s vision of a borderless Internet. Half a decade later, this vision is fast being replaced by the reality of an Internet that is splitting apart and reflecting national borders. Far from flattening the world, the Internet is in many ways conforming to local conditions.[12]

ON BEING "IN" CYBERSPACE

Cyberspace is a place.[13] People live there. They experience all the sorts of things that they experience in real space there, and some experience more. They experience this, not as isolated individuals playing some high-tech computer game, but as part of groups, in communities, among strangers, and among people they come to know and sometimes like—or love.

While they are in that place, cyberspace, they are also here. They are at a terminal screen, eating chips, ignoring the phone. They are downstairs on the computer, late at night, while their husbands are asleep. They are at work, at cyber cafes, and in computer labs. They live this life there, while here, and then at some point in the day they jack out and are only here. They rise from the machine in a bit of a daze, and turn around. They have returned.

So where are they when they are in cyberspace?

We have this desire to pick: We want to say that they are either in cyberspace or in real space. We have this desire because we want to know which space is responsible. Which space has jurisdiction over them? Which space rules?

The answer is both. Whenever anyone is in cyberspace, she is also here, in real space. Whenever one is subject to the norms of a cyberspace community, one is also living within a community in real space. You are always in both places if you are there, and the norms of both places apply. The problem for law is to work out how the norms of the two communities are to apply given that the subject to whom they apply may be in both places at once.

Think again about Jake Baker. The problem with Jake was not that he went to a different place where the norms were different. The problem was that he was simultaneously in a Michigan dorm room and on the Net. He was subject to the norm of civility in the dorm, and he was subject to the norm of indecency in cyberspace. He was subject, that is, to two sets of norms as he sat in that single chair.

So whose norms would apply? How would real-space governments deal with the conflict between these two communities?

Some examples might help to set a context in which that question might be answered. Ordinarily, when you go to Europe you do not bring the federal government with you. You do not carry along a set of rules for Americans while in Europe. In Germany you are generally subject to German law. The United States ordinarily has very little reason to worry about regulating your behavior there.

But sometimes the U.S. government does have a reason to regulate American citizens abroad. When it does, nothing in international law can stop it.[14] For example, there are jurisdictions where pedophilia is not adequately regulated, and for a time they became target tourist spots for pedophiles from around the world. The U.S. government passed a law in 1994 to forbid Americans from engaging in child sex while outside the United States, even in jurisdictions where child sex is permitted.[15]

What justification could there have been for such a law? Obviously, the sense of Congress was that if a person engages in such behavior in a foreign country, they are more likely to do it here as well. If they visit a community where the norms permit such behavior, they are more likely to carry those norms back to their life here. Thus, while the American government generally doesn't much care what you do elsewhere, it does begin to care when what you do elsewhere has an effect on your life here.

Regulations like this are the exception, of course. But they are the exception because the practice of passing into alternative, or alien, communities in real space is also the exception. The frictions of real-space life make it less likely that the norms of an alien culture will bleed into our own; the distance between us and alien cultures is so great that very few can afford to have a life in both places.

But the Net changes this. As the Baker case suggests, and as any number of other cases will press, with cyberspace these other communities are no longer elsewhere. They can be brought home, or more frighteningly, *into* the home. Real-space communities no longer have the buffer of friction to protect them.

Another community can now capture the attention of their citizens without their citizens' ever leaving their living room. People may be in both places at the same time. One affects the other. As Edward Castronova writes, "synthetic worlds are becoming important because events inside them can have effects outside them."[16] The question for government is how far to allow these effects to go.

Now this question has really three different parts—two old, and one new. The old part is how a far a government will allow foreign influences to affect its culture and its people. Cultures at one time isolated are later invaded when the barriers to invasion fall. Think about the plea from Europeans to stop the invasion of American culture, which pours over satellite television into the living rooms of European citizens.[17] Or even more extreme, the Middle East. These places have long fought to protect their culture from certain alien influences, and that fight becomes much more difficult once the Internet becomes ubiquitous.

The second old part is the question of how, or whether, a government will protect its citizens against foreign practices or rules that are inconsistent with its own. For example, the copyright law of France strongly protects the "moral rights" of French authors. If a French author enters into a contract with an American publisher, and that contract does not adequately protect the "moral rights" of the French citizen, how will the French respond?

But the third question—and the new part—is the issue raised by the ability for citizens to live in the alien culture while still at home. This is something more than merely watching foreign television. The alternatives offered by TV are alternatives of the imagination. The interactive life of cyberspace offers alternative ways of living (or at least some cyberspaces do).

My focus in this chapter is not on the first question, which many call cultural imperialism. It is instead upon the conflicts that will be manifested by the second and third. It may well be true that there have always been conflicts between the rules of different governments. It may always have been that those conflicts have bled into particular local disputes. Cyberspace has exploded this third stage of the debate. What was once the exception will become the rule. Behavior was once governed ordinarily within one jurisdiction, or within two coordinating jurisdictions. Now it will systematically be governed within multiple, noncoordinating jurisdictions. How can law handle this?

The integration of cyberspace will produce a profound increase in the incidence of these conflicts. It will produce a kind of conflict that has never happened before: a conflict arising from individuals from different jurisdictions living together in one space while living in these different jurisdictions.

This question has produced a ferocious argument between two extremes. At one end is the work of David Post and David Johnson. Johnson and Post argue that the multiplicity of jurisdictions in which your behavior is subject to regulation (since anything you do in cyberspace has an effect in every other context) should mean that much behavior is presumptively not subject to regulation anywhere. Anywhere, that is, save cyberspace.[18] The inconsistency of any other solution, they argue, would be absurd. Rather than embracing the absurd, we should embrace something far more sensible: life in cyberspace, as Milan Kundera might put it, is life elsewhere.

At the other extreme is the work of scholars such as Jack Goldsmith and Tim Wu, who claim there is nothing new here—at least new from the perspective private international law.[19] For many years the law has worked through these conflicts of authority. Cyberspace may increase the incidence of these conflicts, but it does not change their nature. Old structures may have to be molded to fit this new form, but the pattern of the old will suffice.

While both sides embrace partial truths, in my view both are mistaken. It is true, as Johnson and Post argue, that there is something new here. But what is new is not a difference in kind, only a difference in degree. And it is true, as Goldsmith and Wu argues, that we have always had disputes of this form. But we have not had conflicts at this level. We have not had a time when we could say that people are actually living in two places at once, with no principle of supremacy between them. This is the challenge that we will face in the future.

This duality is a problem because the legal tools we have used to resolve these questions before were not designed to deal with conflicts among citizens. They were designed to deal with conflicts among institutions, or relatively sophisticated actors. They are rules made for businesses interacting with businesses, or businesses interacting with governments. They were not designed for disputes between citizens.

Jessica Litman makes an analogous point in her work on copyright.[20] For much of the last century, Litman argues, copyright has worked fairly well as a compromise between publishers and authors. It is a law that has largely been applied to institutions. Individuals were essentially outside copyright's purview since individuals didn't really "publish."

The Internet, of course, changes all this. Now everyone is a publisher. And Litman argues (convincingly, in my view) that copyright's rules do not necessarily work well when applied to individuals.[21] The ideal rules for individuals may not necessarily be the ideal rules for institutions. The rules of copyright need to be reformed to make them better suited to a world where individuals are publishers.

The same is true of conflicts between sovereigns. The rules for dealing with these conflicts work well when the parties are repeat players—corporations that must do business in two places, for example, or individuals who constantly travel between two places. These people can take steps to conform their behavior to the limited range of contexts in which they live, and the existing rules help them to that end. But it does not follow (as it does not follow in the context of copyright) that the same mix of rules would work best in a world where anyone could be a multinational.

The solution to this change will not come from insisting either that everything is the same or that everything is different. It will take more work than that. When a large number of citizens live in two different places, and when one of those places is not solely within the jurisdiction of a particular sovereign, then what kinds of claims should one sovereign be able to make on others, and what kinds of claims can these sovereigns make on cyberspace?

This question is not yet answered. It is another latent ambiguity in our Constitution's past—but in this case there is no founding international constitutional moment. Even if there had been, it would not have answered this question. At the founding ordinary people were not routinely living in multiple noncoordinating jurisdictions. This is something new.

POSSIBLE RESOLUTIONS

That there will be conflicts in how governments want their citizens to behave is certain. What is not yet certain is how these conflicts will be resolved. In this section, I map three separate strategies. The first was the dream of the early Internet. The second is the reality that many nations increasingly see today. And the third is the world we will slowly become.

The No Law Rule

On February 8, 1996, John Perry Barlow, former lyricist for the Grateful Dead and co-founder of the Electronic Frontier Foundation, published this declaration on EFF's website:

> Governments of the Industrial World, you weary giants of flesh and steel, I come from Cyberspace, the new home of Mind. On behalf of the future, I ask you of the past to leave us alone. You are not welcome among us. You have no sovereignty where we gather.
>
> We have no elected government, nor are we likely to have one, so I address you with no greater authority than that with which liberty itself always speaks. I declare the global social space we are building to be naturally independent of the tyrannies you seek to impose on us. You have no moral right to rule us nor do you possess any methods of enforcement we have true reason to fear.

Governments derive their just powers from the consent of the governed. You have neither solicited nor received ours. We did not invite you. You do not know us, nor do you know our world. Cyberspace does not lie within your borders. Do not think that you can build it, as though it were a public construction project. You cannot. It is an act of nature and it grows itself through our collective actions.

You have not engaged in our great and gathering conversation, nor did you create the wealth of our marketplaces. You do not know our culture, our ethics, or the unwritten codes that already provide our society more order than could be obtained by any of your impositions.

You claim there are problems among us that you need to solve. You use this claim as an excuse to invade our precincts. Many of these problems don't exist. Where there are real conflicts, where there are wrongs, we will identify them and address them by our means. We are forming our own Social Contract. This governance will arise according to the conditions of our world, not yours. Our world is different.

Cyberspace consists of transactions, relationships, and thought itself, arrayed like a standing wave in the web of our communications. Ours is a world that is both everywhere and nowhere, but it is not where bodies live.

We are creating a world that all may enter without privilege or prejudice accorded by race, economic power, military force, or station of birth.

We are creating a world where anyone, anywhere may express his or her beliefs, no matter how singular, without fear of being coerced into silence or conformity.

Your legal concepts of property, expression, identity, movement, and context do not apply to us. They are all based on matter, and there is no matter here.

Our identities have no bodies, so, unlike you, we cannot obtain order by physical coercion. We believe that from ethics, enlightened self-interest, and the commonweal, our governance will emerge. Our identities may be distributed across many of your jurisdictions. The only law that all our constituent cultures would generally recognize is the Golden Rule. We hope we will be able to build our particular solutions on that basis. But we cannot accept the solutions you are attempting to impose.

In the United States, you have today created a law, the Telecommunications Reform Act, which repudiates your own Constitution and insults the dreams of Jefferson, Washington, Mill, Madison, de Tocqueville, and Brandeis. These dreams must now be born anew in us.

You are terrified of your own children, since they are natives in a world where you will always be immigrants. Because you fear them, you entrust your bureaucracies with the parental responsibilities you are too cowardly to confront yourselves. In our world, all the sentiments and expressions of humanity, from the debasing to the angelic, are parts of a seamless whole, the global conversation of bits. We cannot separate the air that chokes from the air upon which wings beat.

In China, Germany, France, Russia, Singapore, Italy and the United States, you are trying to ward off the virus of liberty by erecting guard posts at the frontiers of Cyberspace. These may keep out the contagion for a small time, but they will not work in a world that will soon be blanketed in bit-bearing media.

Your increasingly obsolete information industries would perpetuate themselves by proposing laws, in America and elsewhere, that claim to own speech itself throughout the world. These laws would declare ideas to be another industrial product, no more noble than pig iron. In our world, whatever the human mind may create can be reproduced and distributed infinitely at no cost. The global conveyance of thought no longer requires your factories to accomplish.

These increasingly hostile and colonial measures place us in the same position as those previous lovers of freedom and self-determination who had to reject the authorities of distant, uninformed powers. We must declare our virtual selves immune to your sovereignty, even as we continue to consent to your rule over our bodies. We will spread ourselves across the Planet so that no one can arrest our thoughts.

We will create a civilization of the Mind in Cyberspace. May it be more humane and fair than the world your governments have made before.[22]

Perhaps no single document better reflects an ideal that was dominant on the network a decade ago. Whatever rule governed "our bodies," no government could govern the "virtual selves" that would live in this space. Barlow declared these "virtual selves" "immune" from real space sovereigns. Real-space sovereigns would be lost if they tried to exercise control here.

Though Barlow issued his declaration at a meeting of world leaders at Davos, apparently world governments didn't hear what he said. That very day, the President signed the Communications Decency Act of 1996.[23] And though the Supreme Court would eventually strike down this law, the Supreme Court was certainly not signaling the end of any regulation of "virtual selves." A string of legislation from the United States Congress coincided with a string of regulation from around the world. And that trend has only increased. As one study measured it, the growth of legislative efforts to regulate the Net was slow at first, but has taken off dramatically.[24] These regulations were at first directed to "harness[ing] technology to serve what [were] perceived to be governmental goals unrelated to the net"; then second, "aimed directly at fostering the advancement of Net infrastructure"; and third, "directly concern[ed] control over information."[25]

The reasons Barlow's ideals were not going to be realized might be obvious in retrospect, but they weren't well recognized at the time. Laws are enacted as a result of political action; likewise they can be stopped only by political action. Ideas, or beautiful rhetoric, aren't political action. When Congress confronts impassioned parents demanding it does something to protect their kids on the Net; or when it faces world-famous musicians angry about copyright infringement on the Net; or when it faces serious-seeming government officials talking about the dangers of crime on the Net, the rhetoric of even a Grateful Dead lyricist won't cut it. On Barlow's side, there had to be political action. But political action is just what the Net wasn't ready for.

The One Law Rule

The opposite result of no law is a world where there is but one law. It is the world where one government (or conceivably, all governments working together, but that idea is too ridiculous to even contemplate so I won't discuss it here) dominates the world by enforcing its law everywhere.

As Michael Geist convincingly argues, that's indeed what is happening now. "Governments," Geist writes, are "unwilling to concede that national laws are limited to national borders, [and] are increasingly turning to explicitly extra-territorial legislation."[26]

Here again (unfortunately), the United States is a leader. The United States has a view of proper network behavior. It has asserted the right to enforce that view extraterritorially, and it enforces its rule against citizens from around the world whether or not the U.S. rule conflicts with a local rule. The FTC, for example, is "vested with responsibility for enforcing [the Child Online Privacy Protection Act]," Geist writes, and "its rule-making guidance leaves no doubt that such sites are expected to comply with the statute in their privacy practices toward children."[27] So too does the Department of Justice maintain that the DMCA applies extraterritorially, because it refers to "imports" of technologies.[28] And the USA Patriot Act includes provisions that "are expressly extra-territorial"—including, for example, an expansion of the list of "protected computers" to include "a computer located outside the United States that is used in a manner that affects interstate or foreign commerce or communication of the United States."[29]

Of course, Geist's claim is not that the United States has tamed the Internet. No one would assert that the United States has stopped crime on the network, or even behavior inconsistent with U.S. law. But the attitude and theory that animates U.S. prosecution has no conceptual limit. On the theory the United States advances, there is no behavior anywhere that at least in principle the United States can't reach. (Though there are many who believe international law restricts the United States more than it acknowledges.[30])

It may be that this dominance by the United States will continue for ever. But I doubt it. There is a growing desire among many governments around the world to check the power of the United States. In 2005, some of these government tried to wrest control of ICANN (Internet Corporation for Assigned Names and Numbers) from U.S. influence. This resistance, as well as a healthy dose of sovereign self-respect, will increasingly push for a regime that better balances the interests of the whole world.

The Many Laws Rule (and the technology to make it possible)

So what would a more balanced regime look like?

Return to the conflict that began this chapter. On the one hand, France doesn't want its citizens buying Nazi paraphernalia, the United States doesn't want its citizens watching "free" TV. On the other hand, France doesn't have anything against "free" TV, and the United States doesn't have the constitutional power to block its citizens from buying Nazi paraphernalia. It's some way to give France what it wants (and doesn't want), and to give the U.S. what it wants (and can't want)?

This is not an issue limited to France and the United States. As Victor Mayer-Schonberger and Teree Foster have written, about speech regulation:

> National restrictions of freedom of speech on the [Internet] are commonplace not only in the United States, but also around the globe. Individual nations, each intent upon preserving what they perceive to be within the perimeters of their national interests, seek to regulate certain forms of speech because of content that is considered reprehensible or offensive to national well-being or civic virtue.[31]

Is there a general solution (in the government's eyes at least) to this problem?

Well, imagine first that something like the Identity Layer that I described in Chapter 4 finds its footing. And imagine that the ID layer means that individuals are able to certify (easily and without necessarily revealing anything else) their citizenship. Thus, as you pass across the Web, attached to your presence is a cryptographic object that reveals at least which government claims you.

Second, imagine an international convention to populate a table with any rules that a government wants to apply to its own citizens while those citizens are elsewhere in the world. So the French, for example, would want Nazi material blocked; the Americans would want porn blocked to anyone under 18, etc. The table would then be public and available to any server on the network.

Finally, imagine governments start requiring servers within their jurisdiction to respect the rules expressed in the table. Thus, if you're offering Nazi material, and a French citizen enters your site, you should block her, but if she is a U.S. citizen, you can serve her. Each state would thus be restricting the citizens of other states as those states wanted. But citizens from its nation would enjoy the freedoms that nation guarantees. This world would thus graft local rules onto life in cyberspace.

Consider a particular example to make the dynamic clearer: Internet gambling.[32] Minnesota has a strong state policy against gambling.[33] Its legislature has banned its citizens from gambling, and its attorney general has vigorously enforced this legislative judgment—both by shutting down gambling sites in the state and by threatening legal action against sites outside of the state if they let citizens from Minnesota gamble.

This threat, some will argue, can have no effect on gambling on the Internet, nor on the gambling behavior of Minnesota citizens.[34] The proof is the story of Boral: Imagine a gambling server located in Minnesota. When Minnesota makes gambling illegal, that server can move outside of Minnesota. From the standpoint of citizens in Minnesota, the change has (almost) no effect. It is just as easy to access a server located in Minneapolis as one located in Chicago. So the gambling site can easily move and keep all its Minnesota customers.

Suppose that Minnesota then threatens to prosecute the owner of the Chicago server. It is relatively easy for the attorney general to persuade the courts of Illinois to prosecute the illegal server in Chicago (assuming it could be shown that the behavior of the server was in fact illegal). So the server simply moves from Chicago to Cayman, making it one step more difficult for Minnesota to prosecute but still no more difficult for citizens of Minnesota to get access. No matter what Minnesota does, it seems the Net helps its citizens beat the government. The Net, oblivious to geography, makes it practically impossible for geographically limited governments to enforce their rules.

However, imagine the ID layer that I described above, in which everyone can automatically (and easily) certify their citizenship. As you pass onto a site, the site checks your ID. Thus the gambling site could begin to condition access upon whether you hold the proper ID for that site—if you are from Minnesota and this is a gambling site the site does not let you pass. This process occurs invisibly, or machine to machine. All the user knows is that she has gotten in, or if she has not, then why.[35]

In this story, then, the interests of Minnesota are respected. Its citizens are not allowed to gamble. But Minnesota's desires do not determine the gambling practices of people from outside the state: Only citizens of Minnesota are disabled by this regulation.

This is regulation at the level of one state, for one problem. But why would other states cooperate with Minnesota? Why would any other jurisdiction want to carry out Minnesota's regulation?

The answer is that they wouldn't if this were the only regulation at stake. But it isn't. Minnesota wants to protect its citizens from gambling, but New York may want to protect its citizens against the misuse of private data. The European Union may share New York's objective; Utah may share Minnesota's.

Each state, in other words, has its own stake in controlling certain behaviors, and these behaviors differ. But the key is this: The same architecture that enables Minnesota to achieve its regulatory end can also help other states achieve their regulatory ends. And this can initiate a kind of quid pro quo between jurisdictions.

The pact would look like this: Each state would promise to enforce on servers within its jurisdiction the regulations of other states for citizens from those other states, in exchange for having its own regulations enforced in other jurisdictions. New York would require that servers within New York keep Minnesotans away from New York gambling servers, in exchange for Minnesota keeping New York citizens away from privacy-exploiting servers. Utah would keep EU citizens away from privacy-exploiting servers, in exchange for Europe keeping Utah citizens away from European gambling sites.

This structure, in effect, is precisely the structure that is already in place for regulating interstate gambling. According to federal law, interstate Internet gambling is not permitted unless the user is calling from a gambling-permissive state into another gambling-permissive state.[36] If the user calls from a gambling-restrictive state or into a gambling-restrictive state, he or she has committed a federal offense.

The same structure could be used to support local regulation of Internet behavior. With a simple way to verify citizenship, a simple way to verify that servers are discriminating on the basis of citizenship, and a federal commitment to support such local discrimination, we could imagine an architecture that enables local regulation of Internet behavior.

And if all this could occur within the United States, it could occur between nations generally. There is the same interest internationally in enforcing local laws as there is nationally—maybe even more. And thus in this way, an ID-rich Internet would facilitate international zoning and enable this structure of international control.

Such a regime would return geographical zoning to the Net. It would re-impose borders on a network built without those borders. If would give the regulators in Hungary and Thailand the power to do what they can't do just now—control their citizens as they want. It would leave citizens of the United States or Sweden as free as their government has determined they should be.

To those who love the liberty of the original Net, this regime is a nightmare. It removes the freedom the original architecture of the Internet created. It restores the power to control to a space designed to avoid control.

I too love the liberty of the original Net. But as I have become skeptical of short-cuts to the policy I like—short-cuts, meaning devices that produce a particular result without effective democratic support—I'm hesitant to condemn this regime. Of course, no democratic government should permit the will of a nondemocratic government to be reflected in a zoning table. We shouldn't help totalitarian regimes repress their citizens. But within a family of democracies, such a regime might help promote democracy. If a restriction on liberty is resented by a people, let the people mobilize to remove it.

Of course, my view is that citizens of any democracy should have the freedom to choose what speech they consume. But I would prefer they earn that freedom by demanding it through democratic means than that a technological trick give it to them for free.

But whether or not you, or I, like this regime, my argument at this point is predictive. This regime is a natural compromise between two results, neither of which governments accept—governments will neither accept a world where real space laws don't affect cyberspace, nor a world where the rule of one government, or of a few large governments, controls the world. This regime gives each government the power to regulate its citizens; no government should have the right to do anything more.

This balance is already being struck privately on the Net—though there's significant resistance and unease about it. As I've already described, in January 2005, Google announced that it was giving something to the Chinese government it has refused to give anyone else in the world—a version of the Google search engine that blocks content the Chinese government doesn't want its citizens to see.[37] Thus, if you search on "democracy" or "human rights" on Google.cn, you wouldn't find what you'll find if you search in the same way on Google.com. (Wikipedia now keeps a list of words blocked by search engines in China.[38]) Thus, Google would effectively remake the Internet for the Chinese according to the values the Chinese government pushes.

I understand the motive (profit). I certainly understand the justification (it will speed China to a real democracy). But whether or not you believe this balance is right in the context of Communist China, it certainly has more justification when we're describing agreements among democratic nations. What the Chinese do to its journalists is, in my view, wrong. If a Chinese publisher offered to publish this book in China only on the condition that I omitted this paragraph, I certainly wouldn't. But I have a different view about rules imposed by France or Italy.

One important consequence of this architecture—indeed, perhaps reason enough to oppose it—is that it will make regulation easier. And the easier it is to regulate, the more likely regulation is.

Yet this is the trade-off—between cost and the willingness to regulate—we have seen again and again. Cost for the government is liberty for us. The higher the cost of a regulation, the less likely it will be enforced. Liberty depends on the regulation remaining expensive. Liberty comes with friction.

When it becomes easy or cheap to regulate, however, this contingent liberty is at risk. We can expect more regulation. In these cases, if we want to preserve liberty, we will need to develop affirmative arguments for it. We will need these affirmative arguments to prevent identity-based regulation of the Net. As I explain in the balance of this book, there is both a surprisingly great desire for nations to embrace regimes that facilitate jurisdiction-specific regulation and a significant reason why the costs of regulation are likely to fall. We should expect, then, that there will be more such regulation. Soon.

The effect, in short, would be to zone cyberspace based on the qualifications carried by individual users. It would enable a degree of control of cyberspace that few have ever imagined. Cyberspace would go from being an unregulable space to, depending on the depth of the certificates, the most regulable space imaginable.

PART FIVE

responses

The argument of Part I was that the unregulability of the original Internet will pass. Architectures will develop to make behavior there regulable again. Part II described one aspect of that regulability—technology. "Code" will be an increasingly important part of that regulation, directly enforcing the control the law typically achieves through threats. Part III then considered three contexts in which changing technology would render ambiguous our commitments to fundamental values. This I called a latent ambiguity. How we protect IP, or privacy, or free speech will depend upon fundamental choices our framers didn't make. Part IV then mapped this conflict to jurisdictions. Again, the lesson circles back to Part I: The tendency of government will push to an ever more regulable Net, this time to return the zones of geography to a borderless Internet.

Throughout these four parts, my central objective has been to force a recognition that is obvious once remarked: that there are choices to be made about how this network evolves. These choices will affect fundamentally what values are built into the network.

The question for this part is whether we're capable of making those choices. My argument is that we're not. We have so completely passed off questions of principle to the judicial branch, and so completely corrupted our legislative process with the backhand of handouts, that we confront this moment of extraordinary importance incapable of making any useful decisions. We have been caught off-guard, drunk on the political indulgence of an era, and the most we may be able to do is stay on our feet until we have time to sober up.

SIXTEEN

the problems we face

THERE ARE CHOICES THAT WILL DETERMINE HOW CYBERSPACE IS. BUT, IN MY VIEW, we Americans are disabled from making those choices. We are disabled for three very different reasons. The first is tied to the limits we place on courts; the second to the limits we have realized in legislatures; and the third to the limits in our thinking about code. If choice must be made, these limits mean we will not be making that choice. We are at a time when the most significant decisions about what this space will be are being made, but we don't have the institutions, or practice, to evaluate or readily alter them.

In this chapter, I describe these problems, and in Chapter 17, I sketch three solutions to them. Neither description will be complete, but both should be suggestive. The problems that cyberspace reveals are not problems with cyberspace. They are real-space problems that cyberspace shows us we must now resolve—or maybe reconsider.

PROBLEMS WITH COURTS

There are two types of constitutions, one we could call codifying, and the other transformative. A codifying constitution tries to preserve something essential about the constitutional or legal culture in which it is enacted—to protect that cultural attribute against changes in the future. A transformative constitution (or amendment) does the opposite: It tries to change something essential in the constitutional or legal culture in which it is enacted—to make life different in the future, to remake some part of the culture. The symbol of the codifying regime is Ulysses tied to the mast; the symbol of the transformative is revolutionary France.

Our Constitution has both regimes within it. The Constitution of 1789—before the first ten amendments—was a transformative constitution. It "called into life" a new form of government and gave birth to a nation.[1] The Constitution of 1791—the Bill of Rights—was a codifying constitution. Against the background of the new constitution, it sought to entrench certain values against future change.[2] The Civil War amendments were transformative again. They aimed to remake part of what the American social and legal culture had become—to rip out from the American soul a tradition of inequality and replace it with a tradition and practice of equality.[3]

Of these two regimes, the transformative is clearly the more difficult to realize. A codifying regime at least has inertia on its side; a transformative regime must fight. The codifying regime has a moment of self-affirmation; the transformative regime is haunted with self-doubt and vulnerable to being undermined by targeted opposition. Constitutional moments die, and when they do, the institutions charged with enforcing their commands, such as courts, face increasing political resistance. Flashes of enlightenment notwithstanding, the people retain or go back to their old ways, and courts find it hard to resist.

Our own constitutional history reveals just this pattern. The extraordinary moment after the Civil War—when three amendments committed to civil equality were carved into our Constitution's soul—had passed by 1875. The nation gave up the struggle for equality and turned to the excitement of the Industrial Revolution. Laws enforcing segregation were upheld;[4] the right of African Americans to vote was denied;[5] laws enforcing what was later seen to be a new kind of slavery were allowed.[6] Only after one hundred years of continued inequality did the Supreme Court again take up the cause of the Civil War amendments. It would not be until *Brown v. Board of Education,* in 1954, that the Court again recognized the transformative idea of the Civil War amendments.[7]

One could criticize the Court for this century of weakness. I think it is more important to understand its source. Courts operate within a political context. They are the weakest branch of resistance within that political context. For a time, they may be able to insist on a principle greater than the moment, but that time will pass. If the world does not recognize the wrongness of its racist ways, even a strong statement of principle enacted within our Constitution's text permits a court only so much freedom to resist. Courts are subject to the constraints of what "everyone" with a voice and the resources to make it heard believes is right, even if what "everyone" believes is inconsistent with basic constitutional texts.

Life is easier with a codifying constitution, because there is a tradition that the text is just meant to entrench. If this tradition is long-standing, then there is hope that it will remain solid as well.

But even a codifying constitution faces difficulties. Codification notwithstanding, if the passions of a nation become strong enough, there is often little that courts are willing to do. The clarity of the First Amendment's protection of freedom of speech notwithstanding, when the speech was that of communists and anarchists, the government was allowed the power to punish.[8] The presumption of innocence and equality notwithstanding, when Japan bombed Pearl Harbor, the government was allowed to shuttle every West Coast American of Japanese descent into concentration camps.[9]

These are the realities of courts in a democratic system. We lawyers like to romanticize the courts, to imagine them as above influence. But they have never been so, completely or forever. They are subject to a political constraint that matters. They are an institution within a democracy, and no institution within a democracy can be the enemy of the people for long.

It is against this background that we should think about the problems raised in Parts 3 and 4. In each case, my argument was that we will need to choose the values we want cyberspace to embrace. These questions are not addressed by any clear constitutional text or tradition. In the main, they are questions affecting the codifying part of our tradition, but they are also cases of latent ambiguity. There is no "answer" to them in the sense of a judgment that seems to have been made and that a court can simply report. An answer must be fixed upon, not found; made, not discovered; chosen, not reported.

This creates difficulties for an American court. We live in the shadow of the Supreme Court of Chief Justice Earl Warren. Many people think (but I am not one of this crowd) that his was a wildly activist court, that it "made up" constitutional law and imposed its own "personal values" onto the political and legal system. Many viewed the Rehnquist Court as providing a balance to this activism of old.

I think this view is wrong. The Warren Court was not "activist" in any sense inconsistent with a principle of interpretive fidelity, and the Rehnquist Court was no less activist in that sense than the Warren Court. The question, however, is not what was true; the question is what people believe. What we believe is that the past was marked by activism, and that this activism was wrong.

At least wrong for a court. The opponents of the Warren Court are not just conservatives. Some are liberals who believe that the Court was not acting judicially.[10] These opponents believe that the Court was making, not finding, constitutional law—that it was guided by nothing more than whether it could muster a majority.

Any court risks seeming like a "Warren Court" when it makes judgments that don't seem to flow plainly or obviously from a legal text. Any court is vulnerable when its judgments seem political. Against the background of history, our Supreme Court is particularly vulnerable to this view, and the Court will feel the reaction when its actions seem political.

My point is not that the Court fears retaliation; our Court is secure within our constitutional regime.[11] The Court feels the reaction to its seemingly political decisions because of its own image of its proper role. In its view, its role is not to be "political"; its conception is that it is to be a faithful agent, simply preserving founding commitments until they have changed.[12]

But when—as in the cases of latent ambiguity—there are no founding commitments to preserve, any attempt at translation will seem to be something more. And whenever it seems as if the Court is doing more than simply preserving founding commitments, the perception is created that the Court is simply acting to ratify its own views of a proper constitutional regime rather than enforcing judgments that have been constitutionalized by others.[13] In a word, it seems to be acting "politically."

But what does "political" mean here? It does not mean simply that the Court is making value or policy choices. The claim is not that values are improper reasons for a court to decide a case. To the contrary: Value choices or policy choices, properly ratified by the political process, are appropriate for judicial enforcement. The problem with the choices in cases of latent ambiguity is that they do not seem to have been properly ratified by the political process. They reflect values, but the values do not seem to be taken from the Constitution.

"Political" thus refers to judgments not clearly ratified and presently contested.[14] When the very foundations of a judgment are seen to be fundamentally contested, and when there is no reason to believe that the Constitution takes a position on this contest, then enforcing a particular outcome of translation will appear, in that context, political.[15]

Cyberspace will press this problem intensely. When a framing value can be translated with some clarity or certainty, the Court can act in a way that resists present majorities in the name of founding commitments. But when ambiguities are latent and a choice really seems to be a choice, translation will not suffice. My claim is that the Court will not be the locus for that choice.

This might seem overly pessimistic, especially when we consider the success in striking down the Communications Decency Act.[16] But that case itself reveals the instability that I fear will soon resolve itself into passivity.

Throughout both lower court opinions, the courts spoke as if they were "finding" facts about the nature of cyberspace. The "findings" determined the constitutional result, and both courts reported their findings with a confidence that made them seem set in stone.

These findings, for the most part, were exceptionally good descriptions of where cyberspace was in 1996. But they did not tell us anything about where cyberspace is going or what it could be. The courts spoke as if they were telling us about the nature of cyberspace. But as we've seen, cyberspace has no intrinsic nature. It is as it is designed. By striking down Congress's efforts to zone cyberspace, the courts were not telling us what cyberspace is but what it should be. They were making, not finding, the nature of cyberspace; their decisions are in part responsible for what cyberspace will become.

At first it will not seem this way. When we confront something new, it is hard to know what is natural or given about it, and what part can be changed. But over time courts will see that there is little in cyberspace that is "natural." Limits on the architecture of cyberspace that they have reported as findings in one opinion will be seen to have been "design choices" later on. What was "impossible" will later become possible, and as these shifts in the possible occur, courts will more and more feel that they cannot really say what cyberspace is. They will see that their findings affect what they find. They will see that they are in part responsible for what cyberspace has become.

This is Heisenberg applied to constitutional law. And as courts notice it, as they have in other areas, they will increasingly defer to the political branches: If these judgments are policy, they will be left to policy makers, not judges.[17]

One can hardly blame judges for this. Indeed, in some cases their deference should be encouraged.[18] But we should not underestimate its consequences. In the future legislatures will act relatively unconstrained by courts; the values that we might call constitutional—whether enacted into our Constitution or not—will constrain these legislatures only if they choose to take them into account.

Before we turn to what we might expect from legislatures, consider one other problem with courts—specifically, the problem confronting our constitutional tradition as the Constitution moves into the context of cyberspace. This is the problem of "state action."

Architectures constitute cyberspace; these architectures are varied; they variously embed political values; some of these values have constitutional import. Yet for the most part—and fortunately—these architectures are private. They are constructed by universities or corporations and implemented on wires no longer funded by the Defense Department. They are private and therefore traditionally outside the scope of constitutional review. The constitutional values of privacy, access, rights of anonymity, and equality need not trouble this new world, since this world is "private" and the Constitution is concerned only with "state action."

Why this should be is not clear to me. If code functions as law, then we are creating the most significant new jurisdiction since the Louisiana Purchase. Yet we are building it just outside the Constitution's review. Indeed, we are building it just so that the Constitution will not govern—as if we want to be free of the constraints of value embedded by that tradition.

So far in this book, I have not relied very much on this private/public distinction. You might say I have ignored it.[19] But I have ignored it not because it makes no sense, but because I don't know how it could be carried over to the regulation of cyberspace. The concept of state action itself presents a latent ambiguity, and I don't think we have a clear idea of how to resolve it.

That latent ambiguity is this: The Constitution was drawn at a time when basic architectures were set. The framers found the laws of nature, the laws of economics, the "natural law" of man; they were not made by government or man.

These architectures constrained, of course, and their constraint was a "regulation." But the degree to which they could be used as tools of self-conscious control was limited. Town planning was not limited,[20] and beyond laying out a space, there was little these founders could do about the rules that would govern the built environment of this space.

Cyberspace, however, has different architectures, whose regulatory power are not so limited. An extraordinary amount of control can be built into the environment that people know there. What data can be collected, what anonymity is possible, what access is granted, what speech will be heard—all these are choices, not "facts." All these are designed, not found.

Our context, therefore, is very different. That the scope of constitutional review was limited in the first context does not compel it to be similarly limited in the second. It could be, but we cannot know that merely from its being so limited in a very different context.

We have no answer from the framers, then, about the scope of state action. We must decide on our own what makes better sense of our constitutional tradition. Is it more faithful to our tradition to allow these structures of control, the functional equivalent of law, to develop outside the scope of constitutional review? Or should we extend constitutional review to the structures of private regulation, to preserve those fundamental values within our tradition?

These are hard questions, though it is useful to note that they are not as hard to ask in other constitutional regimes. The German tradition, for example, would have less trouble with the idea that private structures of power must ultimately be checked against fundamental constitutional values.[21] The German tradition, of course, is not our own. But the fact that they have sustained this view suggests that we can make space for the constraint of the Constitution without turning everything into a constitutional dispute. Reasoned decision is possible without turning every private contract into a federal case.

Nevertheless, it will take a revolution in American constitutional law for the Court, self-consciously at least, to move beyond the limits of state action. Scholars have sketched how it could without radically remaking American law, but others have argued it could not without radically remaking the American Constitution.[22]

But my reason for ignoring the state action doctrine is not so much to radically remake law as it is to give us a clearer sense of how we should make the law in this new space in the first place. As Paul Berman puts it, the reason to ignore the state action doctrine for now is that:

> . . . however such questions get resolved, at least we will have been forced to grapple with the substantive constitutional question and to articulate the competing values at stake. The state action doctrine, in contrast, takes such debates off the table altogether by asserting that the activity at issue is private and therefore not a fit subject for the constitutional discourse. If one believes that such discourse, in and of itself, has cultural value, then application of the state action doctrine comes with a significant cost.[23]

Again, it remains likely that we will continue to suffer this cost.

It is in these two ways then that courts are stuck. They cannot be as creative, and the scope of their constitutional review has been narrowed (artificially, I believe) to exclude the most important aspect of cyberspace's law—code. If there are decisions about where we should go, and choices about the values this space will include, then these are choices we can't expect our courts to make.

PROBLEMS WITH LEGISLATORS

At a conference in former Soviet Georgia, sponsored by some Western agency of democracy, an Irish lawyer was trying to explain to the Georgians what was so great about a system of "judicial review" (the system by which courts can strike down the acts of a parliament). "Judicial review," he enthused, "is wonderful. Whenever the court strikes down an act of parliament, the people naturally align themselves with the court, against the parliament. The parliament,

people believe, is just political; the supreme court, they think, is principled."
A Georgian friend, puppy-democrat that he was, asked, "So why is it that in a
democracy the people are loyal to a nondemocratic institution and repulsed
by the democratic institution in the system?" "You just don't understand
democracy," said the lawyer.

When we think about the question of governing cyberspace—when we
think about the questions of choice I've sketched, especially those raised in
Part III—we are likely to get a sinking feeling. It seems impossibly difficult,
this idea of governing cyberspace. Who is cyberspace? Where would it vote?
The very idea seems abhorrent to cyberspace itself.

But the problem here is not with governance in cyberspace. Our problem
is with governance itself. There is no special set of dilemmas that cyberspace
will present; there are only the familiar dilemmas of modern governance, but
in a new place. Some things are different; the target of governance is different;
the scope of international concerns is different. But the difficulty with governance will not come from this different target; the difficulty comes from our
problem with governance.

Throughout this book, I've worked to identify the choices that cyberspace will present. I've argued that its very architecture is up for grabs and
that, depending on who grabs it, there are several different ways it could
turn out. Clearly some of these choices are collective—about how we collectively will live in this space. One would have thought that collective choices
were problems of governance, but very few of us would want government to
make these choices. Government seems the solution to no problem we have,
and we should understand why this is. We should understand the Irish
lawyer in all of us.

Our skepticism is not a point about principle. Most of us are not libertarians. We may be antigovernment, but for the most part we believe that there
are collective values that ought to regulate private action. ("Collective" just in
the sense that all individuals acting alone will produce less of that value than
if that individual action could be coordinated.) We are also committed to the
idea that collective values should regulate the emerging technical world. Our
problem is that we do not know how it should be regulated, or by whom. And
we fear that the values that will be embraced are not the correct ones.

Like the Irish lawyer, we are weary of governments. We are profoundly
skeptical about the product of democratic politics. We believe, rightly or not,
that these processes have been captured by special interests more concerned
with individual than collective values. Although we believe that there is a role
for collective judgments, we are repulsed by the idea of placing the design of
something as important as the Internet into the hands of governments.

The examples here are many, and the pattern is arresting. The single unifying message in the government's own description of its role in cyberspace is that it should simply get out of the way. In the area of Internet commerce, the government says, commerce should take care of itself. (Of course, at the same time, the government is passing all sorts of laws to increase the protections for intellectual property.) The government is also seemingly enthusiastic about regulating "indecent" content regardless of the thriving commerce in it.

A perfect example of this point is the government's hand-off of control of the management of the domain name system. For some time the government had been thinking about how best to continue the governance or control of the domain name system.[24] It had originally farmed the work out under National Science Foundation contracts, first to a California nonprofit organized by the late Jon Postel, and then to a private for-profit corporation, Network Solutions.

The contracts were due to lapse in 1998, however, and for a year the government thought in earnest about what it should do. In June 1998 it released a White Paper calling for the establishment of a nonprofit corporation devoted to the collective interest of the Internet as a whole and charged with deciding the policy questions relating to governing the domain name system. Policy-making power was to be taken away from government and placed with an organization outside its control. In 1998, that policy was effected through the creation of the Internet Corporation for Assigned Names and Numbers (ICANN), which, according to its webpage, is

> dedicated to preserving the operational stability of the Internet; to promoting competition; to achieving broad representation of global Internet communities; and to developing policy appropriate to its mission through bottom-up, consensus-based processes. ICANN, a public benefit, non-profit entity, is the international organization responsible for the management and oversight of the coordination of the Internet's domain name system and its unique identifiers.[25]

Think about the kinds of questions my Georgian friend might ask about this move. A "nonprofit corporation devoted to the collective interest"? Isn't that just what government is supposed to be? A board composed of representative stakeholders? Isn't that what a Congress is? Indeed, my Georgian friend might observe that this corporate structure differs from government in only one salient way—there is no ongoing requirement of elections.

This is policy making vested in what is in effect an independent agency, but one wholly outside the democratic process. And what does this say about us? What does it mean when our natural instinct is to put policy-making power in bodies outside the democratic process?

First, it reflects the pathetic resignation that most of us feel about the products of ordinary government. We have lost faith in the idea that the product of representative government might be something more than mere interest—that, to steal the opening line from Justice Marshall's last Supreme Court opinion, power, not reason, is now the currency of deliberative democracy.[26] We have lost the idea that ordinary government might work, and so deep is this despair that not even government thinks the government should have a role in governing cyberspace.

I understand this resignation, but it is something we must overcome. We must isolate the cause and separate it from the effect. If we hate government, it is not because the idea of collective values is anathema. If we hate government, it is because we have grown tired of our own government. We have grown weary of its betrayals, of its games, of the interests that control it. But we must find a way to get over that weariness.

One central cause of the dysfunction of government is the corruption suggested by the way government is elected. I don't mean "corruption" in the traditional sense that saps the energy from so many developing nations. I don't believe congressmen are on the take (California's Randy Cunningham is an exception, of course[27]); I don't believe their motives are impure. They are trying to do the best they can in the world they inhabit. But it is that world that is the problem.

For with that world, money controls attention. To become a member of the House of Representatives, you have to run. In 2004, if you ran in an open district, then you spent on average $1,086,437. If you won, you spent $1,442,216. If you ran against an incumbent in 2004, then there's a 97.5 percent chance you didn't win. (Only eight challengers won.) In the Senate, only one challenger defeated a sitting senator in 2004. Incumbency means life tenure in the United States. The average term for a member of Congress rivals the average term for a Supreme Court Justice.[28]

To raise this money, members of Congress must spend their time making those with money happy. They do this by listening to their problems, and sometimes, pushing legislation that will solve those problems. That sounds harmless enough, until you begin to realize just how much time they spend doing this fundraising. Former Senator Hollings estimated that one-third of a senator's time is spent fundraising.[29] That's probably a significant underestimate.[30]

Now just think about how absurd these priorities are. Congressmen work for us. If an employee of a restaurant spent 33 percent of her time arranging to get to work, she'd be fired. But that's essentially what happens in Washington. The most significant chunk of time for members of Congress is time spent to raise money to remain members of Congress. Is this really what we pay them for?

The problem here is not so much that members of Congress aren't doing their work. The problem is the way their work gets queered by this need to raise money. The easiest targets for fundraising are the clients of the lobbyists, and the lobbyists have lots of ideas about how to bend the law to benefit their clients.

And so Congress bends, and the law gets changed to benefit the most powerful in the economy. This is not capitalism as much as lobby-ism. Our economy is defined by a combination of laws benefiting some and power benefiting some.

To crack through lobbyism, you need a way to get the attention of members of Congress. But until the system is changed, the only way to get their attention is money. This is the cycle. Its results for democracy are vicious. Our Congress sees only what a small set want them to see. And what they see often has no obvious connection to the truth.

If there is a decision to be made about how cyberspace will grow, then that decision will be made. The only question is by whom. We can stand by and do nothing as these choices are made—by others, by those who will not simply stand by. Or we can try to imagine a world where choice can again be made collectively and responsibly.

PROBLEMS WITH CODE

At a Harvard workshop around the time the first edition of this book was published, Jean Camp, a Harvard computer scientist who taught in the Kennedy School of Government, said that I had missed the point. The problem, she said, is not that "code is law" or that "code regulates." The problem is that "we haven't had a conversation about how code regulates." And then to the rest of the audience, she said, "Did all of you like the debate we had about whether Microsoft Word documents would carry in them a unique identifying number? Was that a satisfying debate?"

Her irony carried with it an important insight, and an interesting mistake. Of course, for the computer scientist code is law. And if code is law, then obviously the question we should ask is: Who are the lawmakers? Who writes this law that regulates us? What role do we have in defining this regulation? What right do we have to know of the regulation? And how might we intervene to check it?

All that is perfectly obvious for someone who thinks and breathes the regulations of code. But to a lawyer, both Camp and I, throughout this book, have made a very basic mistake. Code is not law, any more than the design of an airplane is law. Code does not regulate, any more than buildings regulate. Code is not public, any more than a television is public. Being able to debate and decide is an opportunity we require of public regulation, not of private action.

Camp's mistake is a good one. It is a mistake more of us should make more of the time. Because while of course code is private, and of course different from the U.S. Code, its differences don't mean there are not similarities as well. "East Coast Code"—law—regulates by enabling and limiting the options that individuals have, to the end of persuading them to behave in a certain way. "West Coast Code" does the same. East Coast Code does this by increasing the cost to those who would deviate from the rules required by the code. West Coast Code does the same. And while we might argue that East Coast Code is more prevalent—that it regulates and controls a far larger part of our lives—that is a difference in degree, not kind. It's a reason to be balanced in our concern, not to be unconcerned.

Of course, there are differences between law and code. I don't think that everything is necessarily public, or that the Constitution should regulate every aspect of private life. I don't think it is a constitutional issue when I turn off Rush Limbaugh. But to say that there should be a difference is not to say that the difference should be as absolute as present constitutional thinking makes it. When we lawyers tell the Jean Camps of the world that they are simply making a "mistake" when they bring the values of public law to code, it is rather we who are making the mistake. Whether code should be tested with these constraints of public value is a question, not a conclusion. It needs to be decided by argument, not definition.

This won't be easy, of course. Code is technical; courts aren't well positioned to evaluate such technicality. But even so, the failure is not even to try. The formalism in American law, which puts beyond review these structures of control, is a third pathology that inhibits choice. Courts are disabled, legislatures pathetic, and code untouchable. That is our present condition. It is a combination that is deadly for action—a mix that guarantees that little good gets done.

SEVENTEEN

responses

WE NEED A PLAN. I'VE TOLD A DARK STORY ABOUT THE CHOICES THAT A CHANGING cyberspace is presenting, and about our inability to respond to these choices. I've linked this inability to three features of our present legal and political culture. In this short chapter, I consider three responses. These responses are nothing more than sketches, but they should be enough to suggest the nature of the changes we need to make.

RESPONSES OF A JUDICIARY

I've said that we should understand judicial hesitancy as grounded in prudence. When so much seems possible, and when a rule is not clearly set, it is hard for a court to look like a court as it decides what policies seem best.[1]

Although I agree with this ideal of prudence in general, we need to move its counsel along—to place it in context and limit its reach. We should isolate the source of the judge's difficulty. Sometimes a certain hesitation before resolving the questions of the Constitution in cyberspace finally, or firmly, or with any pretense to permanence, is entirely appropriate. But in other cases, judges—especially lower court judges—should be stronger, because there are many of them and because many are extraordinarily talented and creative. Their voices would teach us something here, even if their rulings were temporary or limited in scope.

In cases of simple translation (where there are no latent ambiguities and our tradition seems to speak clearly), judges should firmly advance arguments that seek to preserve original values of liberty in a new context. In these cases there is an important space for activism. Judges should identify our values and defend them, not necessarily because these values are right, but because if we ignore them, we should do so only because they have been rejected—not by a court but by the people.

In cases where translation is not so simple (cases that have latent ambiguities), judges, especially lower court judges, have a different role. In these cases, judges should kvetch. They should talk about the questions these changes raise, and they should identify the competing values at stake. Even if the decision they must adopt in a particular case is deferential or passive, it should be deferential in protest. These cases may well be a place for prudence, but to justify their passivity and compensate for allowing rights claims to fail, judges should raise before the legal culture the conflict presented by them. Hard cases need not make bad law, but neither should they be treated as if they are easy.

That is the simplest response to the problem of latent ambiguity. But it is incomplete. It forces us to confront questions of constitutional value and to choose. A better solution would help resolve these questions. While it will never be the job of the courts to make final choices on questions of value, by raising these questions the courts may inspire others to decide them.

This is the idea behind the doctrine of a second look outlined twenty years ago by Guido Calabresi, a professor at the time who is now a judge.[2] Brutally simplified, the idea is this: When the Supreme Court confronts issues that present open, yet fundamental questions of value, it should be open about the conflict and acknowledge that it is not plainly resolved by the Constitution. But the Court should nonetheless proceed to resolve it in the way most likely to induce democratic review of the resolution. If the resolution induces the proper review, the Court should let stand the results of that review. The most the Court should do in such cases is ensure that democracy has its say; its job is not to substitute its values for the views of democrats.

Many ridicule this solution.[3] Many argue that the framers clearly had nothing like this in mind when they established a Supreme Court and permitted judicial review. Of course they did not have this in mind. The doctrine of a second look is not designed for the problems the framers had in mind. As a response to the problems of latent ambiguities, it itself reveals a latent ambiguity.

We might deny this ambiguity. We might argue that the framers envisioned that the Court would do nothing at all about latent ambiguities; that in such contexts the democratic process, through Article V, would step in to correct a misapplication or to respond to a changed circumstance. That may well have been their view. But I don't think this intent is clear enough to foreclose our consideration of how we might best confront the coming series of questions on the application of constitutional value to cyberspace. I would rather err on the side of harmless activism than on the side of debilitating passivity. It is a tiny role for courts to play in the much larger conversation we need to have—but to date have not started.

RESPONSES FOR CODE

A second challenge is confronting the law in code—resolving, that is, just how we think about the regulatory power of code. Here are a number of ideas that together would push us toward a world where regulation imposed through code would have to satisfy constitutional norms.

Here again is the link to open code. In Chapter 8, when I described a kind of check that open code would impose on government regulation, I argued that it was harder for government to hide its regulations in open code, and easier for adopters to disable any regulations the government imposed. The movement from closed to open code was a movement from regulable to less regulable. Unless you are simply committed to disabling government's power, this change cannot be unambiguously good.

But there are two parts to the constraint that open code might impose; one is certainly good, and the other is not necessarily terrible. The first part is transparency—the regulations would be known. The second part is resistance—that known regulations could be more easily resisted. The second part need not follow from the first, and it need not be debilitating. It may be easier to disable the regulations of code if the code is in the open. But if the regulation is legitimate, the state can require that it not be disabled. If it wants, it can punish those who disobey.

Compare the regulation of seatbelts. For a time the federal government required that new cars have automatic seatbelts. This was the regulation of code—the car would be made safer by regulating the code to force people to use seatbelts. Many people hated seatbelts, and some disabled them. But the virtue of the automatic seatbelt was that its regulation was transparent. No one doubted who was responsible for the rule the seatbelt imposed. If the state didn't like it when people disabled their seatbelts, it was free to pass laws to punish them. In the end the government did not press the issue—not because it couldn't, but because the political costs would have been too high. Politics checked the government's regulation, just as it should.

This is the most we can expect of the regulation of code in cyberspace. There is a trade-off between transparency and effectiveness. Code regulation in the context of open code is more transparent but also less binding. Government's power to achieve regulatory ends would be constrained by open code.

There is another benefit. Closed code would make it easier for the government to hide its regulation and thus achieve an illicit regulatory end. Thus, there is no simple defeat of government's ends but instead a trade-off—between publicity and power, between the rules' transparency and people's obedience. It is an important check on government power to say that the only rules it should impose are those that would be obeyed if imposed transparently.

Does this mean that we should push for open rather than closed code? Does it mean that we should ban closed code?

No. It does not follow from these observations that we should ban closed code or that we must have a world with only open code. But they do point to the values we should insist on for any code that regulates. If code is a lawmaker, then it should embrace the values of a particular kind of lawmaking.

The core of these values is transparency. What a code regulation does should be at least as apparent as what a legal regulation does. Open code would provide that transparency—not for everyone (not everyone reads code), and not perfectly (badly written code hides its functions well), but more completely than closed code would.

Some closed code could provide this transparency. If code were more modular—if a code writer simply pulled parts off the shelf to plug into her system, as if she were buying spark plugs for a car—then even if the code for these components was closed, the functions and regulation of the end product would be open.[4] Componentized architecture could be as transparent as an open code architecture, and transparency could thus be achieved without opening the code.

The best code (from the perspective of constitutional values) is both modular and open. Modularity ensures that better components could be substituted for worse. And from a competitive perspective, modularity permits greater competition in the development of improvements in a particular coding project.

It is plausible, however, that particular bits of code could not be produced if they were produced as open code, that closed code may sometimes be necessary for competitive survival. If so, then the compromise of a component system would permit something of the best of both worlds—some competitive advantage along with transparency of function.

I've argued for transparent code because of the constitutional values it embeds. I have not argued against code as a regulator or against regulation. But I have argued that we insist on transparency in regulation and that we push code structures to enhance that transparency.

The law presently does not do this. Indeed, as Mark Lemley and David O'Brien argue, the existing structure of copyright protection for software tends to push the development of software away from a modular structure.[5] The law prefers opaque to transparent code; it constructs incentives to hide code rather than to make its functionality obvious.

Many have argued that the law's present incentives are inefficient—that they tend to reduce competition in the production of software.[6] This may well be right. But the greater perversity is again constitutional. Our law creates an incentive to enclose as much of an intellectual commons as possible. It works against publicity and transparency, and helps to produce, in effect, a massive secret government.

Here is a place for concrete legal change. Without resolving the question of whether closed or open code is best, we could at least push closed code in a direction that would facilitate greater transparency. But the inertia of existing law—which gives software manufacturers effectively unlimited terms of protection—works against change. The politics are just not there.

RESPONSES OF A DEMOCRACY

In his rightly famous book *Profiles in Courage*, then-Senator John F. Kennedy tells the story of Daniel Webster, who, in the midst of a fight over a pact that he thought would divide the nation, said on the floor of the Senate, "Mr. President, I wish to speak today, not as a Massachusetts man, nor as a Northern man, but as an American . . ."[7]

When Webster said this—in 1850—the words "not as a Massachusetts man" had a significance that we are likely to miss today. To us, Webster's statement seems perfectly ordinary. What else would he be but an American? How else would he speak?

But these words came on the cusp of a new time in the United States. They came just at the moment when the attention of American citizens was shifting from their citizenship in a state to their citizenship in the nation. Webster spoke just as it was becoming possible to identify yourself apart from your state and as a member of a nation.

As I've said, at the founding citizens of the United States (a contested concept itself) were citizens of particular states first. They were loyal to their own states because their lives were determined by where they lived. Other states were as remote to them as Tibet is to us—indeed, today it is easier for us to go to Tibet than it was then for a citizen of South Carolina to visit Maine.

Over time, of course, this changed. In the struggle leading up to the Civil War, in the battles over Reconstruction, and in the revolution of industry that followed, individual citizens' sense of themselves as Americans grew. In those exchanges and struggles, a national identity was born. Only when citizens were engaged with citizens from other states was a nation created.

It is easy to forget these moments of transformation, and even easier to imagine that they happen only in the past. Yet no one can deny that the sense of being "an American" shifted in the nineteenth century, just as no one can deny that the sense of being "a European" is shifting in Europe today. Nations are built as people experience themselves inside a common political culture. This change continues for us today.

We stand today just a few years before where Webster stood in 1850. We stand on the brink of being able to say, "I speak as a citizen of the world," without the ordinary person thinking, "What a nut." We are just on the cusp of a time when ordinary citizens will begin to feel the effects of the regulations of other governments, just as the citizens of Massachusetts came to feel the effects of slavery and the citizens of Virginia came to feel the effects of a drive for freedom. As Nicholas Negroponte puts it, "Nations today are the wrong size. They are not small enough to be local and they are not large enough to be global." [8] This misfit will matter.

As we, citizens of the United States, spend more of our time and money in this space that is not part of any particular jurisdiction but subject to the regulations of all jurisdictions, we will increasingly ask questions about our status there. We will begin to feel the entitlement Webster felt, as an American, to speak about life in another part of the United States. For us, it will be the entitlement to speak about life in another part of the world, grounded in the feeling that there is a community of interests that reaches beyond diplomatic ties into the hearts of ordinary citizens.

What will we do then? When we feel we are part of a world, and that the world regulates us? What will we do when we need to make choices about how that world regulates us, and how we regulate it?

The weariness with government that I described at the end of the last chapter is not a condition without cause. But its cause is not the death of any ideal of democracy. We are all still democrats; we simply do not like what our democracy has produced. And we cannot imagine extending what we have to new domains like cyberspace. If there were just more of the same there— more of the excesses and betrayals of government as we have come to know it—then better that there should be less.

There are two problems here, though only one that is really tied to the argument of this book, and so only one that I will discuss in any depth. The other I mentioned at the end of the last chapter—the basic corruption in any system that would allow so much political influence to be peddled by those who hand out money. This is the corruption of campaign financing, a corruption not of people but of process. Even good souls in Congress have no choice but to spend an ever-increasing amount of their time raising an ever-increasing amount of money to compete in elections. This is an arms race, and our Supreme Court has effectively said that the Constitution requires it. Until this problem is solved, I have little faith in what our democracy will produce.

The solution to this problem is obvious, even if the details are extremely difficult: Spend public resources to fund public campaigns. The total cost of federal elections in 2004 was probably close to $4 billion.[9] In the same year, we spent $384 billion on defense and $66 billion on the war in Iraq.[10] Whatever you think about the wisdom of defense spending and the war in Iraq, at least the purposes of all three expenditures is the same—to preserve and promote democracy. Is there any doubt if we made campaign contributions essentially irrelevant to policy we'd have a more certain and positive effect on democracy than the other two?

But there is a second, oddly counterintuitive reason for this increasing failure of democracy. This is not that government listens too little to the views of the public; it is that government listens too much. Every fancy of the population gets echoed in polls, and these polls in turn pulse the democracy. Yet the message the polls transmit is not the message of democracy; their frequency and influence is not the product of increased significance. The President makes policy on the basis of overnight polling only because overnight polling is so easy.

This is partly a technology problem. Polls mark an interaction of technology and democracy that we are just beginning to understand. As the cost of monitoring the current view of the population drops, and as the machines for permanent monitoring of the population are built, we are producing a perpetual stream of data about what "the people" think about every issue that government might consider.

A certain kind of code perfects the machine of monitoring—code that automates perfect sample selection, that facilitates databases of results, and that simplifies the process of connecting. We rarely ask, however, whether perfect monitoring is a good.

It has never been our ideal—constitutionally at least—for democracy to be a perfect reflection of the present temperature of the people. Our framers were keen to design structures that would mediate the views of the people. Democracy was to be more than a string of excited utterances. It was to be deliberative, reflective, and balanced by limitations imposed by a constitution.

But maybe, to be consistent with the arguments from Part III, I should say that at least there was a latent ambiguity about this question. In a world where elections were extremely costly and communication was complicated, democracy had to get by with infrequent elections. Nevertheless, we cannot really know how the framers would have reacted to a technology that allows perfect and perpetual polling.

There is an important reason to be skeptical of the flash pulse of the people. The flash pulse is questionable not because the people are uneducated or incapable of good judgment, and not because democracy needs to fail, but because it is often the product of ignorance. People often have ill-informed or partially informed views that they simply repeat as judgments when they know that their judgments are not being particularly noticed or considered.

Technology encourages this. As a consequence of the massive increase in reporting on news, we are exposed to a greater range of information about the world today than ever before. This exposure, in turn, gives us confidence in our judgment. Never having heard of East Timor, people when asked about it might well have said, "I don't know." But having seen ten seconds on TV, or thirty lines on a Web portal news page, gives them a spin they didn't have before. And they repeat this spin, with very little value added.

The solution to this problem is not less news or a ban on polling. The solution is a better kind of polling. The government reacts to bad poll data because that is the only data we have. But these polls are not the only possible kinds of polls. There are techniques for polling that compensate for the errors of the flash poll and produce judgments that are both more considered and more stable.

An example is the "deliberative" poll devised by Professor James Fishkin. Rather than a pulse, Fishkin's polls seek an equilibrium.[11] They bring a cross-section of people together for a weekend at a time. These people, who represent all segments of a society, are given information before the poll that helps ensure that they know something about the subject matter. After being introduced to the topic of the poll, they are then divided into small juries and over the course of a couple of days argue about the topic at issue and exchange views about how best to resolve it. At the end they are asked about their views, and their responses at this point form the "results" of the poll.

The great advantage of this system is not only that information is provided but that the process is deliberative. The results emerge out of the reasoning of citizens debating with other citizens. People are not encouraged to just cast a ballot. They give reasons for their ballot, and those reasons will or will not persuade.

We could imagine (we could dream) of this process extending generally. We could imagine it becoming a staple of our political life—maybe one rule of citizenship. And if it did, it might well do good, as a counterweight to the flash pulse and the perpetually interested process that ordinary government is. It would be a corrective to the process we now have, one that might bring hope.

Cyberspace might make this process more possible; it certainly makes it even more necessary. It is possible to imagine using the architecture of the space to design deliberative forums, which could be used to implement Fishkin's polling. But my message throughout is that cyberspace makes the need all the more urgent.[12]

There is a magic in a process where reasons count—not where experts rule or where only smart people have the vote, but where power is set in the face of reason. The magic is in a process where citizens give reasons and understand that power is constrained by these reasons.

This was the magic that Tocqueville wrote of when he told the world of the amazing system of juries in the United States. Citizens serving on juries must make reasoned, persuasive arguments in coming to decisions that often have extraordinary consequences for social and political life. Writing in 1835, Tocqueville said of juries:

> The jury . . . serves to communicate the spirit of the judges to the minds of all the citizens; and this spirit, with the habits which attend it, is the soundest preparation for free institutions. It imbues all classes with a respect for the thing judged and with the notion of right. . . . It teaches men to practice equity; every man learns to judge his neighbor as he would himself be judged. . . . The jury teaches every man not to recoil before the responsibility of his own actions and impresses him with that manly confidence without which no political virtue can exist. It invests each citizen with a kind of magistracy; it makes them all feel the duties which they are bound to discharge towards society and the part which they take in its government. By obliging men to turn their attention to other affairs than their own, it rubs off that private selfishness which is the rust of society.[13]

It wasn't Tocqueville, however, or any other theorist, who sold me on this ideal. It was a lawyer who first let me see the power of this idea—a lawyer from Madison, Wisconsin, my uncle, Richard Cates.

We live in a time when the sane vilify lawyers. No doubt lawyers are in part responsible for this. But I can't accept it, and not only because I train lawyers for a living. I can't accept it because etched into my memory is a picture my uncle sketched, explaining why he was a lawyer. In 1974 he had just returned from Washington, where he worked for the House Committee on Impeachment—of Nixon, not Clinton, though Hillary Rodham was working with him. I pressed him to tell me everything; I wanted to hear about the battles. It was not a topic that we discussed much at home. My parents were Republicans. My uncle was not.

My uncle's job was to teach the congressmen about the facts in the case—to first learn everything that was known, and then to teach this to the members of the committee. Although there was much about his story that I will never forget, the most compelling part was not really related to the impeachment. My uncle was describing for me the essence of his job—both for the House and for his clients:

> It is what a lawyer does, what a good lawyer does, that makes this system work. It is not the bluffing, or the outrage, or the strategies and tactics. It is something much simpler than that. What a good lawyer does is tell a story that persuades. Not by hiding the truth or exciting the emotion, but using reason, through a story, to persuade.

When it works, it does something to the people who experience this persuasion. Some, for the first time in their lives, see power constrained by reason. Not by votes, not by wealth, not by who someone knows—but by an argument that persuades. This is the magic of our system, however rare the miracles may be.

This picture stuck—not in the elitist version of experts deciding what's best, nor in its populist version of excited crowds yelling opponents down, but in the simple version that juries know. And it is this simple picture that our current democracy misses. Where through deliberation, and understanding, and a process of building community, judgments get made about how to go on.

We could build some of this back into our democracy. The more we do, the less significant the flash pulses will be. And the less significant these flash pulses are, the more we might have faith again in that part of our tradition that made us revolutionaries in 1789—the commitment to a form of government that respects deliberation and the people, and that stands opposed to corruption dressed in aristocratic baubles.

EIGHTEEN

what declan doesn't get

DECLAN MCCULLAGH IS A WRITER WHO WORKS FOR WIRED NEWS. HE ALSO RUNS a mailing list that feeds subscribers bulletins that he decides to forward and facilitates a discussion among these members. The list was originally called "Fight Censorship," and it initially attracted a large number of subscribers who were eager to organize to resist the government's efforts to "censor" the Net.

But Declan has converted the list to far more than a discussion of censorship. He feeds to the list other news that he imagines his subscribers will enjoy. So in addition to news about efforts to eliminate porn from the Net, Declan includes reports on FBI wiretaps, or efforts to protect privacy, or the government's efforts to enforce the nation's antitrust laws. I'm a subscriber; I enjoy the posts.

Declan's politics are clear. He's a smart libertarian whose first reaction to any suggestion that involves government is scorn. In one recent message, he cited a story about a British provider violating fax spam laws; this, he argued, showed that laws regulating e-mail spam are useless. In another, he criticized efforts by Reporters Without Borders to pass laws to protect free speech internationally.[1] There is one unifying theme to Declan's posts: Let the Net alone. And with a sometimes self-righteous sneer, he ridicules those who question this simple, if powerful, idea.

I've watched Declan's list for some time. For a brief time, long ago, I watched the discussion part of the list as well. And throughout the years I have had the pleasure of learning from Declan, a single simple message has dominated the thread: The question is not just, Declan insists again and again, whether there are "market failures" that require government intervention. The question is also whether there are "government failures." (As he said in a

recent post about the Reporters Without Borders, "[Julien Pain's] able to identify all these apparent examples of market failure, but [he's] not as able to
identify instances of *government* failure.") And the consequence for Declan
from asking the second is (just about always) to recommend we do nothing.

Declan's question has a very good pedigree. It was the question Ronald
Coase first started asking as he worked toward his Nobel Prize. Economists
such as Pigou had identified goods that markets couldn't provide. That was
enough for Pigou to show that governments should therefore step in. But as
Coase said,

> [I]n choosing between social arrangements within the context of which individ-
> ual decisions are made, we have to bear in mind that a change in the existing sys-
> tem which will lead to an improvement in some decisions may well lead to a
> worsening of others. Furthermore we have to take into account the costs
> involved in operating the various social arrangements (whether it be the work-
> ing of a market or of a government department) as well as the costs involved in
> moving to a new system. In devising and choosing between social arrangements
> we should have regard for the total effect.[2]

Coase had a discipline to his work. That discipline was to never stop at
theory. Theoretical insight is critical to progress, but testing that theory with
a bit of real-world life is critical as well.

But this is the trouble with the world of at least some libertarians. We can
speculate till the cows come home about what the world would be like if our
government were crafted by a gaggle of pure libertarians. There would be a
government, of course. Libertarians are not anarchists. And no doubt, the
consequences of such a shift are counter-intuitive. It would certainly not be as
bad as statists predict; I doubt it would be as good as libertarians promise.

But the reality is that we're never going to live in libertarian land. And so
the question we should ask is what attitude we should bring to regulation,
given we live in this world where regulation is going to happen. Should our
response in that world—meaning this world, and every possible world we're
ever going to see—be to act as if we oppose all regulation on principle?

Because if this is our response, that attitude will have an effect. It won't
stop all regulation, but it will stop regulation of a certain form. Or, better, it's
certain *not* to stop regulation of a different form—regulation benefiting, for
example, powerful special interests.

Consider an obvious example.

Economists estimate that we as an economy lose billions because of the
burdens of spam. Ferris Research, for example, estimates that the current

costs (including lost productivity) are between $9 and $10 per user per month. That translates into more than $9 billion per year to fight spam.[3] These costs have been borne by everyone who pays for e-mail on the Internet. They don't include the indirect costs of missing a message because it is either filtered or ignored. (Nor does this number reckon the benefit of spam, but as I won't count the benefit in the comparative example either, I'll leave that out for now.)

Economists have also tried to estimate the cost of Internet "piracy" of copyrighted content (excluding software) to the content industry. Some estimate that the costs are actually very low. Felix Oberholzer and Koleman Strumpf, for example, concluded that filesharing has "an effect on sales statistically indistinguishable from zero."[4] Other estimates conclude there is a real loss, but not huge. In 2003, using a sophisticated model to measure the loss from P2P filesharing in 2003, David Blackburn concluded the industry lost $330 million.[5] That number is significantly below the RIAA's estimate of the total annual cost from "all forms of piracy": $4.2 billion.[6]

Suffice it that these estimates are contested. But even so, in this field of contest, one thing is absolutely certain: The cost of "piracy" is significantly less than the cost of spam. Indeed, the total cost of spam—adding consumers to corporations—exceeds the total annual revenues of the recording industry.[7]

So how does this difference in harm calibrate with what Congress has done to respond to each of these two problems?

In the last ten years, Congress has passed exactly one bill to deal with the problem of spam—the CAN-SPAM Act of 2003. Over the same period, Congress has passed 24 laws affecting copyright.[8] Not all of these laws, of course, are directly targeted against "piracy," but they all do aim further to protect copyrighted work in a digital age.

This pattern is not an accident. In a political world that is dominated as ours is, lawmaking happens when special interests benefit. It doesn't happen when special interests oppose. And in these two instances, the lack of regulation and the plethora of regulation is explained by this point precisely. There have been 24 bills about copyright because rock stars lobby for them. There has been one bill about spam because the direct mailers (and many large companies) testified against them.

Now given this reality, I suggest the libertarian should recognize a third important failure that complements "market" and "government" failure: There is "market failure" when markets can't be expected to provide goods efficiently; there's "government failure" when government can't be expected to solve market failures efficiently; and there's "libertarian failure" when the push to do nothing will produce not no regulation at all, but regulation by the most powerful of special interests. Or in a slogan: When it's wrong to push for regulation, only the wrong will get regulation.

I am not a libertarian in the sense Declan is, though I share his skepticism about government. But we can't translate skepticism into disengagement. We have a host of choices that will affect how the Internet develops and what values it will embed. The attitude that eschews government as part of those choices is not one that will stop government; it will simply stop government from making the right choices.

In my view, governments should intervene, at a minimum, when private action has negative public consequences; when shortsighted actions threaten to cause long-term harm; when failure to intervene undermines significant constitutional values and important individual rights; when a form of life emerges that may threaten values we believe to be fundamental; and when we can see that failing to intervene on the side of right will simply strengthen the interventions on the side of wrong. Such intervention must be limited; it must be engaged with all the awareness about the failures of government that right thinking sorts can muster. But action defending right should not be stopped merely because some goes wrong. When those who believe in the liberty of cyberspace, and the values that liberty promotes, refuse to engage with government about how best to preserve those liberties, that weakens liberty. Do-nothingism is not an answer; something can and should be done.

I've argued this, but not with much hope. So central are the Declans in our political culture today that I confess I cannot see a way around them. I have sketched small steps; they seem very small. I've described a different ideal; it seems quite alien. I've promised that something different could be done, but not by any institution of government that I know.

The truth, I suspect, is that the Declans will win—at least for now. We will treat code-based environmental disasters—like the loss of privacy, like the censorship of censorware filters, like the disappearance of an intellectual commons—as if they were produced by gods, not by Man. We will watch as important aspects of privacy and free speech are erased by the emerging architecture of the panopticon, and we will speak, like modern Jeffersons, about nature making it so—forgetting that here, we are nature. We will in many domains of our social life come to see the Net as the product of something alien—something we cannot direct because we cannot direct anything. Something instead that we must simply accept, as it invades and transforms our lives.

Some say this is an exciting time. But it is the excitement of a teenager playing chicken, his car barreling down the highway, hands held far from the steering wheel. There are choices we could make, but we pretend that there is nothing we can do. We choose to pretend; we shut our eyes. We build this nature, then we are constrained by this nature we have built.

It is the age of the ostrich. We are excited by what we cannot know. We are proud to leave things to the invisible hand. We make the hand invisible by looking the other way.

But it is not a great time, culturally, to come across revolutionary technologies. We are no more ready for this revolution than the Soviets were ready for theirs. We, like they, have been caught by a revolution. But we, unlike they, have something to lose.

APPENDIX

In Chapter 7, I sketched briefly an argument for how the four modalities I described constrain differently. In this appendix, I want to extend that argument. My hope is to provide a richer sense of how these modalities—law, the market, norms, and architecture—interact as they regulate. Such an understanding is useful, but not necessary, to the argument of this book. I've therefore put it here, for those with an interest, and too much time. Elsewhere I have called this approach "the New Chicago School."[1]

Law is a command backed up by the threat of a sanction. It commands you not to commit murder and threatens a severe penalty if you do so anyway. Or it commands you not to trade in cocaine and threatens barbaric punishments if you do. In both cases, the picture of law is fairly simple and straightforward: Don't do this, or else.

Obviously law is much more than a set of commands and threats.[2] Law not only commands certain behaviors but expresses the values of a community (when, for example, it sets aside a day to celebrate the birth of Martin Luther King, Jr.);[3] constitutes or regulates structures of government (when the Constitution, for example, establishes in Article I a House of Representatives distinct from a Senate); and establishes rights that individuals can invoke against their own government (the Bill of Rights). All these are examples of law, and by focusing on just one kind of law, I do not mean to diminish the significance of these other kinds. Still, this particular aspect of law provides a well-defined constraint on individuals within the jurisdiction of the law giver, or sovereign. That constraint—objectively—is the threat of punishment.

Social norms constrain differently. By social norms, I mean those normative constraints imposed not through the organized or centralized actions of a state, but through the many slight and sometimes forceful sanctions that members of a community impose on each other. I am not talking about patterns of behavior: It may be that most people drive to work between 7:00 and 8:00 A.M., but this is not a norm in the sense I mean. A norm governs socially salient behavior, deviation from which makes you socially abnormal.[4]

Life is filled with, constituted by, and defined in relation to such norms—some of which are valuable, and many of which are not. It is a norm (and a good one) to thank others for service. Not thanking someone makes you "rude," and being rude opens you up to a range of social sanctions, from ostracism to criticism. It is a norm to speak cautiously to a seatmate on an airplane, or to stay to the right while driving slowly. Norms discourage men from wearing dresses to work and encourage all of us to bathe regularly. Ordinary life is filled with such commands about how we are to behave. For the ordinarily socialized person, these commands constitute a significant portion of the constraints on individual behavior.

Norms, like law, then, are effective rules. What makes norms different is the mechanism and source of their sanction: They are imposed by a community, not a state. But they are similar to law in that, at least objectively, their constraint is imposed after a violation has occurred.

The constraints of the market are different again. The market constrains through price. A price signals the point at which a resource can be transferred from one person to another. If you want a Starbucks coffee, you must give the clerk four dollars. The constraint (the four dollars) is simultaneous with the benefit you want (the coffee). You may, of course, bargain to pay for the benefit later ("I'd gladly pay you Tuesday for a hamburger today"), but the obligation is incurred at the time you receive the benefit. To the extent that you stay in the market, this simultaneity is preserved. The market constraint, unlike law and norms, does not kick in after you have taken the benefit you seek; it kicks in at the same time.

This is not to say that market transactions cannot be translated into law or norm transactions. Indeed, market transactions do not exist except within a context of law and norms. You must pay for your coffee; if you do not, the law of theft applies. Nothing in the market requires that you tip the waiter, but if you do not, norms kick in to regulate your stinginess. The constraints of the market exist because of an elaborate background of law and norms defining what is buyable and sellable, as well as rules of property and contract for how things may be bought and sold. But given these laws and norms, the market still constrains in a distinct way.

The constraint of our final modality is neither so contingent nor, in its full range, so dependent. This is the constraint of architecture—the way the world is, or the ways specific aspects of it are. Architects call it the built environment; those who don't give out names just recognize it as the world around them.

Plainly some of the constraints of architecture are constraints we have made (hence the sense of "architecture") and some are not. A door closes off a room. When locked, the door keeps you out. The constraint functions not as law or norms do—you cannot ignore the constraint and suffer the consequence later. Even if the constraint imposed by the door is one you can overcome—by breaking it down perhaps, or picking the lock—the door still constrains, just not absolutely.

Some architectural constraints, however, are absolute. *Star Trek* notwithstanding, we cannot travel at warp speed. We can travel fast, and technology has enabled us to travel faster than we used to. Nonetheless, we have good reason (or at least physicists do) for believing that there is a limit to the speed at which we can travel. As a T-shirt I saw at MIT put it, "186,282 miles per second. It's not just a good idea. It's the law."

But whether absolute or not, or whether man-made or not, we can consider these constraints as a single class—as the constraints of architecture, or real-space code. What unites this class is the agency of the constraint: No individual or group imposes the constraint, or at least not directly. Individuals are no doubt ultimately responsible for much of the constraint, but in its actual execution the constraint takes care of itself. Laws need police, prosecutors, and courts to have an effect; a lock does not. Norms require that individuals take note of nonconforming behavior and respond accordingly; gravity does not. The constraints of architecture are self-executing in a way that the constraints of law, norms, and the market are not.

This feature of architecture—self-execution—is extremely important for understanding its role in regulation. It is particularly important for unseemly or unjust regulation. For example, to the extent that we can bring about effects through the automatic constraints of real-space code, we need not depend on the continued agency, loyalty, or reliability of individuals. If we can make the machine do it, we can be that much more confident that the unseemly will be done.

The launching of nuclear missiles is a nice example. In their original design, missiles were to be launched by individual crews located within missile launch silos. These men would have been ordered to launch their missiles, and the expectation was that they would do so. Laws, of course, backed up the order—disobeying the order to launch subjected the crew to court-martial.[5]

But in testing the system, the army found it increasingly unreliable. Always the decision to launch was checked by a judgment made by an individual, and always that individual had to decide whether the order was to be obeyed. Plainly this system is less reliable than a system where all the missiles are wired, as it were, to a single button on the President's desk. But we might believe that there is value in this second check, that the agency of the action by the soldier ensures some check on the decision to launch.[6]

This is an important consequence of the automatic nature of the constraints of architecture. Law, norms, and the market are constraints checked by judgment. They are enacted only when some person or group chooses to do so. But once instituted, architectural constraints have their effect until someone stops them.

Agency, then, is one distinction between the four constraints. The temporality of the constraint—when it is imposed—is a second one.

Here I should distinguish between two different perspectives: that of someone observing when a constraint is imposed (the objective perspective), and that of the person who experiences the constraint (the subjective perspective). So far my description of the four constraints in this single model has been from the objective perspective. From that perspective they are quite different, but from a subjective perspective they need not differ at all.

From the objective perspective the difference is between constraints that demand payment up front and constraints that let you play and then pay. Architecture and the market constrain up front; law and norms let you play first. For example, think of the constraints blocking your access to the air-conditioned home of a neighbor who is gone for the weekend. Law constrains you—if you break in, you will be trespassing. Norms constrain you as well—it's not neighborly to break into your neighbor's house. Both of these constraints, however, would be imposed on you after you broke into the house. They are prices you might have to pay later.[7] The architectural constraint is the lock on the door—it blocks you as you are trying to enter the house. The market constrains your ownership of an air conditioner in the same way—it demands money before it will give you one. From an objective perspective, what distinguishes these two classes of constraints is their temporality—when the sanction is imposed.

From a subjective perspective, however, all these differences may disappear. Subjectively, you may well feel a norm constraint long before you violate it. You may feel the constraint against breaking into your neighbor's house just at the thought of doing so. A constraint may be objectively *ex post*, but experienced subjectively *ex ante*.

The point is not limited to norms. Think about a child and fire. Fire is a bit of real-space code: The consequences are felt as soon as the constraint it imposes is violated. A child learns this the first time he puts his hand near a flame. Thereafter, the child internalizes the constraint of fire before putting his hand in one. Burned once, the child knows not to put his hand so near the flame a second time.[8]

We can describe this change as the development of a subjective constraint on the child's behavior. We can then see how the idea extends to other constraints. Think about the stock market. For those who do not shop very much, the constraints of the market may indeed be only the objective constraint of the price demanded when they make a purchase. However, for those who experience the market regularly—who have, as it were, a sense of the market—the constraints of the market are quite different. Such people come to know them as a second nature, which guides or constrains their actions. Think of a stockbroker on the floor of an exchange. To be a great broker is to come to know the market "like the back of your hand," to let it become second nature. In the terms that we've used, this broker has let the market become subjectively part of who she is.

Each constraint, then, has a subjective and an objective aspect. Laws are objectively ex post, but for most of us, the fact that a law directs us in a particular way is sufficient to make it a subjective constraint. (It is not the objective threat of jail that constrains me from cheating on my taxes; instead, I have made subjective the constraints of the law with respect to taxes. Honest, IRS. This is true.) As a subjective constraint, it constrains us before we act.

For those who are fully mature, or fully integrated, all objective constraints are subjectively effective prior to their actions. They feel the constraints of real-space code, of law, of norms, and of the market before they act. For the completely immature, or totally alienated, few objective constraints are subjectively effective. They step in the mud and only then learn about the constraint of mud; they steal bread and only then learn about the punishments of the law; they show up at a wedding in cut-offs and only then learn about the scorn of their friends; they spend all their money on candy and only then learn of the constraint of market scarcity. These two types mark out the extremes; most of us are somewhere in between.

The more subjective a constraint, then, the more effective it is in regulating behavior. It takes work to make a constraint subjective. An individual must choose to make it a part of who he or she is. To the extent that the norm is made subjective, it constrains simultaneously with the behavior it regulates.

This points to one final distinction between law and norms, on the one hand, and real-space code, on the other. Law and norms are more efficient the more subjective they are, but they need some minimal subjectivity to be effective at all. The person constrained must know of the constraint. A law that secretly punishes people for offenses they do not know exist would not be effective in regulating the behavior it punishes.[9]

But this is not the case with architecture. Architecture can constrain without any subjectivity. A lock constrains the thief whether or not the thief knows that it is a lock blocking the door. The distance between two places constrains the intercourse between those two places whether or not anyone in those places understands that constraint. This point is a corollary of the point about agency: Just as a constraint need not be imposed by an agent, neither does the subject need to understand it.

Architectural constraints, then, work whether or not the subject knows they are working, while law and norms work only if the subject knows something about them. If the subject has internalized them, they can constrain whether or not the expected cost of complying exceeds the benefit of deviating. Law and norms can be made more code-like the more they are internalized, but internalization takes work.

Though I have used language invoking architects, my language is not the language of architects. It is instead stolen and bent. I am not a scholar of architecture, but I have taken from architecture its insight about the relationship between the built environment and the practices that environment creates.[10] Neither architects nor I take this relationship to be determinative. Structure X does not determine behavior Y. Instead, these forms are always influences that can change, and when they are changed, they alter the affected behavior.

Like Michael Sorkin, I believe that "meanings inhere in forms, and that the settings for social life can aid its fulfillment." His book *Local Code: The Constitution of a City at 42N Latitude* suggests each feature of the model I am describing, including the ambiguity between law and architecture (building codes) and the constitution the two enable. Whatever the source of the content of these codes, he writes, "their consequences are built."[11] This is the feature to focus on.

My suggestion is that if we relativize regulators—if we understand how the different modalities regulate and how they are subject, in an important sense, to law—then we will see how liberty is constructed, not simply through the limits we place on law, but by structures that preserve a space for individual choice, however that choice may be constrained.

We are entering a time when our power to muck about with the structures that regulate is at an all-time high. It is imperative, then, that we understand just what to do with this power. And, more importantly, what not to do with it.

NOTES

All hypertext links can be located at <http://codev2.cc/links>.

PREFACE TO THE SECOND EDITION

1. The wiki lives on at <http://wiki.codev2.cc>.

PREFACE TO THE FIRST EDITION

1. Sixth Conference on Computers, Freedom and Privacy. See link #1.

CHAPTER ONE

1. See Katie Hafner and Matthew Lyon, *Where Wizards Stay Up Late* (New York: Simon and Schuster, 1996), 10: "Taylor had been the young director of the office within the Defense Department's Advanced Research Projects Agency overseeing computer research . . . Taylor knew the ARPANET and its progeny, the Internet, had nothing to do with supporting or surviving war . . ."

2. Paulina Borsook, "How Anarchy Works," *Wired* 110 (October 1995): 3.10, available at link #2, quoting David Clark.

3. James Boyle, talk at Telecommunications Policy Research Conference (TPRC), Washington, D.C., September 28, 1997. David Shenk discusses the libertarianism that cyberspace inspires (as well as other, more fundamental problems with the age) in a brilliant cultural how-to book that responsibly covers both the technology and the libertarianism; see *Data Smog: Surviving the Information Glut* (San Francisco: Harper Edge, 1997), esp. 174–77. The book also describes technorealism, a responsive movement that advances a more balanced picture of the relationship between technology and freedom.

4. See Kevin Kelley, *Out of Control: The New Biology of Machines, Social Systems, and the Economic World* (Reading, Mass.: Addison-Wesley, 1994), 119. The term "cybernetics" was coined by a founder of much in the field, Norbert Wiener. See *Cybernetics: Or Control and Communication in the Animal and the Machine* (Cambridge, Mass.: MIT Press, 1965). See also Flo Conway and Jim Siegelman, *Dark Hero of the Information Age: In Search of Norbert Wiener, The Father of Cybernetics* (New York: Basic Books, 2004).

5. Siva Vaidhyanathan, "Remote Control: The Rise of Electronic Cultural Policy," *Annals of the American Academy of Political and Social Science* 597, 1 (January 1, 2005): 122.

6. See William J. Mitchell, *City of Bits: Space, Place, and the Infobahn* (Cambridge, Mass: MIT Press, 1995), 111. In much of this book, I work out Mitchell's idea, though I drew the

metaphor from others as well. Ethan Katsh discusses this notion of software worlds in "Software Worlds and the First Amendment: Virtual Doorkeepers in Cyberspace," *University of Chicago Legal Forum* (1996): 335, 338. The best current effort is R. Polk Wagner, "On Software Regulation," *Southern California Law Review* 78 (2005): 457, 470–71.

7. Joel Reidenberg discusses the related notion of "lex informatica" in "Lex Informatica: The Formulation of Information Policy Rules Through Technology," *Texas Law Review* 76 (1998): 553.

8. Oliver Wendell Holmes, Jr., "The Path of the Law," *Harvard Law Review* 10 (1897): 457.

9. Mark Stefik, "Epilogue: Choices and Dreams," in *Internet Dreams: Archetypes, Myths, and Metaphors*, edited by Mark Stefik (Cambridge, Mass.: MIT Press, 1996), 390.

10. Mark Stefik, The Internet Edge: Social, Technical, and Legal Challenges for a Networked World (Cambridge: MIT Press, 1999), 14.

11. *Missouri v. Holland,* 252 US 416, 433 (1920).

12. This debate is nothing new to the American democracy. See *Does Technology Drive History?: The Dilemma of Technological Determinism,* Merritt Roe Smith and Leo Marx eds. (Cambridge: MIT Press, 1994), 1–35 ("If carried to extremes, Jefferson worried, the civilizing process of large-scale technology and industrialization might easily be corrupted and bring down the moral and political economy he and his contemporaries had worked so hard to erect").

13. Richard Stallman, for example, organized resistance to the emergence of passwords at MIT. Passwords are an architecture that facilitates control by excluding users not "officially sanctioned." Steven Levy, *Hackers* (Garden City, N.Y.: Anchor Press/Doubleday, 1984), 422–23.

CHAPTER TWO

1. Second Life—"What is Second Life?", available at link #3. The currently leading game, World of Warcraft, claims more than five million alone. Available at link #4.

2. It is also hypothetical. I have constructed this story in light of what could be, and in places is. I'm a law professor; I make up hypotheticals for a living.

3. Edward Castronova, *Synthetic Worlds: The Business and Culture of Online Games* (Chicago: University of Chicago Press, 2005), 55.

4. Ibid., 2.

5. John Crowley and Viktor Mayer-Schoenberger, "Napster's Second Life?—The Regulatory Challenges of Virtual Worlds" (Kennedy School of Government, Working Paper No. RWP05–052, 2005), 8.

6. "MUD" has had a number of meanings, originally Multi-User Dungeon, or Multi-User Domain. A MOO is a "MUD, object-oriented." Sherry Turkle's analysis of life in a MUD or MOO, *Life on the Screen: Identity in the Age of the Internet* (New York: Simon and Schuster, 1995), is still a classic. See also Elizabeth Reid, "Hierarchy and Power: Social Control in Cyberspace," in *Communities in Cyberspace,* edited by Marc A. Smith and Peter Kollock (New York: Routledge, 1999), 107. The father—or god—of a MUD named LambdaMOO is Pavel Curtis. See his account in "Mudding: Social Phenomena in Text-Based Virtual Realities," in Stefik, *Internet Dreams,* 265–92. For two magical pages of links about the history of MUDs, see Lauren P. Burka, "The MUDline," available at link #5; and Lauren P. Burka, "The MUDdex," available at link #6.

7. This is not a rare feature of these spaces. It is indeed quite common, at least within role-playing games. Julian Dibbell described to me a "parable" he recognized within Ultima Online: As he calls it, the "case of the stolen Bone Crusher."

"I got two offers for a Bone Crusher, which is a powerful sort of mace for bopping monsters over the head. I started dealing with both of them. At a certain point I was informed by one of them that the Bone Crusher had been stolen. So I said, 'I'll go buy it from the other guy. But, by the way, who was it that stole the Bone Crusher, do you know?' He said the name of the other guy. I was faced with this dilemma of was I going to serve as a fence for this other guy knowingly. And so, I turned to my mentor in this business, the guy who had been doing this for years and makes six figures a year on it, and, you know, I thought of him as an honest guy. So I sort of thought and maybe even hoped that he would just say just walk away. We don't do these kinds of deals in our business. We don't need that, you know, blah, blah, blah. But he said, 'Well, you know, thieving is built into the game. It is a skill that you can do. So fair is fair.' It is in the code that you can go into somebody's house and practice your thieving skills and steal something from them. And so, I went ahead and did the deal but there was this lingering sense of, 'Wow, in a way that is completely arbitrary that this ability is in the code here whereas, you know, if it wasn't built into the code it would be another story; they would have stolen it in another way.' . . ."

"But in Ultima Online, it is very explicitly understood that the code allows you to steal and the rules allow you to steal. For me what was interesting was that there remains this gray area. It made it an interesting game, that you were allowed to do something that was actually morally shady and you might have to decide for yourself. I'm not sure that now, going back to the deal, I would have taken the fenced item. I've been stolen from in the game, according to the rules, and it feels like shit."

Audio Tape: Interview with Julian Dibbell (1/6/06) (on file with author).

8. And only theft. If you transferred the property for a different purpose—say, sold the property—then the feature wouldn't change.

9. Compare Susan Brenner, "The Privacy Privilege: Law Enforcement, Technology and the Constitution," *Journal of Technology Law and Policy* 7 (2002): 123, 160. ("Pool tables in cyberspace do not require legs in this place where gravity does not exist"), citing Neal Stephenson, *Snow Crash* (New York: Bantam, 1992), 50 (in the Metaverse, tables only have tops, not legs).

10. Jake Baker's given name was Abraham Jacob Alkhabaz, but he changed his name after his parents' divorce. See Peter H. Lewis, "Writer Arrested After Sending Violent Fiction Over Internet," *New York Times*, February 11, 1995, 10.

11. The seven are comp, misc, news, rec, sci, soc, and talk. See Henry Edward Hardy, "The History of the Net, v8.5," September 28, 1993, available at link #7.

12. I have drawn from Jonathan Wallace and Mark Mangan's vivid account in *Sex, Laws, and Cyberspace* (New York: M&T Books, 1996), 63–81, though more interesting variations on this story circulate on the Net (I'm playing it safe).

13. See *United States v. Baker,* 890 FSupp 1375, 1390 (EDMich 1995); see also Wallace and Mangan, *Sex, Laws, and Cyberspace,* 69–78.

14. See Kurt Eichenwald, "Through His Webcam, a Bot Joins a Sordid Online World," *New York Times*, December 19, 2005, A1.

15. See C. Anderson and B. Bushman, "Effects of Violent Video Games on Aggressive Behavior, Aggressive Cognition, Aggressive Affect, Physiological Arousal, and Prosocial Behavior: A Meta-Analytic Review of the Scientific Literature," *Psychological Science* 12(5) (2001): 353–359, available at link #8; Jonathan L. Freedman, *Media Violence and Its Effect on Aggression* (Toronto: Toronto University Press, 2002).

16. See William J. Stuntz, "The Substantive Origins of Criminal Procedure," *Yale Law Journal* 105 (1995): 393, 406–7.

17. See, for example, Thomas K. Clancy, "The Role of Individualized Suspicion in Assessing the Reasonableness of Searches and Seizures," *University of Memphis Law Review* 25 (1995): 483, 632. "Individualized suspicion . . . has served as a bedrock protection against unjustified and arbitrary police actions."

18. See *United States v. Place,* 462 US 696, 707 (1983).

19. James Boyle, *Shamans, Software, and Spleens: Law and the Construction of the Information Society* (Cambridge, Mass.: Harvard University Press, 1996), 4.

20. See Susan Freiwald, "Uncertain Privacy: Communication Attributes After the Digital Telephony Act," *Southern California Law Review* 69 (1996): 949, 951, 954.

21. Cf. John Rogers, "Bombs, Borders, and Boarding: Combatting International Terrorism at United States Airports and the Fourth Amendment," *Suffolk Transnational Law Review* 20 (1997): 501, n.201.

22. See Mitchell Kapor, "The Software DesignManifesto," available at link #9; David Farber, "A Note on the Politics of Privacy and Infrastructure," November 20, 1993, available at link #10; "Quotations," available at link #11; see also Pamela Samuelson et al., "A Manifesto Concerning the Legal Protection of Computer Programs," *Columbia Law Review* 94 (1994): 2308. Steven Johnson powerfully makes a similar point: "All works of architecture imply a worldview, which means that all architecture is in some deeper sense political"; see *Interface Culture: How New Technology Transforms the Way We Create and Communicate* (San Francisco: Harper Edge, 1997), 44. The Electronic Frontier Foundation, originally cofounded by Mitch Kapor and John Perry Barlow, has updated Kapor's slogan "architecture is politics" to "architecture is policy." I prefer the original.

23. Jed Rubenfeld has developed most extensively an interpretive theory that grounds meaning in a practice of reading across time, founded on paradigm cases; see "Reading the Constitution as Spoken," *Yale Law Journal* 104 (1995): 1119, 1122; and "On Fidelity in Constitutional Law," *Fordham Law Review* 65 (1997): 1469. See also Jed Rubenfeld, *Freedom and Time: A Theory of Constitutional Government* (New Haven: Yale University Press, 2001).

24. See *Minnesota v. Dickerson,* 508 US 366, 380 (1993) (Justice Antonin Scalia concurring: "I frankly doubt . . . whether the fiercely proud men who adopted our Fourth Amendment would have allowed themselves to be subjected, on mere suspicion of being armed and dangerous, to such indignity. . . .").

25. See Steve Silberman, "We're Teen, We're Queer, and We've Got E-Mail," *Wired* (November 1994): 76, 78, 80, reprinted in *Composing Cyberspace: Identity, Community, and Knowledge in the Electronic Age,* edited by Richard Holeton (Boston: McGraw-Hill, 1998), 116.

26. Cf. *United States v. Lamb,* 945 F.Supp 441 (NDNY 1996). (Congress's intent in passing the Child Protection Act was to regulate child pornography via computer transmission, an interest legitimately related to stemming the flow of child pornography.)

CHAPTER THREE

1. David Johnson and David Post, "Law and Borders—The Rise of Law in Cyberspace," *Stanford Law Review* 48 (1996): 1367, 1375.

2. Tom Steinert-Threlkeld, "Of Governance and Technology," *Inter@ctive WeekOnline,* October 2, 1998.

3. J. C. Herz, *Surfing on the Internet: A Nethead's Adventures On-Line* (Boston: Little, Brown, 1995), 2–3.

4. The design of the network has changed slightly in the years since this was written. Some authentication is now required on the Chicago network, but once Ethernet ports have been assigned an IP address, that address remains "as long as it doesn't misbehave, we won't

know that has happened. In that sense, it is much the way it was." Audio Tape: Interview with Greg Jackson (1/9/06) (on file with author).

5. See Helen Nissenbaum, "Values in the Design of Computer Systems," *Computers and Society* (March 1998): 38.

6. As network adminstrator Greg Jackson described to me, while certain ports (including the wireless network) require that the user initially register the machine, there is no ongoing effort to verify the identity of the user. And, more importantly, there are still a significant number of ports which remain essentially unregulated. That doesn't mean that usage, however, isn't regulated. As Jackson described,

> "But the truth is, if we can identify a particular peer-to-peer network that is doing huge movie sharing, we will assign it a lower priority so it simply moves slower and doesn't interfere with other people. So, we do a lot of packet shaping of that sort. Almost never does that extend to actually blocking particular sites, for example, although there are a few cases where we have had to do that just because . . ."

According to Jackson, it is now Columbia that earns the reputation as the free-est network. "Columbia . . . really doesn't ever try to monitor at all who gets on the wired network on campus. They just don't bother with that. Their policy is that they protect applications, not the network."

Audio Tape: Interview with Greg Jackson (1/9/06) (on file with author).

7. For an extremely readable description, see Peter Loshin, *TCP/IP Clearly Explained* (San Francisco: Morgan Kaufmann, 1997), 15–23; see also Craig Hunt, *TCP/IP Network Administration*, 2d ed. (Sebastopol, Cal.: O'Reilly and Associates, 1998), 8–22; *Trust in Cyberspace*, edited by Fred B. Schneider (Washington, D.C.: National Academy Press, 1999), 29–36.

8. Peter Steiner, cartoon, *New Yorker*, July 5, 1993, 61.

9. In some contexts we call a network architecture that solves some of these "imperfections"—that builds in these elements of control—an intranet. Intranets are the fastest-growing portion of the Internet today. They are a strange hybrid of two traditions in network computing—the open system of the Internet, based on TCP/IP, and the control-based capability of traditional proprietary networks layered onto the Internet. Intranets mix values from each to produce a network that is interoperable but gives its controller more control over access than anyone would have over the Internet. My argument in this book is that an "internet" with control is what our Internet is becoming.

CHAPTER FOUR

1. TelecomWorldWire, "Compuserve Moves for Porn Techno Fix," January 11, 1995.

2. See Ed Krol, *The Whole Internet: User's Guide and Catalogue* (Sebastopol, Cal.: O'Reilly and Associates, 1992), 23–25; Loshin, *TCP/IP Clearly Explained*, 3–83; Hunt, TCP/IP, 1–22; see also Ben M. Segal, "A Short History of Internet Protocols at CERN," available at link #12.

3. See Jerome H. Saltzer et al., "End-to-End Arguments in System Design," in *Integrated Broadband Networks*, edited by Amit Bhargava (Norwood, Mass.: Artech House, 1991), 30–41.

4. Shawn C. Helms, "Translating Privacy Values with Technology," *Boston University Journal of Science and Technology Law* 7 (2001): 288, 296.

5. For a description of HTTP Protocols as they were used in the early 1990s, see link #13.

6. For an extraordinarily clear explication of the point, see Dick Hardt—Etech 2006: "Who Is the Dick on My Site?" (2006), available at link #14.

7. Audio Tape: Interview with Kim Cameron (1/9/06) (on file with author).

8. Ibid.

9. Ibid.

10. A number of states have now passed legislation dealing with ID theft. A current listing follows:

Alabama	Alabama Code § 13A-8–190 through 201
Alaska	Alaska Stat § 11.46.565
Arizona	Ariz. Rev. Stat. § 13–2008
Arkansas	Ark. Code Ann. § 5–37–227
California	Cal. Penal Code § 530.5–8
Connecticut	Conn. Stat. § 53a-129a
	Conn. Stat. § 52–571h
Delaware	Del. Code Ann. tit. II, § 854
District of Columbia	Title 22, Section 3227
Florida	Fla. Stat. Ann. § 817.568
Georgia	Ga. Code Ann. § 16–9-120, through 128
Guam	9 Guam Code Ann. § 46.80
Hawaii	HI Rev. Stat. § 708–839.6–8
Idaho	Idaho Code § 18–3126
Illinois	720 Ill. Comp. Stat. 5/16 G
Indiana	Ind. Code § 35–43–5-3.5
Iowa	Iowa Code § 715A.8
Kansas	Kan. Stat. Ann. § 21–4018
Kentucky	Ky. Rev. Stat. Ann. § 514.160
Louisiana	La. Rev. Stat. Ann. § 14:67.16
Maine	ME Rev. Stat. Ann. tit. 17-A §905-A
Maryland	Md. Code Ann. art. 27 § 231
Massachusetts	Mass. Gen. Laws ch. 266, § 37E
Michigan	Mich. Comp. Laws § 750.285
Minnesota	Minn. Stat. Ann. § 609.527
Mississippi	Miss. Code Ann. § 97–19–85
Missouri	Mo. Rev. Stat. § 570.223
Montana	Mon. Code Ann § 45–6-332
Nebraska	NE Rev. Stat. § 28–608 and 620
Nevada	Nev. Rev. State. § 205.463–465
New Hampshire	N.H. Rev. Stat. Ann. § 638:26
New Jersey	N.J. Stat. Ann. § 2C:21–17
New Mexico	N.M. Stat. Ann. § 30–16–24.1
New York	NY CLS Penal § 190.77–190.84
North Carolina	N.C. Gen. Stat. § 14–113.20–23
North Dakota	N.D.C.C. § 12.1–23–11
Ohio	Ohio Rev. Code Ann. § 2913.49
Oklahoma	Okla. Stat. tit. 21, § 1533.1
Oregon	Or. Rev. Stat. § 165.800
Pennsylvania	18 Pa. Cons. Stat. § 4120
Rhode Island	R.I. Gen. Laws § 11–49.1–1
South Carolina	S.C. Code Ann. § 16–13–510
South Dakota	S.D. Codified Laws § 22–30A-3.1.
Tennessee	TCA § 39–14–150
	TCA § 47–18–2101

Texas	Tex. Penal Code § 32.51
Utah	Utah Code Ann. § 76–6-1101–1104
Virginia	Va. Code Ann. § 18.2–186.3
Washington	Wash. Rev. Code § 9.35.020
West Virginia	W. Va. Code § 61–3-54
Wisconsin	Wis. Stat. § 943.201
Wyoming	Wyo. Stat. Ann. § 6–3-901

11. Stewart A. Baker and Paul R. Hurst, *The Limits of Trust: Cryptography, Governments, and Electronic Commerce* (Boston: Kluwer Law International, 1998), xv.

12. Ibid.

13. See Hal Abelson et al., "The Risks of Key Recovery, Key Escrow, and Trusted Third-Party Encryption," *World Wide Web Journal* 2 (1997): 241, 245: "Although cryptography has traditionally been associated with confidentiality, other cryptographic mechanisms, such as authentication codes and digital signatures, can assure that messages have not been tampered with or forged."

14. Whitfield Diffie and Martin E. Hellman, "New Directions in Cryptography," *IEEE Transactions on Information Theory it–22* (November 1976): 29–40. The idea had apparently been discovered earlier by James Ellis at the British Government Communication Headquarters, but it was not then published; see Baker and Hurst, *The Limits of Trust,* xvii–xviii.

15. Even if the wires are tapped, this type of encryption still achieves its magic. We can get a hint of how in a series of cases whose accumulating impact makes the potential clear.

A. If I want to send a message to you that I know only you will be able to read, I can take your public key and use it to encrypt that message. Then I can send that message to you knowing that only the holder of the private key (presumably you) will be able to read it. Advantage: My message to you is secure. Disadvantage: You can't be sure it is I who sent you the message. Because anyone can encrypt a message using your public key and then send it to you, you have no way to be certain that I was the one who sent it. Therefore, consider the next example.

B. Before I send the message I have encrypted with your public key, I can encrypt it with my private key. Then when you receive the message from me, you can first decrypt it with my public key, and then decrypt it again with your private key. After the first decryption, you can be sure that I (or the holder of my private key) was the one who sent you the message; after the second decryption, you can be sure that only you (or other holders of your private key) actually read the content of the message. But how do you know that what I say is the public key of Larry Lessig is actually the public key of Larry Lessig? How can you be sure, that is, that the public key you are using is actually the public key it purports to be? Here is where the next example comes in.

C. If there is a trustworthy third party (say, my bank, or the Federal Reserve Board, or the ACLU) with a public key (a fact I am able to verify because of the prominence of the institution), and that third party verifies that the public key of Larry Lessig is actually the public key of Larry Lessig, then along with my message sent to you, encrypted first in your public key and second in my private key, would be a certificate, issued by that institution, itself encrypted with the institution's private key. When you receive the message, you can use the institution's public key to decrypt the certificate; take from the certificate my public key (which you now are fairly confident is my public key); decrypt the message I sent you with the key held in the certificate (after which you are fairly confident comes from me); and then decrypt the message encrypted with your public key (which you can be fairly confident no one else has read). If we did all that, you would know that I am who I say I am and that the message was sent by me; I would know that only you read the message; and you would know that no one else read the message along the way.

16. Shawn C. Helms, "Translating Privacy Values with Technology," *Boston University Journal of Science and Technology Law* 7 (2001): 288, 299.

17. Ipanema Technologies, "Automatically discover applications running over your network." Available at link #15.

18. iProtectYou Pro Web Filter v7.10. See link #16.

19. Nmap ("Network Mapper"). See link #17.

20. *American Library Association v. Pataki,* 969 F. Supp. 160 (S.D.N.Y. 1997), cited in Michael Geist, *Cyberlaw 2.0,* 44 *Boston College Law Review* 323, 326–27 (2003).

21. Jack Goldsmith and Timothy Wu, *Who Controls the Internet: Illusions of a Borderless World* (New York: Oxford University Press, 2006), 44.

22. MaxMind Home Page, available at link #18.

23. Hostip.info Home Page, available at #19.

24. Seth Finkelstein, Barbara Nitke and the National Association for Sexual Freedom v. Ashcroft—Declaration of Seth Finkelstein (last updated Fri April 28, 2006), available at link #20.

25. *Plato's Republic, Book II* (Agoura Publications, Inc. 2001).

CHAPTER FIVE

1. Joel R. Reidenberg, "Technology and Internet Jurisdiction," *University of Pennsylvania Law Review* 153 (2005): 1951.

2. Since *Code* v1, there has been an extensive debate about whether government intervention will be needed to effect important public values. See, e.g., Thomas B. Nachbar, "Paradox and Structure: Relying on Government Regulation to Preserve the Internet's Unregulated Character," *Minnesota Law Review* 85 (2000): 215 (suggesting intervention needed); Neil Weinstock Netanel, "Cyberspace Self-Governance: A Skeptical View from Liberal Democratic Theory," *California Law Review* 88 (2000): 395 (surveying and emphasizing democratic deliberation); Jay P. Kesan, "Private Internet Governance," *Loyola University Chicago Law Journal* 35 (2003): 87 (surveying failed examples of private regulation); Thomas Schultz, "Does Online Dispute Resolution Need Governmental Intervention? The Case for Architectures of Control and Trust," *North Carolina Journal of Law and Technology* 6 (2004): 71; Carl Shapiro, "Will E-Commerce Erode Liberty?," *Harvard Business Review* (May-June 2000): 195. (optimistic about market's regulatory effect); Brett Frischmann, "Privatization and Commercialization of the Internet Infrastructure: Rethinking Market Intervention into Government and Government Intervention into the Market," *Columbia Science and Technology Law Review* 2 (2000/2001): 1 (supporting intervention); Cass R. Sunstein, "Code Comfort," *New Republic,* Jan. 10, 2002 (optimistic about market response); Henry H. Perritt, Jr., "Towards a Hybrid Regulatory Scheme for the Internet," *University of Chicago Legal Forum 215* (2001) (supporting gov't backed private solutions); Jay P. Kesan and Andres A. Gallo, "Optimizing Regulation of Electronic Commerce," *University of Cincinnati Law Review* 72 (2004): 1497 (brilliant integration of game theory to understand when intervention is required).

3. Michael Geist, "Cyberlaw 2.0," *Boston College Law Review* 44 (2003): 323, 332.

4. Transport for London, "Congestion Charging." Available at link #21; Center for Transportation Studies, "London's Congestion Charge Cuts Traffic Delays, Spurs Bus Use" (December 2004), available at link #22 and link #23; Transport for London, "London Congestion Charging Technology Trials." (February 2005), available at link #24.

5. See Katie Hafner and Matthew Lyon, *Where Wizards Stay Up Late: The Origins of the Internet* (New York: Simon and Schuster, 1996), 62–63.

6. CALEA authorized distribution of $500 million to cover modifications to telecommunications systems installed or deployed before January 1, 1995. That was estimated to be

about 25 percent of the total costs of the modification. House of Representatives, Subcommittee on Crime, Committee on the Judiciary, Testimony on the Implementation of CALEA. Wednesday, October 23, 1997, Testimony of RoyUSTA (available at link #25).

7. Susan P. Crawford, "Symposium, Law and the Information Society, Panel V: Responsibility and Liability on the Internet, Shortness of Vision: Regulatory Ambition in the Digital Age," 74 *Fordham Law Review* (2005): 695, 723–24.

8. Ibid., 720.

9. Susan P. Crawford, "Someone to Watch Over Me: Social Policies for the Internet" 37 (Cardozo Law School Legal Studies Research Paper, No. 129, 2006).

10. This is just what happened, Seventh Circuit Court of Appeals Chief Judge Richard Posner argues, when the Warren Court constitutionalized criminal procedure. To compensate for the increased difficulty in convicting a criminal, Congress radically increased criminal punishments. See Richard A. Posner, "The Cost of Rights: Implications for Central and Eastern Europe—and for the United States," *Tulsa Law Journal* 32 (1996): 1, 7–9. Professor William Stuntz has made a similar point. William J. Stuntz, "The Uneasy Relationship Between Criminal Procedure and Criminal Justice," *Yale Law Journal* 107 (1997): 1, 4. The Constitution, in this story, acted as an exogenous constraint to which Congress could adjust. If the protections of the Constitution increased, then Congress could compensate by increasing punishments.

11. Initially, the CALEA requirements extended to "facilities based" VOIP services only, though the push more recently is to extend it to all VOIP services. See Daniel J. Solove, Marc Rotenberg, and Paul M. Schwartz, *Information Privacy Law,* 2nd edition (New York: Aspen Publishers, 2006), they summarize the VOIP situation on pp. 287–88: "Voice over Internet Protocol (VoIP)."

12. See Federal Communications Commission, Further Notice of Proposed Rulemaking, Released November, 5 1998, at p. 25 ("In the matter of: Communications Assistance for Law Enforcement Act") ("J-STD-025 includes a 'location' parameter that would identify the location of a subject's 'mobile terminal' whenever this information is reasonably available at the intercept access point and its delivery to law enforcement is legally authorized. Location information would be available to the LEA irrespective of whether a call content channel or a call data channel was employed."). The FBI's desire to gather this information was challenged by civil liberties groups and industry associations. See *United States Telecom Association, et al. v. FCC,* 227 F.3d 450 (D.C. Cir. 2000). The Court permitted the cell tower information to be revealed, but only with a more substantial burden placed on the government.

13. See Center for Democracy and Technology, "FBI Seeks to Impose Surveillance Mandates on Telephone System; Balanced Objectives of 1994 Law Frustrated: Status Report," March 4, 1999, available at link #26.

14. Declan McCullagh, "ISP Snooping Gaining Support," CNET News, Apr. 14, 2006, available at link #27. On March 15, 2006, the European Parliament passed a directive concerning the obligations of publicly available communications services with respect to the retention of data. See Eur. Parl. Doc. (COD/2005/0182). Members of Congress have been mulling over similar legislation. See Anne Broache, "U.S. attorney general calls for 'reasonable' data retention," CNET News, Apr. 20, 2006, available at link #28.

15. Directive on the Retention of Data Generated or Processed in Connection with the Provision of Publicly Available electronic Communications Services or of Public Communications Networks and Amending Directive 2002/58/EC, available at link #29.

16. Declan McCullagh, "Bill Would Force Websites to Delete Personal Info," CNET News, Feb. 8, 2006, available at link #30.

17. For a good discussion of the Clipper controversy, see Laura J. Gurak, *Persuasion and Privacy in Cyberspace: The Online Protests over Lotus Marketplace and the Clipper Chip*

(New Haven: Yale University Press, 1997), 32–43. For a sample of various views, see Kirsten Scheurer, "The Clipper Chip: Cryptography Technology and the Constitution," *Rutgers Computer and Technology Law Journal* 21 (1995): 263; cf. Howard S. Dakoff, "The Clipper Chip Proposal: Deciphering the Unfounded Fears That Are Wrongfully Derailing Its Implementation," *John Marshall Law Review* 29 (1996): 475. "Clipper was adopted as a federal information-processing standard for voice communication" in 1994; see *Gurak, Persuasion and Privacy in Cyberspace,* 125.

18. See Electronic Frontier Foundation (EFF), *Cracking DES: Secrets of Encryption Research, Wiretap Politics, and Chip Design* (Sebastopol, Cal.: Electronic Frontier Foundation, 1998), ch. 1.

19. For a good summary of the Clipper scheme, see Baker and Hurst, *The Limits of Trust,* 15–18; A. Michael Froomkin, "The Metaphor Is the Key: Cryptography, the Clipper Chip, and the Constitution," *University of Pennsylvania Law Review* 143 (1995): 709, 752–59. For a more technical discussion, see Bruce Schneier, *Applied Cryptography: Protocols, Algorithms, and Source Code in C,* 2d ed. (New York: Wiley, 1996): 591–93.

20. See Richard Field, "1996: Survey of the Year's Developments in Electronic Cash Law and the Laws Affecting Electronic Banking in the United States," 46 *American University Law Review* (1997): 967, 993, n.192.

21. See A. Michael Froomkin, "It Came from Planet Clipper: The Battle over Cryptographic Key 'Escrow,'" *University of Chicago Legal Forum 1996* (1996): 15, 32.

22. Anick Jesdanun, "Attacks Renew Debate Over Encryption Software," *Chicago Tribune,* September 28, 2001, available at link #31.

23. Jay P. Kesan and Rajiv C. Shah, Shaping Code, 18 *Harvard Journal of Law and Technology* 319, 326–27 (2005).

24. Former Attorney General Richard Thornburgh, for example, has called a national ID card "an infringement on rights of Americans"; see Ann Devroy, "Thornburgh Rules Out Two Gun Control Options; Attorney General Objects to Registration Card for Gun Owners, National Identification Card," *Washington Post,* June 29, 1989, A41. The Immigration Reform and Control Act of 1986 (Public Law 99–603, 100 Stat 3359 [1986], 8 USC 1324a[c] [1988]) eschews it: "Nothing in this section shall be construed to authorize directly or indirectly, the issuance or use of national identification cards or the establishment of national identification cards." Given the power of the network to link data, however, this seems to me an empty protection. See also Real ID Act, Pub. L. No. 109–13, Title II §202 (2005). The Real ID Act requires citizens to go to the DMV in person, bringing with them several pieces of identification to the DMV, including birth certificates, and face consumers with higher fees and tougher background check. Supporters feel the act targets the link between terrorists, illegal immigrants, and identification standards.

25. Jack Goldsmith and Timothy Wu, "Digital Borders," *Legal Affairs,* Jan./Feb. 2006, 44.

26. Notice that this would be an effective end-run around the protections that the Court recognized in *Reno v. American Civil Liberties Union,* 117 SCt 2329 (1997). There are many "activities" on the Net that Congress could easily regulate (such as gambling). Regulation of these activities could require IDs before access to these activities would be permitted. To the extent that such regulation increases the incidence of IDs on the Net, other speech-related access conditions would become easier to justify.

27. Arthur Cordell and T. Ran Ide have proposed the consideration of a bit tax; see Arthur J. Cordell et al., *The New Wealth of Nations: Taxing Cyberspace* (Toronto: Between the Lines, 1997). Their arguments are compelling from the perspective of social justice and economics, but what they do not account for is the architecture that such a taxing system would require. A Net architected to meter a bit tax could be architected to meter just about anything.

28. Countries with such a requirement have included Argentina, Australia, Belgium, Greece, Italy, and Switzerland; see Richard L. Hasen, "Symposium: Law, Economics, and Norms: Voting Without Law?" *University of Pennsylvania Law Review* 144 (1996): 2135.

29. See the description in Scott Bradner, "The Internet Engineering Task Force," in *Open Sources: Voices from the Open Source Revolution,* edited by Chris DiBona et al. (Sebastopol, Cal.: O'Reilly and Associates, 1999).

30. Michael Froomkin makes a similar point: "Export control rules have had an effect on the domestic market for products with cryptographic capabilities such as e-mail, operating systems, and word processors. Largely because of the ban on export of strong cryptography, there is today no strong mass-market standard cryptographic product within the U.S. even though a considerable mathematical and programming base is fully capable of creating one"; "It Came from Planet Clipper," 19.

31. See "Network Associates and Key Recovery," available at link #32.

32. Cisco has developed products that incorporate the use of network-layer encryption through the IP Security (IPSec) protocol. For a brief discussion of IPSec, see Cisco Systems, Inc., "IP Security–IPSec Overview," available at link #33. For a more extensive discussion, see Cisco Systems, Inc., "Cisco IOS Software Feature: Network-Layer Encryption—White Paper"; Cisco Systems, Inc. "IPSec—White Paper," available at link #34; see also Dawn Bushaus, "Encryption Can Help ISPs Deliver Safe Services," *Tele.Com*, March 1, 1997; Beth Davis and Monua Janah, "Cisco Goes End-to-End," *Information Week,* February 24, 1997, 22.

33. See Internet Architectural Board statement on "private doorbell" encryption, available at link #35.

34. Little, but not nothing. Through conditional spending grants, the government was quite effective initially in increasing Net participation, and it was effective in resisting the development of encryption technologies; see Whitfield Diffie and Susan Eva Landau, *Privacy on the Line: The Politics of Wiretapping and Encryption* (Cambridge, Mass.: MIT Press, 1998). Steven Levy tells of a more direct intervention. When Richard Stallman refused to password-protect the MIT AI (artificial intelligence) machine, the Department of Defense threatened to take the machine off the Net unless the architectures were changed to restrict access. For Stallman, this was a matter of high principle; for the Department of Defense, it was business as usual; see Steven Levy, *Hackers: Heroes of the Computer Revolution* (Garden City, N.Y.: Anchor Press/Doubleday, 1984), 416–18.

35. On virtual private networks, see Richard Smith, *Internet Cryptography* (Boston: Addison-Wesley, 1997) chs. 6, 7; on biometric techniques for security, see *Trust in Cyberspace,* edited by Fred B. Schneider (Washington, D.C.: National Academy Press, 1999), 123–24, 133–34.

36. Jonathan L. Zittrain, "The Generative Internet," 119 *Harvard Law Review* 1974 (2006).

37. Ibid., 2010.

38. Ibid., 2012.

39. Ibid.

40. Ibid.

41. Ibid., 2011.

42. Ibid.

43. Uniting and Strengthening America by Providing Appropriate Tools Required to Intercept and Obstruct Terrorism (USA PATRIOT ACT) Act, Pub. L. No. 107–56, 155 STAT. 272 (2001); American Civil Liberties Union, *Seeking Truth From Justice: PATRIOT Propaganda—The Justice Department's Campaign to Mislead the Public About the USA PATRIOT Act* (American Civil Liberties Union, July 9, 2003).

44. Roberto Mangabeira Unger, *Social Theory: Its Situation and Its Task* (New York: Cambridge University Press, 1987).

45. In Bruce Ackerman, *Social Justice in the Liberal State* (New Haven: Yale University Press, 1980), the core analytic device is dialogue: every assertion of power is met with a demand for justification.

46. William J. Mitchell, *City of Bits: Space, Place, and the Infobahn"* (Cambridge, Mass.: MIT Press, 1996), 112.

47. David Brin, *The Transparent Society: Will Technology Force Us to Choose Between Privacy and Freedom?* (Boulder: Perseus, 1999), 324.

48. Though the plan remains uncertain. In June 2006, Google co-founder Sergey Brin expressed some doubts about Google's plans. See Thomas Crampton, "Google Is Voicing Some Doubt Over China," *International Herald Tribune,* June 7, 2006.

CHAPTER SIX

1. Mike Godwin, *Cyber Rights: Defending Free Speech in the Digital Age* (New York: Times Books, 1998), 15. See also Esther Dyson, *Release 2.0: A Design for Living in the Digital Age* (New York: Broadway Books, 1997), who asserts: "Used right, the Internet can be a powerful enabling technology fostering the development of communities because it supports the very thing that creates a community—human interaction" (32); see also Stephen Doheny-Farina, *The Wired Neighborhood* (New Haven, Conn.: Yale University Press, 1996), 121–37. For an important collection examining community in cyberspace, see Marc A. Smith and Peter Kollock, *Communities in Cyberspace* (New York: Routledge, 1999). The collection ranges across the social issues of community, including "social order and control," "collective action," "community structure and dynamics," and "identity." The same relationship between architecture and norms assumed in this chapter guides much of the analysis in Smith and Kollock's collection.

2. As I explored in *Code* v1, the newest "communitarian" on the Net might be business. A number of influential works have argued that the key to success with online businesses is the development of "virtual communities"; see, for example, Larry Downes and Chunka Mui, *Unleashing the Killer App: Digital Strategies for Market Dominance* (Boston: Harvard Business School Press, 1998), 101–9; John Hagel and Arthur G. Armstrong, Net Gain: Expanding Markets Through Virtual Communities (Boston: Harvard Business School Press, 1997). The explosion of essentially community based entities, such as Wikipedia and MySpace, in the time since confirms the insight of these authors.

3. For a detailed study of Internet demographics, see E-Consultancy, *Internet Statistics Compendium,* April 12, 2006, available at link #36.

4. For a great sense of how it was, see the articles by Rheingold, Barlow, Bruckman, and Ramo in part 4 of Richard Holeton, *Composing Cyberspace: Identity, Community, and Knowledge in the Electronic Age* (Boston: McGraw-Hill, 1998). Howard Rheingold's book (the first chapter of which is excerpted in Holeton's book) is also an early classic; see *The Virtual Community: Homesteading on the Electronic Frontier* (Reading, Mass.: Addison-Wesley, 1993). Stacy Horn's book is a brilliant text taken more directly from the interchange (and more) online; see *Cyberville: Clicks, Culture, and the Creation of an Online Town* (New York: Warner Books, 1998).

5. For an excellent description, see Jonathan Zittrain, "The Rise and Fall of Sysopdom," *Harvard Journal of Law and Technology* 10 (1997): 495.

6. As Steven Johnson puts it: "In theory, these are examples of architecture and urban planning, but in practice they are bound up in broader issues: each design decision echoes and amplifies a set of values, an assumption about the larger society that frames it"; *Interface Culture: How New Technology Transforms the Way We Create and Communicate* (San Francisco: Harper, 1997), 44. See also Nelson Goodman, "How Buildings Mean," in *Reconceptions in Phi-*

losophy and Other Arts and Sciences, edited by Nelson Goodman and Catherine Z. Elgin (London: Routledge, 1988), 31–48. The same insight applies to things as well as spaces. See Langdon Winner, "Do Artifacts Have Politics?," in *The Whale and the Reactor: A Search for Limits in an Age of High Technology* (Chicago: University of Chicago Press, 1986), 19–39. To say a space or thing has values, however, does not say it determines any particular result. Influences and agency are many.

7. Mark Stefik, *The Internet Edge,* 14–15.

8. Cf. Godwin, *Cyber Rights: Defending Free Speech in the Digital Age* (New York: Times Books, 1998): ("If you're face-to-face with someone, you're exposed to countless things over which the other person may have had no conscious control—hair color, say, or facial expressions. But when you're reading someone's posted ASCII message, everything you see is a product of that person's mind") 42; see also ibid., 44.

9. See Martha Minow, *Making All the Difference: Inclusion, Exclusion, and American Law* (Ithaca, N.Y.: Cornell University Press, 1990), 79–97.

10. See Laura J. Gurak, *Persuasion and Privacy in Cyberspace: The Online Protests over Lotus, Marketplace, and the Clipper Chip* (New Haven: Yale University Press, 1997), 12–16. Gurak notes that "pseudonyms, for example, can be used to mask the name of a speaker, so that often it is the ethos of the texts, not the character of the speaker, that does or does not convince others." Cf. Lori Kendall, "MUDder? I Hardly Know 'Er!: Adventures of a Feminist MUDder," in *Wired Women: Gender and New Realities in Cyberspace,* edited by Lynn Cherny and Elizabeth Reba Weise (Seattle: Seal Press, 1996), 207–233. Godwin describes another possibility, as the ASCII channel on the Net shuts down: "Then, perhaps, the world of ASCII communications will become a preserve for the edgy exchanges of tense text maniacs. Like me"; *Cyber Rights,* 45.

11. This is what economists would call a "separating equilibrium": "players of different types adopt different strategies and thereby allow an uninformed player to draw inferences about an informed player's type from that player's actions"; Douglas G. Baird, Robert H. Gertner, and Randal C. Picker, *Game Theory and the Law* (Cambridge, Mass.: Harvard University Press, 1994), 314. William Mitchell argues that the advance back to synchronous communication is not necessarily an advantage: "As much more efficient asynchronous communications systems have become commonplace, though, we have seen that strict synchrony is not always desirable; controlled asynchrony may have its advantages"; *City of Bits,* 5–16.

12. On making the Web accessible, see Judy Brewer and Daniel Dardailler, "Web Accessibility Initiative (WAI)," available at link #37; cf. "Note: Facial Discrimination: Extending Handicap Law to Employment Discrimination on the Basis of Physical Appearance," *Harvard Law Review* 100 (1987): 2035.

13. Dawn C. Nunziato, "The Death of the Public Forum in Cyberspace," *Berkeley Technology Law Journal* 20 (2005): 1115, 1125.

14. See AOL, "About the Company: Profile," available at link #38, and now available at link #39.

15. Nunziato, "The Death of the Public Forum in Cyberspace," 1125.

16. See Kara Swisher, Aol.com: How Steve Case Beat Bill Gates, Nailed the Netheads, and Made Millions in the War for the Web (New York: Times Business, 1998), 65.

17. As stated in AOL's Terms of Service (TOS): "As an AOL member you are required to follow our TOS no matter where you are on the Internet." Some of the other terms of service include the following rules: "Language: Mild expletives and nonsexual anatomical references are allowed, but strong vulgar language, crude or explicit sexual references, hate speech, etc., are not. If you see it, report it at Keyword: Notify AOL. Nudity: Photos containing revealing attire or limited nudity in a scientific or artistic context are okay in some places (not all). Partial or full frontal nudity is not okay. If you see it, report it at Keyword: Notify AOL. Sex/Sen-

suality: There is a difference between affection and vulgarity. There is also a difference between a discussion of the health or emotional aspects of sex using appropriate language, and more crude conversations about sex. The former is acceptable, the latter is not. For example, in a discussion about forms of cancer, the words breast or testicular would be acceptable, but slang versions of those words would not be acceptable anywhere. Violence and Drug Abuse: Graphic images of humans being killed, such as in news accounts, may be acceptable in some areas, but blood and gore, gratuitous violence, etc., are not acceptable. Discussions about coping with drug abuse in health areas are okay, but discussions about or depictions of illegal drug abuse that imply it is acceptable are not."

18. See Amy Harmon, "Worries About Big Brother at America Online," *New York Times,* January 31, 1999, 1.

19. Just as version 2 of this book was being completed, AOL switched to a free online service. The full scope of the change that this will involve is not yet clear. I have therefore framed this discussion in the past tense.

20. Swisher, *Aol.com,* 314–15. Available at link #40.

21. Ibid., 96–97.

22. See Robert C. Post, *Constitutional Domains: Democracy, Community, Management* (Cambridge, Mass.: Harvard University Press, 1995), 199–267.

23. See *CyberPromotions, Inc. v. America Online, Inc.,* 948 FSupp 436 (EDPa 1996) (holding that a company has no free speech right under the United States, Pennsylvania, or Virginia Constitutions to send unsolicited e-mail over the Internet to a competitor's customers).

24. Nunziato, "The Death of the Public Forum in Cyberspace," 1121.

25. Ibid., 1122.

26. E-mail from Alan Rothman to David R. Johnson (February 5, 2006) (on file with author): "When CC permanently went offline in June 1999, several members had established two new forums over on in anticipation of this on Delphi called Counsel Cafe and Counsel Politics. The end was approaching and this was viewed as a virtual lifeboat for the devoted and cohesive community that had thrived on CC. About 100 CC survivors washed up together to settle in these new forums. Both were established as being private but members were allowed to invite friends."

27. Ibid.

28. Ibid.

29. See Elizabeth Reid, "Hierarchy and Power: Social Control in Cyberspace," in *Communities in Cyberspace,* edited by Marc A. Smith and Peter Kollock (London: Routledge, 1999), 109.

30. See Josh Quittner, "Johnny Manhattan Meets the Furry Muckers," *Wired* (March 1994): 92, available at link #41.

31. See Julian Dibbell, "A Rape in Cyberspace," *Village Voice,* December 23, 1993, 36, 37, available at link #42.

32. Ibid.

33. In particular, see Dibbell's extraordinary *My Tiny Life: Crime and Passion in a Virtual World* (London: Fourth Estate, 1998).

34. Ibid., 13–14.

35. If anything, the sexuality of the space invited adolescent responses by adolescents; see Scott Bukatman, *Terminal Identity: The Virtual Subject in Postmodern Science Fiction* (Durham, N.C.: Duke University Press, 1993), 326. On MOOs in particular, see Dibbell, *My Tiny Life.* The challenge for the community was to construct norms that would avoid these responses without destroying the essential flavor of the space.

36. Dibbell, *My Tiny Life,* 24–25.

37. See Rebecca Spainhower, *"Virtually Inevitable": Real Problems in Virtual Communities* (Evanston, Ill.: Northwestern University Press, 1994), available at link #43.

38. Ibid.

39. For a rich account of both the democracy and how it functions, and the implications for self-regulation with a MUD, see Jennifer Mnookin, "Virtual(ly) Law: The Emergence of Law on LambdaMOO," *Journal of Computer-Mediated Communication* 2 (1996): 1.

40. Hafner and Lyon, *Where Wizards Stay Up Late,* 216. "Flaming" is e-mail or other electronic communication that expresses exaggerated hostility; see Gurak, *Persuasion and Privacy in Cyberspace,* 88.

41. Mnookin, "Virtual(ly) Law," 14.

42. One student of mine studied this behavior and concluded that the difference was significant. That study was limited, however, by a relatively small sample. On the question more generally, Gurak reaches a different conclusion about whether cyberspace remedies gender imbalances; *Persuasion and Privacy in Cyberspace,* 104–13.

43. Audio Tape: Interview with Julian Dibbell (1/6/06) (on file with author).

44. MMOGCHART.com Home Page, available at link #44.

45. Audio Tape: Interview with Philip Rosedale (1/13/06) (on file with author).

46. Castronova, *Synthetic Worlds,* 2.

47. Julian Dibbell, "Dragon Slayers or Tax Evaders?," *Legal Affairs* (Jan./Feb. 2006): 47.

48. Castronova, *Synthetic Worlds,* 19.

49. Audio Tape: Interview with Philip Rosedale (1/16/06) (on file with author).

50. Lawrence Lessig, *Free Culture: The Nature and Future of Creativity* (New York: Penguin, 2004), 2–3, discussing *United States v. Causby,* U.S. 328 (1946): 256, 261. The Court did find that there could be a "taking" if the government's use of its land effectively destroyed the value of the Causbys' land. This example was suggested to me by Keith Aoki's wonderful piece, "(Intellectual) Property and Sovereignty: Notes Toward a Cultural Geography of Authorship," *Stanford Law Review* 48 (1996): 1293, 1333. See also Paul Goldstein, *Real Property* (Minneola, N.Y.: Foundation Press, 1984), 1112–13.

51. St. George Tucker, *Blackstone's Commentaries 3* (South Hackensack, N.J.: Rothman Reprints, 1969), 18.

52. J. D. Lasica, *Darknet: Hollywood's War Against the Digital Generation* (New York: Wiley, 2005), 248.

53. Ibid., 246.

54. See Jerome H. Saltzer et al., "End-to-End Arguments in System Design," in *Integrated Broadband Networks,* edited by Amit Bhargava (New York: Elsevier Science Publishing Co., 1991), 30.

55. Susan P. Crawford, "Symposium, Law and the Information Society, Panel V: Responsibility and Liability on the Internet, Shortness of Vision: Regulatory Ambition in the Digital Age," *Fordham Law Review* 74 (2005) 695, 700–701.

56. Audio Tape: Interview with Philip Rosedale (1/13/06) (on file with author).

57. See Lessig, *Free Culture: The Nature and Future of Creativity,* 330, n.9: Fisher's proposal is very similar to Richard Stallman's proposal for DAT. Unlike Fisher's, Stallman's proposal would not pay artists directly proportionally, though more popular artists would get more than the less popular. See link #45.

58. See Audio Home Recording Act, 17 USC 1002 (1994) (requiring the serial copy management system); see also U.S. Department of Commerce, *Intellectual Property and the National Information Infrastructure: Report of the Working Group on Intellectual Property Rights* (Washington, D.C.: Information Infrastructure Task Force, 1995), 179, 189–90.

59. See 47 CFR 15.120; see also Telecommunications Act of 1996 Pub.L. 104–104, 551, 110 Stat. 56, 139–42 (1996), 47 USC 303 (1998) (providing for study and implementation of video blocking devices and rating systems).

60. The consequence of an efficient v-chip on most televisions would be the removal of the standard justification for regulating content on broadcasting. If users can self-filter, then the

FCC need not do it for them; see Peter Huber, *Law and Disorder in Cyberspace: Abolish the FCC and Let Common Law Rule the Telecosm* (New York: Oxford University Press, 1997), 172–73.

61. Digital Millenium Copyright Act, 17 U.S.C. §§ 512, 1201–1205, 1201(a)(2), 1201(b)(1)(A) (1998).

62. See Electronic Frontier Foundation, "DVD-CCA v. Bunner and DVD-CCA v. Pavlovich" available at link #46; *DVD Copy Control Association, Inc. v. Bunner,* 31 Cal. 4th 864 (Cal. 2003); *Pavlovich v. Superior Court,* 29 Cal. 4th 262 (Cal. 2002); *Universal Studios, Inc. v. Corley,* 273 F.3d 429 (2d Cir. 2001).

63. Archive of developments involving Dmitri Sklyarov, his arrest, and trial, available at link #47.

64. Electronic Frontier Foundation, "Unintended Consequences: Seven Years Under the DMCA," available at link #48.

65. See Chamberlain Group, Inc. v. Skylink Technologies, Inc., 544 U.S. 923 (2005).

66. Crawford, "Symposium, Law and the Information Society, Panel V," 695, 710.

67. The most significant cost is on innovation. If the broadcast flag requirement reaches any device capable of demodulating digital television, then its requirement reaches any digital device on the network. It would be the first time network applications would have to comply with a technical mandate of such breadth, and it would be an unmanageable burden for open source and free software deployments.

68. R. Polk Wagner, *On Software Regulation, Southern California Law Review* 78 (2005): 457, 470–71. See also Joel R. Reidenberg, "Technology and Internet Jurisdiction," *University of Pennsylvania Law Review* 153 (2005): 1951; Joshua A. T. Fairfield, "Cracks in the Foundation: The New Internet Legislation's Hidden Threat to Privacy and Commerce," *Arizona State Law Journal* 36 (2004): 1193 (arguing Congress should be more jurisdictionally exceptional and less content exceptional in its regulation of cyberspace).

69. Timothy Wu, "When Code Isn't Law," *Virginia Law Review* 89 (2003): 679, 707–8.

70. Ibid., 682.

CHAPTER SEVEN

1. Or more precisely, against a certain form of government regulation. The more powerful libertarian arguments against regulation in cyberspace are advanced, for example, by Peter Huber in *Law and Disorder in Cyberspace.* Huber argues against agency regulation and in favor of regulation by the common law. See also Thomas Hazlett in "The Rationality of U.S. Regulation of the Broadcast Spectrum," *Journal of Law and Economics* 33 (1990): 133, 133–39. For a lawyer, it is hard to understand precisely what is meant by "the common law." The rules of the common law are many, and the substantive content has changed. There is a common law process, which lawyers like to mythologize, in which judges make policy decisions in small spaces against the background of binding precedent. It might be this that Huber has in mind, and if so, there are, of course, benefits to this system. But as he plainly understands, it is a form of regulation even if it is constituted differently.

2. The primary examples are the convictions under the Espionage Act of 1917; see, for example, *Schenck v. United States,* 249 US 47 (1919) (upholding conviction for distributing a leaflet attacking World War I conscription); *Frohwerk v. United States,* 249 US 204 (1919) (upholding conviction based on newspaper alleged to cause disloyalty); *Debs v. United States,* 249 US 211 (1919) (conviction upheld for political speech said to cause insubordination and disloyalty).

3. See, for example, the work of John R. Commons, *Legal Foundations of Capitalism* (1924), 296–98, discussed in Herbert Hovenkamp, *Enterprise and American Law, 1836–1937*

(Cambridge, Mass.: Harvard University Press, 1991), 235; see also John R. Commons, *Institutional Economics: Its Place in Political Economy* (1934) (New Brunswick, N.J.: Transaction Publishers reprint, 1990).

4. The general idea is that the tiny corrections of space enforce a discipline, and that this discipline is an important regulation. Such theorizing is a tiny part of the work of Michel Foucault; see *Discipline and Punish: The Birth of the Prison* (New York: Vintage, 1979), 170–77, though his work generally inspires this perspective. It is what Oscar Gandy speaks about in *The Panoptic Sort: A Political Economy of Personal Information* (Boulder: Westview Press, 1993), 23. David Brin makes the more general point that I am arguing—that the threat to liberty is broader than a threat by the state; see *The Transparent Society,* 110.

5. See, for example, *The Built Environment: A Creative Inquiry into Design and Planning,* edited by Tom J. Bartuska and Gerald L. Young (Menlo Park, Cal.: Crisp Publications, 1994); *Preserving the Built Heritage: Tools for Implementation,* edited by J. Mark Schuster et al. (Hanover, N.H.: University Press of New England, 1997). In design theory, the notion I am describing accords with the tradition of Andres Duany and Elizabeth Plater-Zyberk; see, for example, William Lennertz, "Town-Making Fundamentals," in *Towns and Town-Making Principles,* edited by Andres Duany and Elizabeth Plater-Zyberk (New York: Rizzoli, 1991): "The work of . . . Duany and . . . Plater-Zyberk begins with the recognition that design affects behavior. [They] see the structure and function of a community as interdependent. Because of this, they believe a designer's decisions will permeate the lives of residents not just visually but in the way residents live. They believe design structures functional relationships, quantitatively and qualitatively, and that it is a sophisticated tool whose power exceeds its cosmetic attributes" (21).

6. Elsewhere I've called this the "New Chicago School"; see Lawrence Lessig, "The New Chicago School," *Journal of Legal Studies* 27 (1998): 661. It is within the "tools approach" to government action (see John de Monchaux and J. Mark Schuster, "Five Things to Do," in Schuster, *Preserving the Built Heritage,* 3), but it describes four tools whereas Schuster describes five. I develop the understanding of the approach in the Appendix to this book.

7. These technologies are themselves affected, no doubt, by the market. Obviously, these constraints could not exist independently of each other but affect each other in significant ways.

8. Lasica, *Darknet,* 16. See also Lior Jacob Strahilevitz, "Charismatic Code, Social Norms and the Emergence of Cooperation on the File-Swapping Networks," 89 *Virginia Law Review* (2003), 505 (arguing that charismatic code creates an illusion of reciprocity that accounts for why people contribute to a filesharing network).

9. Jay Kesan has offered a related, but more expansive analysis. See Jay P. Kesan and Rajiv C. Shah, "Shaping Code," *Harvard Journal of Law and Technology* 18 (2005): 319, 338.

10. See Michelle Armond, "Regulating Conduct on the Internet: State Internet Regulation and the Dormant Commerce Clause," *Berkeley Technology Law Journal* 17 (2002): 379, 380.

11. See, for example, the policy of the Minnesota attorney general on the jurisdiction of Minnesota over people transmitting gambling information into the state; available at link #49.

12. See, for example, *Playboy Enterprises v. Chuckleberry Publishing, Inc.,* 939 FSupp 1032 (SDNY 1996); *United States v. Thomas,* 74 F3d 701 (6th Cir 1996); *United States v. Miller,* 166 F3d 1153 (11th Cir 1999); *United States v. Lorge,* 166 F3d 516 (2d Cir 1999); *United States v. Whiting,* 165 F3d 631 (8th Cir 1999); *United States v. Hibbler,* 159 F3d 233 (6th Cir 1998); *United States v. Fellows,* 157 F3d 1197 (9th Cir 1998); *United States v. Simpson,* 152 F3d 1241 (10th Cir 1998); *United States v. Hall,* 142 F3d 988 (7th Cir 1998); *United States v. Hockings,* 129 F3d 1069 (9th Cir 1997); *United States v. Lacy,* 119 F3d 742 (9th Cir 1997); *United States v. Smith,* 47 MJ 588 (CrimApp 1997); *United States v. Ownby,* 926 FSupp 558 (WDVa 1996).

13. See Julian Dibbell, "A Rape in Cyberspace," *Village Voice,* December 23, 1993, 36.

14. Norms are something different—more directly regulating user behavior. See Daniel Benoliel, *Technological Standards, Inc.: Rethinking Cyberspace Regulative Epistemology*, 92 *California Law Review* 1069, 1077 (2004).

15. See, for example, "AOL Still Suffering but Stock Price Rises," *Network Briefing,* January 31, 1997; David S. Hilzenrath, "'Free' Enterprise, Online Style; AOL, CompuServe, and Prodigy Settle FTC Complaints," *Washington Post,* May 2, 1997, G1; "America Online Plans Better Information About Price Changes," *Wall Street Journal,* May 29, 1998, B2; see also Swisher, *Aol.com,* 206–8.

16. USENET postings can be anonymous; see Henry Spencer and David Lawrence, Managing USENET (Sebastopol, Cal.: O'Reilly and Associates, 1998), 366–67.

17. Web browsers make this information available, both in real time and archived in a cookie file; see link #50. They also permit users to turn this tracking feature off.

18. PGP is a program to encrypt messages that is offered both commercially and free.

19. Encryption, for example, is illegal in some international contexts; see Baker and Hurst, *The Limits of Trust,* 130–36.

20. Mitchell, *City of Bits,* 159.

21. See Ethan Katsh, "Software Worlds and the First Amendment," 335, 340. "If a comparison to the physical world is necessary, one might say that the software designer is the architect, the builder, and the contractor, as well as the interior decorator."

22. See *Rummel v. Estelle,* 445 US 263, 274 n.11 (1980).

23. Interestingly—and again, a reason to see the future of regulation talk located elsewhere—this is not true of architects. An example is the work of John de Monchaux and J. Mark Schuster. In their essay "Five Things to Do" and in the collection that essay introduces, *Preserving the Built Heritage,* they describe the "five and only five things that governments can do—five distinct tools that they can use—to implement their" policies (4–5): ownership and operation (the state may own the resource); regulation (of either individuals or institutions); incentives; property rights; information. Monchaux and Schuster's five tools map in a complex way on the structure I have described, but significantly, we share a view of regulation as a constant trade-off between tools.

24. See, for example, James C. Carter, *The Provinces of the Written and the Unwritten Law* (New York: Banks and Brothers, 1889), who argues that the common law cannot be changed (38–41).

25. See, for example, the discussion of wage fund theory in Hovenkamp, *Enterprise and American Law,* 193–96.

26. For a fascinating account of the coming of age of the idea that the natural environment might be tamed to a productive and engineered end, see John M. Barry, *Rising Tide: The Great Mississippi Flood of 1927 and How It Changed America* (New York: Simon and Schuster, 1997).

27. As Roberto Unger puts it, "Modern social thought was born proclaiming that society is made and imagined, that it is a human artifact rather than the expression of an underlying natural order"; *Social Theory,* 1.

28. The idea of a free market was the obsession of the realists, especially Robert Hale; see Barbara H. Fried, *The Progressive Assault on Laissez-Faire: Robert Hale and the First Law and Economics Movement* (Cambridge, Mass.: Harvard University Press, 1998): "Economic life, like Clark's moral market, was constituted by a regime of property and contract rights that were neither spontaneously occurring nor self-defining, but were rather the positive creation of the state" (2–3). For a modern retelling, see Cass R. Sunstein, *The Partial Constitution* (Cambridge, Mass.: Harvard University Press, 1993), 51–53.

29. Americans with Disabilities Act (ADA) of 1990, 42 USC §§ 12101 et seq. (1994).

30. See Alain Plessis, *The Rise and Fall of the Second Empire, 1852–1871* (1979) translated by Jonathan Mandelbaum (English-language edition, New York: Cambridge University Press,

1985), 121; "Haussmann, Baron Georges-Eugène," in *Encyclopedia Britannica*, 5th ed., (1992). Steven Johnson criticizes other aspects of the change in *Interface Culture*, 63–64.

31. See Robert A. Caro, *The Power Broker: Robert Moses and the Fall of New York* (New York: Alfred A. Knopf, 1974), 318.

32. Ralph Nader, *Unsafe at Any Speed: The Designed-In Dangers of the American Automobile* (New York: Grossman, 1965), xciii.

33. See Neal Kumar Katyal, "Architecture as Crime Control," 111 *Yale Law Journal* 1039 (2002).

34. Ibid., 1047.

35. Ibid., 1048.

36. Brin, *The Transparent Society*, 293.

37. Consider civil rights in the American South. During the legislative hearings on the Civil Rights Act of 1964, supporters of the bill called before the committee white, southern employers and business owners whose discrimination against blacks was the prime target of the legislation. Some of these employers and businessmen supported the bill because business would improve: The labor pool would increase, causing wages to decrease, and the demand for services would increase—so long, that is, as whites did not shift their custom. This last point is what set the stage for business support for the Civil Rights Act. What business leaders feared was the retaliation of whites against their voluntary efforts to integrate. The Civil Rights Act changed the context to make discrimination against blacks illegal. The businessman could then—without fear of the retaliation of whites—hire or serve a black because of either his concern for the status of blacks or his concern to obey the law. By creating this ambiguity, the law reduced the symbolic costs of hiring blacks. This example demonstrates how law can change norms without government having control over the norms. In this case, the norm of accommodating blacks was changed by giving it a second meaning—the norm of simply obeying the law; see Lessig, "The Regulation of Social Meaning," 965–67.

38. Thurgood Marshall, Esq., oral argument on behalf of respondents, *Cooper v. Aaron*, 358 US 1 (1958) (no. 1), in *Fifty-four Landmark Briefs and Arguments of the Supreme Court of the United States: Constitutional Law*, edited by Philip B. Kurland and Gerhard Casper (Washington, D.C.: University Publications of America, 1975), 533, 713.

39. See, for example, Dyson, *Release 2.0:* "Government can play a divisive role vis-à-vis communities. Often, the more government provides, the less community members themselves contribute" (43); in "The Regulation of Groups: The Influence of Legal and Nonlegal Sanctions on Collective Action" (*University of Chicago Law Review* 63 [1996]: 133), Eric A. Posner argues that government help to a community can undermine the community.

40. R. Polk Wagner, "On Software Regulation," *Southern California Law Review* 78 (2005): 457, 487.

41. Ibid., 474.

42. Ibid., 465.

43. Cass Sunstein points to seatbelt law as a hypothetical of "government regulation permit[ing] people to express preferences by using the shield of the law to lessen the risk that private actors will interfere with the expression [through normative censure]"; "Legal Interference with Private Preferences," *University of Chicago Law Review* 53 (1986): 1129, 1145. Alternatively, seatbelt laws have been used as the factual basis for critiques of norm sponsorship as ineffective and no substitute for direct regulation; see Robert S. Alder and R. David Pittle, "Cajolery or Command: Are Education Campaigns an Adequate Substitute for Regulation?" *Yale Journal on Regulation* 1 (1984): 159, 171–78. However, the observations may have been premature. John C. Wright, commenting on television's normative content, claims that "we have won the battle on seatbelts, just by a bunch of people getting together and saying, 'It is indeed macho to put on a seatbelt. It is macho and it is smart and it is manly and it is also feminine and smart and

savvy and charming to put on a seatbelt'"; Charles W. Gusewelle et al., "Round Table Discussion: Violence in the Media," *Kansas Journal of Law and Public Policy* 4 (1995): 39, 47.

44. The analysis here was in part suggested by Minow, *Making All the Difference*.

45. See Tracey L. Meares, "Social Organization and Drug Law Enforcement," *American Criminal Law Review* 35 (1998): 191.

46. Eric Posner ("The Regulation of Groups") points to contexts within which government action may have had this effect.

47. See Tracey L. Meares, "Charting Race and Class Differences in Attitudes Toward Drug Legalization and Law Enforcement: Lessons for Federal Criminal Law," *Buffalo Criminal Law Review* 1 (1997): 137.

48. In the mid-1970s the U.S. government sponsored a campaign to spray paraquat (a herbicide that causes lung damage to humans) on the Mexican marijuana crop. This sparked a public outcry that resulted in congressional suspension of funding in 1978. However, following a congressional amendment in 1981, paraquat spraying was used on the domestic marijuana crop during the 1980s. The publicity surrounding the use of paraquat in Mexico is generally believed to have created a boom in the domestic marijuana industry and also an increase in the popularity of cocaine during the 1980s. See generally Michael Isikoff, "DEA Finds Herbicides in Marijuana Samples," *Washington Post*, July 26, 1989, 17. In "Drug Diplomacy and the Supply-Side Strategy: A Survey of United States Practice" (*Vanderbilt Law Review* 43 [1990]: 1259, 1275 n.99), Sandi R. Murphy gives a full history of the laws passed relevant to paraquat; see also "A Cure Worse Than the Disease?," *Time*, August 29, 1983, 20.

49. *Roe v. Wade*, 410 US 113 (1973).

50. *Rust v. Sullivan*, 500 US 173 (1991).

51. *Maher v. Roe*, 432 US 464 (1977).

52. *Hodgson v. Minnesota*, 497 US 417 (1990).

53. This distinction between "direct" and "indirect" regulation, of course, has a long and troubled history in philosophy as well as in law. Judith J. Thomson describes this difference in her distinction between the trolley driver who must run over one person to save five and the surgeon who may not harvest the organs from one healthy person to save five dying people; see "The Trolley Problem," *Yale Law Journal* 94 (1985): 1395, 1395–96. This difference is also known as the "double effect doctrine," discussed in Philippa Foot, "The Problem of Abortion and the Doctrine of the Double Effect," in *Virtues and Vices and Other Essays in Moral Philosophy* (Berkeley: University of California Press, 1978), 19. See also Thomas J. Bole III, "The Doctrine of Double Effect: Its Philosophical Viability," *Southwest Philosophy Review* 7 (1991): 91; Frances M. Kamm, "The Doctrine of Double Effect: Reflections on Theoretical and Practical Issues," *Journal of Medicine and Philosophy* 16 (1991): 571; Warren Quinn, "Actions, Intentions, and Consequences: The Doctrine of Double Effect," *Philosophy and Public Affairs* 18 (1989): 334. The trouble in these cases comes when a line between them must be drawn; here I do not need to draw any such line.

54. Richard Craswell suggests other examples making the same point: The government could (a) regulate product quality or safety directly or (b) disclose information about different products' quality or safety ratings, in the hope that manufacturers would then have an incentive to compete to improve those ratings; the government could (a) allow an industry to remain monopolized and attempt directly to regulate the price the monopolist charged or (b) break up the monopolist into several competing firms, in the hope that competition would then force each to a more competitive price; the government could (a) pass regulations directly requiring corporations to do various things that would benefit the public interest or (b) pass regulations requiring that corporate boards of directors include a certain number of "independent" representatives, in the hope that the boards would then decide for themselves to act more consistently with the public interest.

55. See *New York v. United States*, 505 US 144 (1992).

56. Lee Tien identifies other important problems with architectural regulation in "Architectural Regulation and the Evolution of Social Norms," *International Journal of Communications Law and Policy* 9 (2004): 1.

57. Aida Torres, "The Effects of Federal Funding Cuts on Family Planning Services, 1980–1983," *Family Planning Perspectives* 16 (1984): 134, 135, 136.

58. *Rust v. Sullivan*, USNY (1990) WL 505726, reply brief, *7: "The doctor cannot explain the medical safety of the procedure, its legal availability, or its pressing importance to the patient's health."

59. See *Madsen v. Women's Health Center, Inc.*, 512 US 753, 785 (1994) (Justice Antonin Scalia concurring in the judgment in part and dissenting in part: "Today's decision . . . makes it painfully clear that no legal rule or doctrine is safe from ad hoc nullification by this Court when an occasion for its application arises in a case involving state regulation of abortion" [quoting *Thornburgh v. American College of Obstetricians and Gynecologists*, 476 US 747, 814 (1986) (Justice Sandra Day O'Connor dissenting)]).

60. *Shelley v. Kraemer*, 334 US 1 (1948).

61. See Herman H. Long and Charles S. Johnson, *People Versus Property: Race-Restrictive Covenants in Housing* (Nashville: Fisk University Press, 1947), 32–33. Douglas S. Massey and Nancy A. Denton point out that the National Association of Real Estate Brokers adopted an article in its 1924 code of ethics stating that "a Realtor should never be instrumental in introducing into a neighborhood . . . members of any race or nationality . . . whose presence will clearly be detrimental to property values in that neighborhood" (citing Rose Helper, *Racial Policies and Practices of Real Estate Brokers* [1969], 201); they also note that the Fair Housing Authority advocated the use of race-restrictive covenants until 1950 (citing Kenneth T. Jackson, *Crabgrass Frontier: the Suburbanization of the United States* [1985], 208); *American Apartheid: Segregation and the Making of the Under Class* (Cambridge, Mass.: Harvard University Press, 1993), 37, 54.

62. See Massey and Denton, *American Apartheid*.

63. Michael Froomkin points to the Clipper chip regulations as another example. By using the standards-setting process for government purchases, the federal government could try to achieve a standard for encryption without adhering to the Administrative Procedure Act. "A stroke of bureaucratic genius lay at the heart of the Clipper strategy. Congress had not, and to this date has not, given the executive branch the power to control the private use of encryption. Congress has not even given the executive the power to set up an escrow system for keys. In the absence of any formal authority to prevent the adoption of unescrowed cryptography, Clipper's proponents hit upon the idea of using the government's power as a major consumer of cryptographic products to rig the market. If the government could not prevent the public from using nonconforming products, perhaps it could set the standard by purchasing and deploying large numbers of escrowed products"; "It Came from Planet Clipper," 15, 24, 1–33.

64. See *The Industry Standard*, available at link #51.

65. See "Legal Eagle" (letter to the editor), *The Industry Standard*, April 26, 1999 (emphasis added).

CHAPTER EIGHT

1. Castronova, *Synthetic Worlds*, 207.

2. Declan McCullagh, "It's Time for the Carnivore to Spin," *Wired News*, July 7, 2000, available at link #52.

3. Ann Harrison, "Government Error Exposes Carnivore Investigators; ACLU Blasts Team for Close Ties to Administration," *Computerworld*, October 5, 2000, available at link #53. This concern was strongly criticized. See Center for Democracy and Technology, "Cryptography," available at link #54.

4. The Mitre Corporation did examine a related question for the military. See Carolyn A. Kenwood, *A Business Case Study of Open Source Software* (Mitre Corporation: 2001).

5. See *Bush v. Gore*, 531 U.S. 98, 126 (2000) (Stevens, J., dissenting).

6. Di Franco et al., "Small Vote Manipulations Can Swing Elections," *Communications of the ACM*, Volume 47, Number 10 (2004), 43–45, available at link #55.

7. For an extraordinarily troubling account that raises much more than suspicion, see Robert F. Kennedy, Jr., "Was the 2004 Election Stolen?," *Rolling Stone* (June 2006).

8. David E. Ross, *PGP: Backdoors and Key Escrow*, 2003, available at link #56.

9. Craig Hunt, *TCP/IP: Network Administration* (Sebastopol, Calif.: O'Reilly and Associates, 1997), 1–22, 6, 8; Loshin, *TCP/IP: Clearly Explained*, 13–17.

10. There is no standard reference model for the TCP/IP layers. Hunt refers to the four layers as the "network access," "internet," "host-to-host transport," and "application" layers; *TCP/IP: Network Administration*, 9. Loshin uses the terminology I follow in the text; *TCP/IP: Clearly Explained*, 13–17. Despite the different moniker, the functions performed in each of these layers are consistent. As with any protocol stack model, data are "passed down the stack when it is being sent to the network, and up the stack when it is being received from the network." Each layer "has its own independent data structures," with one layer "unaware of the data structures used by" other layers; Hunt, *TCP/IP: Network Administration*, 9.

11. Hunt, TCP/IP: Network Administration, 9; Loshin, TCP/IP: Clearly Explained, 13–17.

12. As Hafner and Lyon explain: "The general view was that any protocol was a potential building block, and so the best approach was to define simple protocols, each limited in scope, with the expectation that any of them might someday be joined or modified in various unanticipated ways. The protocol design philosophy adopted by the NWG [network working group] broke ground for what came to be widely accepted as the 'layered' approach to protocols"; *Where Wizards Stay Up Late*, 147.

13. The fights over encryption at the link level, for example, are fights over the TCP/IP protocols. Some within the network industry have proposed that encryption be done at the gateways, with a method for dumping plain text at the gateways if there were proper legal authority—a kind of "private doorbell" for resolving the encryption controversy; see Elizabeth Kaufman and Roszel Thomsen II, "The Export of Certain Networking Encryption Products Under ELAs," available at link #57. This has been opposed by the Internet Architectural Board (IAB) as inconsistent with the "end-to-end" architecture of the Internet; see IAB statement on "private doorbell" encryption, available at link #58.

Since *Code* v1, there has been an explosion of excellent work extending "layer theory." Perhaps the best academic work in this has been Lawrence B. Solum and Minn Chung, "The Layers Principle: Internet Architecture and the Law," University of San Diego Public Law Research Paper No. 55, available at link #59. Solum and Chung have used the idea of Internet layers to guide regulatory policy, locating appropriate and inappropriate targets for regulatory intervention. This is an example of some of the best work integrating technology and legal policy, drawing interesting and important implications from the particular, often counter intuitive, interaction between the two. I introduce "layers" in my own work in *The Future of Ideas: The Fate of the Commons in a Connected World* (New York: Random House, 2001), 23–25. See also Yochai Benkler, *The Wealth of Networks: How Social Production Transforms Markets and Freedom* (New Haven: Yale University Press, 2006), 391–97. For other very useful work extending this analysis, see Craig McTaggart, "A Layered Approach to Internet Legal Analysis," *McGill Law Journal* 48 (2003): 571; Thomas A. Lane, "Of Hammers and Saws: The

Toolbox of Federalism and Sources of Law for the Web," *New Mexico Law Review* 33 (2003): 115; Jane Bailey, "Of Mediums and Metaphors: How a Layered Methodology Might Contribute to Constitutional Analysis of Internet Content Regulation," *Manitoba Law Journal* 30 (2004): 197.

14. See Hafner and Lyon, *Where Wizards Stay up Late,* 174.

15. A 1994 HTML manual lists twenty-nine different browsers; see Larry Aronson, *HTML Manual of Style* (Emeryville, Cal.: Ziff-Davis Press, 1994), 124–26.

16. Source code is the code that programmers write. It sometimes reads like a natural language, but it is obviously not. A program is (ordinarily) written in source code, but to be run it must be converted into a language the computer can process. This is what a "compiler" does. Some source code is converted on the fly—BASIC, for example, is usually interpreted, meaning the computer compiles the source code as it is run. "Object code" is machine-readable. It is an undifferentiated string of 0s and 1s that instructs the machines about the tasks it is to perform.

17. Hypertext is text that is linked to another location in the same document or in another document located either on the Net or on the same computer.

18. T. Berners-Lee and R. Cailliau, *WorldWideWeb: Proposal for a HyperText Project,* 1990, available at link #60.

19. Of course, not always. When commercial production of computers began, software was often a free addition to the computer. Its commercial development as proprietary came only later; see Ira V. Heffan, "Copyleft: Licensing Collaborative Works in the Digital Age," *Stanford Law Review* 49 (1997): 1487, 1492–93.

20. At the time Linux was developed, the dominant thinking among computer scientists was against a monolithic operating system operating out of a single kernel and in favor of a "microkernel"-based system. MINIX, a microkernel system, was the primary competitor at the time. Torvalds consciously rejected this "modern" thinking and adopted the "traditional" model for Linux; see "The Tanenbaum-Torvalds Debate," in *Open Sources: Voices from the Open Source Revolution,* edited by Chris DiBona et al. (Sebastopol, Cal.: O'Reilly and Associates, 1999), 221–51.

21. See the lists, "Ports of Linux" and Linux Online, "Hardware Port Projects" available at link #61 and link #62.

22. Technically, it does not sit in the public domain. Code from these open source projects is copyrighted and licensed. GNU/Linux is licensed under the GNU GPL, which limits the possible use you can make of Linux; essentially, you cannot take the public part and close it, and you cannot integrate the open part with the closed; see Bruce Perens, "The Open Source Definition," in DiBona et al., *Open Sources,* 181–82. But for purposes of future open source development, the code sits in the commons. On the idea and values of the commons, see, for example, Michael A. Heller, "The Tragedy of the Anticommons: Property in the Transition from Marx to Markets," *Harvard Law Review* 111 (1998): 621; Stephen M. McJohn, "Fair Use and Privatization in Copyright," *San Diego Law Review* 35 (1998): 61; Mark A. Lemley, "The Economics of Improvement in Intellectual Property Law," *Texas Law Review* 75 (1997): 989; Mark A. Lemley, "Romantic Authorship and the Rhetoric of Property," *Texas Law Review* 75 (1997): 873; Jessica Litman, "The Public Domain," *Emory Law Journal* 39 (1990): 965; Carol M. Rose, "The Several Futures of Property: Of Cyberspace and Folk Tales, Emission Trades and Ecosystems," *Minnesota Law Review* 83 (1998): 129.

23. Daniel Benoliel, "Technological Standards, Inc.: Rethinking Cyberspace Regulatory Epistemology," *California Law Review* 92 (2004): 1069, 1114.

24. Peter Harter, "The Legal and Policy Framework for Global Electronic Commerce," comments at the Berkeley Center for Law and Technology Conference, March 5–6, 1999.

25. For an argument to the opposite conclusion, see Stephen M. McJohn, "The Paradoxes of Free Software," *George Mason Law Review* 9 (2000): 25, 64–65. Mathias Strasser extends the

analysis here in a useful way in "A New Paradigm in Intellectual Property Law? The Case Against Open Sources," *Stanford Technology Law Journal* 2001 (2001): 4.

26. I am grateful to Hal Abelson for this point.

PART III

1. For a related practice that focuses upon principles in context rather than application, see Andrew L. Shapiro, "The 'Principles in Context' Approach to Internet Policymaking," *Columbia Science and Technology Law Review* 1 (2000): 2.

CHAPTER NINE

1. Justice Holmes himself called the wiretapping a "dirty business"; *Olmstead v. United States,* 277 US 438, 470 (1928) (Justice Oliver Wendell Holmes Jr. dissenting).

2. Ibid., 457 (Chief Justice William H. Taft: the obtaining of evidence by wiretaps inserted along telephone wires was done without trespass and thus did not violate the Fourth Amendment).

3. Ibid., 471 (Justice Louis D. Brandeis dissenting; Justices Holmes, Stone, and Butler also filed dissents).

4. There is an extensive debate about the original meaning of the Fourth Amendment and how it should be applied today. For the two camps, see Akhil Reed Amar, "Fourth Amendment First Principles," *Harvard Law Review* 107 (1994): 757; Tracey Maclin, "The Complexity of the Fourth Amendment: A Historical Review," *Boston University Law Review* 77 (1997): 925 (critiquing Amar's argument).

5. See *California v. Acevedo,* 500 US 565, 582 (1991) (Justice Antonin Scalia concurring: describing warrant requirement as "riddled with exceptions").

6. See Bradford P. Wilson, "The Fourth Amendment as More Than a Form of Words: The View from the Founding," in *The Bill of Rights: Original Meaning and Current Understanding,* edited by Eugene W. Hickok Jr. (Charlottesville: University Press of Virginia, 1991), 151, 156–57. As many have pointed out, there were not really any "police" at that time in the sense that we understand the term today. The modern police force is a creation of the nineteenth century; see Carol S. Steiker, "Second Thoughts About First Principles," *Harvard Law Review* 107 (1994): 820, 830–34; William J. Stuntz, "The Substantive Origins of Criminal Procedure," *Yale Law Journal* 105 (1995).

7. See Amar, "Fourth Amendment First Principles," 767; Stuntz, "The Substantive Origins of Criminal Procedure," 400.

8. Indeed, as Professor William Stuntz argues quite effectively, one danger with warrants in general is that judges become lax and yet the product of their work (the warrant) receives great deference in subsequent proceedings; "Warrants and Fourth Amendment Remedies," *Virginia Law Review* 77 (1991): 881, 893.

9. See Stuntz, "The Substantive Origins of Criminal Procedure," 396–406.

10. See *United States v. Virginia,* 518 US 515, 566–67 (1996) (Justice Antonin Scalia dissenting: "Closed-minded they were—as every age is . . . with regard to matters it cannot guess, because it simply does not consider them debatable").

11. See Lawrence Lessig, "Fidelity in Translation," *Texas Law Review* 71 (1993): 1165, 1230.

12. *Olmstead v. United States,* 277 US 438, 470 (1928), 464–65.

13. Ibid., brief for the Pacific Telephone and Telegraph Company (nos. 493, 532, 533).

14. Ibid., 473 (Justice Louis Brandeis dissenting).

15. "Translation" is not Brandeis's term, though it is a term of the courts. The idea is best captured by Justice Robert H. Jackson in *West Virginia State Board of Education v. Barnette,* 319 US 624, 639–40 (1943): "Nor does our duty to apply the Bill of Rights to assertions of official authority depend upon our possession of marked competence in the field where the invasion of rights occurs. True, the task of translating the majestic generalities of the Bill of Rights, conceived as part of the pattern of liberal government in the eighteenth century, into concrete restraints on officials dealing with the problems of the twentieth century, is one to disturb self-confidence. These principles grew in soil which also produced a philosophy that the individual was the center of society, that his liberty was attainable through mere absence of governmental restraints, and that government should be entrusted with few controls and only the mildest supervision over men's affairs. We must transplant these rights to a soil in which the laissez-faire concept or principle of non-interference has withered at least as to economic affairs, and social advancements are increasingly sought through closer integration of society and through expanded and strengthened governmental controls. These changed conditions often deprive precedents of reliability and cast us more than we would choose upon our own judgment. But we act in these matters not by authority of our competence but by force of our commissions. We cannot, because of modest estimates of our competence in such specialties as public education, withhold the judgment that history authenticates as the function of this Court when liberty is infringed."

16. See Robert Post, *Constitutional Domains: Democracy, Community, Management* (Cambridge, Mass.: Harvard University Press, 1995), 60–64.

17. See Lessig, "Fidelity in Translation," 1214–68; Lawrence Lessig, "Translating Federalism: United States v Lopez," *Supreme Court Review* 1995 (1995): 125, 146. For a more sophisticated analysis of how changing technologies in the context of telecommunications is affecting legislation and judicial doctrine, see Monroe E. Price and John F. Duffy, "Technological Change and Doctrinal Persistence: Telecommunications Reform in Congress and the Court," *Columbia Law Review* 97 (1997): 976.

18. So, for example, the translations to support federalism are translations on the right, while the translations to support criminal rights are translations on the left.

19. *Katz v. United States,* 389 US 347, 353 (1967).

20. Laurence H. Tribe, "The Constitution in Cyberspace: Law and Liberty Beyond the Electronic Frontier," address at the First Conference on Computers, Freedom, and Privacy, March 26, 1991, reprinted in *The Humanist* (September-October 1991): 15, 20–21.

21. *Katz v. United States,* 389 US 347, 351 (1967).

22. As the history of the Fourth Amendment's protection of privacy since Katz will attest, the technique used by Stewart was in the end quite ineffectual. When tied to property notions, no doubt the reach of the Fourth Amendment was narrow. But at least its reach went as far as the reach of property. Because "property" is a body of law independent of privacy questions, it was resilient to the pressures that privacy placed on it. But once the Court adopted the "reasonable expectation of privacy" test, it could later restrict these "reasonable expectations" in the Fourth Amendment context, with little consequence outside that context. The result has been an ever-decreasing scope for privacy's protection.

23. See Lessig, "Translating Federalism," 206–11.

24. Tribe, "The Constitution in Cyberspace," 15.

25. See Lawrence Lessig, "Reading the Constitution in Cyberspace," *Emory Law Journal* 45 (1996): 869, 872.

26. This example is drawn from *Maryland v. Craig,* 497 US 836 (1990).

27. See Tribe, "The Constitution in Cyberspace," 15.

28. "A latent ambiguity arises from extraneous or collateral facts which make the meaning of a written instrument uncertain although the language thereof be clear and unambiguous.

The usual instance of a latent ambiguity is one in which a writing refers to a particular person or thing and is thus apparently clear on its face, but upon application to external objects is found to fit two or more of them equally"; *Williston on Contracts,* 3d ed., edited by Walter H. E. Jaeger (Mount Kisco, N.Y.: Baker, Voorhis, 1957), 627, 898.

29. See *United States v. Virginia,* 518 US 515, 566–67 (1996) (Justice Antonin Scalia dissenting).

30. Related work has been done under the moniker the "New Judicial Minimalism." See Christopher J. Peters and Neal Devins, "Alexander Bickel and the New Judicial Minimalism," in *The Judiciary and American Democracy,* Kenneth D. Ward and Cecilia R. Castillo, eds. (Albany: State University of New York Press, 2005).

31. See Bernard Williams, "The Relations of Philosophy to the Professions and Public Life," unpublished manuscript.

32. For a strong argument against a strong role for judicial review in matters such as this, see Orin Kerr, "The Fourth Amendment and New Technologies: Constitutional Myths and the Case for Caution," *Michigan Law Review* 102 (March 2004): 801.

CHAPTER TEN

1. Harold Smith Reeves, "Property in Cyberspace," *University of Chicago Law Review* 63 (1996): 761.

2. This in the end was not his conclusion. He concluded instead, not that boundaries should not be protected in cyberspace, but rather that the unconventional nature of cyberspace requires that boundaries be set along nontraditional context-specific lines. This conclusion, Reeves asserts, requires the law to understand both the environment of cyberspace and the interests of those who transact in that space; see ibid., 799.

3. Cf. Yochai Benkler, "Free as the Air to Common Use: First Amendment Constraints on Enclosure of the Public Domain," *New York University Law Review* 74 (1999): 354.

4. Maureen O'Rourke has extended the idea of the technological fences that cyberspace might provide, describing techniques that websites, for example, might use to control, or block, links from one site to another; see "Fencing Cyberspace: Drawing Borders in a Virtual World," *Minnesota Law Review* 82 (1998): 610, 645–47. See, e.g., *Thrifty-Tel, Inc. v. Bezenek,* 46 Cal. App. 4th 1559 (Cal. Ct. App. 1996) (Trespass to chattel claim involving defendant's children hacking plaintiff's confidential code to make long distance phone calls); *Intel v. Hamidi,* 30 Cal. 4th 1342 (Cal. 2003) (Trespass to chattels claim involving Hamidi, a former employee, using Intel's employee list-serve to send e-mails to employees); *eBay v. Bidder's Edge,* 100 F. Supp. 2d 1058 (D. Cal. 2000) (eBay sought to prevent Bidder's Edge, an Internet-based auction aggregation site, from use of an automated query function without eBay's authorization); *Register.com v. Verio,* 356 F. 3d 393 (2d. Cir. 2004) (Register.com sought to prevent Verio from using its trademark or online databases to solicit business from lists provided on the Register.com website); *America Online, Inc. v. IMS,* 1998 U.S. Dist. LEXIS 20645 (D. Va. 1998) (America Online alleged that IMS was sending unsolicited bulk e-mail advertisements to its members in violation of the Lanham Act, 15 U.S.C.S 1125).

5. See, for example, Stephen Breyer, "The Uneasy Case for Copyright: A Study of Copyright in Books, Photocopies, and Computer Programs," *Harvard Law Review* 84 (1970): 281.

6. There is a ferocious debate about whether these separate forms of regulation—copyright, patent, and trademark—should be referred to together as "Intellectual Property." I myself have gone both ways on this question, but currently believe it is harmful not to refer to these distinct bodies of law as "intellectual property." Though of course these domains are different, calling them by the same name doesn't necessarily confuse (no one is confused

about the difference between a tiger and a kitty cat, even if they're both called "cats"). More importantly, by not calling them by the same name, we lose a chance to point out inconsistencies in the way these different forms of property are treated. For example, both patent and trademark benefit from significant formalities built into each system; when you notice those formalities are absent from "copyright," one is led to wonder why one form of "intellectual property" is free of formalities, while the other two are not.

7. Paul Goldstein, *Copyright's Highway: From Gutenberg to the Celestial Jukebox* (Stanford: Stanford University Press, 2003) 64, 103: "Little did I realize at the time that this was all going to have its effect on television and motion pictures and VCRs, and the whole gamut of things which are affected by copyright law, which of course weren't even thought of when we made our move. We were dealing with a fairly simple operation—Xerox. Now it's become horribly complicated."

8. "Intellectual Property and the National Information Infrastructure: The Report of the Working Group on Intellectual Property Rights," U.S. Department of Commerce, 1995; hereafter "White Paper." George Smirnoff III ("Copyright on the Internet: A Critique of the White Paper's Recommendation for Updating the Copyright Act and How the Courts Are Already Filling in Its Most Important Shortcoming, Online Service Provider Liability," *Cleveland State Law Review* 44 [1996]: 197) criticizes the White Paper's lack of completeness, inconsistencies, and apparent lack of adequate consideration; see also Pamela Samuelson, "The Copyright Grab," *Wired* (January 1996): 134, 136. By contrast, Gary W. Glisson ("A Practitioner's Defense of the White Paper," *Oregon Law Review* 75 [1996]: 277) argues that the White Paper is neither a misleading summary of the state of intellectual property law nor a proposal for dramatic changes. For an extensive analysis of the copyright issues raised by cyberspace, see Trotter Hardy, "Project Looking Forward: Sketching the Future of Copyright in a Networked World," U.S. Copyright Office final report (1998), available at link #63.

9. For a summary of the changes called for by the White Paper, see Bruce Lehman, address before the Inaugural Engelberg Conference on Culture and Economics of Participation in an International Intellectual Property Regime, reprinted in *New York University Journal of International Law and Politics* 29 (1996–97): 211, 213–15; "White Paper," 17.

10. The most important such threat is the anticircumvention provision of the Digital Millennium Copyright Act, which makes it a crime (subject to complex exceptions) to manufacture code to circumvent a copyright protection mechanism, even if the use of the underlying material itself would be a fair use; see Pub.L. 105–304, 112 Stat 2877 (1998) (prohibiting the manufacture, importation, or distribution of "devices, products, components" that "defeat technological methods of preventing unauthorized use").

11. See John Perry Barlow, "The Economy of Ideas," *Wired* (March 1994), 129; see also John Perry Barlow, "Papers and Comments of a Symposium on Fundamental Rights on the Information Superhighway," *Annual Survey of American Law* 1994 (1994): 355, 358. Barlow argues that "it is not so easy to own that which has never had any physical dimension whatsoever," unlike traditional forms of property. "We have tended to think," he adds, "that copyright worked well because it was physically difficult to transport intellectual properties without first manifesting them in some physical form. And it is no longer necessary to do that."

12. See Mark Stefik, "Shifting the Possible: How Trusted Systems and Digital Property Rights Challenge Us to Rethink Digital Publishing," *Berkeley Technology Law Journal* 12 (1997): 137; Mark Stefik, "Trusted Systems," *Scientific American* (March 1997): 78; Mark Stefik, "Letting Loose the Light: Igniting Commerce in Electronic Publication," in Stefik, *Internet Dreams,* 220–22, 226–28.

13. See Joel R. Reidenberg, "Governing Networks and Rule-Making in Cyberspace," *Emory Law Journal* 45 (1996): 911.

14. See Mark Stefik, "Shifting the Possible: How Trusted Systems and Digital Property Rights Challenge Us to Rethink Digital Publishing," *Berkeley Technology Law Journal* 12 (1997).

15. In "Shifting the Possible" (142–44), Stefik discusses how trusted printers combine four elements—print rights, encrypted online distribution, automatic billing for copies, and digital watermarks—in order to monitor and control the copies they make.

16. Ibid.

17. Stefik, *The Internet Edge*, 91.

18. Sony v. Universal Studios, Inc., 464 U.S. 417, 432 (1984).

19. See David Hackett Fischer, *Albion's Seed: Four British Folkways in America* (New York: Oxford University Press, 1989), 765.

20. See *American Legal Realism,* edited by William W. Fisher III et al. (New York: Oxford University Press, 1993), 98–129; John Henry Schlegel, *American Legal Realism and Empirical Social Science* (Chapel Hill: University of North Carolina Press, 1995). For a nice modern example of the same analysis, see Keith Aoki, "(Intellectual) Property and Sovereignty: Notes Toward a Cultural Geography of Authorship," *Stanford Law Review* 48 (1996): 1293.

21. See Fried, *The Progressive Assault on Laissez-Faire,* 1–28; see also Joel P. Trachtman ("The International Economic Law Revolution," *University of Pennsylvania Journal of International Economic Law* 17 [1996]: 33, 34), who notes that many realists and critical legal theorists have asserted that "private law" is an oxymoron.

22. Judges have also made this argument; see *Lochner v. New York,* 198 US 45, 74 (1905) (Justice Oliver Wendell Holmes Jr. dissenting).

23. This is the epistemological limitation discussed in much of Friedrich A. von Hayek's work; see, for example, *Law, Legislation, and Liberty,* vol. 2 (Chicago: University of Chicago Press, 1978).

24. Boyle, Shamans, Software, and Spleens, 174.

25. I am hiding a great deal of philosophy in this simplified utilitarian account, but for a powerful economic grounding of the point, see Harold Demsetz, "Toward a Theory of Property Rights," *American Economics Review* 57 (1967): 347.

26. For a wonderfully clear introduction to this point, as well as a complete analysis of the law, see Robert P. Merges et al., *Intellectual Property in the New Technological Age* (New York: Aspen Law and Business, 1997), ch. 1.

27. Thomas Jefferson, letter to Isaac Mcpherson, August 13, 1813, reprinted in *Writings of Thomas Jefferson, 1790–1826,* vol. 6, edited by H. A. Washington (1854), 180–81, quoted in *Graham v. John Deere Company,* 383 US 1, 8–9 n.2 (1966).

28. For the classic discussion, see Kenneth J. Arrow, "Economic Welfare and the Allocation of Resources for Invention," in *The Rate and Direction of Inventive Activity: Economic and Social Factors* (Princeton, N.J.: Princeton University Press, 1962), 609, 616–17.

29. For a powerfully compelling problematization of the economic perspective in this context, see Boyle, "Intellectual Property Policy Online," 35–46. Boyle's work evinces the indeterminacy that economics ought to profess about whether increasing property rights over information will also increase the production of information.

30. Some insist on calling this "property"; see Frank H. Easterbrook, "Intellectual Property Is Still Property," *Harvard Journal of Law and Public Policy* 13 (1990): 108.

31. This is the message of Justice Stephen Breyer's work on copyright, for example, "The Uneasy Case for Copyright."

32. See *Eldred v. Ashcroft,* 537 U.S. 186 (2003).

33. For an extensive and balanced analysis, see William M. Landes and Richard A. Posner, "An Economic Analysis of Copyright Law," *Journal of Legal Studies* 18 (1989): 325, 325–27, 344–46. These authors note that because ideas are a public good—that is, an infinite number

of people can use an idea without using it up—ideas are readily appropriated from the creator by other people. Hence, copyright protection attempts to balance efficiently the benefits of creating new works with the losses from limiting access and the costs of administering copyright protection; copyright protection seeks to promote the public benefit of advancing knowledge and learning by means of an incentive system. The economic rewards of the marketplace are offered to authors in order to stimulate them to produce and disseminate new works (326). See also Richard Posner, *Law and Literature* (Cambridge, Mass.: Harvard University Press, 1998), 389–405; William M. Landes and Richard Posner, *The Economic Structure of Intellectual Property Law* (Cambridge, Mass.: Harvard University Press, 2003), 8–9.

34. These limits come from both the limits in the copyright clause, which sets its purposes out quite clearly, and the First Amendment; see, for example, *Feist Publications, Inc. v. Rural Telephone Service Co.*, 499 US 340, 346 (1991).

35. The "first sale" doctrine was developed under 27 of the former Copyright Act (17 USC [1970]) and has since been adopted under 109(a) of the present Copyright Act; see *United States v. Goss*, 803 F2d 638 (11th Cir 1989) (discussing both versions of the Copyright Act).

36. Europeans like to say that "moral rights" have been part of their system since the beginning of time, but as Professor Jane C. Ginsburg has shown with respect to France, they are actually a nineteenth-century creation; see "A Tale of Two Copyrights: Literary Property in Revolutionary France and America," *Tulane Law Review* 64 (1990): 991.

37. Daniel Benoliel, "Technological Standards, Inc.: Rethinking Cyberspace Regulative Epistemology," 92 *California Law Review* 1069, 1114 (2004).

38. See *Universal Studios, Inc. v. Corley*, 273 F.3d 429 (2d Cir. 2001).

39. Stefik, *The Internet Edge*, 99–100.

40. See, e.g., *People v. Network Associates, Inc.*, 195 Misc. 2d 384 (N.Y. Misc. 2003).

41. See William W. Fisher III, "Compulsory Terms in Internet-Related Contracts," *Chicago-Kent Law Review* 73 (1998). Fisher catalogs public policy restrictions on freedom of contract, which he characterizes as "ubiquitous."

42. Stefik, *The Internet Edge*, 91–7.

43. See Lessig, *Free Culture: The Nature and Future of Creativity*, xiv–xvi.

44. Yochai Benkler, "Net Regulation: Taking Stock and Looking Forward," *University of Colorado Law Review* 71 (2000): 1203, 1254.

45. See *Campbell v. Acuff-Rose Publishing*, 510 U.S. 569 (1994). Gordon ("Fair Use as Market Failure") argues that the courts should employ fair use to permit uncompensated transfers that the market is incapable of effectuating; see also Wendy J. Gordon, "On Owning Information: Intellectual Property and Restitutionary Impulse," *Virginia Law Review* 78 (1992): 149. In "Reality as Artifact: From Feist to Fair Use" (*Law and Contemporary Problems* 55 5PG [1992]: 93, 96), Gordon observes that, while imaginative works are creative, they may also comprise facts, which need to be widely available for public dissemination. Gordon's "Toward a Jurisprudence of Benefits: The Norms of Copyright and the Problem of Private Censorship" (*University of Chicago Law Review* 57 [1990]: 1009) is a discussion of the ability of copyright holders to deny access to critics and others; see also Wendy Gordon, "An Inquiry into the Merits of Copyright: The Challenges of Consistency, Consent, and Encouragement Theory," *Stanford Law Review* 41 (1989): 1343.

46. See *Gibbons v. Ogden*, 22 US 1 (1824) (striking down New York's grant of a monopoly of steamboat navigation on the Hudson River as inconsistent with the federal Coasting Act of 1793); *McCulloch v. Maryland*, 17 US 316 (1819) (pronouncing that Congress has the power to do what is "necessary and proper" to achieve a legitimate end, like the regulation of interstate commerce).

47. See Bernard C. Gavit, *The Commerce Clause of the United States Constitution* (Bloomington, Ind.: Principia Press, 1932), 84.

48. See Pensacola Telegraph Company v. Western Union Telegraph Company, 96 US 1, 9 (1877).

49. As one commentator put it near the turn of the century: "If the power of Congress has a wider incidence in 1918 than it could have had in 1789, this is merely because production is more dependent now than then on extra-state markets. No state liveth to itself alone to any such extent as was true a century ago. What is changing is not our system of government, but our economic organization"; Thomas Reed Powell, "The Child Labor Law, the Tenth Amendment, and the Commerce Clause," *Southern Law Quarterly* 3 (1918): 175, 200–201.

50. See Alexis de Tocqueville, *Democracy in America,* vol. 1 (New York: Vintage, 1990), 158–70, on the idea that the framers' design pushed states to legislate in a broad domain and keep the local government active.

51. See *Maryland v. Wirtz,* 392 US 183, 201 (1968) (Justice William O. Douglas dissenting: The majority's bringing of employees of state-owned enterprises within the reach of the commerce clause was "such a serious invasion of state sovereignty protected by the Tenth Amendment that it . . . [was] not consistent with our constitutional federalism"); *State Board of Insurance v. Todd Shipyards Corporation,* 370 US 451, 456 (1962) (holding that "the power of Congress to grant protection to interstate commerce against state regulation or taxation or to withhold it is so complete that its ideas of policy should prevail") (citations omitted).

52. See Michael G. Frey, "Unfairly Applying the Fair Use Doctrine: Princeton University Press v Michigan Document Services, 99 F3d 1381 (6th Cir 1996)," *University of Cincinnati Law Review* 66 (1998): 959, 1001; Frey asserts that "copyright protection exists primarily for the benefit of the public, not the benefit of individual authors. Copyright law does give authors a considerable benefit in terms of the monopolistic right to control their creations, but that right exists only to ensure the creation of new works. The fair use doctrine is an important safety valve that ensures that the benefit to individual authors does not outweigh the benefit to the public"; Marlin H. Smith ("The Limits of Copyright: Property, Parody, and the Public Domain," *Duke Law Journal* 42 [1993]: 1233, 1272) asserts that "copyright law is better understood as that of a gatekeeper, controlling access to copyrighted works but guaranteeing, via fair use, some measure of availability to the public."

53. Stefik, "Letting Loose the Light," 244. For an excellent use of the general analysis of Code to argue that the specific analysis of this chapter is mistaken, see John Tehranian, "All Rights Reserved? Reassessing Copyright and Patent Enforcement in the Digital Age," *University of Cincinnati Law Review* 72 (2003): 45.

54. Efficient here both in the sense of cheap to track and in the sense of cheap to then discriminate in pricing; William W. Fisher III, "Property and Contract on the Internet," *Chicago-Kent Law Review* 74 (1998).

55. Julie E. Cohen, "A Right to Read Anonymously: A Closer Look at 'Copyright Management' in Cyberspace," *Connecticut Law Review* 28 (1996): Reading anonymously is "so intimately connected with speech and freedom of thought that the First Amendment should be understood to guarantee such a right" (981, 982). Cohen has extended her analysis in the context of technology that didn't gather private information. See Julie E. Cohen, "DRM and Privacy," *Berkeley Technology Law Journal* 18 (2003): 575. See also Helen Nissenbaum, "Securing Trust Online: Wisdom or Oxymoron," *Boston University Law Review* 81 (2001): 635 (describing the dynamic of trust emerging systems will evoke). For related, and powerful work, see Sonia K. Katyal, "The New Surveillance," *Case Western Reserve Law Review* 54 (2003): 297.

56. "The freedom to read anonymously is just as much a part of our tradition, and the choice of reading materials just as expressive of identity, as the decision to use or withhold one's name" (Cohen, "A Right to Read Anonymously," 1012).

57. See *Olmstead v. United States* 277 US 438, 474 (1928) (Justice Louis Brandeis dissenting: "Can it be that the Constitution affords no protection against such invasions of individual security?").

58. See Jessica Litman, "The Exclusive Right to Read," *Cardozo Arts and Entertainment Law Journal* 13 (1994): 29.

59. See Dan Hunter and F. Gregory Lastowka, "Amateur-to-Amateur," *William and Mary Law Review* 46 (December 2004): 951, 1026–27.

60. Lasica, *Darknet: Hollywood's War Against the Digital Generation* 18. ("The director of MIT's Comparative Media Studies Program and author of nine books on popular culture, [Henry] Jenkins says that from an early age, children reimagine what you can do with characters and settings from movies and TV. They play video games that permit control over a character within limited boundaries. Newer games allow an even broader range of interactivity and behaviors. When they get online, they can share stories, and children as young as seven are posting to fan fiction sites with simple but interesting stories about Harry Potter and Pokemon.")

61. Siva Vaidhyanathan, "Remote Control: The Rise of Electronic Cultural Policy," *Annals of the American Academy of Political and Social Science* 597, 1 (January 1, 2005): 126.

62. Lasica, *Darknet: Hollywood's War Against the Digital Generation*, 78, quoting Ernest Miller.

63. From DJ Danger Mouse Web 2.0 Conference presentation "Music Is a Platform," October 6, 2004, quoted in Lasica, *Darknet: Hollywood's War Against the Digital Generation*, 211.

64. See, for example, anime music videos, available at link #64.

65. Peter Huber relies explicitly on the high costs of control in his rebuttal to Orwell's *1984;* see *Orwell's Revenge: The 1984 Palimpsest* (New York: Maxwell Macmillan International, 1994). But this is a weak basis on which to build liberty, especially as the cost of networked control drops. Frances Cairncross (*The Death of Distance: How the Communications Revolution Will Change Our Lives* [Boston: Harvard Business School Press, 1997], 194–95) effectively challenges the idea as well.

66. Lessig, *The Future of Ideas: The Fate of the Commons in a Connected World*, 19–23.

67. A founding work is David Lange, "Recognizing the Public Domain," *Law and Contemporary Problems* 44 (1981): 147. There are many important foundations, however, to this argument. See, for example, Benjamin Kaplan, *An Unhurried View of Copyright* (New York: Columbia University Press, 1967). Gordon ("Fair Use as Market Failure") argues that the courts should employ fair use to permit uncompensated transfers that the market is incapable of effectuating; see also Wendy J. Gordon, "On Owning Information: Intellectual Property and Restitutionary Impulse," *Virginia Law Review* 78 (1992): 149. In "Reality as Artifact: From Feist to Fair Use" (*Law and Contemporary Problems* 55 5PG [1992]: 93, 96), Gordon observes that, while imaginative works are creative, they may also comprise facts, which need to be widely available for public dissemination. Gordon's "Toward a Jurisprudence of Benefits: The Norms of Copyright and the Problem of Private Censorship" (*University of Chicago Law Review* 57 [1990]: 1009) is a discussion of the ability of copyright holders to deny access to critics and others; see also Wendy Gordon, "An Inquiry into the Merits of Copyright: The Challenges of Consistency, Consent, and Encouragement Theory," *Stanford Law Review* 41 (1989): 1343.

68. In the first edition to this book, in addition to Boyle, I acknowledged broadly the work that had informed my understanding, including Keith Aoki, "Foreword to Innovation and the Information Environment: Interrogating the Entrepreneur," *Oregon Law Review* 75 (1996): 1; in "(Intellectual) Property and Sovereignty," Aoki discusses the challenges to the traditional concept of property that arise from the growth of digital information technology; in "Authors, Inventors, and Trademark Owners: Private Intellectual Property and the Public Domain" (*Columbia-VLA Journal of Law and the Arts* 18 [1993]: 1), he observes the shifting boundaries in intellectual property law between "public" and "private" realms of information and argues

that trends to increase the number of exclusive rights for authors are converting the public domain into private intellectual property and constraining other types of socially valuable uses of expressive works that do not fit the "authorship" model underlying American copyright traditions; he also argues that recent expansion of trademark law has allowed trademark owners to obtain property rights in their trademarks that do not further the Lanham Act's goal of preventing consumer confusion. Benkler, "Free as the Air to Common Use"; Yochai Benkler, "Overcoming Agoraphobia: Building the Commons of the Digitally Networked Environment," *Harvard Journal of Law and Technology* 11 (1998): 287; Julie E. Cohen, "Copyright and the Jurisprudence of Self-Help," *Berkeley Technology Law Journal* 13 (1998): 1089; Julie E. Cohen, "Lochner in Cyberspace: The New Economic Orthodoxy of 'Rights Management,'" *Michigan Law Review* 97 (1998): 462; Julie E. Cohen, "Some Reflections on Copyright Management Systems and Laws Designed to Protect Them," *Berkeley Technology Law Journal* 12 (1997): 161, 181–82; Julie E. Cohen, "Reverse-Engineering and the Rise of Electronic Vigilantism: Intellectual Property Implications of 'Lock-Out' Programs," *Southern California Law Review* 68 (1995): 1091. Niva Elkin-Koren, "Contracts in Cyberspace: Rights Without Laws," *Chicago-Kent Law Review* 73 (1998); Niva Elkin-Koren, "Copyright Policy and the Limits of Freedom of Contract," *Berkeley Technology Law Journal* 12 (1997): 93, 107–10 (criticizing the ProCD decision); Niva Elkin-Koren, "Cyberlaw and Social Change: A Democratic Approach to Copyright Law in Cyberspace," *Cardozo Arts and Entertainment Law Journal* 14 (1996): 215; in "Copyright Law and Social Dialogue on the Information Superhighway: The Case Against Copyright Liability of Bulletin Board Operators" (*Cardozo Arts and Entertainment Law Journal* 13 [1995]: 345, 390–99), Elkin-Koren analyzes the problems created by applying copyright law in a digitized environment. In "Goodbye to All That—A Reluctant (and Perhaps Premature) Adieu to a Constitutionally Grounded Discourse of Public Interest in Copyright Law" (*Vanderbilt Journal of Transnational Law* 29 [1996]: 595), Peter A. Jaszi advocates the development of new, policy-grounded arguments and constitutionally based reasoning to battle expansionist legislative and judicial tendencies in copyright to diminish public access to the "intellectual commons"; see also Peter A. Jaszi, "On the Author Effect: Contemporary Copyright and Collective Creativity," *Cardozo Arts and Entertainment Law Journal* 10 (1992): 293, 319–20; Peter A. Jaszi, "Toward a Theory of Copyright: The Metamorphoses of 'Authorship,'" *Duke Law Journal* 1991 (1991): 455. On the misuse of copyright, see Mark A. Lemley, "Beyond Preemption: The Law and Policy of Intellectual Property Licensing," 87 *California Law Review,* 111 (1999); Mark A. Lemley, "The Economics of Improvement in Intellectual Property Law," *Texas Law Review* 75 (1997): 989, 1048–68; in "Intellectual Property and Shrink-wrap Licenses" (*Southern California Law Review* 68 [1995]: 1239, 1239), Lemley notes that "software vendors are attempting en masse to 'opt out' of intellectual property law by drafting license provisions that compel their customers to adhere to more restrictive provisions than copyright . . . law would require." Jessica Litman ("The Tales That Article 2B Tells," *Berkeley Technology Law Journal* 13 [1998]: 931, 938) characterizes as "dubious" the notion that current law enables publishers to make a transaction into a license by so designating it. In her view, article 2B is "confusing and confused" about copyright and its relationship with that law, and would make new law. She believes that "whatever the outcome" of the debate over whether copyright makes sense in the digital environment (see "Reforming Information Law in Copyright's Image," *Dayton Law Review* 22 [1997]: 587, 590), "copyright doctrine is ill-adapted to accommodate many of the important interests that inform our information policy. First Amendment, privacy, and distributional issues that copyright has treated only glancingly are central to any information policy." See also Jessica Litman, "Revising Copyright Law for the Information Age," *Oregon Law Review* 75 (1996): 19; and "The Exclusive Right to Read" (*Cardozo Arts and Entertainment Law Journal* 13 [1994]: 29, 48), in which Litman states that "much of the activity on the net takes place on the mistaken assumption that any material on the Internet is free from copyright unless expressly declared to be otherwise." In "Copyright as Myth" (*University of Pittsburgh Law Review* 53 [1991]: 235, 235–37), Litman provides a general overview of the issues of authorship and infringement in copyright law, indicating that debate continues regarding the definition of "authorship" (she defines "author" "in the copyright sense of anyone who creates copyrightable works, whether they be books, songs, sculptures, buildings, computer programs, paintings or films" [236, n.5]); she also discusses why copyright law is counterintuitive to the authorship process. See also "The Public Domain" (*Emory Law Journal* 39 [1990]: 965, 969), in which Litman recommends a broad definition of the public domain ("originality is a keystone of copyright law" [974]). Neil Weinstock Netanel, "Asserting Copyright's Democratic Principles in the Global Arena," *Vanderbilt Law Review* 51 (1998): 217, 232 n.48, 299 n.322; Neil Netanel, "Alienability Restrictions and the Enhancement of Author Autonomy in United States and Continental Copyright Law," *Cardozo Arts and Entertainment Law Journal* 12 (1994): 1, 42–43; in "[C]opyright and a Democratic Civil Society" (*Yale Law Journal* 106 [1996]: 283, 288, 324–36), Netanel analyzes copyright law and policy in terms of its democracy-enhancing function: "Copyright is in essence a state measure that uses market institutions to enhance the democratic character of society." Margaret Jane Radin and Polk Wagner, "The Myth of Private Ordering: Rediscovering Legal Realism in Cyberspace," *Chicago-Kent Law Review* 73 (1998); Margaret Jane Radin, *Reinterpreting Property* (Chicago: University of Chicago Press, 1993), 56–63. Pam Samuelson, "Encoding the Law into Digital Libraries," *Communications of the ACM* 41 (1999): 13, 13–14; Pamela Samuelson, foreword to "Symposium: Intellectual Property and Contract Law for the Information Age," *California Law Review* 87 (1998): 1; Pamela Samuelson observes in "Embedding Technical Self-Help in Licensed Software" (Communications of the ACM 40 [1997]: 13, 16) that "licensors of software or other information . . . will generally invoke self-help"; see also the criticism of the European database directive in J. H. Reichman and Pamela Samuelson, "Intellectual Property Rights in Data?," *Vanderbilt Law Review* 50 (1997): 51, 84–95; Samuelson, "The Copyright Grab," 134; Pamela Samuelson, "Fair Use for Computer Programs and Other Copyrightable Works in Digital Form: The Implications of Sony, Galoob and Sega," *Journal of Intellectual Property Law* 1 (1993): 49.

There is much more that I have learned from in the last seven years. But rather than replicating the listing style, I would point to Jessica Litman, *Digital Copyright: Protecting Intellectual Property on the Internet* (Amherst, N.Y.: Prometheus Books, 2000); Vaidhyanathan, *Copyrights and Copywrongs;* William Fisher, *Promises to Keep: Technology, Law, and the Future of Entertainment* (Stanford: Stanford University Press, 2004), and Benkler, *The Wealth of Networks.*

69. Boyle, *Shamans, Software, and Spleens.* For other compelling accounts of the general movement to propertize information, see Debora J. Halbert, *Intellectual Property in the Information Age: The Politics of Expanding Ownership Rights* (Westport, Conn.: Quorum, 1999). Seth Shulman's *Owning the Future* (Boston: Houghton Mifflin, 1999) gives the story its appropriate drama. *Internet Publishing and Beyond: The Economics of Digital Information and Intellectual Property* (Brian Kahin and Hal R. Varian, eds., Cambridge, Mass.: MIT Press, 2000) (Internet publishing and intellectual property). *A Handbook of Intellectual Property Management: Protecting, Developing and Exploiting Your IP Assets* (Adam Jolly and Jeremy Philpott eds. [London: Kogan Page, 2004]) (intellectual property and intangible property).

70. "We favor a move away from the author vision in two directions; first towards recognition of a limited number of new protections for cultural heritage, folkloric productions, and biological 'know-how.' Second, and in general, we favor an increased recognition and protection of the public domain by means of expansive 'fair use protections,' compulsory licensing, and narrower initial coverage of property rights in the first place"; Boyle, *Shamans, Software, and Spleens,* 169.

71. James Boyle, "A Politics of Intellectual Property: Environmentalism for the Net?," *Duke Law Journal* 47 (1997): 87.

CHAPTER ELEVEN

1. See Jonathan Zittrain, "What the Publisher Can Teach the Patient: Intellectual Property and Privacy in an Era of Trusted Privication," *Stanford Law Review* 52 (2000): 1201.

2. Olmstead v. United States, 277 US 438 (1928).

3. *International News Service v. Associated Press,* 248 U.S. 215, 250 (1918) (Brandeis, dissenting).

4. Declan MCullagh and Elinor Mills collected the practices of all major search engines in "Verbatim: Search Firms Surveyed on Privacy," *CNET NEWS,* February 3, 2006, available at link #65.

5. Stefik, *The Internet Edge,* 20.

6. The government too can snoop on e-mail conversation, but only with a warrant. Ordinarily, notice of the snooping is required. But the government can get a 90 day delay on giving that notice. See US Code Title 18, Section 2705(a)(i).

7. See Richard Posner, "Our Domestic Intelligence Crisis," *Washington Post,* December 21, 2005, available at link #66.

8. See, e.g., L. Grossman, "Welcome to the Snooper Bowl," *Time,* February 12, 2001, available at link #67; D. McCullagh, "Call It Super Bowl Face Scan I," *Wired,* February 2, 2001., available at link #68.

9. C-VIS, "What is Face Recognition Technology?", available at link #69. For an argument that face recognition technology should be seen to violate the Fourth Amendment, see Alexander T. Nguyen, "Here's Looking at You, Kid: Has Face-Recognition Technology Completely Outflanked The Fourth Amendment?" *Virginia Journal of Law and Technology* 7 (2002): 2.

10. See Face Recognition Vendor Test Home Page, available at link #70.

11. Jeffrey Rosen, The Naked Crowd: Reclaiming Security and Freedom in an Anxious Age (New York: Random House, 2004), 34–53.

12. Lawrence Lessig, "On the Internet and the Benign Invasions of Nineteen Eighty-Four," in *On "Nineteen Eighty-Four": Orwell and Our Future,* Abbott Gleason, Jack Goldsmith, and Martha C. Nussbaum eds. (Princeton: Princeton University Press, 2005), 212.

13. We've learned that the Defense Department is deeply involved in domestic intelligence (intelligence concerning threats to national security that unfold on U.S. soil). The department's National Security Agency has been conducting, outside the framework of the Foreign Intelligence Surveillance Act, electronic surveillance of U.S. citizens within the United States. Other Pentagon agencies, notably the one known as Counterintelligence Field Activity (CIFA), have, as described in Walter Pincus's recent articles in the *Washington Post,* been conducting domestic intelligence on a large scale. Although the CIFA's formal mission is to prevent attacks on military installations in the United States, the scale of its activities suggests a broader concern with domestic security. Other Pentagon agencies have gotten into the domestic intelligence act, such as the Information Dominance Center, which developed the Able Danger data-mining program. Richard Posner, "Our Domestic Intelligence Crisis," *Washington Post,* December 21, 2005, at A31.

14. Jeffrey Rosen, *The Naked Crowd: Reclaiming Security and Freedom in an Anxious Age* (New York: Random House, 2004), 34–53.

15. See American Civil Liberties Union, "The Government is Spying on Americans," available at link #71.

16. See *Minnesota v. Dickerson,* 508 US 366, 381 (1993) (Justice Antonin Scalia concurring).

17. See, for example, William J. Stuntz, "Privacy's Problem and the Law of Criminal Procedure," *Michigan Law Review* 93 (1995): 1016, 1026; in "The Substantive Origins of Criminal Procedure," Stuntz discusses the origins of the Fourth Amendment.

18. Stuntz, "Privacy's Problem and the Law of Criminal Procedure," 1026.

19. Alien and Sedition Acts of 1798, Act of June 18, 1798, ch. 59, 1 Stat. 566 (repealed 1802), Act of June 25, 1798, ch. 63, 1 Stat. 570 (expired); Act of July 6, 1798, ch. 70, 1 Stat. 577 (expired), Act of July 14, 1798, ch. 77, 1 Stat. 596 (empowering the president to deport anyone he deems dangerous to the country's peace and safety) (expired). The Alien and Sedition Acts were declared unconstitutional in *New York Times Co. v. Sullivan*, 376 US 254, 276 (1964), though, of course, by then their terms they had expired. See Neal Devins, *Constitutional Values* (Baltimore: Johns Hopkins University Press, 1996), on overruling (13); and James Morton Smith, *Freedom's Fetters: The Alien and Sedition Laws and American Civil Liberties* (Ithaca, N.Y.: Cornell University Press, 1956), on the history, enforcement, and impact of the Alien and Sedition Acts.

20. Stuntz, "Substantive Origins," 395.

21. See Cass Sunstein, *Legal Reasoning and Political Conflict* (Oxford University Press, 1996), 35–61.

22. Frank Main, "Blogger Buys Presidential Candidate's Call List," *Chicago Sun-Times*, January 13, 2006, available at link #72.

23. Peter H. Lewis, "Forget Big Brother," *New York Times*, March 19, 1998, G1.

24. Brin, *The Transparent Society*, 8–15.

25. For a good story that effectively summarizes the state of Web advertising, and for a discussion of how DoubleClick operates and the case study of 3M's sale of projectors through the advertising placement company, see Aquantive, available at link #73 and 24-7 Real Media, available at link #74.

26. See Federal Trade Commission, "Privacy Online: A Report to Congress," June 1998, n.107, available at link #75.

27. See Gandy, *The Panoptic Sort*, 1–3.

28. Johnson, *Interface Culture*, 192–205. Andrew Shapiro calls this the "feedback effect" but argues that it narrows the range of choices; see Andrew Shapiro, *The Control Revolution: How the Internet is Putting Individuals in Charge and Changing the World We Know* (New York: PublicAffairs, 1999), 113.

29. See, for example, *McIntyre v. Ohio Elections Commission*, 514 US 334, 341–43 (1995).

30. See Janai S. Nelson, "Residential Zoning Regulations and the Perpetuation of Apartheid," *UCLA Law Review* 43 (1996): 1689, 1693–1704.

31. Examples of laws that aim at segregation based on social or economic criteria include: regulations requiring a minimum lot size for housing; single-family ordinances prohibiting "nontraditional" families from living in certain areas; and residential classifications that exclude apartment housing. All such restrictions significantly increase the cost of housing for lower-income individuals; see ibid., 1699–1700.

32. In 1926 the Supreme Court held zoning to be a valid exercise of local governmental power. See *Village of Euclid v. Ambler Realty Company*, 272 US 365 (1926) (holding that a state has the right to separate incompatible uses). Not until the twentieth century were municipalities given much power to regulate areas of law such as zoning decisions; see Richard Briffault, "Our Localism: Part I—The Structure of Local Government Law," *Columbia Law Review* 90 (1990): 1, 8–11, 19.

33. In 1917 the Supreme Court outlawed racial zoning as a violation of the Fourteenth Amendment; see *Buchanan v. Warley*, 245 US 60 (1917). However, "nonexclusionary" zoning regulation was used to preserve residential segregation; even though racially neutral and based on economic factors (ostensibly to prevent property devaluation), various laws and regulations have resulted in de facto segregation; see Briffault, "Our Localism," 103–4; Meredith Lee Bryant, "Combating School Resegregation Through Housing: A Need for a Reconceptualization of American Democracy and the Rights It Protects," *Harvard BlackLetter Journal* 13 (1997): 127, 131–32.

34. See Joel Kosman, "Toward an Inclusionary Jurisprudence: A Reconceptualization of Zoning," *Catholic University Law Review* 43 (1993): 59, 77–86, 101–3.

35. See Gordon S. Wood, *The Radicalism of the American Revolution* (New York: Alfred A. Knopf, 1992), 5–8, 271–86.

36. See Lynne G. Zucker, "Production of Trust: Institutional Sources of Economic Structure, 1840–1920," *Research in Organizational Behavior* 8 (1986): 53.

37. Price discrimination is the ability to charge different prices for the same good. Airplane tickets are the best example—the same seat can cost hundreds of dollars more for a traveler who cannot stay over Saturday night. See, for example, Joseph Gregory Sidak, "Debunking Predatory Innovation," *Columbia Law Review* 83 (1983): 1121, 1132–35; see also Easterbrook, "Intellectual Property Is Still Property"; Fisher, "Reconstructing the Fair Use Doctrine," 1659; but see Janusz A. Ordover et al., "Predatory Systems Rivalry: A Reply," *Columbia Law Review* 83 (1983): 1150, 1158–64.

38. Viviana A. Zelizer, *The Social Meaning of Money*, 2d ed. (Princeton: Princeton University Press, 1994), 94–95 (footnote omitted).

39. Susan Brenner puts the point very powerfully. As she frames the question, "is it reasonable to translate the values incorporate in the Fourth Amendment into a context created and sustained by technology?" Susan Brenner, "The Privacy Privilege: Law Enforcement, Technology and the Constitution," *Journal of Technology Law and Policy* 7 (2002): 123, 162. The question isn't simply whether anonymity has a value—plainly it does. The question instead is "how to translate rights devised to deal with real world conduct into [a world where] greater degrees of anonymity are possible. . . ." Ibid., 139–40. "Because the technology alters the contours of the empirical environment in which the right to remain anonymous is exercised, it creates a tension between this aspect of the right to be let alone and the needs of effective law enforcement." Ibid., 144.

40. Shawn C. Helms, "Translating Privacy Values with Technology," *Boston University Journal of Science and Technology Law* 7 (2001): 288, 314. ("We should approach the translation of anonymity on the Internet through 'code' by developing and implementing privacy-enhancing technologies.")

41. As William McGeveran writes, Marc Rotenberg, one of privacy's most important advocate, doesn't view P3P as a PET "because Rotenberg defines a PET as technology that inherently reduces transfer of personal data." William McGeveran, "Programmed Privacy Promises: P3P and Web Privacy Law," *New York University Law Review* 76 (2001): 1813, 1826–27 n.80. I share McGeveran's view that P3P is a PET. If privacy is control over how information about you is released, then a technology that enhances that control is a PET even if it doesn't "reduce[the] transfer of personal data"—so long as that reduction is consistent with the preferences of the individual. No doubt, a PET could be a bad PET to the extent it fails to enable choice. But it isn't a bad PET because it fails to enable the choice of someone other than the consumer.

For a wonderful account of how norms have risen to change data privacy practice, see Steven A. Hetcher, "Norm Proselytizers Create a Privacy Entitlement in Cyberspace," *Berkeley Technology Law Journal* 16 (2001): 877.

42. See U.S. Department of Health, Education and Welfare, Secretary's Advisory Committee on Automated Personal Data Systems, Records, Computers, and the Rights of Citizens viii (1973), cited at link #76.

43. Ibid.

44. Lior Jacob Strahilevitz nicely explores this fundamentally "empirical" question in "A Social Networks Theory of Privacy," *University of Chicago Law Review* 72 (2005): 919, 921.

45. See Guido Calabresi and A. Douglas Melamed, "Property Rules, Liability Rules, and Inalienability: One View of the Cathedral," *Harvard Law Review* 85 (1972): 1089, 1105–6. "Property rules involve a collective decision as to who is to be given an initial entitlement but

not as to the value of the entitlement. . . . Liability rules involve an additional stage of state intervention: not only are entitlements protected, but their transfer or destruction is allowed on the basis of a value determined by some organ of the state rather than by the parties themselves" (1092).

46. Ibid.

47. See, e.g., Mark A. Lemley, "Private Property," *Stanford Law Review* 52 (2000): 1545, 1547; Paul M. Schwartz, "Beyond Lessig's Code for Internet Privacy: Cyberspace Filter, Privacy-Control, and Fair Information Practices," *Wisconsin Law Review* 2000 (2000): 743; Julie E. Cohen, "DRM and Privacy," *Berkeley Technology Law Journal* 18 (2003): 575, 577; Marc Rotenberg, "Fair Information Practices and the Architecture of Privacy: (What Larry Doesn't Get)," *Stanford Technology Law Review* (2001): 1, 89–90. Andrew Shapiro discusses a similar idea in *The Control Revolution*, 158–65.

48. See Neil M. Richards, "Reconciling Data Privacy and the First Amendment," *UCLA Law Review* 52 (2005): 1148, 116. Richards rightly identifies the brilliant Eugene Volokh as the strongest proponent of the view that the First Amendment restricts privacy property. But the comprehensive view Richards offers of the range of rules regulating privacy is quite persuasive against the Volokh position.

49. William McGeveran, "Programmed Privacy Promises: P3P and Web Privacy Law," *New York University Law Review* 76 (2001): 1813, 1843.

50. The important limit to contracts, however, is that they typically bind only people "within privity," meaning parties to the contract. Thus, an agreement I enter in with you about how you promise not to use a book I've sold you (e.g., a promise not to review it before a certain date) won't bind someone else who comes across the book and reads it.

51. As described above, the weakness is linked to the point above about "privity." Unlike a rule of property that travels automatically with the property, a rule built out of agreements reaches only as far as the agreements.

52. Barlow, "The Economy of Ideas," *Wired* (March 1994), available at link #77 ("information wants to be free").

CHAPTER TWELVE

1. See 47 CFR 73.658(e) (1998); see also Herbert J. Rotfeld et al., "Television Station Standards for Acceptable Advertising," *Journal of Consumer Affairs* 24 (1990): 392.

2. See Strafgesetzbuch (penal code) (StGB) 130–31, reprinted in *German Criminal Law*, vol. 1, edited by Gerold Harfst, translated by Otto A. Schmidt (Würzburg: Harfst Verlag, 1989), 75–76.

3. Built by industry but also especially by Cypherpunks—coders dedicated to building the tools for privacy for the Internet. As Eric Hughes writes in "A Cypherpunk's Manifesto" (in *Applied Cryptography,* 2d ed., by Bruce Schneier [New York: Wiley, 1996], 609): "We the Cypherpunks are dedicated to building anonymous systems. We are defending our privacy with cryptography, with anonymous mail forwarding systems, with digital signatures, and with electronic money. Cypherpunks write code. We know that someone has to write software to defend privacy, and since we can't get privacy unless we all do, we're going to write it. We publish our code so that our fellow Cypherpunks may practice and play with it. Our code is free for all to use, worldwide."

4. John Perry Barlow has put into circulation the meme that, "in cyberspace, the First Amendment is a local ordinance"; "Leaving the Physical World," available at link #78.

5. Or it may well be that our understanding of First Amendment doctrine is insufficiently focused on its history with electronic media. See Marvin Ammori, "Another Worthy Tradition:

How the Free Speech Curriculum Ignores Electronic Media and Distorts Free Speech Doctrine," *Missouri Law Review* 70 (2005): 59.

6. See David Rudenstine, *The Day the Presses Stopped: A History of the Pentagon Papers Case* (Berkeley: University of California Press, 1996), 101, 139.

7. Ibid., 100.

8. See ibid., 2.

9. See ibid., 2, 42.

10. Ibid., 47–63.

11. Sanford J. Ungar, *The Papers and the Papers: An Account of the Legal and Political Battle over the Pentagon Papers* (New York: Columbia University Press, 1989), 120; cited in Rudenstine, *The Day the Presses Stopped*, 92.

12. See Rudenstine, *The Day the Presses Stopped*, 105.

13. *Near v. Minnesota*, 283 US 697, 716 (1931); cf. *United States v. Noriega*, 917 F2d 1543 (11th Cir 1990) (affirming the prior restraint of audiotapes of the defendant's conversations with his US 976 (1990) (Justice Thurgood Marshall dissenting).

14. See, for example, Organization for a Better Austin v. Keefe, 402 US 415, 418–19 (1971); Bantam Books, Inc., v. Sullivan, 372 US 58, 70 (1963); Near v. Minnesota, 283 US 697, 713–14.

15. The standard arguments are summarized well by Kathleen M. Sullivan and Gerald Gunther: "(1) It is easier for an official to restrict speech 'by a simple stroke of the pen' than by the more cumbersome apparatus of subsequent punishment. . . . (2) Censors will have a professional bias in favor of censorship, and thus will systematically overvalue government interests and undervalue speech. (3) Censors operate more informally than judges and so afford less procedural safeguards to speakers. (4) Speech suppressed in advance never reaches the marketplace of ideas at all. (5) When speech is suppressed in advance, there is no empirical evidence from which to measure its alleged likely harms"; *First Amendment Law* (New York: Foundation Press, 1999), 339–40, citing Thomas Emerson, "The Doctrine of Prior Restraint," *Law and Contemporary Problems* 20 (1955): 648. Frederick Schauer offers a nice balance to this commonplace theory; see "Fear, Risk, and the First Amendment: Unraveling the 'Chilling Effect,'" *Boston University Law Review* 58 (1978): 685, 725–30.

16. In a particularly telling exchange, Justice Stewart asked Professor Bickel about a case in which disclosure "would result in the sentencing to death of a hundred young men whose only offense had been that they were nineteen years old and had low draft numbers. What should we do?" Bickel replied that his "inclinations of humanity overcome the somewhat more abstract devotion to the First Amendment in a case of that sort"; *May It Please the Court: The Most Significant Oral Arguments Made Before the Supreme Court Since 1955*, edited by Peter Irons and Stephanie Guitton (New York: Free Press, 1993), 173.

17. In a concurring opinion, Justice Potter Stewart wrote that the prior restraint at issue was invalid since he could not "say that disclosure of [the Pentagon Papers] will surely result in direct, immediate, and irreparable damage to our Nation or its people"; *New York Times Company v. United States*, 403 US 713, 730 (1971) (per curiam). This standard has frequently been thought to reflect the position of the Court; see Laurence H. Tribe, *American Constitutional Law* (Mineola, N.Y.: Foundation Press, 1978), 731; Morton H. Halperin and Daniel N. Hoffman, *Top Secret: National Security and the Right to Know* (Washington, D.C.: New Republic Books, 1977), 147 n.22; see also *Alderman v. Philadelphia Housing Authority*, 496 F2d 164, 170 (3d Cir 1974), cert. denied, 419 US 844 (1974) (prior restraint must be supported by "compelling proof" that it is "essential to a vital government interest").

18. See *United States v. Progressive, Inc.*, 467 FSupp 990 (WDWis 1979); see also L. A. Powe Jr., "The H-Bomb Injunction," *University of Colorado Law Review* 61 (1990): 55, 56.

19. The *Milwaukee Sentinel* and *Fusion* magazine had published articles dealing with similar concepts; see A. DeVolpi et al., *Born Secret: The H-Bomb, The Progressive Case, and National*

Security (New York: Pergamon Press, 1981), 102, 106; see also Howard Morland, *The Secret That Exploded* (New York: Random House, 1981), 223, 225–26.

20. See Floyd Abrams, "First Amendment Postcards from the Edge of Cyberspace," *St. John's Journal of Legal Commentary* 11 (1996): 693, 699.

21. NTSB Chairman Jim Hall announced later that investigations confirmed that a fuel tank explosion caused the crash; see "Statement of Jim Hall, Chairman, National Transportation Safety Board," July 16, 1998, available at link #79.

22. See Robert E. Kessler, "TWA Probe: Submarines off Long Island/Sources: But No Link to Crash of Jetliner," *Newsday*, March 22, 1997, A8.

23. See, for example, James Sanders, *The Downing of TWA Flight 800* (New York: Kensington Publishing, 1997), 131–37; Accuracy in Media et al., "TWA 800—Missile Website Roadmap," available at link #80; Mark K. Anderson, "Friendly Ire," available at link #81; Ian W. Goddard, "TWA Flight 800 and Facts Pertaining to U.S. Navy Culpability," available at link #82.

24. See Sanders, *The Downing of TWA Flight 800*, 29–30, 75, 70–79, 171–73.

25. We can tell that it is false, of course, as in, "The cat was alive and not alive."

26. Initial CBS article on controversy: available at link #83; CBS acknowledgment of mistake: available at link #84.

27. See Howard Kurtz, "Rather Admits 'Mistake in Judgment,'" *Washington Post*, September 21, 2004, A01. (". . . ending a nearly two-week-long defense of the network's journalistic conduct that media analysts say has badly hurt its credibility.")

28. Jim Giles, "Internet Encyclopedias Go Head to Head," news@nature.com, December 12, 2005, available at link #85.

29. See Cass Sunstein, *Infortopia: How Many Minds Produce Knowledge* (New York: Oxford University Press, 2006).

30. See Seth Finkelstein, Al Gore "invented the Internet"—resources, transcript: Vice President Gore on CNN's *Late Edition* (last updated Fri April 28, 2006), available at link #86.

31. Ibid.

32. Ibid

33. *Ginsburg v. New York*, 390 US 629 (1968). Obscenity is not constitutionally protected speech, and federal laws prohibit the transportation of obscene materials; see 18 USCA 1462 (1984), amended by 18 USCA 1462 (Supp 1999). In *Miller v. California*, the Supreme Court described the test for obscenity as: "(a) whether 'the average person, applying contemporary community standards' would find that the work, taken as a whole, appeals to the prurient interest; (b) whether the work depicts or describes, in a patently offensive way, sexual conduct specifically defined by the applicable state law; and (c) whether the work, taken as a whole, lacks serious literary, artistic, political, or scientific value"; *Miller v. California*, 413 US 15, 24 (1973) (5–4 decision), rehearing denied, 414 US 881 (1973). Porn, on the other hand, is protected by the First Amendment but may be regulated to promote the state's interest in protecting children from harmful materials so long as the regulation is the least restrictive means to further the articulated interest; see *Ginsberg v. New York*, 390 US 629, 637–40 (1968). Child porn may be prohibited as obscene material even if it is not obscene under the Miller test, owing to the strong state interest in preventing the sexual exploitation of children; see *New York v. Ferber*, 458 US 747, 764 (1982). Child porn is not constitutionally protected, and federal law prohibits the transportation of child porn; see 18 USCA 2252 (1984), amended by 18 USCA 2252 (Supp 1999).

34. Justice Sandra Day O'Connor listed more than 40 states with such law in her concurrence in *Reno v. ACLU*, 521 US 844, 887 n.2.

35. *Ginsberg v. New York*, 390 US 629 (1968).

36. See Blake T. Bilstad, "Obscenity and Indecency in a Digital Age: The Legal and Political Implications of Cybersmut, Virtual Pornography, and the Communications Decency Act of 1996," *Santa Clara Computer and High Technology Law Journal* 13 (1997): 321, 336–37.

37. Marty Rimm, "Marketing Pornography on the Information Superhighway: A Survey of 917,410 Images, Descriptions, Short Stories, and Animations Downloaded 8.5 Million Times by Consumers in over 2,000 Cities in Forty Countries, Provinces, and Territories," *Georgetown University Law Journal* 83 (1995): 1849. Godwin provides the whole history of the Rimm article, describing the most significant problems and consequences of the "misleading" and "false" statements, and its eventual demise; *Cyber Rights*, 206–59; see also Jonathan Wallace and Mark Mangan, *Sex, Laws, and Cyberspace* (New York: M&T Books, 1996), ch. 6.

38. See Philip Elmer-DeWitt, "On a Screen Near You: Cyberporn—It's Popular, Pervasive, and Surprisingly Perverse, According to the First Survey of Online Erotica—And There's No Easy Way to Stamp It Out," *Time*, July 3, 1995.

39. 47 USCA 223(e)(5)(A) (Supp 1999).

40. The law was extinguished (at least in part) at 521 US 844 (1997); see Eugene Volokh, "Freedom of Speech, Shielding Children, and Transcending Balancing," *Supreme Court Review* 1997 (1997): 141.

41. See *Federal Communications Commission v. Pacifica Foundation*, 438 US 726, 748–50 (1978) (plurality). Though Pacifica has been criticized strongly, see Steven H. Shiffrin, *The First Amendment, Democracy, and Romance* (Cambridge, Mass.: Harvard University Press, 1990), 80, as Jonathan Weinberg convincingly argues, Pacifica continues to have influence in the broadcasting context; "Cable TV, Indecency, and the Court," *Columbia-VLA Journal of Law and the Arts* 21 (1997): 95.

42. *Ashcroft v. ACLU*, 540 U.S. 1072 (2003). Child Online Privacy Protection Act of 1998, Title XIV, Section 1401.

43. *Ashcroft v. ACLU*, 540 U.S. 1072 (2003).

44. *Ginsberg v. New York*, 390 U.S. 629 (1968).

45. There is also a doctrine within First Amendment law that might limit the ability of the government to regulate when the regulation is ineffective. See *Reno v. ACLU*, 929 F. Supp 824, 848 (D. Pa.1996), where the court talks about how this regulation wouldn't work in foreign jurisdictions anyway.

46. Ann Beeson and Chris Hansen, "Fahrenheit 451.2: Is Cyberspace Burning?" (American Civil Liberties Union White Paper, March 17, 2002).

47. Not all of these filters function by using blacklists. Two examples of filtering programs that use an algorithmic approach rather than blacklists are PixAlert's SafeScreen (available at link #87) and LTU Technologies' ImageSeeker (available at link #88), the latter of which is supposedly being used by the FBI and DHS in child pornography investigations.

48. Paul Resnick, "PICS-Interest@w3.0rg, Moving On," January 20 1999, available at link #89; Paul Resnick, "Filtering Information on the Internet," *Scientific American* 106 (March 1997), also available at link #90; Paul Resnick, "PICS, Censorship, and Intellectual Freedom FAQ," available at link #91; Paul Resnick and Jim Miller, "PICS: Internet Access Controls Without Censorship," Communications of the ACM 39 (1996): 87, also available at link #92; Jim Miller, Paul Resnick, et al., "PICS 1.1 Rating Services and Rating Systems—and Their Machine-Readable Descriptions," October 31, 1996, available at link #93); Tim Krauskopf, Paul Resnick, et al., "PICS 1.1 Label Distribution—Label Syntax and Communication Protocols," October 31, 1996, available at link #94; Christopher Evans, Paul Resnick, et al., "W3C Recommendation: PICS Rules 1.1, REC-PICS, Rules-971229," December 29, 1997, available at link #95.

49. See Jonathan Weinberg, "Rating the Net," *Hastings Communications and Entertainment Law Journal* 19 (1997): 453, 478 n.108.

50. This claim, of course, is too strong. The site could block deceptively, making it seem as if the user were gaining access but actually not giving her access to what she believes she is gaining access to.

51. See Richard Thompson Ford ("The Boundaries of Race: Political Geography in Legal Analysis," *Harvard Law Review* 107 [1994]: 1841, 1844), who asserts that jurisdictional boundaries perpetuate racial segregation and inequality; Gerald E. Frug ("Universities and Cities," *Connecticut Law Review* 30 [1998]: 1199, 1200), explains how universities erect borders to divorce themselves from surrounding poverty and argues that universities should critique these borders; Lani Guinier ("More Democracy," *University of Chicago Legal Forum* 1995 [1995]: 1, 3) advocates a cross-racial participatory democracy that demands a concern for, and a familiarity with, the views of others.

52. See Regents of the *University of California v. Bakke,* 438 US 265, 312 (1978) (Justice Lewis F. Powell, quoting *Keyishian v. Board of Regents,* 385 US 589, 603 [1967]: "The Nation's future depends upon leaders trained through wide exposure to that robust exchange of ideas which discovers truth 'out of a multitude of tongues, [rather] than through any kind of authoritative selection'").

53. See Sunstein, *Democracy and the Problem of Free Speech,* xvi–xx; Fiss, *The Irony of Free Speech,* 3, 37–38; Andrew Shapiro's powerful analysis of Sunstein's point is better tuned to the realities of the Net; see *The Control Revolution,* 107–12.

54. Sunstein, *Democracy and the Problem of Free Speech,* xvi–xx.

55. Ithiel de Sola Pool, *Technologies Without Boundaries: On Telecommunications in a Global Age,* edited by Eli M. Noam (Cambridge, Mass.: Harvard University Press, 1990), 15.

56. See Geoffrey R. Stone, "Imagining a Free Press," *Michigan Law Review* 90 (1992): 1246, 1264.

57. Dan Hunter argues it is not our choice anyway. See Dan Hunter, "Philippic.com," *California Law Review* 90 (2002): 611. Greg Laughlin is convinced the concerns are overstated. See Gregory K. Laughlin, "Sex, Lies, and Library Cards: The First Amendment Implications of the Use of Software Filters to Control Access to Internet Pornography in Public Libraries," *Drake Law Review* 51 (2003): 213, 267–68 n.287. For a review of Congress's latest effort to facilitate filtering, see Susan P. Crawford, Symposium, "Law and the Information Society, Panel V: Responsibility and Liability on the Internet, Shortness of Vision: Regulatory Ambition in the Digital Age," *Fordham Law Review* 74 (2005): 1, 6. ("The next information-flow membrane mandate to pass Congress—again, prompted by legislators' fixation on indecent (but legal) content online—was the Children's Internet Protection Act ("CIPA"), which required libraries to install filtering software on all their computers capable of accessing the Internet in order to hold on to their federal funding. The goal of this 2000 legislation was to condition provision of such funding on libraries' use of filters that block access to visual depictions that are harmful to minors (when accessed by a minor). On June 23, 2003, after another three years of litigation, the Supreme Court upheld CIPA, with two "swing" Justices (Anthony Kennedy and Stephen Breyer) suggesting that adults would be able to ask libraries to unblock legal sites (legal for adult viewing, if harmful to minors) that had been blocked by the installed filters. Even though the tie to the CDA was clear—this was another congressional attempt to eliminate online sexual material using technology that would also inevitably filter out protected speech—the link to federal funding made this case one the Justices could decide differently. Indeed, the federal funding element may have been the crucial difference between CDA and CIPA. One European commentator noted the CIPA opinion as an 'important shift' by an American legal system that had been 'previously critical of government's attempts to regular Internet access.'")

58. Compare Jonathan Zdziarski, "Ending Spam: Bayesian Content Filtering and the Art of Statistical Language Classification 31 (2005) and DSPAM, available at link #96.

59. Zdziarski, Ibid., 25.

60. Ibid., 31. But a related point can be made about Bayesian filtering as well, since many of the tools are themselves open source or free software. DSPAM, for example, is licensed under the GPL.

61. This is being charitable. Zdziarski is much more critical of "vigilantes who don't adhere to any form of proper procedure before blacklisting networks." Ibid., 28.

62. See Arik Hesseldahl, *U.S. Congress Makes No Progress on Spam*, December 26, 2003, available at link #97. Also Todd Bishop, Software Notebook: Is Gates' prediction on spam a bust? *Seattle Post-Intelligencer* (1/23/06). Estimates of success here differ dramatically. Microsoft estimates it blocks 95 percent of spam from reaching e-mail inboxes.

63. Jonathan Zdziarski, *Ending Spam: Bayesian Content Filtering and the Art of Statistical Language Classification* (San Francisco: No Starch Press, 2005) 23.

64. See CAN-SPAM Act of 2003, Public Law 108-187 (2003). For a review of European legislation, see D. I. Cojocarasu, *Anti-spam Legislation Between Privacy and Commercial Interest: An Overview of the European Union Legislation Regarding the E-mail Spam* (Oslo: University of Oslo, 2006).

In my view, we define spam as "unsolicited bulk commercial e-mail." Each element is necessary. Unsolicited, meaning there is no agreement to receive such e-mail. If there is an agreement, the requirements would be removed. Bulk meaning it would not be intended to regulate circulations to friends or within small groups. Cf. Sonia Arrison, "Canning Spam: An Economic Solution to Unwanted Email" 9 (Pacific Research Institute, Feb. 2004). Commercial meaning it would not regulate social or political e-mail. And e-mail, meaning maybe more than e-mail—perhaps, for example, including blog spam.

65. In my view, Congress should be permitted to discriminate in favor of political speech, and should thus be permitted to exempt political speech from any "spam" regulation. This is not only because of the special value in this speech, but also, and more importantly, because abuse with political speech is more naturally regulated. If I am trying to win your vote, I'm not likely to annoy you with spam. But if I'm trying to sell you Viagra, whether I annoy you or not won't matter much to me.

66. This was the law in many states before the federal CAN-SPAM Act preempted this state law. But as those laws didn't have the enforcement remedy I propose here, they are not directly relevant to the argument I am making here. See "Subject Line Labeling as a Weapon Against Spam," A CAN-SPAM Act Report of Congress (FTC June 2005).

This solution is just one instance of a general form which aims to shift the burden of revealing information to the sender. For a much more sophisticated proposal, see Theodore Loder, Marshall Van Alstyne, and Rick Wash (2006) "An Economic Response to Unsolicited Communication", *Advances in Economic Analysis and Policy* Vol. 6, No. 1, Article 2, available at link #98.

67. See Spammer-X, Jeffrey Polsuns and Stu Sjouwerman, *Inside the Spam Cartel: Trade Secrets from the Dark Side* (New York: Syngress Publishing, 2004).

68. R. Polk Wagner, "On Software Regulation," *Southern California Law Review* 78 (2005): 457, 516.

69. Lessig, *Free Culture: The Nature and Future of Creativity*, xiii–xvi.

70. Yochai Benkler, "Net Regulation: Taking Stock and Looking Forward," *University of Colorado Law Review* 71 (2000): 1203, 1249.

71. See, e.g., *United States v. Dunifer*, 219 F.3d 1004 (9th Cir. 2000). (FCC closure of pirate radio station Free Radio Berkeley); *United States v. Any & All Radio Station Transmission Equip.*, 2004 U.S. Dist. LEXIS 24899 (D.N.Y. 2004); *United States v. Szoka*, 260 F3d 516 (6th Cir. 2001). See 47 CFR 73.277 (1998).

72. 47 USCA 81–119 (1927) (repealed by the Communications Act of 1934).

73. See *Red Lion Broadcasting Company v. Federal Communications Commission*, 395 US 367, 375–77 (1969); *National Broadcasting Company v. United States*, 319 US 190, 212–13 (1943). Thomas Hazlett makes a powerful critique of Frankfurter's history of the emergence of any necessity for FCC regulation; see Thomas W. Hazlett, "Physical Scarcity, Rent Seeking, and the First Amendment," *Columbia Law Review* 97 (1997): 905, 933–34.

74. See Turner Broadcasting System, Inc. v Federal Communications Commission, 512 US 622, 637–38 (1997); see also Huber, Law and Disorder in Cyberspace.

75. See National Broadcasting Company, Inc. v. Columbia Broadcasting System, 213.

76. See Ronald H. Coase, "The Federal Communications Commission," *Journal of Law and Economics* 2 (1959): 1.

77. Paul Starr, *The Creation of Media: Political Origins of Modern Communications* (Basic Books, 2004), 25–46.

78. Yochai Benkler, "Net Regulation: Taking Stock and Looking Forward," *University of Colorado Law Review* 71 (2000): 1203.

79. See, for example, research at MIT to build viral mesh networks which increase in capacity as the number of users increases. Collaborative (Viral) Wireless Networks, available at link #99.

80. Ethernet effectively functions like this. Data on an Ethernet network are streamed into each machine on that network. Each machine sniffs the data and then pays attention to the data intended for it. This process creates an obvious security hole: "sniffers" can be put on "promiscuous mode" and read packets intended for other machines; see Loshin, *TCP/IP Clearly Explained*, 44–46.

81. See Yochai Benkler and Lawrence Lessig, "Net Gains," *New Republic*, December 14, 1998.

82. The founder of this argument must be Eli Noam; see "Spectrum Auctions: Yesterday's Heresy, Today's Orthodoxy, Tomorrow's Anachronism—Taking the Next Step to Open Spectrum Access," *Journal of Law and Economics* 41 (1998): 765. Benkler has spiced it up a bit (in my view, in critical ways) by adding to it the value of the commons. For an extraordinarily powerful push to a similar political (if not technological) end, see Eben Moglen, "The Invisible Barbecue," *Columbia Law Review* 97 (1997): 945. Moglen notes the lack of debate regarding the sociopolitical consequences of carving up telecommunication rights at the "Great Barbecue" and draws a parallel with the Gilded Age's allocation of benefits and privileges associated with the railroad industry.

CHAPTER FOURTEEN

1. Audio Tape: Interview with Philip Rosedale 2 (1/13/06) (transcript on file with author).

2. Ibid., 4–6.

3. Ibid., 5.

4. Castronova, *Synthetic Worlds*, 207.

5. Ibid., 216.

6. Ibid., 213.

7. See Judith N. Shklar, *American Citizenship: The Quest for Inclusion* (Cambridge, Mass.: Harvard University Press, 1991), 25–62; James A. Gardner, "Liberty, Community, and the Constitutional Structure of Political Influence: A Reconsideration of the Right to Vote," *University of Pennsylvania Law Review* 145 (1997): 893; *Quiet Revolution in the South,* edited by Chandler Davidson and Bernard Grofman (Princeton, N.J.: Princeton University Press, 1994): 21–36.

8. See Lani Guinier, *The Tyranny of the Majority: Fundamental Fairness in Representative Democracy* (New York: Free Press, 1994); Richard Thompson Ford, "Beyond Borders: A Partial Response to Richard Briffault," *Stanford Law Review* 48 (1996): 1173; Richard Thompson Ford, "Geography and Sovereignty: Jurisdictional Formation and Racial Segregation," *Stanford Law Review* 49 (1997): 1365; Jerry Frug, "Decentering Decentralization," *University of Chicago Law Review* 60 (1993): 253; Jerry Frug, "The Geography of Community," *Stanford Law Review* 48 (1996): 1047.

9. See Michael Walzer, *Spheres of Justice: A Defense of Pluralism and Equality* (New York: Basic Books, 1983).

10. See Charles M. Tiebout, "A Pure Theory of Local Expenditures," *Journal of Political Economy* 64 (1956): 416; see also Clayton P. Gillette, *Local Government Law: Cases and Materials* (Boston: Little, Brown, 1994), 382; Vicki Been, "'Exit' as a Constraint on Land Use Exactions: Rethinking the Unconstitutional Conditions Doctrine," *Columbia Law Review* 91 (1991): 473, 514–28.

11. See David G. Post, "Governing Cyberspace," *Wayne Law Review* 43 (1996): 155; David Post, "The New Electronic Federalism," *American Lawyer* (October 1996): 93; David G. Post, "The 'Unsettled Paradox': The Internet, the State, and the Consent of the Governed," *Indiana Journal of Global Legal Studies* 5 (1998): 521, 539; David R. Johnson and Kevin A. Marks, "Mapping Electronic Data Communications onto Existing Legal Metaphors: Should We Let Our Conscience (and Our Contracts) Be Our Guide?," *Villanova Law Review* 38 (1993): 487; Johnson and Post, "Law and Borders"; David G. Post, "Anarchy, State, and the Internet: An Essay on Law-Making in Cyberspace," *Journal of Online Law* (1995): article 3, available at link #100.

12. See Phillip E. Areeda et al., *Antitrust Law,* vol. 2A (Boston: Little, Brown, 1995), 85–87.

13. See Post, "Anarchy, State, and the Internet," 29–30.

14. In the time since *Code* v1, this point has become much more questionable. The ability of people playing games to effectively move from one game to another has increased. Here again, real space and cyberspace are becoming more alike.

15. F. Gregory Lastowka and Dan Hunter, "The Laws of Virtual Worlds," *California Law Review* 92 (2004): 1, 73.

16. Or at least three of the four regions in the early United States shared this history; see Fischer, *Albion's Seed,* 827–28.

17. Article V of the Constitution states (obscurely no doubt) that "provided that no Amendment which may be made prior to the Year One thousand eight hundred and eight shall in any Manner affect the first and fourth Clauses in the Ninth Section of the first Article." These clauses state: "(1) The Migration or Importation of such Persons as any of the States now existing shall think proper to admit, shall not be prohibited by the Congress prior to the Year one thousand eight hundred and eight, but a Tax or duty may be imposed on such Importation, not exceeding ten Dollars for each Person"; and "(4) No Capitation, or other direct, Tax shall be laid, unless in Proportion to the Census or Enumeration herein before directed to be taken."

18. See John F. Kennedy, *Profiles in Courage* (New York: Harper, 1956), ch. 3.

CHAPTER FIFTEEN

1. The story of the suit is told in *Yahoo! Inc. v. La Ligue Contre le Racisme,* 433 F.3d 1199 (9th Cir. 2006). See also Jack Goldsmith and Timothy Wu, *Who Controls the Internet: Illusions of a Borderless World*; Michael Geist, "Is There a There There? Towards Greater Certainty for Internet Jurisdiction," 16 *Berkeley Technology Law Journal* 1345 (2001). For criticism of the conflict (and its significance) see Marc H. Greenberg, "A Return to Lilliput: The LICRA v. Yahoo! Case and the Regulation of Online Content in the World Market," *Berkeley Technology Law Journal* 18 (2003): 1191.

2. Yahoo! Inc. v. La Ligue Contre le Racisme, 433 F.3d 1199, 1202 (9th Cir. 2006).

3. Ibid., 1223.

4. See "France Bans Internet Nazi Auctions," BBC NEWS, May 23, 2000, available at link #101.

5. Yahoo! Inc. v. La Ligue Contre le Racisme, 433 F.3d 1199, 1203 (9th Cir. 2006).

6. Adam D. Thierer, "Web Restrictions Unlikely to Muzzle Neo-Nazi Speech," Cato Institute Web Site (Jan 15, 2001) (available at link #102).

7. Available at link #103. John Borland, "Broadcasters Win Battle Against iCraveTV.com," *CNET NEWS,* Jan. 28, 2000, available at link #104.

8. Michael Geist, "Is There a There There? Towards Greater Certainty for Internet Jurisdiction," *Berkeley Technology Law Journal* 16 (2001): 1345.

9. Yahoo! Inc. v. La Ligue Contre le Racisme, 433 F.3d 1199 (9th Cir. 2006).

10. Reidenberg points out that the translation of the French ruling offered to the District Court in the United States was flawed. Joel R. Reidenberg, "Technology and Internet Jurisdiction," *University of Pennsylvania Law Review* 153 (2005): 1951, 1959.

11. Yahoo! Inc. v. La Ligue Contre le Racisme, 433 F.3d 1199, 1203 (9th Cir. 2006).

12. Jack Goldsmith and Timothy Wu, *Who Controls the Internet: Illusions of a Borderless World* (2006), 41.

13. There has been a rich, and sometimes unnecessary, debate about whether indeed cyberspace is a "place." I continue to believe the term is useful, and I am confirmed at least partly by Dan Hunter, "Cyberspace as Place and the Tragedy of the Digital Anti-commons," *California Law Review* 91 (2003): 439. Michael Madison adds a valuable point about what the place metaphor misses in Michael J. Madison, "Rights of Access and the Shape of the Internet," *Boston College Law Review* 44 (2003): 433. Lemley too adds an important perspective. See "Place and Cyberspace," *California Law Review* 91 (2003): 521.

14. See Restatement (Third) of Foreign Relations Law (1986), 402(2) and comment (e).

15. Child Sexual Abuse Prevention Act, 18 USC 2423(b) (1994). See Margaret A. Healy, "Prosecuting Child Sex Tourists at Home: Do Laws in Sweden, Australia, and the United States Safeguard the Rights of Children as Mandated by International Law?," *Fordham International Law Journal* 18 (1995): 1852, 1902–12.

16. Castronova, *Synthetic Worlds* (2005), 7.

17. See Bill Grantham, "America the Menace: France's Feud With Hollywood," *World Policy Journal* 15, 2 (Summer 1998): 58; Chip Walker, "Can TV Save the Planet?," *American Demographics* (May 1996): 42.

18. See, for example, David R. Johnson and David Post, "Law and Borders: The Rise of Law in Cyberspace," *Stanford Law Review* 48 (1996): 1379–80.

19. Jack Goldsmith and Timothy Wu, *Who Controls the Internet.* See Jack L. Goldsmith, "Against Cyberanarchy," *University of Chicago Law Review* 65 (1998): 1199; Jack L. Goldsmith, "The Internet and the Abiding Significance of Territorial Sovereignty," *Indiana Journal of Global Legal Studies* 5 (1998): 475; see also David Johnston, Sunny Handa, and Charles Morgan, *Cyberlaw: What You Need to Know About Doing Business Online* (Toronto: Stoddart, 1997), ch. 10. Allan R. Stein ("The Unexceptional Problem of Jurisdiction in Cyberspace," *The International Lawyer* 32 [1998]: 1167) argues that the jurisdictional problems in cyberspace are like those found in real-space international law.

20. See Jessica Litman, "The Exclusive Right to Read," *Cardozo Arts and Entertainment Law Journal* 13 (1994): 29.

21. Ibid.

22. See John Perry Barlow, "A Declaration of the Independence of Cyberspace" (1996), available at link #105.

23. See Communications Decency Act, PL 104-104, 110 Stat. 56 (1996).

24. Yochai Benkler, "Net Regulation: Taking Stock and Looking Forward," *University of Colorado Law Review* 71 (2000): 1203, 1206–07 (15 in 101; 23 in 102; 34 in 103; 66 in 104; 275 in 105; 348 for first session of 106).

25. Ibid., 1203, 1232, 1234, 1237.

26. Michael Geist, "Cyberlaw 2.0," *Boston College Law Review* 44 (2003): 323, 332. For a related point, see Matthew Fagin, "Regulating Speech Across Borders: Technology vs. Values," *Michigan Telecommunications Technology Law Review* 9 (2003): 395.

27. Geist, Ibid., 343.

28. Ibid., 338.

29. Ibid., 344–45.

30. Patricia L. Bellia, "Chasing Bits Across Borders," *University of Chicago Legal Forum* 35, 100 (2001).

31. Viktor Mayer-Schönberger and Teree E. Foster, *A Regulatory Web: Free Speech and the Global Information Infrastructure,* 3 Mich. Telecomm. Tech. L. Rev. 45, 45 (1997).

32. I describe this example at the state level, but the regime I'm imagining would work at the level of nation-states, not U.S. states.

33. See Minnesota Statute 609.75, subd. 2–3, 609.755(1) (1994), making it a misdemeanor to place a bet unless done pursuant to an exempted, state-regulated activity, such as licensed charitable gambling or the state lottery. Internet gambling organizations are not exempted.

34. See Scott M. Montpas, "Gambling Online: For a Hundred Dollars, I Bet You Government Regulation Will Not Stop the Newest Form of Gambling," *University of Dayton Law Review* 22 (1996): 163.

35. Or at least it could work like this. Depending on the design, it could reveal much more.

36. See 18 USC 1955 (regulating businesses, defining interstate "illegal gambling" as gambling that occurs in a state in which it is illegal).

37. As described above, see supra Chapter 5, note 38, within six months, one of the founders of Google was having second thoughts. See Clive Thompson, "Google's China Problem (And China's Google Problem)," *New York Times,* April 23, 2006, Section 6, p. 64.

38. See Wikipedia, "List of Words Censored by Search Engines in Mainland China," available at link #106.

CHAPTER SIXTEEN

1. *Missouri v. Holland,* 252 US 416, 433 (1920).

2. See, for example, Jack N. Rakove, *Original Meanings: Politics and Ideas in the Making of the Constitution* (New York: Alfred A. Knopf, 1996), 289–90; see also Akhil Reed Amar, "The Bill of Rights as a Constitution" (*Yale Law Journal* 100 [1991]: 1131), for another such understanding of the Bill of Rights.

3. This is not to deny that some aspects of the equality delineated in the Civil War amendments echoed in our constitutional past. The abolitionists, of course, made great weight of the Declaration of Independence's claims to equality; see, for example, Trisha Olson, "The Natural Law Foundation of the Privileges or Immunities Clause of the Fourteenth Amendment," *Arkansas Law Review* 48 (1995): 347, 364. An amendment can be transformative, however, even if it is simply recalling a part of the past and reestablishing it—as Germany did, for example, after World War II.

4. See *Plessy v. Ferguson,* 163 US 537 (1896).

5. See A. Leon Higginbotham Jr., "Racism in American and South African Courts: Similarities and Differences," *New York University Law Review* 65 (1990): 479, 495–96.

6. These laws permitted compelled labor to pay a debt; see *Bailey v. Alabama,* 219 US 219 (1911) (striking peonage laws under the Thirteenth Amendment).

7. Brown v. Board of Education, 347 US 483 (1954).

8. See, for example, *Dennis v. United States,* 341 US 494 (1951) (upholding convictions under the Smith Act, which banned certain activities of the Communist Party).

9. See Korematsu v. United States, 323 US 214 (1944).

10. See, for example, John Hart Ely, *Democracy and Distrust: A Theory of Judicial Review* (Cambridge, Mass.: Harvard University Press, 1980).

11. I've overstated the security of the American judiciary. An incident with District Court Judge Harold Baer suggests continued insecurity, especially in the context of the war on drugs. Baer released a criminal defendant after suppressing a search that had discovered eighty pounds of narcotics; Don Van Natta Jr., "Judge's Drug Ruling Likely to Stand," *New York Times,* January 28, 1996, 27. The decision was then attacked by presidential candidate Robert Dole, who called for Baer's impeachment; Katharine Q. Seelye, "A Get Tough Message at California's Death Row," *New York Times,* March 24, 1996, 29. President Clinton then joined the bandwagon, suggesting that he might ask for Baer's resignation if Baer did not reverse his decision; Alison Mitchell, "Clinton Pressing Judge to Relent," *New York Times,* March 22, 1996, 1. Baer then did reverse his decision; Don Van Natta Jr., "Under Pressure, Federal Judge Reverses Decision in Drug Case," *New York Times,* April 2, 1996, 1. Chief Judge Jon Newman, of the Second Circuit Court of Appeals, along with other judges, then criticized Dole's criticism of Baer, arguing that he went "too far"; Don Van Natta Jr., "Judges Defend a Colleague from Attacks," *New York Times,* March 29, 1996, B1.

12. I describe the Court's conception of its role in more detail in Lessig, "Translating Federalism."

13. Robert H. Bork, *The Antitrust Paradox: A Policy at War with Itself* (New York: Basic Books, 1978), 83.

14. See, for example, Felix Frankfurter, *The Commerce Clause Under Marshall, Taney, and Waite* (Chapel Hill: University of North Carolina Press, 1937), 82.

15. The relationship between a contested ground and a political judgment is more complex than this suggests. I discuss it more extensively in Lawrence Lessig, "Fidelity and Constraint," *Fordham Law Review* 65 (1997): 1365.

16. *ACLU v. Reno,* 929 FSupp 824 (EDPa 1996); *Shea v. Reno,* 930 FSupp 916 (SDNY 1996).

17. I discuss this in Lessig, "Fidelity and Constraint."

18. One could well argue that during the crisis of the Depression deference by the Court to the Congress would have been well advised; see, for example, Sunstein, *Democracy and the Problem of Free Speech,* 39.

19. For the clearest statement of a contrary position, see Charles Fried, "Book Review: Perfect Freedom or Perfect Control?," *Harvard Law Review* 114 (2000): 606.

20. Fischer *(Albion's Seed)* shows how town planning in the United States followed habits in Europe.

21. David P. Currie, *The Constitution of the Federal Republic of Germany* (Chicago: University of Chicago Press, 1994), 182–87. See also Dawn C. Nunziato, "The Death of the Public Forum in Cyberspace," *Berkeley Technology Law Journal* 20 (2005): 1115, 1170 n.2 (describing first amendment review of anti-dilution law).

22. Charles Fried, "Book Review: Perfect Freedom or Perfect Control?," *Harvard Law Review* 114 (2000): 606.

23. Paul Schiff Berman, "Cyberspace and the State Action Debate: The Cultural Value of Applying Constitutional Norms to 'Private' Regulation," *University of Colorado Law Review* 71 (2000): 1263, 1269.

24. A. Michael Froomkin, "The Collision of Trademarks, Domain Names, and Due Process in Cyberspace," *Communications of the ACM* 44 (2001): 91. See also Jonathan Weinberg, "ICANN and the Problem of Legitimacy," *Duke Law Journal* 50 (2000): 187.

25. Internet Corporation for Assigned Names and Numbers, available at link #107.

26. *Payne v. Tennessee,* 501 U.S. 808, 844 (1991) (Marshall, dissenting).

27. See Wikipedia, "Duke Cunningham," available at link #108.

28. The average term for a Supreme Court justice is 15 years. See link #109. The average term for a Senator in the 109th Congress was 12.1 years, and for a member of the House, 9.3 years. See link #109. The figures for campaign spending are derived from link #110.

29. Ernest F. Hollings, "Stop the Money Chase," *Washington Post,* Page B07, Feb. 19, 2006, available at link #112.

30. Peter Francia and Paul Herrnson, "The Impact of Public Finance Laws on Fundraising in State Legislative Elections," 31 *American Politics Research* 5 (September 2003), confirms Hollings's numbers.

CHAPTER SEVENTEEN

1. Deborah Hellman, in "The Importance of Appearing Principled" (*Arizona Law Review* 37 [1995]: 1107), describes the illegitimacy costs that courts incur when they overrule precedents for apparently political reasons.

2. Guido Calabresi, *A Common Law for the Age of Statutes* (Cambridge, Mass.: Harvard University Press, 1982), 16–32; Guido Calabresi, "The Supreme Court, 1990 Term—Foreword: Antidiscrimination and Constitutional Accountability (What the Bork-Brennan Debate Ignores)," *Harvard Law Review* 105 (1991): 80, 83, 103–7, 119–20.

3. Or come close to doing so; see Richard A. Posner, *The Problems of Jurisprudence* (Cambridge, Mass.: Harvard University Press, 1990), 300–301.

4. I am grateful to Viktor Mayer-Schoenberger for demonstrating this point to me. Hal Abelson points out that the components would have to be verifiable if they were not themselves open. Otherwise, components could function as Trojan Horses—pretending to be one thing while in reality being something else.

5. See Mark A. Lemley and David W. O'Brien, "Encouraging Software Reuse," *Stanford Law Review* 49 (1997): 255. See also, e.g., James Boyle, "A Politics of Intellectual Property: Environmentalism for the Net," available at link #113.

6. For an extraordinary account of the damage done by copyright law to software development, see Mark Haynes, "Black Holes of Innovation in the Software Arts," *Berkeley Technology Law Journal* 14 (1999): 503. See also David McGowan, "Legal Implications of Open Source Software," *Illinois University Law Review* 241 (2001).

7. Kennedy, Profiles in Courage, 71.

8. See Nicholas Negroponte, *Being Digital* (New York: Alfred A. Knopf, 1995), 18, 238.

9. Center for Responsive Politics, "'04 Elections Expected to Cost Nearly $4 Billion," October 21, 2004, available at link #114.

10. Chris Edwards, "Bush's Overspending Problem," CATO Institute, February 6, 2003, available at link #115.

11. See, for example, James S. Fishkin, *The Voice of the People* (New Haven, Conn.: Yale University Press, 1995). For excellent work exploring how cyberspace might advance this general project, see Beth Simone Noveck, "Designing Deliberative Democracy in Cyberspace: The Role of the Cyber-Lawyer," *Boston University Journal of Science and Technology Law* 9 (2003): 1.

12. Dean Henry H. Perritt Jr. provides a well-developed picture of what "self-regulation" in the Internet context might be, drawing on important ideals of democracy; see "Cyberspace Self-government: Town Hall Democracy or Rediscovered Royalism?," *Berkeley Technology Law Journal* 12 (1997): 413. As he describes it, the possibility of self-governance depends importantly on architectural features of the Net—not all of which are developing in ways that will

support democracy; see also Shapiro (*The Control Revolution*, 150–57, 217–30), who discusses "push-button politics" and tools of democracy.

13. Tocqueville, *Democracy in America*, vol. 1, 284–85.

CHAPTER EIGHTEEN

1. Posting of Declan McCullagh, "Reporters Without Borders calls for regulation of U.S. Internet companies," available at link #116.

2. Ronald Coase, "The Problem of Social Cost," *Journal of Law and Economics* (October 1960).

3. "Study: Spam Costs Businesses $13 Billion," CNN.COM, January 5, 2003, available at link #117.

4. Felix Oberholzer and Koleman Strumpf, "The Effect of File Sharing on Record Sales: An Empirical Analysis" 3 (Working Paper 2004).

5. David Blackburn, "On-line Piracy and Recorded Music Sales" (Harvard University, Job Market Paper, 2004.

6. Recording Industry Association of America Home Page, "Issues—Anti-Piracy: Old as the Barbary Coast, New as the Internet," available at link #118.

7. David Blackburn, "On-line Piracy and Recorded Music Sales" (Harvard University, Job Market Paper, 2004), available at link #119.

8. Family Entertainment and Copyright Act of 2005 (P.L. 109–9), signed April 27, 2005. (Adds § 2319B to Title 17, which makes it a crime punishable with imprisonment to copy in a movie theater, without authorization, motion pictures or any audiovisual work protected under Title 17.); Intellectual Property Protection and Courts Amendment Act of 2004 (P.L. 108–482), signed December 23, 2004. (Amends the Trademark Act of 1946 to provide for increased criminal and civil penalties for individuals who willfully submit false information to a domain name registration authority in connection with an Internet address used to commit a crime or engage in online copyright or trademark infringement.); Satellite Home Viewer Extension and Reauthorization Act of 2004 (contained in Consolidated Appropriations Act, 2005, P.L. 108–447), signed December 8, 2004. (In addition to extending for an additional five years the statutory license for satellite carriers retransmitting over-the-air television broadcast stations to their subscribers and making a number of amendments to the existing section 119 of the Copyright Act, SHVERA directs the Copyright Office to conduct two studies and report its findings to the Committee on the Judiciary of the House of Representatives and the Committee on the Judiciary of the Senate. One study, due by December 31, 2005, required the Office to examine select portions of the section 119 license and to determine what, if any, impact sections 119 and 122 have had on copyright owners whose programming is transmitted by satellite carriers.); Individuals with Disabilities Education Improvement Act of 2004 (P.L. 108–446), signed December 3, 2004. (Modifies § 121 of Title 17, providing for the establishment of the National Instructional Materials Accessibility Center ("NIMAS") and the free accessibility of certain materials—such as Braille, audio or digital text for use by the blind—via NIMAS.); Copyright Royalty and Distribution Reform Act of 2004 (P.L. 108–419), signed November 30, 2004. (Amends the Copyright Act to replace the Copyright Office copyright arbitration royalty panel system, created under the Copyright Royalty Tribunal Reform Act of 1993, with three copyright royalty judges to oversee adjustment of compulsory license royalty rates and distribution of copyright royalties.); Small Webcaster Settlement Act of 2002 (P.L. 107–321), enacted December 4, 2002. (Amends the Copyright Act to establish performance royalty rights for sound recordings transmitted through electronic digital technology.); Technology, Education, and Copyright Harmonization Act of 2002 (P.L. 107–273, Subtitle C of the

21st Century Department of Justice Appropriations Authorization Act), enacted November 2, 2002. (Introduces provisions relating to the use of copyrighted works for distance education purposes.); Intellectual Property and High Technology Technical Amendments Act of 2002 (P.L. 107–273, Subtitle B of the 21st Century Department of Justice Appropriations Authorization Act), enacted November 2, 2002. (Makes technical corrections to Title 17 and to the IP and Communications Omnibus Reform Act of 1999, also known as the Satellite Home Viewer Improvement Act of 1999.); Work Made for Hire and Copyright Corrections Act of 2000 (P.L. 106–379), enacted October 27, 2000. (Amends definition of works made for his in Title 17.); Digital Theft Deterrence and Copyright Damages Improvement Act of 1999 (P.L. 106–160), enacted December 9, 1999. (Increases statutory damages for copyright infringement by amending chapter 5 of Title 17.); Satellite Home Viewer Improvement Act of 1999 (P.L. 106–113), enacted November 29, 1999. (Amends chapters 12 and 13 of Title 17.); Copyright Amendments and Amendments to the Vessel Hull Design Protection Act (P.L. 106–44), enacted August 5, 1999. (Makes technical corrections to Title 17.); Vessel Hull Design Protection Act (P.L. 105–304, Title V of the Digital Millennium Copyright Act), enacted October 28, 1998. (Introduces design protection for vessel hulls.); Computer Maintenance Competition Assurance Act (P.L. 105–304, Title III of the Digital Millennium Copyright Act), enacted October 28, 1998. (Amends § 117 of Title 17.); Online Copyright Infringement Liability Limitation Act (P.L. 105–304, Title III of the Digital Millennium Copyright Act), enacted October 28, 1998. (Adds § 512 to Title 17.); WIPO Copyright and Performances and Phonograms Treaties Implementation Act of 1998 (P.L. 105–304, Title I of the Digital Millennium Copyright Act), enacted October 28, 1998). (Adds a new chapter 12 to Title 17, which prohibits circumvention of CR protection systems and provides protection for CR management information.); Digital Millennium Copyright Act (P.L. 105–304), enacted October 28, 1998; Fairness in Music Licensing Act of 1998 (P.L. 105–298), enacted October 27, 1998. (Amending § 110 and adding § 513 to provide a music licensing exemption for food service and drinking establishments.); Sonny Bono Copyright Term Extension Act (P.L. 105–298, Title I), enacted October 27, 1998. (Extends term of copyright protection for most works to life plus 70 years.); No Electronic Theft (NET) Act (P.L. 105–147), enacted December 16, 1997; Copyright Amendments and Amendments to Semiconductor Chip Protection act of 1984 (P.L. 105–80), enacted November 13, 1997. (Introduces technical amendments to certain provisions of Title 17.); Legislative Branch Appropriations Act (P.L. 104–197), enacted September 16, 1996. (Adds a new version of § 121 concerning the limitation on exclusive copyrights for literary works in specialized format for the blind and disabled.); Anticounterfeiting Consumer Protection Act of 1996 (P.L. 104–153), enacted July 2, 1996. (Amends § 603 of Title 17 and § 2318 of Title 18.); Digital Performance Right in Sound Recordings Act of 1995 (104–39), enacted November 1, 1995. (Amends §§ 114 and 115 of Title 17.).

APPENDIX

1. Lessig, "The New Chicago School," 661.

2. See H. L. A. Hart, *The Concept of Law,* 2d ed. (New York: Oxford University Press, 1994), 6–13, 27–33.

3. For example, Illinois law states: "The third Monday in January of each year is a holiday to be observed throughout the State and to be known as the birthday of Dr. Martin Luther King, Jr. Within 10 days before the birthday of Dr. Martin Luther King, Jr., in each year the Governor shall issue a proclamation announcing the holiday and designating the official events that shall be held in honor of the memory of Dr. Martin Luther King, Jr., and his contributions to this nation"; 5 Illinois Comprehensive Statutes Annotated 490/65 (West 1998).

4. See Robert Cooter, "Expressive Law and Economics," *Journal of Legal Studies* 27 (1998): 585.

5. Cf. Paul N. Bracken, *The Command and Control of Nuclear Forces* (New Haven: Yale University Press, 1983), 179–237; Christopher Chant and Ian Hogg, *The Nuclear War File* (London: Ebury Press, 1983), 68–115.

6. On the other side, the military built into the system technological brakes on the ability to launch, to ensure that no decision to launch was ever too easy; see also Daniel Ford, *The Button: The Nuclear Trigger—Does It Work?* (London: Allen and Unwin, 1985), 118–21.

7. "The phenomena of social meaning and incommensurability constrain rational choice (individual and collective). Generalizing, it is irrational to treat goods as commensurable where the use of a quantitative metric effaces some dimension of meaning essential to one's purposes or goals. It would be irrational, for example, for a person who wanted to be a good colleague within an academic community to offer another scholar cash instead of comments on her manuscript. Against the background of social norms, the comment's signification of respect cannot be reproduced by any amount of money; even to attempt the substitution conveys that the person does not value his colleague in the way appropriate to their relationship"; Dan M. Kahan, "Punishment Incommensurability," *Buffalo Criminal Law Review* 1 (1998): 691, 695.

8. Many scholars, Robert Cooter most prominently among them, argue that norms are special because they are "internalized" in a sense that other constraints are not; see Robert D. Cooter, "Decentralized Law for a Complex Economy: The Structural Approach to Adjudicating the New Law Merchant," *University of Pennsylvania Law Review* 144 (1996): 1643, 1662; Robert D. Cooter, "The Theory of Market Modernization of Law," *International Review of Law and Economics* 16 (1996): 141, 153. By internalization, Cooter is just describing the same sort of subjectivity that happens with the child and fire: the constraint moves from being an objectively ex post constraint to a subjectively ex ante constraint. The norm becomes a part of the person, such that the person feels its resistance before he acts, and hence its resistance controls his action before he acts. Once internalized, norms no longer need to be enforced to have force; their force has moved inside, as it were, and continues within this subjective perspective. In my view, we should see each constraint functioning in the same way: We subjectively come to account for the constraint through a process of internalization. Some internalization incentives may be stronger than others, of course. But that is just a difference.

9. Cf. Dan M. Kahan, "Ignorance of Law Is an Excuse—But Only for the Virtuous," *Michigan Law Review* 96 (1997): 127.

10. See, for example, Schuster et al., Preserving the Built Heritage; Peter Katz, *The New Urbanism: Toward an Architecture of Community* (New York: McGraw-Hill, 1994); Duany and Plater-Zyberk, *Towns and Town-Making Principles.*

11. Michael Sorkin, *Local Code: The Constitution of a City at 42N Latitude* (New York: Princeton Architectural Press, 1993), 11, 127.

INDEX

Page references in **bold** refer to text graphics.